INTIMUS
Interior Design Theory Reader

Edited by Mark Taylor and Julieanna Preston

John Wiley & Sons, Ltd

Other Wiley Editorial Offices

John Wiley & Sons Inc., 111 River Street, Hoboken, NJ 07030, USA

Jossey-Bass, 989 Market Street, San Francisco, CA 94103-1741, USA

Wiley-VCH Verlag GmbH, Boschstr. 12, D-69469 Weinheim, Germany

John Wiley & Sons Australia Ltd, 42 McDougall Street, Milton, Queensland 4064, Australia

John Wiley & Sons (Asia) Pte Ltd, 2 Clementi Loop #02-01, Jin Xing Distripark, Singapore 129809

John Wiley & Sons Canada Ltd, 5353 Dundas Street West, Suite 400, Etobicoke, Ontario M9B 6H8

Wiley also publishes its books in a variety of electronic formats. Some content that appears in print may not
be available in electronic books.

ISBN-13 978-0-470-01570-4 (HB)   978-0-470-01571-1 (PB)

Cover image Henri Matisse (1869-1954), The Red Studio © Photo SCALA, Florence, The Museum of
Modern Art (MoMA), New York

Design and prepress by Artmedia Press Ltd, UK

Acknowledgements

We thank all contributors, living and deceased, for committing their thoughts and practice to words and images, in effect founding the territory of our research. Appreciation is also extended to all those contributors and colleagues who have provided positive comment and encouragement as the collection unfolded. We are indebted to our very capable research assistants Monique van Alphen Fyfe, Nuala Collins and Hannah Davies for their hard work and dedication.

Our thanks go to Helen Castle at Wiley (UK) for her faith in the publication; particularly her encouragement in the early and latter stages of the work.

This project was supported by research funding from Massey University College of Creative Arts and Victoria University of Wellington, School of Architecture without which this project would not have been possible.

Finally, to David and Chora, Vanessa, Oliver, Imogen and Sebastian, our thanks for being here and there.

Contents

Proximities

Mark Taylor and Julieanna Preston

The collection of texts contained in this volume stems from a proposition that as an emerging discipline interior design draws from a body of theory specific to its creative practice. Initial informal surveys of interior design/interior architecture and spatial arts university programmes revealed that not only do approaches, outlooks and pedagogical philosophy differ, but also the scope of theoretical texts rarely repeat or identify a distinct set of readings. Feedback from respondents indicated that most interior design programmes identify theoretical sources that span across several disciplines, including material from cultural geography, sociology, anthropology, philosophy and gender studies. The material offers positions and insights that operate beyond architectural canons and interior design's marginalisation within that discourse. This is not to suggest the interior as an inside is possible without architectural context or another form of enframing, particularly as Elizabeth Grosz has discussed the impossibility of having an inside without some form of demarcation that distinguishes the outer from the inner.[1] Our search for theory related to the specifics of inhabitation and bodily presence confirms that the interior and its design constitute a wider field of cultural production.

There is a wealth of material about the interior spanning a spectrum of geographies and histories in the form of paintings, drawings, illustrations, film and other visual representations. Conscious of the close affinity between the way the interior is spatially conceptualised and visualised, many recent critical historical texts have explored the correlation between image and spatial conditions. While we made an intentional decision to place these issues outside the territory of this book, these artefacts offer a tremendous resource for future analysis and observation of the convention of interior design as decorated and inhabited rooms relevant to many disciplines.

However, one image in particular harboured virtual potentials pertinent to our inquiry.

Within the pages of Emily Post's book *The Personality of a House*, is a photographic plate attributed to New York architect William Lawrence Bottomley.[2] This seemingly unassuming image gently frames the prevailing issues, topics and texts of this volume.

A pale timber-panelled wall stretches across the image. It is articulated from the ceiling by a deep cornice moulding inscribed with cosmological signs. Garnished by an elaborate keystone, the centre of the image is marked by two figures sitting back to back, the

Gemini twins. Characterised as dual-natured, elusive, complex and contradictory, this sign aptly describes this masked space. Cancer, another star sign, is also visible to the right indicating that the remainder of the room might be aligned with the cosmos. Two arched doors peel open away from the surface of the wall in perfect symmetry with the ornament above. Their mirror-lined inner faces offer a vague reflection of the greater room.

The doors reveal a space behind the opaque panelling, a space within the wall occupied by a small vanity or dressing-table. Another mirror backs the niche which doubles the light, and the ruffles and tassels of swagged curtains are softly gathered at the boundary of this closet and cloister. A small clock is placed on a horizontal marbled surface next to a few indistinct trinkets, perhaps a dish, a perfume jar or bottle; the necessary artefacts for dressing and grooming. Cosmos becomes cosmetic. Equally poised, a lightly upholstered rectangular stool stands in front of the table and parted doors, ready to be slipped behind the table's flounced skirt before the doors are closed and the wall absorbs the secrets of the situation.

This pretty scene, this quaint proscenium, this decorated hideaway, provokes a myriad questions pertinent to the interior as evidenced in our collection of texts. For whom was this dressing-table made? Most certainly a woman, perhaps the lady of the house, who relished the activity of reviewing her dress and hair from multiple vantage points but who could not resolve its objectified presence in the room or refuse the architect's ingenious solution to clutter. As such female activities associated with beauty have been enveloped by the panelled wall, where has this female body gone? For the stool's skewed position indicates that she may have just left the frame, perhaps to select from her wardrobe across the room or attend to other household duties. Evidence of her presence is latently implied in the photograph. And what is it to sit in this aperture of space, dwelling in the margin of the room, looking outwards and inwards simultaneously? Do the curtains gild one's image in like manner to the interiority of intellectual musing? Is there a collapse and merging of philosophic values and physical virtues? The room seems to be dressed in parity to the self-reflective body that inhabits it.

And yet, it is a private space, a space for one, a space for an individual. The mirrors reflect very little of the greater surroundings, but the scale of the panelling and the floor- to-ceiling height help to extrapolate that this secret space occurs as an informality among the far more social and self-conscious home atmosphere. How might this 'PERFECT EXAMPLE OF DRESSING-TABLE HIDDEN BEHIND PANELING WHEN NOT IN USE' be physically, socially and theoretically constructed? How are the intricate details of curved timber work on the doors and stool indicative of current and historical values on ornament, surface, gender and politics? While the doors mask the presence of the dressing-table, the mirrored interior expands infinitely. What appears as a small enclosure is a mode of liberation. What one might assume to be self-indulgent or decadent decoration may be found to be a sign of self-expression. While the architectural room is wrapped with abstract notions of time and space, this small alcove inhabits its periphery as a pocket where body is central, maybe even fluid, and space is temporal, perhaps even subjective.

What is being teased out here is a multifaceted dialogue between that which is theoretical in nature, abstract, knowledge-based and immaterial and that which is grounded, physical, phenomenal and concrete. Not wishing to pull these apart, but rather to encourage convergence, this book identifies a territory of emerging points that collectively register connections of understanding with reference to a field tentatively named as the theoretical domain of interior design. This conception forms a working method for searching and organising texts, and for mapping their locations as a relational matrix. Described in other theoretical discourse as rhizomatic, networked or diagrammatic, matrices foster the formation of connections among notions as opposed to defining or creating singular isolated entities.

This matrix or diagram mediates between the virtual potentials generated by the data (the field of essays/excerpts) and the actual book. The matrix is to some extent graphic shorthand used to declare latent structures of organisation. The diagram is also generative, and can be used to order possible readings.

This in hand, we sought theory informative to interior design by trusting that through the act of searching various sources/databases a range of associations and connections would verify an emergent practice. Such associations are fuelled by the abstract and diagrammatic quality of an organising tactical matrix in its flexibility to seek casual and coincidental links among related and sometimes assumed disparate disciplines. That is, we looked for correspondence between seemingly unrelated research and practice, moving laterally between existing systems and categories, not in a haphazard manner but through productive leaps generated by rules that had consequential and significant outcomes. This process enabled the gathering of material from several disciplines when the linear historical model seemed inapplicable, and thematic structures too constraining.

Coupled with its ability to engage the complexity of the real, the matrix assists in making sense of the found texts and their potential reformations. Conceptually, such order is made not towards the specificity or hegemony of a discipline, but rather to turn outwards and mobilise forces of action and imagination between matter and information. Pragmatically, the matrix positions each text relative to a disciplinary body of knowledge (social, political, philosophical, technological, gender and psychological) and then relative to prominent interior design practice issues (material, colour, light, space, decoration and furnishing). Within this methodology we acknowledge the interpretive role we played in ordering these texts and the multiple locations in which each text could be placed. The matrix is intended to be used as a surveying instrument and ordering device with the purpose to catalyse cross- and inter-disciplinary insights.

An interdisciplinary database search using terms typically associated with interior design as a decorative craft, an architectural speciality, a spatial art or a physical articulation of social interaction located essays framed by a wide range of types of theory, genres of writing and sources of textual discourse. Many of the researched essays did not declare that they are concerned with 'interior theory', but instead they either operated critically on spaces, places and inhabitation of the built environment's interiors, or offered observations and abstractions of use and inhabitation that engender a criticality in this collection of texts. To include this material raises questions of what constitutes theory, and how theory relates to the critical study of the interior.

In their book *Intersections: Architectural Histories and Critical Theories*, Iain Borden and Jane Rendell outline nine epistemological tendencies on which theory is constituted within critical discourse.[3] Rather than champion a narrow definition or description, their categories are expansive and inclusive, and when considered relative to the scope of our book assist in substantiating numerous items that would normally fall outside the limits of architectural or design theory, most notably some that take the form of turn-of-the-century advice literature or historical analysis of a place or activity. We are also pointing to those texts that are observational in nature or assert new paradigms of dwelling in light of technology. In most cases, selection of such texts proved a matter of locating the speculative mode of inquiry within the written work, registering the inferences and extending them as conduits to other contemporary works or notions. In other cases, it became an exercise in dwelling in the period, revelling in the detail specific to when the text was written and recognising that theory and critical history have been defined and couched differently across time. For if theory is conditioned by inquiries and speculation about what occurs between events, situations, objects and actions, then the method of inquiry or the analytical device employed is of primary concern.

This matter was very apparent when we were faced with many texts across several disciplines that, despite fostering connective tissue between points, approached the manner of writing in very different styles and genres. Looking back, we should have expected this occurrence as it appears that many disciplines have, for various reasons, adopted a primary form and voice specific to the nature of their practice and audience. The nature of speaking theoretically in archaeology may necessitate the survey of cultural and geographical material, while the presentation of studies on social behaviour may include a review of statistical data gathered through direct observation. A theoretical discussion about colour from a psychological viewpoint may veer towards comparative analysis, while in architectural theory the text may rely on narrative or historical data from field studies or phenomenological discourse on perception and experience. While these do not form an equal and level 'reading' field (it is often a challenge to read from one to the next without mitigating the difference of voice, tone, word usage, historical perspective and so on.), we felt that it was important to include texts of different writing styles and genres not only to demonstrate Borden and Rendell's analysis of critical theory but also to defend the field as plural, multiplicitous and interdisciplinary.

Establishing a field of potential connections and crossings as a fertile catalyst for intellectual inquiry is really only fruitful if it can be inhabited, tested and stretched beyond its own means. For example, an examination of the essays held within the matrix reveals several latent structures, issues, themes or traces that span several disciplines and territories. Surfacing as interconnected points, they operate beyond the stratification of disciplinary boundaries, revealing the complexity/extent of the interior when viewed as an interdisciplinary activity. Of these, the two following examples test this notion against the stereotypical image of interior design's short history, which often situates it as female, domestic and decorative; and the domain of objects and furnishing – a bias that can not be avoided. Most certainly, any book on theory surrounding interior design can not escape discussion about feminism, gender, race and sexuality, if not because of interior design's own history as a practice stemming from the upholsterer's trade then for its alliances (or stereotype associations) with domestic, residential and feminine decorative practice. While these are complex issues tangled with political and social events, and historical gender roles within Western culture including post-colonialism and racial affairs, evidence in the found texts indicates that such issues not only reside within designed works but are impacted by them.

The historical identification of women with the domestic interior, and subsequent cultural conflation of women, dress and the interior environment are subject to discourses on power. Whether enacted through metaphoric relations between women and the imprint of female character on the domestic room, or semi-autobiographic examinations of entrapment, they move beyond the structure/ornament dialectic that so fervently governs many architectural treatises. We acknowledge that there are a number of noteworthy publications within the discipline of architecture that address issues of architecture and feminism. These comprise both recovered histories and feminist readings of architecture as a gendered discourse of power, patriarchy and phallocentrism.

What is being provoked here is not just the suppression of ornament but the identification of the female body with the domestic and with the decorative, which forms a lingering and significant field of inquiry, and perhaps prejudice, towards what defines interior design historically. The exploration of such themes occurs through both gendered and sexed readings of architectural space as they intersect with discourses on power. Several critical theoretical essays in this book offer gendered readings of architectural history and the spaces associated with women. These essays characterise the impossibility of ignoring

10

the role feminism and feminist theory has in any discussion of the interior. In addition, recent developments in feminist and human geographic studies also investigate the relationship between particular bodies and their environment. Focusing on sexed corporeality, particular located bodies are examined through the ways a body's desires and capacities are produced or created by specific spaces. It is this identification of specific space to specific body that is relevant to any theorising of the interior that intends engaging with immanence, rather than masculine transcendent values. These critical theoretical essays use queer theory not to reify the lesbian or homosexual but to discuss complexities of public and private space and the containment of an identity. Positioning notions of 'other' or outside, they challenge traditional 'normal' ontologies of home, for example, home, privacy and publicity. This is not to substitute one universalising value for another, but to destabilise implicit homogeneities.

Although this example links numerous 'body' issues, it also veers in the direction of interiority – the conscious and reflexive awareness of self, identity, community and others within a social environment. Situated among philosophy and psychology, this cluster of associated points in the interdisciplinary arena of 'interiority' examines the innerness of interior design as that which is felt and projected upon and within the interior environment via body as a culturally lived organism.

An equally significant but not oppositional constellation of connections explores all that is concrete, material and objectified in the physical interior environment. Here the historiographic project that aligns interior decoration with furnishing generally operates through image-based texts and literary narratives that provide descriptions of great manors, castles and homes, inadvertently commenting on wealth, social status, worldliness and craft. A political and social engagement with all matters of style, taste and décor is enacted from positions of conformity or individuality. Moreover, rooms comprising plush textiles, gilded frames, polished floors and floriated wallpaper are indexical indicators of the infrastructure of inhabitation. As objects in space they are responsible for creating atmospheric effect but it is the latent effect that is seething behind the detail.

Among texts recording the historical development of the interior, including Mario Praz,[4] Charlotte Gere[5] and Peter Thornton,[6] there is a tendency to perpetuate the style- manual documentation of furnishings and accessories. This propensity has contributed to the suppression and relegation of the decorative to a lesser understood architectural activity. Although primarily based on representation, and lacking a sense of criticality, such works model the predisposition for humans to decorate as an inherent impulse of self-expression. What lingers about this material is the manner in which things, objects and artefacts frame interior spaces, influence behaviour, reflect imagination and mark prevailing political and social notions of the time. Hence, this book includes several essays that explore the constitutional understanding of furnishing over and above its representational or ergonomic value.

This anthology unabashedly includes texts that dwell on the core business of interior design practice as anything from the selection of cushions to the coordination of adjacent rooms measured in the light of popular style trends of the time. Such works speak to the ever-changing and elusive nature of taste, and its likely alliance to consumption and the acquisition of possessions as a symbol of social status. Several working definitions of what qualifies as tasteful and appropriate room design expose the extent to which such attributes may be subjectively grounded but socially influenced; issues of order and composition vacillate between unifying space via harmony and repose and charging the space with an array of eclectic objects. This wide range of approaches to decorating or furnishing the interior, the conventional practice of interior design, appears to extend through historical advice literature to popular interior magazines and journals of today.

Outside of issues to do with décor is a collection of texts that expose the various ways in which notions and principles of function form and inform interior space and, furthermore, inhabitation and behaviour. The functional characteristics of interior spaces prove as diverse as the acquisition of bodily comfort, aesthetic proportion and programme facilitation. Furniture, as a bodily interface, dictates posture and as a signifier of social gathering it indicates a performative event. We are made acutely aware that such interior objects are neither neutral nor nullifying. Consistent with issues of power, this collection of points in the matrix culls a portion of the field more familiar and less volatile than those surrounding body, gender and spatial and social interaction. For the most part, these issues and modes of inquiry related to concrete matter have acted as the mainstay of design and architectural practice. Even as physical things are inert inanimate matter, their power to absorb and exert influence over the spatial environment is exposed.

With a focus on specific spaces, some of these essays 'read' objects through ritual, metaphor and narrative as surrogates for technological progress and commodity, and conditioners of human behaviour. While some use historical and ethnographic methods of inquiry to examine social variables relative to ordering domestic space, others map social interaction as a space of specific inquiry. Here modernism and modernist paradigms are subject to cultural and aesthetic criticism. These essays subject transcendent metaphors of order and function to philosophical inquiry in order to engage the mundane and the ordinary and, subsequently, reframe the discussion through specificity and the implication of the body in space.

Declaring a field of inquiry that lies beyond disciplinary boundaries of design and architecture, all of the texts included in this reader establish generative and active exploration of interior design as a practice informed by the intellectual scholarship surrounding its cultural production and creative practice. They are not foundational in that they do not recognise or declare an originary state or propose any fundamental canon. Collected in order to catalyse creative associations within this operational field, the texts in this volume are presented via an organisational strategy that refuses both chronologic and thematic structure. Connectivity to do with inhabitation and spatial presence as outlined in the examples above is at once distant, by discipline, and intimate, by content.

William Lawrence Bottomley, Architect. A Perfect Example of Dressing-Table Hidden Behind Paneling When Not in Use

Notes
1   Elizabeth Grosz, 'Chaos, Territory, Art. Deleuze and the Framing of the Earth', *IDEA Journal*, 2005, pp 15–28.
2   William Lawrence Bottomley, Architect, 'A Perfect Example of Dressing-Table Hidden Behind Paneling When Not in Use', (Plate 31) in Emily Post, *The Personality of a House: The Blue Book of Home Charm*, Funk & Wagnalls (New York), 1945.
3   Iain Borden and Jane Rendell (eds), *Intersections: Architectural Histories and Critical Theories*, Routledge (London and New York), 2000, pp 1–24.
4   Mario Praz, *An Illustrated History of Interior Decoration from Pompeii to Art Nouveau* [1964], Thames and Hudson (London), 1981. First published as *La filosofia dell'arredamento*, Documente, Libraio Editore (Rome), 1945.
5   Charlotte Gere, *Nineteenth-century Decoration: The Art of the Interior*, HN Abrams (New York), 1989; and Charlotte Gere, *Nineteenth Century Interiors: An Album of Watercolours*, Thames and Hudson (London), 1992.
6   Peter Thornton, *Authentic Decor: The Domestic Interior, 1620–1920*, Weidenfeld & Nicolson (London), 1984.

13

Matrix Key

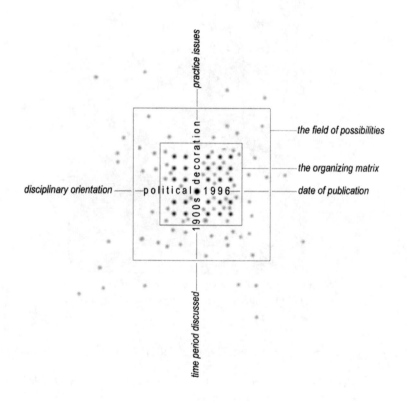

The Partition of Space

Shirley Ardener

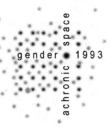

As a cross-cultural researcher of anthropological issues, Shirley Ardener reminds us that space defines the people in it, and reflexively, people define space. Under this conception she notes there is a cultural relationship between 'real' physical space and 'social reality' in which perceptions and patterns are mediated through spatial terms. Having noted that boundaries on the ground are negotiated through rules, she later questions the neutrality of bounded space. The shape and size of space is shown to exert an influence so that behaviour and space are not mutually exclusive. In this text, the special relevance to women is demonstrated through the link between space and gender as ordering systems that impose restraints on mobility. It discusses the space of the interior beyond its physical dimensions and its social and symbolic aspects, as experienced by women.

A restricted area like a club, a theatre or a nation-state has a set of rules to determine how its boundary shall be crossed and who shall occupy that space. Those who enter it will share certain defining features: they will perhaps have met specific criteria of club membership, bought a ticket or passed a citizenship test. In some way they must be recognised, say by a gate-keeper, such as a hall porter, an usherette or an Immigration Officer, or by the other members of the category. So, too, other systems of classification will be decided by taxonomic rules of some kind, which will define 'X' in contrast to 'non-X.' Thus, in studying the way people pattern their perceptions, attention has been especially drawn to the significance of the perimeters of the categories that we make in order to codify and confront the worlds we create, in which we then live, and how we cope with some of the problems that arise from the existence of these boundaries.[1]

These few words have already found us deeply involved with the point on which the chapters in this volume depend: space. For in discussing ways in which humans perceive and pattern their social worlds, a notion (the boundary) has been seized and applied to the meaning of concepts, and to classification into groups, whose label is taken from the register of terms which is used primarily for the three-dimensional 'real' world. The extended use of such spatial terms is firmly embedded in the language in which this is written. Obvious cases would be 'high society,' 'wide application,' 'spheres of interest,' 'narrow-mindedness,' 'political circles,' 'deep divides of opinion,' and so forth. Such practices merely remind us that much of social life is given shape, and that when dimension or location are introduced we assert a correspondence between the so-called 'real' physical world and its 'social reality.'[2] There is, of course, an interaction such that appreciation of the *physical* world is in turn dependent on *social* perceptions of it. Measurements, and what is measured, for instance, are neither totally imperative nor just random; choice enters 'reality,' Societies have generated their own rules, culturally determined, for making boundaries on the ground, and have divided the social into spheres, levels and territories with invisible fences and platforms to be scaled by abstract ladders and crossed by intangible bridges with as much trepidation or exultation as on a plank over a raging torrent.

This brief preamble is by way of indicating why this book on 'women and space' links 'ground rules' with 'social maps' and why such ambiguous pairs of terms were selected for the sub-title. As a preliminary to introducing the chapters and to giving special consideration to women, a few more general points may quickly be raised, in condensed form. It will become apparent that, while divisions of space and social formations are intimately associated, no simple one-way 'cause and effect' pertains, and their cumulative interdependence suggests that we should think rather in terms of 'simultaneities,'[3] and this should be remembered when considering the following section.

Communication systems are primarily associated in our minds with words. Nevertheless, it is by now well recognised, of course, that society has also devised many other symbolic codes. Of one, Edwin Ardener has written: 'We might visualise a semiotic system that depended, in the absence of the power of speech, upon the apperception by the human participants of contextually defined logical relations among themselves in space. Let us say: the relevant position of each participant to another in a gathering, and to items in a fixed environment.'[4] Thus people may 'jockey for position' knowing that their fellows may 'read' from this their social importance. Thus, as Hall puts it, *space speaks*.

Goffman suggests that 'the division and hierarchies of social structure are depicted microecologically, that is, through the use of small-scale spatial metaphors.'[5] This suggests that *space reflects social organisation*, but of course, once space has been bounded and shaped it is no longer merely a neutral background: it exerts its own influence. A dozen people in a small room 'is not the same thing' as a dozen people in a great hall; seating-space shaped by a round, rather than square, table, may influence the nature of social interaction among those seated. The 'theatre of action' to some extent determines the action. The environment imposes certain restraints on our mobility, and, in turn, our perceptions of space are shaped by our own capacity to move about, whether by foot or by mechanical or other transport. So: *behaviour and space are mutually dependent*.

As Judy Matthews in her study of community action has noted, social identity is partly determined by 'the physical and spatial constituents of the groups' environment;'[6] that is to say: *space defines the people in it.* At the same time, however (again reflexively), the presence of individuals in space in turn determines its nature. For example, the entry of a stranger may change a private area into a public one;[7] similarly, 'the Court is where the king is.' Thus: *people define space.*

Not only people, but, as Goffman has said, 'Objects are thought to structure the environment immediately around themselves; they cast a shadow, heat up the surround, strew indications, leave an imprint, they impress a part of themselves, a portrait that is unintended and not dependent on being attended, yet, of course, informing nonetheless to whomsoever is properly placed, trained and inclined.'[8] Further, as anyone who has played chess will know, *objects are affected by the place in space of other objects;* not only their presence, and their position, but even their absence, or 'negative presence,' may be important.[9]

Structural relationships, such as in hierarchies or other ranking patterns, and systems of relationships like those of kinship, are treated in this volume as 'social maps,' which are frequently, but not necessarily, realised on 'the ground' by the placing of individuals in space. In many situations we find (real or metaphysical) 'spaces within spaces,' or 'overlapping universes.' To understand them we may be required to 'pull them apart' in order first to identify each simple map (of, say 'X' and 'non-X'), before reconsidering the way these correspond or are interrelated. It is as if we provide one map showing only where the roads are (or are not), and another setting out the water courses, and so on, before we compile a complex map of all the features of the terrain. Correspondingly, ideally we may 'map,' say, the relationships between a wife and her husband (where they draw the various limits) before 'mapping' the same woman's relationships to her children, in order to compile a complete picture of her family life.

Individuals (and things) belong, then, to many pairs, groups or sets, each of which may be thought of as occupying its own 'space,' or as sharing a particular 'universe.' Members of one group may be 'dominant' relative to members of another group in one 'universe,' while in turn being 'muted' in relation to members of a third group sharing with them a universe differently defined.[10] A woman may be 'muted' relative to her husband and 'dominant' in relation to her children; gypsy men are 'dominant' in their own culture and structurally 'muted' *vis-à-vis* the English.[11] In a society where, say, (a) men take precedence over women and (b) the religious is dominant in relation to the secular, the following ordering is possible: *monks ← lay-men ← nuns ← lay-women* (where *gender* is the predominant critical distinction). Alternatively (as in some Buddhist processions), where the space is primarily *religious* (but gender counts), we may find a redistribution of space between the poles: *monks ← lay-men–nuns ← lay-women*. The second ordering is interesting because the (religious) precedence of *nuns* over *lay-women* may tend to obscure the priority of males between the sexes. This might be particularly so if, at any time or place, no *monks* or *lay-women* are present (that is, the sequence is incomplete). This may account for the inability of some to distinguish asymmetries, that even bear upon them disadvantageously. In other 'real' or 'social' spaces femaleness may be the dominant determinant, but in others yet again, gender may be irrelevant, or insignificant. Age, class and many other features, may add further complexities in situations of multiple dimensions).[12] If relationships (say between *monks*, *nuns* and *lay-persons*) are expressed by the distribution of people on the ground, then the application of the term 'map' is probably unambiguous to most readers of this book. If, however, the relationships cannot be actually 'seen' in physical arrangements, but only detected in other ways (such as by who speaks first, or in what manner, or by who bows to whom) then possibly the use of the term 'map' may be challenged. Even when an ordering is 'jumbled up' to the eye, or intangible, it may, however, still be *convenient* to our understanding to think of that ordering as a 'map' on which the 'jumble' has been simplified by a logical rearrangement of the information. No map corresponds to what can be seen: the London underground system is not accurately and completely portrayed on the map provided to the public.

Thus, in this volume the term 'social map' has been used broadly, and sometimes in different ways. The concept is applied to 'historical time' (in which 'yesterday' may seem 'closer' than the 'distant' past; just as some kin, living or dead, may seem 'close' relative to other kin). The notion of 'private' as opposed to 'public' is seen as a criterion for 'mapping' metaphysical space, as 'inner' does in opposition to 'outer,' *regardless* of the fact that some 'private places' can really be walked into. No emphasis has been given to the distinction between 'place' and 'space,' as used by geographers. The term 'social map,' as used in this book, may be taken, perhaps, as a temporary and handy 'folk' term, rather than as having the status of a definitive scientific label.

Space, then, is not a simple concept. In certain societies it is coloured. Thus, among the Zuni of America, north is thought of as blue, south as red, and east as white.[13] Among the Atoni of Indonesia, south is again red (it is also associated with rulers), east is again white (and is connected with warriors, west is black (and is associated with village headman) and the north is – not blue (Zuni) – but yellow. The Irish have coloured space.[14] Here, however, south is black (and the sphere of music, slaves, witches and the dead).

If space is an ordering principle, so, of course, is gender. These principles are often also linked, though not always in the same way. For the Irish, south is associated with women. In contrast, the Chinese see the south as male and the north as female.

In 1909 Robert Hertz wrote a classic text 'The Pre-eminence of the Right Hand.' It is available in Needham's 1973 translation from French into English. Thus over 80 years ago Hertz wrote:

Society and the whole universe have a side which is sacred, noble and precious, and another which is profane and common; a male side, strong and active, and another, female, weak and passive; or, in two words, a right side and a left side ... [15]

He also equated the right with 'rectitude,' 'dexterity,' 'the juridical norm' (p 11), 'life' (p 12), the 'inside' (p 13), the 'sacred' (p 12), 'good,' and 'beauty' (p 12).

He associated the left with the 'profane' (p 12), the 'ugly' (p 12); with 'bad' (p 12), 'death' (p 12), the 'outside, the infinite, hostile and the perpetual menace of evil' (p 13).

Hertz (drawing on Wilson's report of 1891) noted that among North American Indians 'The right hand stands for me, the left for not-me, others.' Drawing on Mallery (1881) Hertz noted that 'The raised right hand signifies bravery, power, and virility, while on the contrary the same hand, carried to the left and placed below the left hand, signifies, according to context, the ideas of death, destruction, and burial.'

After discussing Australian beliefs (of the Wulwanga), Hertz concludes it is not chance that God took one of Adam's left ribs to create Eve, 'for one and the same essence characterises woman and the left side of the body – two parts of a weak and defenceless being, somewhat ambiguous and disquieting, destined by nature to a passive and receptive role and to a subordinate condition.'

Since Hertz, social anthropologists have travelled the world collecting world-views from different cultures. Many have described systems of dual classification, and a selection of studies can be found in Needham.[16] These schemes of perception which elsewhere Bourdieu speaks of finding, include those 'which divide the world up in accordance with the oppositions between male and female, east and west, future and past, top and bottom, right and left ...'[17] To which we may add public/private and inside/outside (a particular concern of modern Greeks, as shown by Hirschon).[18] Thus Faron provides two lists from Chile demonstrating the 'Mapuche inferior-superior, left-right hand associations' adding that 'There are many indications of male superiority and association with the right as well as with good and the sacred.'[19] There is also 'an unmistakable and literal connection between left and evil, right and good.' Again, van der Kroef correlates pairs of oppositions among the people of Amboyna in Indonesia ... [20]

Now it would be a diversion to go into further details on dual classification here; it is a field requiring delicate handling – especially of the relationship between concepts placed in vertical lists. There is, indeed, no attempt here at a comprehensive analysis of all the characteristics of space; the literature is in any case already extensive. McDowell, for example, has provided a useful review of material on the gender division of urban space.[21] For some Marxist analyses of place and space see the work of David Harvey.

The few simple, but fundamental points raised above are merely reminders of the general context in which the following discussions are to be viewed. The chapters below provide illustrations of them, and give some examples of their special relevance to women. Although there is no pretence to comprehensiveness, one more aspect must, nevertheless, be mentioned: the relationship of time and space. When we speak of 'the world getting smaller' through the advent of air travel, or of a distance being 'five minutes' walk away,' we clearly acknowledge that time and space are 'mutually affecting spheres of reality,' where 'reality' is understood to depend upon human apperceptions. Paine quotes a resident of Israel who felt that by settling in Israel he had taken a leap back in time which made him closer to David and Uzziah than to the contemporary *shtetl* in Poland.[22] One could say that by a change of place time had been collapsed, or elided. This reminds us of Harvey's comment that 'nearness does not consist of shortness of distance' and Edwin Ardener's study of 'remoteness.'[23] 'Time-systems occupy spaces which are generated by and with the physical and social space.'[24]   (...p 6)

Notes

1 See for example, M Douglas, *Purity and Danger: An Analysis of Concepts of Pollution and Taboo*, Routledge and Kegan Paul (London), 1966; S Ardener (ed), *Defining Females*, Halstead (London, Croom Helm; New York), 1978, Reprint Berg, 1993.

2 See for example, E Durkheim and M Mauss, *Primitive Classification* [1903] trans R Needham, Cohen and West (London), 1963. First published in France 1901–2. Speaking of various indigenous groups in Australia and America, Durkheim and Mauss wrote: 'Cosmic space and tribal space are thus only very imperfectly distinguished and the mind passes from one to the other without difficulty, almost without being aware of doing so' (p 65). 'Shape' and 'space' are used in this book in the sense of 'topological space,' where alterations in the boundaries may still preserve the integrity of the space: thus a Regency chair may occupy the same 'conceptual slot' or 'conceptual space' as a Victorian chair, though their actual forms may differ; we can assume them both to be 'chair-shaped' nevertheless; similarly a tree may grow, and change its appearance in other ways, while remaining a tree.

3 See for example, 'Introductory Essay', EW Ardener (ed), *Social Anthropology and Language*, Tavistock Press (London), 1971; E W Ardener (ed), *The Voice of Prophecy*, Malcolm Chapman, (ed), Blackwell (Oxford), 1989.

4 E Ardener, *Social Anthropology*, pp xliii–xliv.

5 E Goffman, *Gender Advertisements*, Macmillan (London), 1979, p 1. First published in America in 1976.

6 JA Matthews, 'Environment, Change and Community Identity,' paper delivered at Conference on Threatened Identities, under the auspices of the British Psychological Society, Oxford, April 1980. Forthcoming in a volume to be edited by Glynis Breakwell for John Wiley.

7 See S Ardener, *Defining Females*, 1978, p 32, 1993, p 18; and S Rodgers, 'Women's Space in a Men's House: The British House of Commons', S Ardener (ed), *Women and Space: Ground Rules and Social Maps*, Oxford, Berg, 1993.

8 Goffman, *Gender Advertisements*, p 1.

9 See F de Saussure, *Cours de Linguistique Générale* [1916] English trans, reprinted Owen (London), 1964. The study of sign systems ('semiology') was advocated by Saussure in the period around the turn of the century (see his posthumous work: 1916) and has been elaborated by many scholars subsequently.

10 For the original presentation and extensive discussions of the notion of 'mutedness' and who generates social concepts and the words that label them, see E Ardener, 'Belief and the Problem of Women', J La Fontaine (ed), *The Interpretation Ritual*, Tavistock Press (London), 1972; E Ardener,

'The Problem Revisited', S Ardener (ed), *Perceiving Women*, Halstead (London, Dent; New York), 1975; E Ardener, 'Some Outstanding Problems in the Analysis of Events', E Schwimmer (ed), *Yearbook of Symbolic Anthropology*, Hirst (London), 1975; S Ardener, *Perceiving Women*; S Ardener, *Defining Females*. The concept has since been taken up and documented in Spender and applied by other researchers. See D Spender, *Man Made Language*, Routledge and Kegan Paul (London), 1980.

11 J Okely, 'Privileged Schooled and Finished: Boarding Education for Girls', S Ardener, *Defining Females*, 1978, pp 109–39; 1993, pp 93–122.

12 See S Ardener (ed), *Persons and Powers of Women in Diverse Cultures*, Berg (Oxford and Providence), 1992.

13 E Durkheim and M Mauss, *Primitive Classification* [1903] trans R Needham, Cohen and West (London), 1963, p 44; R Needham (ed), *Introduction to Right and Left, Essays on Dual Symbolic Classification*, University of Chicago Press (Chicago), 1973, p 33.

14 S Ardener, *Perceiving Women*.

15 Needham, *Introduction to Right and Left*, p 10.

16 Needham, *Introduction to Right and Left*.

17 P Bourdieu, *Outline of a Theory of Practice*, Cambridge University Press (Cambridge), 1977, p 15.

18 Renée Hirschon, 'Essential Objects and the Sacred: Interior and Exterior Space in an Urban Greek Locality', S Ardener, *Women and Space*.

19 Needham, *Introduction to Right and Left*, p 196.

20 Needham, *Introduction to Right and Left*, p 180.

21 L McDowell, 'Towards an Understanding of the Gender Division of Urban Space', *Environment and Planning D: Society and Space*, 1, 1983, pp 59–72.

22 R Paine, 'Ethnicity of Place and Time Among Zionists', paper given to History and Ethnicity Conference of the ASA, Spring 1947.

23 D Harvey, 'Between Space and Time: Reflections on the Geographical Imagination', *Annals* of the Association of American Geographers, vol 3, September, 1990; D Harvey, 'From Space to Place and Back Again; Reflections on the Condition of Postmodernity', Futures' Symposium, Tate Gallery, November, 1990; E Ardener, 'Remote Areas: Some Theoretical Considerations', A Jackson (ed), *Anthropology at Home*, Tavistock (London), 1987.

24 E Ardener, 'The Voice of Prophecy', The Munro Lecture, delivered in Edinburgh, 1975, p 11. See also section 'Time and Space', E Ardener, 'The Voice of Prophecy'. For 'simultaneities' see E Ardener, 'Some Outstanding Problems in the Analysis of Events', E Schwimmer, *Yearbook of Symbolic Anthropology*. The phrase 'mutually affecting spheres of reality' is borrowed from K Hastrup, 'The Semantics of Biology: Virginity', S Ardener, *Defining Females*, 1978, pp 49–65; 1993, pp 34–50.

Article originally published as extracts p 1–6 'The Partition of Space', from *Women and Space: Ground Rules and Social Maps* (ed Shirley Ardener), by Berg Publishers (Oxford and New York), April 1993, www.bergpublishers.com
Reprinted by permission of Berg Publishers.
(Excerpt pp 1–6)

The Dialectics of Outside and Inside

Gaston Bachelard

philosophical space 1958 achronic

This selection from The Poetics of Space *demonstrates Gaston Bachelard's ability to bridge scientific logic with poetic analysis. As a phenomenological reading of the poetic image, it probes the geometrical divide between inside and outside through an analysis of the imagination of matter. It resists simplification, engaging with both physical and psychological body-space relations, and describes an exchange between interior and exterior in which the latter might be 'an old intimacy'. The dialectical condition of 'interior immensity' and the 'immeasurable outside', attests to the spatiality of being as a reflexive inquiry on interiority, what Bachelard calls intimate geometry grounded in imagination.*

Once we have been touched by the grace of super-imagination, we feel it in the presence of the simpler images through which the exterior world deposits virtual elements of highly-colored space in the heart of our being. The image with which Pierre Jean Jouve constitutes his secret being is one of these. He places it in his most intimate cell:

La cellule de moi-même emplit d'étonnement
La muraille peinte à la chaux de mon secret.
(Les Noces, p 50)[1]

(The cell of myself fills with wonder
The white-washed wall of my secret.)

The room in which the poet pursues such a dream as this is probably not 'white-washed.' But this room in which he is writing is so quiet, that it really deserves its name, which is, the 'solitary' room! It is inhabited thanks to the image, just as one inhabits an image which is 'in the imagination.' Here the poet inhabits the cellular image. This image does not transpose a reality. It would be ridiculous, in fact, to ask the dreamer its dimensions. It does not lend itself to geometrical intuition, but is a solid framework for secret being. And secret being feels that it is guarded more by the whiteness of the lime-wash than by the strong walls. The cell of the secret is white. A single value suffices to coordinate any number of dreams. And it is always like that, the poetic image is under the domination of a heightened quality. The whiteness of the walls, alone, protects the dreamer's *cell*. It is stronger than all geometry. It is a part of the cell of intimacy.

Such images lack stability. As soon as we depart from expression as it is, as the author gives it, in all spontaneity, we risk relapsing into literal meaning. We also risk being bored by writing that is incapable of condensing the intimacy of the image. And we have to withdraw deep into ourselves, for instance, to read this fragment by Maurice Blanchot in the tonality of being in which it was written: 'About this room, which was plunged in utter darkness, I knew everything, I had entered into it, I bore it within me, I made it live, with a life that is not life, but which is stronger than life, and which no force in the world can vanquish.'[2] One feels in these repetitions, or to be more exact, in this constant strengthening of an image into which one has entered (and not of a room into which one has entered, a room which the author bears within himself, and which he has made live with a life that does not exist in life) one feels, as I said, that it is not the writer's intention merely to describe his *familiar* abode. Memory would *encumber* this image by stocking it with *composite memories* from several periods of time. Here everything is simpler, more radically simple. Blanchot's room is an abode of intimate space, it is his inner room. We share the writer's image, thanks to what we are obliged to call a *general image*, that is, an image which participation keeps us from confusing with a *generality*. We individualize this general image right away. We live in it, we enter into it the way Blanchot enters into his. Neither word nor idea suffices, the writer must help us to reverse space, and shun description, in order to have a more valid experience of the hierarchy of repose.

Often it is from the very fact of concentration in the most restricted intimate space that the dialectics of inside and outside draws its strength. One feels this elasticity in the following passage by Rilke:[3] 'And there is almost no space here; and you feel almost calm at the thought that it is impossible for anything very large to hold in this narrowness.' There is consolation in knowing that one is in an atmosphere of calm, in a narrow space. Rilke achieved this narrowness intimately, in inner space where everything is commensurate with inner being. Then, in the next sentence, the text continues dialectically:

> But outside, everything is immeasurable. And when the level rises outside, it also rises in you, not in the vessels that are partially controlled by you, or in the phlegm of your most unimpressionable organs: but it grows in the capillary veins, drawn upward into the furthermost branches of your infinitely ramified existence. This is where it rises, where it overflows from you, higher than your respiration, and, as a final resort, you take refuge, as though on the tip of your breath. Ah! where, where next? Your heart banishes you from yourself, your heart pursues you, and you are already almost beside

yourself, and you can't stand it any longer. Like a beetle that has been stepped on, you flow from yourself, and your lack of hardness or elasticity means nothing any more.

Oh night without objects. Oh window muffled on the outside, oh, doors carefully closed; customs that have come down from times long past, transmitted, verified, never entirely understood. Oh silence in the stair-well, silence in the adjoining rooms, silence up there, on the ceiling. Oh mother, oh one and only you, who faced all this silence, when I was a child.

I have given this long passage without cuts for the reason that it has dynamic continuity. Inside and outside are not abandoned to their geometrical opposition. From what overflow of a ramified interior does the substance of being run, does the outside call? Isn't the exterior an old intimacy lost in the shadow of memory? In what silence does the stair-well resound? In this silence there are soft foot-steps: the mother comes back to watch over her child, as she once did. She restores to all these confused, unreal sounds their concrete, familiar meaning. Limitless night ceases to be empty space. This passage by Rilke, which is assailed by such frights, finds its peace. But by what a long, circuitous route! In order to experience it in the reality of the images, one would have to remain the contemporary of an osmosis between intimate and undetermined space.

I have presented texts that were as varied as possible, in order to show that there exists a play of values, which makes everything in the category of simple determinations fall into second place. The opposition of outside and inside ceases to have as coefficient its geometrical evidence.

To conclude this chapter, I shall consider a fragment in which Balzac defines determined opposition in the face of affronted space. This text is all the more interesting in that Balzac felt obliged to correct it.

In an early version of *Louis Lambert*, we read: 'When he used his entire strength, he grew unaware, as it were, of his physical life, and only existed through the all-powerful play of his interior organs, the range of which he constantly maintained and, according to his own admirable expression, he made *space withdraw before his advance*.'[4]

In the final version, we read simply: 'He left space, as he said, behind him.'

What a difference between these two movements of expression! What decline of power of being faced with space, between the first and second forms! In fact, one is puzzled that Balzac should have made such a correction. He returned, in other words, to 'indifferent space.' In a meditation on the subject of being, one usually puts space between parentheses, in other words, one leaves space 'behind one.' As a sign of the lost 'tonalization' of being, it should be noted that 'admiration' subsided. The second mode of expression is no longer, according to the author's own admission, *admirable*. Because it really was admirable, this power to make *space withdraw*, to put space, all space, outside, in order that meditating being might be free to think.   (... p 231)

Notes

1   [Editors' note: See Pierre Jean Jouve, *Poésie: Les Noces, Sueur de Sang, Matière Céleste, Kyrie*, Mercure de France (Paris), 1964, p 43.]

2   Maurice Blanchot, *L'arrêt de mort*, p 124. [Editors' note: See Maurice Blanchot, *L'arrêt de mort*, Gallimard (Paris), 1948, p 124.]

3   Rilke, French translation, p 106, of *Les Cahiers*. [Editors' note: For another English translation see: Rainer Maria Rilke, *The Notebooks of Malte Laurids Brigge* [1910], Oxford University Press (Oxford, New York), 1984, pp 70–1.]

4   Ed Jean Pommier, Corti, p 19. [Editors' note: See Honoré de Balzac, *Louis Lambert: édition critique établie par Marcel Bouteron et Jean Pommier avec la collaboration de Madame Robert Siohan*, J Corti (Paris), 1954, p 19. For an English translation see Honoré de Balzac, *Louis Lambert* (electronic resource), trans Clara Bell and James Waring, Champaign, Ill, Project Gutenberg, Boulder, Colo, NetLibrary, p 4, http://www.gutenberg.org/etext/1943.]

'The Dialectics of Outside and Inside', from *The Poetics of Space* by Gaston Bachelard, translated by Maria Jolas, The Orion Press (London), 1964. © 1964 by The Orion Press, Inc. Original copyright © 1958 by Presses Universitaires de France. Reprinted by permission of Viking Penguin, a division of Penguin Group (USA) Inc. (Excerpt pp 227–31)

The Sterility of Perfection + The Rule Breaker's Success

Billy Baldwin

social ● 1972

mid 20th century furnish

In sharp contrast to advice literature of the nineteenth century, Billy Baldwin's designs freely play with history, form and finish, each in service to the comfort and expression of living. To this extent he breaks with a tradition that promoted homogeneity, but advances on those seeking individuality and personality so that all aspects of interior decoration are used for effect. In these two excerpts, he rallies against the tyranny of perfection and questions those who advocate rules for interior decoration. His own signature interiors for New York's wealthy and famous demonstrate this thinking, and are recognisable for his flare to mix and match period styles in an effort to charge their individual characteristics and create a uniquely decorated room. This text reveals Baldwin's attitudes and values against pretentious design and demonstrates his commitment to reconcile his clients' needs with lifestyle.

The Sterility of Perfection

I know a magnificent French apartment in New York that someone has brilliantly described as 'a series of foyers leading to nothing.' How sad to see rooms so beautiful, yet so cold. You must walk through the austere living room and out again in search of a small haven of comfort to sit in. Even the master bedroom looks like an unwelcoming guest room.

A young client of mine expressed the same feelings another way. We were discussing his library, where he works during the evening while his wife reads or does needlepoint. They had just returned from visiting a newly decorated house with a library that had made them cringe with horror – shiny walnut paneling, yards and yards of brand-new untouched books, a new desk without a trace of evidence that it had ever been used. The young man said, 'I hope you understand that we do not want our house to be perfect.' This young couple had glimpsed the awful sterility of perfection, and realized at once what I have always maintained: Nothing is interesting unless it is personal. So their library has a superb Louis XVI desk, and sitting unashamedly beside it, an efficient filing cabinet.

Everyone has his own needs, his own preferences, his own ways of using space. When a decorator disregards these needs, or tries to superimpose an alien personality, he cannot bring off that wonderful warm atmosphere of a private, personal place.

I, for one, cannot imagine a fireplace without a fire burning whenever there is the slightest excuse for it. I cannot conceive of a house in the country without dogs, or of any house without books – the greatest decoration of all. These give a room heart – along with lighted candles and the smell of fresh flowers, or bowls of potpourri in open windows.

There is nothing quite so boring as false refinement, or so vulgar as misplaced elegance. I have often quoted Cole Porter, who said to me: 'Please don't try to hide my television, or make slipcovers for my piano.' I had a client once who was infuriated when I put flowers on her grand piano. 'Do you know who plays that piano?' she said. 'Rubinstein! Get those flowers off.' 'Well,' I replied, 'does he play it every night?' It wasn't as if I had put a Spanish shawl on it, or a crowd of photographs. How pretentious to object to movable blossoms!

A woman whose house Elsie de Wolfe had decorated years ago always kept twelve red roses on her hall console. Elsie had probably said, 'Wouldn't it be nice to have some red roses there,' and the woman had taken it as an unalterable dictum. But the roses never looked as if she had fallen in love with them in the florist's window. They were just furniture.

One of the greatest sterilizers of the would-be perfectionist is fashion. There's no reason for rooms and houses to change as often as hairdos and skirt lengths. All rooms should begin as outgrowths of the owner's personality, then become lovelier, more personal, and more welcoming with every year. I haven't much interest in a client who asks me what I have just done in someone else's living room, or worse yet, what the 'latest trends' are. If I find that something I am doing is becoming a trend, I run from it like the plague.

A client has no one but herself to blame for a sterile, uninteresting house if she hasn't the gumption or self-assurance to assert herself. Ruby Ross Wood once took me to visit one of her clients who lived in a beautiful house with superb furniture and lots of lovely little objects and flowers around. But the woman was frantic. 'I'm going out of my mind,' she said. 'Someone has given me this little box, and I don't know where to put it.' Ruby snatched the box from her and thumped it on the first table she came to. 'Put it there,' she said. The woman had become so afraid of her own room, she felt everything in it had to be an arrangement.

Some people add enormously to a room in a way that no decorator ever could. They can move into a newly decorated house and make it look as if they have lived there for thirty years. And a year later, you see still more wonderful growth. I know several people with this precious knack – I work out the colors and fabric and furniture arrangement, and when everything is in place I say, 'All right. Now go ahead and mess it up,' Then they buy and arrange the paintings and objects, make needlepoint pillows, fix flowers, move a chair to a place where it really is more comfortable. They break up the hardness of the perfect look, and make the room their own.

The way people accumulate and display objects can add immeasurably to a room's vitality. For a decorator to go out and buy a whole collection at one fell swoop is almost an invasion of privacy. To display it formally in some ghostly lighted cabinet, as the French often do, makes me shudder. I love to see collections that have been gathered over the years kept right out in the open as the English keep them – on tables and commodes where you can see them and touch them.

A touch of wit can help a great deal to ward off the sterile look. I don't mean that a room should make you roar with laughter, but as you sit in it, you might be struck suddenly by some unexpected object, an entertaining picture, some little eccentricity of the owner. In my window there sits a foolish little wooden monkey holding a globe covered with chips of mirror that shoot sparks of sunlight all over the room. It is a very silly thing, but a good friend gave it to me and I like it. The Duke di Verdura found a little fieldstone, split it in half, and polished the insides. When you open the two halves, you discover a little green-enamel lizard that he tucked between them. It is a shock every time! Things like that are fun to collect for your own house, and delightful to come upon in someone else's. But I would never go out and buy something 'funny' for a room. No object should 'wink' at us.

A good friend of mine served Chinese fortune cookies at her husband's sixtieth birthday party. The wife laughed when she read her own fortune: 'Your marriage will be prosperous.' Next time I visited them, I happened to notice quite by accident something that struck me as the essence of making a room warm and alive. On a table sat a little glass box – a French box with gold edges, probably of great value. And there in the box, like a jewel, was that crinkled message from the fortune cookie.

The Rule Breaker's Success
The first rule of decoration is that you can break almost all the other rules. A room arranged absolutely according to the book, with little *i*'s dotted and big *t*'s crossed, is all very well in its impersonal way. But the rooms that are really successful declare the owner's independence, carry the owner's signature, his very private scrawl.

It's a rule that pattern should not be played against pattern, that figured curtains need a plain wall. But nothing is more enchanting than the indoor garden that grows from flowering chintz, flowered walls, flowery needlework rugs. One of the pleasantest drawing rooms on Long Island has a flowered Bessarabian rug, all muted reds and faded greens, with furniture slipcovered in pale-green and cream flower chintz, and a flourish of books, pictures, bunches of flowers. Another handsome room, this one in town, spreads a soft ancient Oriental rug across the floor, and surprises it by overlaying another, much smaller and higher in key, in front of the little French mantel.

It's a rule that one chintz is a charmer – two's a crowd. But maybe you want to cover two chairs in chintz, and can find only enough of a fabric to cover one. Well, use it – and for the second chair use another chintz, of equal caliber but different design. No one hesitates to hang two flower paintings in the same room, so why not allow two flower chairs, like distinct and lovely bouquets?

There's a great distinction in no pattern at all. Consider a room all the dark fresh green of gardenia leaves. The walls might be highly lacquered; the curtains dull, roughly woven; the sofas and chairs covered in damask and needlework – all wearing the green, but with their own textures giving their own value to it. The variety would be subtle, but very real. And don't forget that one person puts pattern and movement into a room, and the intricacy of the design grows with the size of the party.

There's chic in repetition – a splurge of the same fabric for curtains, sofas, chairs. Don't be timid about making this an all-out effort, or your friends will suspect that you undercalculated your yardage. In Connecticut, there's a wonderful salon, its style a kind of Norwegian Louis XVI. On a polished Fontainebleau floor is ranged a levee of chairs and sofas, all painted chalk white, all covered with a pale-blue, gray, and white checked fabric. The curtains are of the same fabric, the walls are a misty gray-blue, and the effect is fabulous.

There's chic in not repeating. One very grand drawing room has walls of glowing red flock-paper, gold satin curtains, gold and white furniture – nowhere another flicker of red. And one chair in a high clear tone makes its point more conclusively if its color is not echoed. In a gray monochrome room, a chair covered in poison-green satin will lose its fine sting if the green is recalled in a pillow or two on the little gray sofa. It's superfluous to repeat the green at all, but if you must, do it in an off-shade and another medium – perhaps an emerald-green chandelier.

A few decorating principles seem safe from contradiction. When you are arranging furniture, it's always wise to put pieces of equal value together. Don't hang a contemporary painted mirror over an elegant old commode. The mirror may have its decoration virtue, but in that false position it will insult the antique, and show itself for an upstart. If you are looking for a mantel garniture, choose something that has the same quality as the mantel itself, and the picture or mirror over it. (There's a seeming exception to this rule – one lovely mantel arrangement involves a beige marble Louis XV mantel, and on it a row of purple violets in modest clay pots, reflected in a superb gilt mirror. But this makes sense, because the pots don't pretend to be more than they are; they are, in their own way, just as authentic).

If you spend most of your decorating money on a Chippendale table or a Chinese lacquer screen, don't fill in the gaps with mediocrity. Forget the gaps for a while; just have simple slipcovers in one pretty color. Then, as you can, acquire other good pieces that are compatible with your first extravagance. Let the room grow slowly to maturity. There is 'costume' decoration as well as 'costume' jewelry – in itself, it may have charm, but it tends to destroy the charm of the Real Thing, if used with it.

No one object should dominate a room. A great work of art is the richest endowment a room can have, and it should be given a dominating position – but if it is really great, it will have the grace of all great things, and won't be too obtrusive. Today we don't want to be too conscious of the *mise en scène*; don't want to have curtains, chairs, paintings thrust themselves forward as topics of conversation.

It's far more important to have three rooms that are beautifully done and beautifully run than to have ten or twenty that are dreary and neglected. Some of the most distinguished buildings in the world are the little villas, pavilions, orangeries. If we live in small-scale rooms, we needn't be limited to small-style decoration. A tiny library – with boiserie and double doors – can have as much style as a ballroom, and can offer more stimulus to conversation.   (... p 27)

Billy Baldwin, *Billy Baldwin Decorates*, Chartwell Books (Secaucus, NJ), 1972. (Excerpt pp 24–7)

Chromophobia

David Batchelor

Artist and critical theorist David Batchelor has written widely on colour and contemporary art as well as exhibiting his own research projects on both colour and urbanism. In the book, Chromophobia, he argues that contemporary culture exhibits a Western tradition of resistance to colour that can be traced back to antiquity. This is characterised by a desire to deny its significance, complexity and value, by assigning it negative values such as primitive, vulgar and feminine, while equating it with the superficial and cosmetic; it is dangerous and trivial. The chosen extract discusses how Le Corbusier's rationalism – the rhetoric of order, purity and truth – is inscribed in a pure blinding white surface. Colour is subordinate to the rule of line and the mind so its purpose is to reveal whiteness. Batchelor's text evidences how this sense of order remains a persistent factor in contemporary popular and design culture particularly in interiors.

If it started with a short visit to an inside-out interior of a colourless whiteness where clarity was confusion, simplicity was complication, and art was uniformly grey, then it would be comforting to think that it might also end there. After all, there can't be many places like this interior which was home only to the very few things that had submitted to its harsh regime. And those few things were, in effect, sealed off from the unwanted and uncertain contingencies of the world outside. No exchange, no seepage, no spillage. Rather: isolation, confinement. But this shutting-off began to speak more and more about what it excluded than what it contained. What did this great white hollow make me think about? Not, for long, its whiteness. Rather, its colour.

If colour is unimportant, I began to wonder, why is it so important to exclude it so forcefully? If colour doesn't matter, why does its abolition matter so much? In one sense, it doesn't matter, or it wouldn't if we could say for certain that this inside really was as self-contained and isolated as it looked. But this house was a very *ambitious* inside. It was not a retreat, it was not a monastic emptiness. Its 'voluntary poverty' – that's how its architect likes to talk – was altogether more righteous and evangelical. It looked like it wanted to impose its order upon the disorder around it. Like neoclassicism, like the manifestoes of Adolf Loos or Le Corbusier, it wanted to rescue a culture and lead it to salvation. In which case, colour does matter. It mattered to Melville and Conrad, and it mattered to Pater and Winkelmann; it mattered to Le Corbusier, and, it turns out, it has mattered to many others for whom, in one way or another, the fate of Western culture has mattered. It mattered because it got in the way. And it still matters because it still does.

The notion that colour is bound up with the fate of Western culture sounds odd, and not very likely. But this is what I want to argue: that colour has been the object of extreme prejudice in Western culture. For the most part, this prejudice has remained unchecked and passed unnoticed. And yet it is a prejudice that is so all-embracing and generalized that, at one time or another, it has enrolled just about every other prejudice in its service. If its object were a furry animal, it would be protected by international law. But its object is, it is said, almost nothing, even though it is at the same time a part of almost everything and exists almost everywhere. It is, I believe, no exaggeration to say that, in the West, since Antiquity, colour has been systematically marginalized, reviled, diminished and degraded. Generations of philosophers, artists, art historians and cultural theorists of one stripe or another have kept this prejudice alive, warm, fed and groomed. As with all prejudices, its manifest form, its loathing, masks a fear: a fear of contamination and corruption by something that is unknown or appears unknowable. This loathing of colour, this fear of corruption through colour, needs a name: chromophobia.

Chromophobia manifests itself in the many and varied attempts to purge colour from culture, to devalue colour, to diminish its significance, to deny its complexity. More specifically: this purging of colour is usually accomplished in one of two ways. In the first, colour is made out to be the property of some 'foreign' body – usually the feminine, the oriental, the primitive, the infantile, the vulgar, the queer or the pathological. In the second, colour is relegated to the realm of the superficial, the supplementary, the inessential or the cosmetic. In one, colour is regarded as alien and therefore dangerous; in the other, it is perceived merely as a secondary quality of experience, and thus unworthy of serious consideration. Colour is dangerous, or it is trivial, or it is both. (It is typical of prejudices to conflate the sinister and the superficial.) Either way, colour is routinely excluded from the higher concerns of the Mind. It is other to the higher values of Western culture. Or perhaps culture is other to the higher values of colour. Or colour is the corruption of culture. (... p 23)

What colour was the Parthenon in Le Corbusier's dream? Not, as one might expect from his later writings, a magnificent, triumphant, all-embracing white. Or not immediately. Rather, in his description of the great temple, next to the form, volume, mass and space of the architecture, colour begins to *give way*; colour no longer appears to be such a significant force; it no longer has the same power to intoxicate; it no longer has quite the same intensity. His description becomes more muted: 'I shall give this entire account an ochre cast;' the marbles adopt the colour of the landscape and 'seem as reddish-brown as terra-cotta.' And yet in this *reflected* colour, there is still something awesome: 'Never in my life have I experienced the subtleties of such monochromy.' Only later, during a storm, does the Parthenon whiten: 'I saw through the large drops of rain the hill becoming suddenly white and the temple sparkle like a diadem against the ink-black Hymettus and the Pentelicus ravaged by downpours.' Once again, the Parthenon absorbs and reflects the colours of its surroundings and atmosphere, but it does not seem to have colour of its own; the Parthenon is somehow beyond colour.

In Le Corbusier's earlier evocations, just about every object had brilliant local colour, and these intense hues were often intermingled with strong blacks and dazzling whites. White was the precondition for colour; colour was intensified by its proximity to white; there was no sense of opposition between the two; they were co-dependent and co-operative. That was certainly part of the brilliance of Le Corbusier's early writing on colour. The *separation* of whiteness and colour would come later. Le Corbusier in 1925 in *The Decorative Art of Today*:

> What shimmering silks, what fancy, glittering marbles, what opulent bronzes and golds! What fashionable blacks, what striking vermilions, what silver lamés from Byzantium and the Orient! Enough. Such stuff founders in a narcotic haze. Let's have done with it ... It is time to crusade for whitewash and Diogenes.[1]

The architect was done with drugs. He had been off them since at least 1920; the Great War had seen to that. In their place: Order. Reason. Purity. Truth. Architecture. Whitewash.

In his evangelical *Rappel à l'ordre* tirade against 'the flourish, the stain, the distracting din of colours and ornaments', and in his campaign for a world shaped by the New Spirit and a new architecture, Le Corbusier aligned himself with the earlier but equally evangelical Adolf Loos: 'We have gone beyond ornament, we have achieved plain, undecorated simplicity. Behold, the time is at hand, fulfilment awaits us. Soon the streets of the city will shine like white walls! Like Zion, the Holy City, Heaven's capital. The fulfilment will be ours.'[2] Heaven is white; that which gets closest to God – the Parthenon, the Idea, Purity, Cleanliness – also sheds its colour. But for Le Corbusier, ornament, clutter, glitter and colour were not so much signs of primitive 'degeneracy,' as they had been for Loos, as they were the particularly modern form of degeneration that we now call kitsch. The difference is important, because at no time did Le Corbusier attack what he saw as the authentic 'simplicity' of the folk cultures of the past, cultures which, he conceded, had their own whiteness: 'Whitewash has been associated with human habitation since the birth of mankind.' The problem was, rather, modern industrialized ornamentation and colouring, a problem which, for Le Corbusier, reeked of confusion, disorder, dishonesty, imbalance, subservience, narcosis and dirt.

Thus, under the chapter title 'A Coat of Whitewash: The Law of Ripolin' (a phrase that is constantly repeated and usually capitalized):

we would perform a moral act: *to love purity!*
we would improve our condition: *to have the power of judgement!*
An act which leads to the joy of life: the pursuit of perfection.
Imagine the results of the Law of Ripolin. Every citizen is required to replace his hangings, his damasks, his wall-papers, his stencils, with a plain coat of white ripolin. *His home* is made clean. There are no more dirty, dark corners. *Everything is shown as it is.* Then comes *inner* cleanness, for the course adopted leads to refusal to allow anything which is not correct, authorised, intended, desired, thought-out: no action before thought. When you are surrounded with shadows and dark corners you are at home only as far as the hazy edges of the darkness your eyes cannot penetrate. You are not *master in your own house.* Once you have put ripolin on your walls you will be master of your own house.

White is clean, clear, healthy, moral, rational, masterful … White, it seems, was everywhere, at least in the minds of Le Corbusier's contemporaries and followers. Theo van Doesburg, for example:

WHITE is the spiritual colour of our times, the clearness which directs all our actions. It is neither grey white nor ivory white, but pure white.
WHITE is the colour of modern times, the colour which dissipates a whole era; our era is one of perfection, purity and certitude.
WHITE it includes everything.
We have superseded both the 'brown' of decadence and classicism and the 'blue' of divisionism, the cult of the blue sky, the gods with green beards and the spectrum.
WHITE pure white.[3]

In Le Corbusier's intoxicated rationalism, the rhetoric of order, purity and truth is inscribed in a pure, blinding white surface. So blinding, in fact, that the discourse of modern architecture has almost entirely failed to notice that most of his buildings are actually *coloured.* This marvellous paradox in the rhetoric of whiteness has been carefully picked apart by Mark Wigley, who has observed, for example, that Le Corbusier's manifesto building, the Pavilion de l'Esprit Nouveau, built in the same year as *The Decorative Arts of Today* was written, was actually painted in ten different colours: white, black, light grey, dark grey, yellow ochre, pale yellow ochre, burnt sienna, dark burnt sienna and light blue. Wigley has noted that Le Corbusier only ever made one white building. In spite of this, he has argued, there is 'a self-imposed blindness … shared by almost all of the dominant historiographies … Colour is detached from the master narrative' of architecture. Once again, it appears that we are not dealing with something as simple as white things and white surfaces, with white as an empirically verifiable fact or as a colour. Rather, we are in the realm of *whiteness*. White as myth, as an aesthetic fantasy, a fantasy so strong that it summons up negative hallucinations, so intense that it produces a blindness to colour, even when colour is literally in front of your face.

In *Purism*, a manifesto for painting co-written in 1920 with Amédée Ozenfant, Le Corbusier writes of painting as a kind of architecture: 'A painting is an association of purified, related, and architectured elements;' 'Painting is a question of architecture'.[4] In later writing, he often describes architecture as a kind of painting, a process that follows the academic logic from 'composition,' through 'contour,' to 'light and shade.' If this is the case, if architecture is a kind of painting as much as painting is a kind of architecture, then Le Corbusier, like Blanc before him, was forced by his own logic to recognize the presence of colour in a work. This he did, and in a very similar way to Blanc. *Purism* is ultra-rationalist; the text is speckled with terms such as 'logic,' 'order,' control,' 'constant,' 'certainty,' 'severe,' 'system,' 'fixed,' 'universal,' 'mathematical' and so on. But, as the authors acknowledge, 'when one says painting, inevitably he says colour.' And in the Purist universe, colour is a problem, a 'perilous agent;' it has the 'properties of shock' and a 'formidable fatality;' it often 'destroys or disorganises' an art which aims to address itself 'to the elevated faculties of the mind.'

Colour, then, must be controlled. It must be ordered and classified; a hierarchy must be established. And so it is. Le Corbusier and Ozenfant come up with three 'scales' for colour: the 'major scale', the 'dynamic scale' and the 'transitional scale'. The major scale is made up of 'ochre yellows, reds, earths, white, black, ultramarine blue and … certain of their derivatives'. This scale is 'strong' and 'stable;' it gives 'unity' and 'balance;' these colours are 'constructive' and are employed 'in all the great periods.' And they are also almost exactly the colours employed by Le Corbusier in his 1925 Pavilion. The dynamic scale is made up of 'disturbing elements:' citron yellow, oranges, vermilions and other 'animated,' 'agitated' colours; the transitional scale, 'the madders, emerald green, and all the lakes,' are simply 'not of construction.' A painting 'cannot be made without colour,' but the painter is advised to stick with the major scale; therein lies the tradition of great painting. The further one drifts down the scale of colour, the further one drifts from the 'architectural aesthetic' to the 'aesthetic of printed cloth' – that is, the further one drifts from art to mere decoration. This, in the end, was Cézanne's 'error,' for he 'accepted without examination the attractive offer of the colour-vendor, in a period marked by a fad for colour-chemistry, a science with no possible effect on great painting.' Such 'sensory jubilations of the paint tube' were best left 'to the clothes-dyers,' because while painting could not be made without colour, 'in a true and durable plastic work, it is *form* which comes first and everything else should be subordinated to it.' The 'architectural' aesthetic of painting was concerned with the unified representation of volumes (whereas the clothes-dyers' aesthetic was limited to flat patterns); colours of the 'major scale' were strong and stable insofar as they served and emphasized this representation of volume. The same logic applies to the 'painterly' aesthetic of Le Corbusier's architecture: the function of coloured planes in a space is to render the volumes and spaces more balanced and coherent, more exact and, in the end, more white: 'To tell the truth, my house does not seem white unless I have disposed the active forces of colours and values in the appropriate places.' White must be whiter than white, and to achieve that, colour must be added.

It doesn't much matter whether this hierarchy of colours is coherent, any more than it matters whether Blanc's cosmology of colour makes any real sense. What matters is the show of force: the rhetorical subordination of colour to the rule of line and the higher concerns of the mind. No longer intoxicating, narcotic or orgasmic, colour is learned, ordered, subordinated and tamed. Broken.   (... p 49)

Notes
1   Le Corbusier, *The Decorative Art of Today*, in *Essential Le Corbusier: L'Esprit Nouveau Articles*, trans J Dunnett (Oxford), 1998, p 135.
2   Adolf Loos, 'Ornament and Crime', *The Architecture of Adolf Loos*, trans W Wang (London), 1985, p 168.
3   Theo van Doesburg, quoted in Mark Wigley, *White Walls, Designer Dresses: The Fashioning of Modern Architecture* (Cambridge, MA, and London), 1995, p 239.
4   Le Corbusier and Amédée Ozenfant, 'Purism', RL Herbert (ed), *Modern Artists on Art: Ten Unabridged Essays* (New Brunswick, NJ), 1964, pp 67, 70. Subsequent quotations are from pp 67–71.

Structures of Atmosphere

Jean Baudrillard

philosophical • 1996
achronic light

In his examination of the role colour plays in creating atmosphere, sociologist and theorist Jean Baudrillard exposes a cultural inheritance linking material, form and space. Colour's proclivity towards embellishment is revealed to affect bodily function and yet, within the modern interior environment, it is abstract. Baudrillard points to interior furnishing, inclusive of colour, as a cultural system of signs that is reliant upon the contrast of 'hot and cold' and the interplay between objects and the humans that live among them. As such, the interior is understood outside of its historical frame as an applied, disjunctive and randomly accumulative space of inhabitation.

The term 'interior design' sums up the organizational aspect of the domestic environment, but it does not cover the entire system of the modern living space, which is based on a counterpoint between DESIGN and ATMOSPHERE. In the discourse of advertising the technical need for design is always accompanied by the cultural need for atmosphere. The two structure a single practice; they are two aspects of a single *functional* system. And both mobilize the values of play and of calculation – calculation of function in the case of design, calculation of materials, forms and space in the case of atmosphere.[1]

Atmospheric Values: Colour

Traditional Colour
In the traditional system colours have psychological and moral overtones. A person will 'like' a particular colour, or have 'their' colour. Colour may be dictated by an event, a ceremony, or a social role; alternatively, it may be the characteristic of a particular material – wood, leather, canvas or paper. Above all it remains circumscribed by form; it does not seek contact with other colours, and it is not a free value. Tradition confines colours to its own parochial meanings and draws the strictest of boundary-lines about them. Even in the freer ceremonial of fashion, colours generally derive their significance from outside themselves: they are simply metaphors for fixed cultural meanings. At the most impoverished level, the symbolism of colours gets lost in mere psychological

resonance: red is passionate and aggressive, blue a sign of calm, yellow optimistic, and so on; and by this point the language of colours is little different from the languages of flowers, dreams or the signs of the Zodiac.

The traditional treatment of colour negates colour as such, rejects it as a complete value. Indeed, the bourgeois interior reduces it for the most part to discreet 'tints' and 'shades'. Grey, mauve, garnet, beige – all the shades assigned to velours, woollens and satins, to the profusion of fabrics, curtains, carpets and hangings, as also to heavier materials and 'period' forms, imply a moral refusal of both colour and space. But especially of colour, which is deemed too spectacular, and a threat to inwardness. The world of colours is opposed to the world of values, and the 'chic' invariably implies the elimination of appearances in favour of being:[2] black, white, grey – whatever registers zero on the colour scale – is correspondingly paradigmatic of dignity, repression, and moral standing.

'Natural' Colour

Colours would not celebrate their release from this anathema until very late. It would be generations before cars and typewriters came in anything but black, and even longer before refrigerators and washbasins broke with their universal whiteness. It was painting that liberated colour, but it still took a very long time for the effects to register in everyday life. The advent of bright red armchairs, sky-blue settees, black tables, multicoloured kitchens, living-rooms in two or three different tones, contrasting inside walls, blue or pink facades (not to mention mauve and black underwear) suggests a liberation stemming from the overthrow of a global order. This liberation, moreover, was contemporary with that of the functional object (with the introduction of synthetic materials, which were polymorphous, and of non-traditional objects, which were polyfunctional). The transition, however, did not go smoothly. Colour that loudly announced itself as such soon began to be perceived as over-aggressive, and before long it was excluded from model forms, whether in clothing or in furnishing, in favour of a somewhat relieved return to discreet tones. There is a kind of obscenity of colour which modernity, after exalting it briefly as it did the explosion of form, seems to end up apprehending in much the same way as it apprehends pure functionality: labour should not be discernible anywhere – neither should instinct be allowed to show its face. The dropping of sharp contrasts and the return to 'natural' colours as opposed to the violence of 'affected' colours reflects this compromise solution at the level of model objects. At the level of serially produced objects, by contrast, bright colour is always apprehended as a sign of emancipation – in fact it often compensates for the absence of more fundamental qualities (particularly a lack of space). The discrimination here is obvious: associated with primary values, with functional objects and synthetic materials, bright, 'vulgar' colours always tend to predominate in the serial interior. They thus partake of the same anonymity as the functional object: having once represented something approaching a liberation, both have now become signs that are merely traps, raising the banner of freedom but delivering none to direct experience.

Furthermore – and this is their paradox – such straightforward and 'natural' colours turn out to be neither. They turn out to be nothing but an impossible echo of the state of nature, which explains why they are so aggressive, why they are so naïve – and why they so very quickly take refuge in an order which, for all that it is no longer the old moral order with its complete rejection of colour, is nevertheless a puritanical order of compromise with nature. This is the order, or reign, of pastels. Clothing, cars, showers, household appliances, plastic surfaces – nowhere here, it seems, is the 'honest' colour that painting once liberated as a living force now to be found. Instead we encounter only the *pastels*, which aspire to be living colours but are in fact merely signs for them, complete with a dash of moralism.   (… p 33)

Hot and Cold

So far as colours are concerned, 'atmosphere' depends upon a calculated balance between hot and cold tones. This is a fundamental distinction which – along with a few others (components/seats,[3] design/atmosphere) – helps to endow the discursive system of furnishing with a high degree of coherence, and thus makes it into a determining category of the overall system of objects. (We shall see that this coherence is perhaps merely that of a manifest discourse beneath which a latent discourse is continually deploying its contradictions.) To get back to the warmth of warm tones: this is clearly not a warmth grounded in confidence, intimacy or affection, nor an organic warmth emanating from colours or substances. Warmth of that kind once had its own density and required no opposing cold tones to define it negatively. Nowadays, on the other hand, both warm and cold tones are required to interact, in each ensemble, with structure and form. When we read that 'The warmth of its materials lends intimacy to this well-designed bureau,' or when we are told of 'doors of matte oiled Brazilian rosewood traversed by chrome-plated handles [and] chairs covered in a buff leatherette that blends them perfectly into this austere and warm ensemble,' we find that warmth is always contrasted with rigour, organization, structure, or something of the sort, and that every 'value' is defined by this contrast between two poles. 'Functional' warmth is thus a warmth that no longer issues forth from a warm substance, nor from a harmonious juxtaposition of particular objects, but instead arises from the systematic oscillation or abstract synchrony of a perpetual 'warm-and-cold' which in reality continually defers any real 'warm' feeling. This is a purely signified warmth – hence one which, by definition, is never realized: a warmth characterized, precisely, by the absence of any source.

Atmospheric Values: Materials

Natural Wood/Cultural Wood

The same sort of analysis applies to materials – to wood, for example, so sought after today for nostalgic reasons. Wood draws its substance from the earth, it lives and breathes and 'labours.' It has its latent warmth; it does not merely reflect, like glass, but burns from within. Time is embedded in its very fibres, which makes it the perfect container, because every content is something we want to rescue from time. Wood has its own odour, it ages, it even has parasites, and so on. In short, it is a material that has being. Think of the notion of 'solid oak' – a living idea for each of us, evoking as it does the succession of generations, massive furniture and ancestral family homes. The question we must ask, however, is whether this 'warmth' of wood (or likewise the 'warmth' of freestone, natural leather, unbleached linen, beaten copper, or any of the elements of the material and maternal dream that now feeds a high-priced nostalgia) still has any meaning.

By now functional substitutes for virtually all organic and natural materials have been found in the shape of plastic and polymorphous substances: wool, cotton, silk and linen are thus all susceptible of replacement by nylon and its countless variants, while wood, stone and metal are giving way to concrete and polystyrene.[4] There can be no question of rejecting this tendency and simply dreaming of the ideal warm and human substance of the objects of former times. The distinction between natural and synthetic substances, just like that between traditional colours and bright colours, is strictly a value judgement. Objectively, substances are simply what they are: there is no such thing as a true or a false, a natural or an artificial substance. How could concrete be somehow less 'authentic' than stone? We apprehend old synthetic materials such as paper as altogether natural – indeed, glass is one of the richest substances we can conceive of. In the end, the inherited nobility of a given material can exist only for a cultural ideology analogous to that of the aristocratic myth itself in the social world – and even that cultural prejudice is vulnerable to the passage of time.

The point is to understand, apart from the vast horizons opened up on the practical level by these new substances, just how they have changed the 'meaning' of the materials we use.

Just as the shift to shades (warm, cold or intermediate) means that colours are stripped of their moral and symbolic status in favour of an abstract quality which makes their systematization and interplay possible, so likewise the manufacture of synthetics means that materials lose their symbolic naturalness and become polymorphous, so achieving a higher degree of abstractness which makes possible a universal play of associations among materials, and hence too a transcendence of the formal antithesis between natural and artificial materials. There is thus no longer any difference 'in nature' between a Thermoglass partition and a wooden one, between rough concrete and leather: whether they embody 'warm' or 'cold' values, they all now have exactly the same status as component materials. These materials, though disparate in themselves, are nevertheless homogeneous as cultural signs, and thus susceptible of organization into a coherent system. Their abstractness makes it possible to combine them at will.[5]

The Logic of Atmosphere

This 'discourse of atmosphere' concerning colours, substance, volume, space, and so on mobilizes all these elements simultaneously in a great systematic reorganization: it is because furniture now comprises movable elements in a decentralized space, and because it has a correspondingly lighter structure based on assembly and veneers, that there is a case for more 'abstract' woods – teak, mahogany, rosewood or certain Scandinavian woods.[6] And it so happens that the colours of these woods are not traditional either, but lighter or darker variations, often varnished, lacquered, or left deliberately unfinished; the main point, though, is that the colour in question, like the wood itself, is always *abstract* – an object of mental manipulation along with everything else. The entire modern environment is thus transposed onto the level of a sign system, namely ATMOSPHERE, which is no longer produced by the way any particular element is handled, nor by the beauty or ugliness of that element. That used to be true for the inconsistent and subjective system of tastes and colours, of *de gustibus non est disputandum*, but under the present system the success of the whole occurs in the context of the constraints of abstraction and association.

Whether or not you care for teak, for example, you are obliged to acknowledge that its use is consistent with the organization of component elements, that its shade is consistent with a plane surface, hence also with a particular 'rhythm' of space, etc, etc – and that this is indeed the law of the system. There is nothing at all – not antiques, not rustic furniture in solid wood, not even precious or craft objects – that cannot be incorporated into the interactions of the system, thus attesting to the boundless possibilities of such abstract integration. The current proliferation of such objects does not constitute a contradiction in the system:[7] they enter the system precisely as the most 'modern' materials and colours, and as atmospheric elements. Only a traditional and fundamentally naïve view would find inconsistency in the encounter, on a teak-veneered chest, of a futuristic cube in raw metal and the rotten wood of a sixteenth-century carving. The point is, though, that *the consistency here is not the natural consistency of a unified taste but the consistency of a cultural system of signs*. Not even a 'Provençal' room, not even an authentic Louis XVI drawing-room, can attest to anything beyond a vain nostalgic desire to escape from the modern cultural system: both are just as far removed from the 'style' they ape as any formica-topped table or any black-metal and leatherette tubular chair. An exposed ceiling beam is every bit as abstract as a chrome-plated tube or an Emauglas partition. What nostalgia paints as an authentic whole object is still nothing but a combining variant, as is indeed signalled by the language used in speaking of provincial or period 'ensembles.' The word 'ensemble,' closely related to 'atmosphere,' serves to reintroduce any conceivable element, whatever subjective associations it may carry, into the logic of the system. That this system is affected by ideological connotations and latent motives is indisputable, and we shall return to this question later. But it is incontestable, too, that its logic, which is that of a combination of

41

signs, is irreversible and limitless. No object can escape this logic, just as no product can escape the formal logic of the commodity.   (... p 41)

Notes

1 To the extent that arrangement involves dealing with space, it too may be considered a component of atmosphere.

2 'Loud' colours are meant to strike the eye. If you wear a red suit, you are more than naked – you become a pure object with no inward reality. The fact that women's tailored suits tend to be in bright colours is a reflection of the social status of women as objects.

3 See below, pp 44 ff. [Editors' note: This reference is to Baudrillard's discussion of 'seats' which appears later in the text.]

4 This development at least partially realizes the substantialist myth which, beginning in the sixteenth century, informed the stucco and the worldly demiurgy of the baroque style: the notion that the whole world could be cast from a single ready-made material. This substantialist myth is one aspect of the functionalist myth that I discuss elsewhere, and the equivalent on the material plane of automatism on the functional one. The idea is that a 'machine of machines' would replace all human gestures and institute a synthetic universe. It should be borne in mind, however, that the 'substantialist' dream is the most primitive and repressive aspect of the myth as a whole, for it continues to enshrine a pre-mechanist alchemy of transubstantiation.

5 And this is the difference, for instance, between the 'solid oak' of old and the present-day use of teak. Teak is not fundamentally distinct from oak in respect of origin, exoticism or cost; it is its use in the creation of atmosphere which means that it is no longer a primary natural material, dense and warm, but, rather, *a mere cultural sign of such warmth*, and by virtue of that fact reinstated qua sign, like so many other 'noble' materials, in the system of the modern interior: no longer wood-as-material but wood-as-component. And now, instead of the quality of presence, it has atmospheric value.

6 Certainly these woods are technically better suited than oak to the needs of veneering and assembling. It must also be said that exoticism plays the same role here as the idea of holidays does in the use of bright colours: it evokes the myth of an escape via 'naturalness'. The essential point, however, is that for all these reasons these woods are 'secondary' woods, embodying a cultural abstraction that enables them to partake of the logic of the system.

7 It does indicate a *shortcoming* of the system – but a successfully integrated one. On this point, see the discussion of antiques below. [Editors' note: This reference is to Baudrillard's discussion of 'antiques', which appears later in the text.]

Jean Baudrillard, *The System of Objects*, trans James Benedict, Verso (London), 1996. Reprinted by permission of Verso.
(Excerpts pp 30–3, 36–41)

A Christian House

Catharine E Beecher and Harriet Beecher Stowe

social 1869 · mid 19th century space

In one of the earliest treatise on the home, Catharine E Beecher and Harriet Beecher Stowe advance a clear agenda towards aligning the home with Christian ethics of family life and family work. Under this conception of home, the interior is not for display but provides for health, industry and economy. Hence the Beechers' own design is aimed at supporting the family as an institution rather than societal custom. Their carefully planned practical considerations for the home included 'scientific' kitchen planning to accommodate changes in food preparation and management. For both sisters, managing a home in the industrial age was associated with female-led domestic government, rather than domestic slavery, and echoed their concern for women's advancement through education. More specifically, their detailed examination of everyday household objects indicates a familiarity with the role the household played within Christian society.

In the Divine Word it is written, 'The wise woman buildeth her house.' To be 'wise,' is 'to choose the best means for accomplishing the best end.' It has been shown that the best end for a woman to seek is the training of God's children for their eternal home, by guiding them to intelligence, virtue, and true happiness. When, therefore, the wise woman seeks a home in which to exercise this ministry, she will aim to secure a house so planned that it will provide in the best manner for health, industry, and economy, those cardinal requisites of domestic enjoyment and success. To aid in this, is the object of the following drawings and descriptions, which will illustrate a style of living more conformed to the great design for which the family is instituted than that which ordinarily prevails among those classes which take the lead in forming the customs of society. The aim will be to exhibit modes of economizing labor, time, and expenses, so as to secure health, thrift, and domestic happiness to persons of limited means, in a measure rarely attained even by those who possess wealth.

At the head of this chapter is a sketch of what may be properly called a Christian house; that is, a house contrived for the express purpose of enabling every member of a family to labor with the hands for the common good, and by modes at once healthful, economical, and tasteful. Of course, much of the instruction conveyed in the following pages is chiefly applicable to the wants and habits of those living either in the country or in such suburban vicinities as give space of ground for healthful outdoor occupation in the family service, although the general principles of house-building and house-keeping are of necessity universal in their application – as true in the busy confines of the city as in the freer and purer quietude of the country. So far as circumstances can be made to yield the opportunity, it will be assumed that the family state demands some outdoor labor for all. The cultivation of flowers to ornament the table and house, of fruits and vegetables for food, of silk and cotton for clothing, and the care of horse, cow, and dairy, can be so divided that each and all of the family, some part of the day, can take exercise in the pure air, under the magnetic and healthful rays of the sun. Every head of a family should seek a soil and climate which will afford such opportunities. Railroads, enabling men toiling in cities to rear families in the country, are on this account a special blessing. So, also, is the opening of the South to free labor, where, in the pure and mild climate of the uplands, open-air labor can proceed most of the year, and women and children labor out of doors as well as within.

In the following drawings are presented modes of economizing time, labor, and expense by the close packing of conveniences. By such methods, small and economical houses can be made to secure most of the comforts and many of the refinements of large and expensive ones. The cottage at the head of this chapter is projected on a plan which can be adapted to a warm or cold climate with little change. By adding another story, it would serve a large family.

Fig. 1 shows the ground-plan of the first floor. On the inside it is forty-three feet long and twenty-five wide, excluding conservatories and front and back projections. Its inside height from floor to ceiling is ten feet. The piazzas each side of the front projection have sliding-windows to the floor, and can, by glazed sashes, be made green-houses in winter. In a warm climate, piazzas can be made at the back side also.

In the description and arrangement, the leading aim is to show how time, labor, and expense are saved, not only in the building but in furniture and its arrangement. With this aim, the ground-floor and its furniture will first be shown, then the second story and its furniture, and then the basement and its conveniences. The conservatories are appendages not necessary to housekeeping, but useful in many ways pointed out more at large in other chapters.

The entry has arched recesses behind the front doors, furnished with hooks for over-clothes in both – a box for over-shoes in one, and a stand for umbrellas in the other. The roof of the recess is for statuettes, busts, or flowers. The stairs turn twice with broad steps, making a recess at the lower landing, where a table is set with a vase of flowers. On one side of the recess is a closet, arched to correspond with the arch over the stairs.

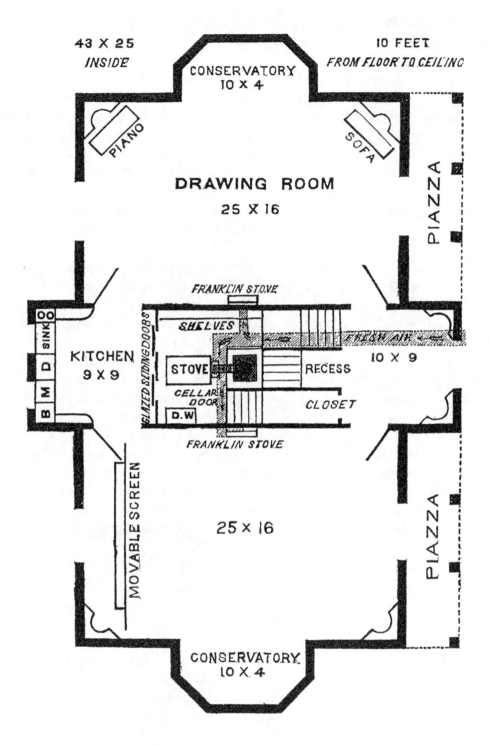

Fig. 1. Ground plan of the first floor. With permission of Mount Holyoke College Archives and Special Collections.

A bracket over the first broad stair, with flowers or statuettes, is visible from the entrance, and pictures can be hung as in the illustration.

The large room on the left can be made to serve the purpose of several rooms by means of a *movable screen*. By shifting this rolling screen from one part of the room to another, two apartments are always available, of any desired size within the limits of the large room. One side of the screen fronts what may be used as the parlor or sitting-room; the other side is arranged for bedroom conveniences. Of this, the front side [is] covered first with strong canvas, stretched and nailed on. Over this is pasted panel-paper, and the upper part is made to resemble an ornamental cornice by fresco-paper. Pictures can be hung in the panels, or be pasted on and varnished with white varnish. To prevent the absorption of the varnish, a wash of gum isinglass (fish-glue) must be applied twice.

Fig. 2 shows the back or inside of the movable screen, toward the part of the room used as the bedroom. On one side, and at the top and bottom, it has shelves with *shelf boxes*, which are cheaper and better than drawers, and much preferred by those using them. Handles are cut in the front and back side. Half an inch space must be between the box and the shelf over it, and as much each side so that it can be taken out and put in easily. The central part of the screen's interior is a wardrobe. This screen must be so high as nearly to reach the ceiling, in order to prevent it from overturning. It is to fill the width of the room, except two feet on each side. A projecting cleat or strip, reaching nearly to the top of the screen, three inches wide, is to be screwed to the front sides, on which light frame doors are to be hung, covered with canvas and panel-paper like the front of the screen. The inside of these doors is furnished with hooks for clothing, for which the projection makes room. The whole screen is to be eighteen inches deep at the top and two feet deep at the base, giving a solid foundation. It is moved on four wooden rollers, one foot long and four inches in diameter. The pivots of the rollers and the parts where there is friction must be rubbed with hard soap, and then a child can move the whole easily.

A curtain is to be hung across the whole interior of the screen by rings, on a strong wire. The curtain should be in three parts, with lead or large nails in the hems to keep it in place. The wood-work must be put together with screws, as the screen is too large to pass through a door.

At the end of the room, behind the screen, are two couches, to be run one under the other. The upper one is made with four posts, each three feet high and three inches square, set on casters two inches high. The frame is to be fourteen inches from the floor, seven feet long, two feet four inches wide, and three inches in thickness. At the head, and at the foot, is to be screwed a notched two-inch board, three inches wide. The mortises are to be one inch wide and deep, and one inch apart, to receive slats made of ash, oak, or spruce, one inch square, placed lengthwise of the couch. The slats being small, and so near together,

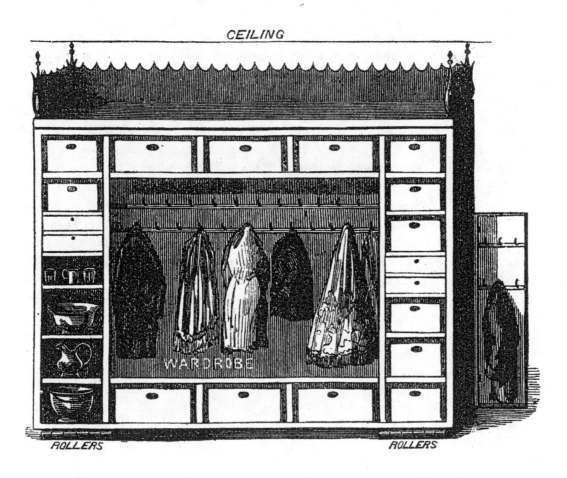

Fig. 2. The back or inside of the movable screen. With permission of Mount Holyoke College Archives and Special Collections.

and running lengthwise, make a better spring frame than wire coils. If they warp, they can be turned. They must not be fastened at the ends, except by insertion in the notches. Across the posts, and of equal height with them, are to be screwed head and foot-boards.

The under couch is like the upper, except these dimensions: posts, nine inches high, including castors; frame, six feet two inches long, two feet four inches wide. The frame should be as near the floor as possible, resting on the casters.

The most healthful and comfortable mattress is made by a case, open in the centre and fastened together with buttons; to be filled with oat straw, which is softer than wheat or rye. This can be adjusted to the figure, and often renewed.   (... p 31)

Let us suppose a colony of cultivated and Christian people, having abundant wealth, who now are living as the wealthy usually do, emigrating to some of the beautiful Southern uplands, where are rocks, hills, valleys, and mountains as picturesque as those of New-England, where the thermometer but rarely reaches 90° in summer, and in winter as rarely sinks below freezing point, so that out-door labor goes on all the year, where the fertile soil is easily worked, where rich tropical fruits and flowers abound, where cotton and silk can be raised by children around their home, where the produce of vineyards and orchards finds steady markets by railroads ready made; suppose such a colony, with a central church and schoolroom, library, hall for sports, and a common laundry, (taking the most trying part of domestic labor from each house), – suppose each family to train the children to labor with the hands as a healthful and honorable duty; suppose all this, which is perfectly practicable, would not the enjoyment of this life be increased, and also abundant treasures be laid up in heaven, by using the wealth thus economized in diffusing similar enjoyments and culture among the poor, ignorant, and neglected ones in desolated sections where many now are perishing for want of such Christian example and influences?   (... p 42)

Catharine E Beecher and Harriet Beecher Stowe, *The American Woman's Home: or Principles of Domestic Science; Being A Guide to the Formation and Maintenance of Economical, Healthful, Beautiful, and Christian Homes*, JB Ford and Company (New York), 1869.
(Excerpts pp 23–42)

Thick Edge: Architectural Boundaries and Spatial Flows

Iain Borden

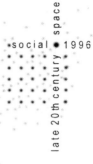

Having long been relegated to the domain of the 'inside,' interior design often confronts the issue of boundary crossing in the form of both literal and theoretical thresholds. But as architectural historian and urban commentator Iain Borden suggests, boundaries can be social and spatial ordering devices, particularly within the public urban realm. Noting a disparity in the idea of spatiality as the simple relation between objects and forms, Borden realigns spatiality as a force, or flow, among social elements, including all forms of inhabitation. In this way boundaries are defined as permeable, temporal and political markers of bodily negotiation.

Clear Blue Water

On London's Kingsway in Holborn sits the church of Holy Trinity. A theatrical inwardly-curved facade grandly enfolds a semicircular portico. Beyond splendorous Edwardian aesthetics, Belcher and Joass' design also provides a public micro-retreat from the motorcycle couriers and taxis on Kingsway. As a church, Holy Trinity welcomed visitors, drawing them onto the ambiguous stage defined by its facade, then into the portico, and onwards to the interior. Forsaken by 1991 as a place of worship, it rapidly became a focus for Holborn's many homeless, a semi permanent sitting and sleeping place away from the exposed doorways in the Strand. Holy Trinity was now a different stage set, at once public domain and private to those seeking defensible space and their own appropriated form of illegal real estate.[1] Clusters of homeless recomposed a niche space from layers of clothes, cardboard and classical architecture.

Except that a line has just been drawn: a three metres high plane of wood, painted a striking resonant blue, spanning the Holy Trinity front, and shutting off the semi-public stage set from the street and passers-by. Yet it is not so much that the building is shut off from people, but that people – particularly the homeless – are divorced from it. To the cognoscenti, the screen may suggest a Christoesque device or even Derek Jarman's reductive film screen 'Blue,' and certainly it inserts a startling colourist disjunction to the grainy grey of Holborn. But for the new owners of the church, the Post Office, this is a considered attempt to keep architecture as things, and space as the distance between objects; they have constructed a boundary of exclusion, a brutally frontal relation which physically repels the unwanted and the unwashed. It is the architecture of separation, of clear blue water between spaces and peoples.

I learned much of this from a man called Bob, a small Geordie with a flat cap and weathered lines from decades of life on the streets of London.[2] To him and other former residents of the Holy Trinity portico, this is indeed a divisive boundary, demarcating the uncrossable chasm between private ownership and public use, recent history and immediate future. Architectural boundaries like this have social effects which cannot be denied.

But what is the boundary's socio-spatial nature? Architecture has too often been conceived solely as the product of design intention, from which social effects simply follow. The 'second nature'[3] of architecture is posited as simply the artificial replacement for Nature, the pre-given space to which people come and respond. But this view of space ultimately offers little more than what Soja terms the 'illusion of opacity,' by which 'spatiality is reduced to physical objects and forms.'

Since the 1970s, a politically-minded approach to architectural history has emerged, in which space assumes a more social character. The focus, however, still tends to the notion of function, in which buildings remain primarily designed objects, and the social activities are simply accommodated in architectural design (particularly in plan), or to the notion of social history, whereby buildings form backdrops to the drama of everyday life. In either case, the essential interrelation of buildings, spaces and people is reduced to a false dualism between object and social use.[4]

In contradistinction to this dualism, and taking their cue from sources as diverse as anthropologist Marc Augé, urban geographers Edward Soja and David Harvey, historian Michel Foucault, and, in particular, the philosopher Henri Lefebvre, more anthropologically-minded historians and theorists are now reconceptualising architecture as what I call a 'space of flows' – not as objects, but as the interrelation between things, spaces, individuals and ideas. Bernard Tschumi is the most persistent architect here, arguing that 'architecture ... could not be dissociated from the events that "happened" in it.'[5] Similarly, Adrian Forty remarks of the 'Strangely Familiar' project that architecture 'is not made just once, but is made and remade over and over again each time it is represented through another medium, each time its surroundings change, each time different people experience it.'[6] Architecture is both produced and reproduced, designed and experienced. It is a medium not a message, a system of power relations not a force, a flow not a line.

So what is the boundary? Georg Simmel noted that boundaries make social orders more concrete, more intensely experienced; indeterminate in themselves, they stand in contrast to the physical boundaries of nature, their significance springing from interaction on either side of the line. For Simmel, the 'boundary is not a spatial fact with sociological consequences but a sociological fact that is formed spatially.' Boundaries do not cause sociological effects in themselves, but are formed between social elements.[7]

The Holy Trinity blue screen shows precisely this. The social effects on those who experience the boundary change its historical nature, dislocating significance away from the object itself. Furthermore, these effects are simultaneously an attempt by the Post Office to patrol the social relation between the homeless and its own property. The Post Office renegotiates that relationship by erecting a physical screen which hides – metaphorically and literally – its own concerns; in experiencing the screen-as-object we should remember with Guy Debord that such things are also spectacles, and thus 'not a collection of images, but a social relation among people, mediated by images.'[8] The conception of the blue screen purely as object is then reductive.

There is also another way in which the boundary is socio-spatial – through its materiality. The blue screen's obvious function is to keep undesirables off the stage-space beyond, hindering the transition of the human body. Apart from this, it offers another, more pervasive control over the space and time of the would-be-invasive body. In front of the stage-set space is a low wall, of the right depth and height to sit and, potentially, to sleep upon, To prevent this, the vertical screen makes a sudden 45 degrees deviation, such that instead of resting behind the low wall it terminates halfway across its depth, leaving only 150 millimetres clear in front. The condition produced is subtle and important; through the precise control of screen and wall in relation to the thickness of the human body, the low wall becomes too shallow for a person to sleep upon, or to sit upon for any length of time. Many similar edge-hardenings have begun to sprout up around London, where spiked windowsills, 'decorative' railings, studded flower-planters and night-time automatic sprinkler systems to 'clean' shop and office doorways are being used to repel the public from the edge of the street.

In the case of the Holy Trinity screen, even the 'respectable' pedestrian is discouraged from stopping. Beside erasing a temporary resting space, the smooth surface of the blue screen is devoid of detail interest and exactly that tactility which Maurice Merleau-Ponty reasserted against the domination of vision.[9] It deflects attention away, presenting a blank nothing to the interrogative eye. There is no occasion to linger, observe or inspect.

What appears to be a simple, planar boundary, is then quite different; the blue screen discloses the boundary as a zone of negotiation, in which vision is just one of a series of body-centric architectural devices. The space of the body is used to control its interrelation with the screen and, by extension, the influence of the screen's surface is projected onto the pavement. Passers-by continue to pass by, discouraged from stopping by the screen's materiality. The boundary is not a surface but a thick edge, a five metre deep in-between zone in which social relations are challenged and controlled through architectural materiality.

Rights of Passage

If the Holy Trinity screen frontally controls property and social relations through physicality, what of boundaries that see control in a more ambiguous manner?[10] What of those new urban spaces – the shopping mall, plaza and transport concourse – those spaces at once public and private?

One of the most prominent of these spaces is the Broadgate office development, constructed for the post 'Big Bang' (1986) financial centre in the City of London.[11] Developed by Rosehaugh Stanhope and British Rail over the lines of Liverpool Street and the old Broad Street train station, the 29 acre site provides 4 million square feet of high-quality office space and three internalised urban squares.

Broadgate is also an area which strives to define its social ethos, and the dominant temper of well-salaried and besuited office workers is reinforced by many different measures. An aesthetic enclave within the fragmented postmodern city, Broadgate contains Americanised 'fashion effect' architecture designed by Arup Associates and SOM, generating a pervasive ambience of prestige and wealth. There are no 'festival' or 'liminal' spaces here, nor the crowded conflicts of pedestrians and pavement cafés in Soho. Carefully delimited shops, golfing emporia, health clubs, restaurants and bars cater for middle-manager tastes and pockets, while displaying signs barring entry to those not in 'smart' dress. The *Broadgate Broadsheet* newspaper furnishes a booster guide to news and events, like the much-publicised 'Broomball' contests on the Arena ice rink. In contrast, the army of service workers are kept out of sight, hidden in a subterranean undercroft of access roads and maintenance circuits, while in a similarly Disneyfied scopic regime undesirables are escorted off the scheme, litter is instantly removed, and hawks are brought in weekly to scare away pigeons. Social difference within the 20,000 working population is accommodated, but only within a class, gender and race framework predicated on the middle class Oxbridge-educated businessman.

Following the two IRA bombs in the City of 1992 and 1993 both within 400 metres of Broadgate, and the later Canary Wharf attack in 1996, it might be expected that Broadgate would toughen the outer walls of its enclave. However, because the 'Ring of Steel' armed road-checks and 24-hour 'Camerawatch' CCTV networks organised by the City police have successfully (for the City) redirected both terrorism and armed robbery to other parts of London, Broadgate's managers are content to rely on their own extensive system of private security guards and surveillance cameras.[12]

Broadgate's boundaries are therefore free to be configured toward more social ends, installing a further social ring of defence within the City's militaristic frontier. Subtle yet distinctive signs mark this inner social cordon: brass rails let into the pavement signify the edge of the property line, public art like Serra's 45-tonne 'Fulcrum' signals entrances, armorial devices record the borough thresholds, and various gates denote the transition from public to private realms.

Prominent among these gates is a very curious device marking the northern edge of Broadgate Arena. Designed by the artist Alan Evans, the 'Go-Between Screens' seemingly provide the usual boundary control – open during daytime and closed at night. Except that these are not normal gates, for even when 'closed' one can walk around their sides, a 2 metre gap being left for this purpose. The boundary here is never sealed, operating in a manner other than physical exclusion. This feeling is reinforced by the artful materiality of the 'Go-Between Screens' which, in contrast to the highly-machined surrounding buildings, are fabricated of mild steel, with line forging used to create a 'soft' visibly hammered surface.

What the Broadgate gates do is not so much obstruct horizontal movement of the body, as to challenge the visitor's self-perception as to whether they are permitted to enter. As privatised urban space under corporate control, Broadgate in effect has no resident-owners, and everyone who enters is either a worker, visitor or trespasser. As Foucault notes, '[a]nyone can enter one of these heterotopian locations, but, in reality, they are nothing more than an illusion: one thinks one has entered and, by the sole fact of entering, one is excluded.'[13] To control this ambiguity, the combination of hard architecture and soft gates, unlike the exclusionary physicality of the Holy Trinity blue screen, provokes in the visitor's mind as they momentarily pass through the thickness of the edge the questions, 'Should I be here, and now? Do I have the right of passage?'

The temporality of the through-passage is also critical, providing the momentary yet urgent actuality of this questioning process. The gates are not just the space but the lived time of several seconds through which the visitors validate themselves in relation to Broadgate. As a result, space, temporality, body and identity are mutually confronted and constructed, in a version of Augé's 'non-place as a turning back on the self,' checking the contractual relation between the individual and that non-place.[14] More material and mental suggestion than brute physicality, this is the ultimate extension of the Benthamite project of surveillance, in which each and every citizen surveys and disciplines themselves.

The 'Go-Between Screens' are a form of mirror, by which the visitor is ultimately returned not a view of Broadgate but, in Augé's terms, of themselves playing a role within it:

What he is confronted with, finally, is an image of himself, but in truth it is a pretty strange image ... The passenger through non-places retrieves his identity only at Customs, at the tollbooth, at the check-out counter. Meanwhile, he obeys the same code as others, receives the same messages, responds to the same entreaties. The space of non-place creates neither singular identity nor relations; only solitude, and similitude.[15]

Visitors reconfigure themselves in the normative character of Broadgate, such that, as with Disneyland's staff, everyone becomes a 'cast member.'[16]

We might even consider that if Broadgate's architecture, as mirror, acts as a kind of Sartrean 'other's look,' conferring spatiality on the viewer, then it too is looked back upon, the gaze being returned. This architecture is then absorbed within the self, dissolving the organic space of the body and the social space in which it lives, and entering that 'betweenness of place' beyond objectivity and subjectivity. As such, the boundary is validated by the anthropological ritual of passing through – its presence does not act upon visitors, but is a projection outward by visitors considering themselves in relation to the architecture.   (... p 86)

Notes

1 Neil Smith, 'Homeless/Global: Scaling Places,' Jon Bird *et al* (eds), *Mapping the Futures: Local Cultures, Global Change*, Routledge (London), 1993, p 89.
2 Conversation, Kingsway, London, January 1996.
3 Henri Lefebvre, *The Production of Space*, Blackwell (Oxford), 1991 and Edward W Soja, *Postmodern Geographies: the Reassertion of Space in Critical Social Theory*, Verso (London), 1989, p 123.
4 See for example, Iain Borden and D Dunster (eds), *Architecture and the Sites of History*, Butterworth Architecture (Oxford), 1995; Adrian Forty, *Objects of Desire*, Thames and Hudson (London), 1986; Dolores Hayden, *Grand Domestic Revolution*, MIT Press (Cambridge, Mass), 1981.
5 Bernard Tschumi, 'Spaces and Events', *Questions of Space: Lectures on Architecture*, Architectural Association (London), 1990, p 88.
6 Adrian Forty, 'Foreword' to Iain Borden, Joe Kerr, Alicia Pivaro and Jane Rendell (eds), *Strangely Familiar: Narratives of Architecture and the City*, Routledge (London), 1996, p 5. See also Iain Borden, Joe Kerr, Alicia Pivaro and Jane Rendell (eds), *The Unknown City: Contesting Architecture and Social Space*, MIT Press (Cambridge, MA), 1997.
7 Frank J Lechner, 'Simmel on Social Space', *Theory, Culture and Society*, vol 8 no 3, August 1991, p 197; and David Frisby, 'Social Space, the City and the Metropolis', *Simmel and Since: Essays on George Simmel's Social Theory*, Routledge (London), 1992, p 105.
8 Guy Debord, *Society of the Spectacle*, Black & Red (Detroit), 1983, para 4.
9 Maurice Merleau-Ponty, *Phenomenology of Perception*, Routledge and Kegan Paul (London), 1962, pp 207–42.
10 This section of the paper has benefited from studies carried out by students at the School of Architecture and Interior Design, University of North London, and at the Bartlett, University College London. I am particularly grateful to A Keightley-Moore, N Murray, S Warren, W Whyte.
11 Jane M Jacobs, *Edge of Empire: Postcolonialism and the City*, Routledge (London), 1996.
12 City of London Police, *Camerawatch*, City of London Police (London), 1994.
13 Michel Foucault, 'Of Other Spaces: Utopias and Heterotopias', Joan Ockman (ed), *Architecture Culture 1943–1968: a Documentary Anthology*, Rizzoli (New York), 1993, p 425.

14 Marc Augé, *Non-Places: Introduction to an Anthology of Supermodernity*, Verso (London), 1995, pp 92, 101–2, and Michel Foucault, 'Panopticism' in *Discipline and Punish: the Birth of the Prison*, Penguin (Harmondsworth), 1979, pp 195–228.
15 Marc Augé, *Non-Places*, p 103.
16 Michael Sorkin, 'See You in Disneyland', Michael Sorkin (ed), *Variations on a Theme Park*, Noonday Press (New York, 1992, p 228.

Iain Borden, 'Thick Edge: Architectural Boundaries and Spatial Flows', *Architectural Design*, vol 66 no 11–12, 1996, pp 84–7.

A Wall of Books: The Gender of Natural Colors in Modern Architecture

William W Braham

gender · colour
early 20th century
1999

William Braham's essay weaves a path through a complex series of occasions and circumstances that link interior design's historical alliance with decoration, including more recent negations of ornament fostered by modernism. Central to this discussion is Braham's interest in the genealogy of colour, including its effacement through architecture's promotion of 'natural finishes'. Writing as both academic and architect, Braham notes that the authority of the natural generates an opposition between natural and applied, a situation that also contributes to the bifurcation between interior design and architecture as professional domains. In this excerpt the discussion is grounded in an examination of books as displayed collections and their reading as decorative wall elements.

This essay examines a decorative convention – the display of books in modern interiors – that appears in both *The International Style* (1932) by Henry-Russell Hitchcock and Philip Johnson and *The Personality of a House* (1930) by Emily Post. Looking at books in this way constitutes a partial history of the architectural palette that arises from the privileging of natural over applied finishes. The internal logic of that practice and its class and gender characterizations are discussed in the context of the separation of architecture from interior design. The 'natural' palette and its host of attendant conventions is everywhere visible in contemporary architecture and interior design and even helps to define the boundary between the two practices, to explain what is and is not architectural.   (… p 4)

At present applied color is used less. The color of natural surfacing materials and the natural metal color of detail is definitely preferred. Where the metal is painted, a dark neutral tone minimizes the apparent weight of the window frame. In surfaces of stucco, white or off-white, even where it is obtained with paint, is felt to constitute the natural color. The earlier use of bright color had value in attracting attention to the new style, but it could not long remain pleasing. It ceased to startle and began to bore; its mechanical sharpness and freshness became rapidly tawdry. If architecture is not to resemble billboards, color should be both technically and psychologically permanent.[1]

While the errors, exaggerations, and omissions of the exhibition have been examined and debated since its inception, the fact remains that it produced a startlingly successful manual of style, similar in approach to the numerous home and interior design manuals that preceded it.[2] *The International Style* promoted a highly refined and selective taste that relied directly on the distinction between natural and applied color, explicitly deploring the artifice and impermanence of paint, and boldly claiming the status of a natural finish for white and off-white tones. Those conventions continue to persuade. The logic of the natural/neutral palette still appears in contemporary 'high-tech' buildings and expensive consumer products, visible also throughout architecture, interior design, and shelter magazines. It is not the only decorative palette that is observed, but it retains a particular authority. It is the palette of architecture in its 'return to basics,' resonating with the environmental, the preindustrial, and somewhat paradoxically, with the primitive, known equally well for bright colors. (... p 5)

The closed bookcase has its own history, traceable to the time when books were rare and required protection. As Edith Wharton described it in *The Decoration of Houses*, the 'natural bookcase was a chest with a strong lock.'[3] The open and decorative display of books only became common with their increased production and availability in the eighteenth and, especially, the nineteenth centuries. The decorative convention derived initially from private libraries where different forms of storage and their decoration had been explored by those privileged enough to own substantial collections. Books still suggest something of that aristocratic provenance, and their public display in the homes of the middle class – designed or not – owes much to that formation. As the numbers of books, the kinds of literature, and literacy itself expanded, so too did the means of storage and display, as well as the social meaning of books. Like the displays of other collections – ceramics, stuffed animals, and musical recordings – objects are deployed, in part, to represent the character of the occupants, but books exceed the personal statement and have attained the status of an *objet-type*, a decorative convention that can be deployed even in the homes of nonreaders ...

Two aspects of the decorative formation of concern to this inquiry are the representation of architectural authenticity and the development of interior design as a distinct and separate practice in the late nineteenth and early twentieth century.[4] These two aspects are deeply intertwined: When decorative elements are deemed artificial, they and their advocates are excised from mainstream architectural practice, and displaced into interior design. The resistance of books to that displacement, even in decorative application, suggests other distinctions by which plainly decorative elements can remain architectural. Certainly the actual reading of books preserves their affiliation with other objects of utility, but the strongly polarized conventions of modern gender roles play their part as well. Although interior design constitutes one of the many divisions of labor within the modern building trades, the distinction is a highly gendered one, in which the activities and individuals engaged in it are implicitly assumed to be feminine. The gender connotation derives partly from the fact that women dominate the profession of interior design, a situation conditioned by the removal of men and their work from the home in the nineteenth and twentieth centuries.   (... p 7)

It is Ruskin's warning about exterior paint that indicates one of the operational principles by which natural and applied colors are distinguished.

> The true colours of architecture are those of natural stone, and I would fain see them taken advantage of to the full ... [L]et the painter's work be reserved for the shadowed loggia and inner chamber ... [5]

This is a real distinction of craft; the demands on exterior finishes differ substantially from those of the interior, the facts of endurance and weathering draw a line precisely between colorful natural materials and applied colors. Fifty years of experimentation with modern polychromy had taught nineteenth-century architects the importance of 'structural' colors, not only through the experiences with paint in their colder, wetter climate, but from the recognition that the applied coloring of ancient and medieval buildings had been lost to time.[6]

But what, operationally, is a natural color? The processes of finishing, of dressing, cutting, polishing, curing, sealing, and so on, can modify the visual appearance of materials every bit as much as any opaque coating. In practice, materials like wood, stone, brick, metal, and leather grown or produced through natural processes are valued as such when their finishes enhance or at least do not obscure the complexity, depth, or variety of their appearance. Technically, there is little difference between a stain and a paint, except that the latter obscures the material, reducing it to the thin, surface color of the finely ground substances suspended in the binder. ... The natural can only be understood as a somewhat flexible category of finishes, not by a single principle of use, manufacture, or appearance. ... It is little wonder that the efforts of Owen Jones, Gottfried Semper, or Adolf Loos to regulate the logic of coating materials turns on the question of imitation.[7] Excluding it, as Loos's Law of Cladding sought to do, leads directly to the difficult pursuit of authenticity that characterizes the natural/neutral palette. Admitting the imitative practices *faux-bois* or *faux-marbre*, for example, opens the door to all applied ornament.

These questions are not meant to eliminate or undermine the concept of natural materials and finishes in construction or design. They derive from a host of very real physical and phenomenal observations and, more importantly perhaps, they hold a useful place in the everyday discussion of materials and finishes. As such, they offer one of the sites or topics with which architecture must contend, the topics that architects should approach with humility because they result from the kinds of broad cultural negotiation to which public constructions aspire.[8] That does not mean that critical investigations should be suspended by reifying the everyday or the primitive. Shifting authority to 'other' sources of that kind is precisely the problem. The difficult question raised by the authority of the natural has two aspects, the one concerns the opposition between the natural and the applied/artificial, the other concerns the related opposition between architecture and interior design. Why are applied, surface colors allied with artifice in the opposition to the equally contrived finishing of natural materials? And why are similar terms used in the opposition between two disciplines whose actual work so often overlaps and coincides? (... p 9)

The contemporary polarization of the natural and the artificial aligns ornament and applied colors with artifice, complexity, curviness, and femininity, building on the now apparently common-sense distinction made in German aesthetic theory between the 'Core-form' and 'Art-form,' between the essential, working aspect of an artifact and its supplemental, aesthetic features.[9] The fully gendered distrust of ornament is the dark side of aesthetics. It informed the growing ethic of simplicity, as expressed in German building culture, for example, by Heinrich Tessenow, when he observed that 'ornament has, and this is said with some apprehension, a lady-like quality.'[10] Not surprisingly, he was trying to distinguish 'artistic' from 'aesthetic' qualities, following the terms of the Arts and Crafts movement to which he had been converted through the writings of Morris and Ruskin, and then Hermann Muthesius's 1904 report on *The English House*.[11] Tessenow, however, recognized the historical nature of his characterization, noting that 'the actual value of ornament can be found in the same place as the actual values of lady-like qualities ... Today real lady-like qualities – distinctly opposed to feminine ones – are rare; we lack the necessary appreciation for them.'[12] 'Lady-like' ornament, in common with the clothing and manners of the eighteenth century courtier for example, was simply out of place in the modern building.

But of course the ornament of the nineteenth century differs radically from that of the eighteenth century. If Giedion made no other point, it was that we had to be redeemed from the excesses of nineteenth-century industrialized ornament. The proliferation of mass-produced decorative goods and the successive movements of reform and education are bound together; manuals of interior design and programs of public art education attempt to manage or suppress the proliferation of kitsch, camp, and low art.[13] Canons of taste like *The International Style* must everywhere negotiate the political and class distinctions inherent in this process. As Hitchcock and Johnson explained about their work, '[T]he current style sets a high, but not impossible standard for decoration: better none at all unless it be good. The principle is aristocratic rather than puritanical.'[14] Oscar Wilde would have agreed with the standard if not the specifics of the style. Edith Wharton's book has also been criticized as a design guide only for the wealthy, while Elsie de Wolfe used her career as a professional designer to transform herself into an English peer. Like gender formations, the 'aristocratic' standard of decoration is both an emblem or badge and a shifting collection of principles and artifacts with which it is discovered, negotiated, and enforced.

A remarkable book that illustrates these methods and exemplifies the fully developed class and gender characterizations of interior design is Emily Post's book, *The Personality of a House: The Blue Book of Home Design and Decoration*, which was published just prior to the mounting of Hitchcock and Johnson's exhibition.[15]   (... p 11)

Her general ethic, 'emptiness is always an essential of classic beauty and dignity,' is virtually identical to de Wolfe's 'simplicity and reticence,' and the 'better none at all' of *The International Style*. Although she devotes one chapter to the formal rules for color combination, implicit terms for the distinction between natural and artificial colors are developed throughout the book. They receive special emphasis in her chapter on the design of 'A Room for a Man,' in which she articulates the now familiar gendered assumptions about colors, finishes, and books that had crystallized since the turn of the century:

> All plain wood-lined rooms are good, as are also walls painted or papered in neutral tones of putty, or sand, or olive-gray, or wrapping-paper brown, made colorful by many books (red ones!). For a man's study – unless he never reads – the most furnishing decorations are well-filled book-shelves, not too closely matched. Odd lots of books, reference books in calf or leather, or at most, sets of favorite authors in cloth bindings, are far more suggestive of the man who reads than are even rows of splendidly-tooled bindings – unless bindings are his hobby.[16]

Elsie de Wolfe, too, understood books as a means of introducing colorful variety into the neutral/natural palette acceptable for the masculine stereotype of the library. 'Here, if anywhere, you would think a monotony of brown wood would be obvious, but think of thousands of books with brilliant bindings. ... Can't you see that this cypress room is simply glowing with color.'[17] Books provide a subversive decoration, introducing colorful variety under the guise of craftsmanship and scholarship, apparently slipping a feminine note of decoration into obviously masculine interiors.   (... p 12)

But the importance of color in the convention of the masculine library cannot be overstated. In *Style-Architecture and Building-Art* Muthesius had earlier observed that because previous styles of architecture had no distinctly interior decoration, transferring exterior features to the interior, that 'color becomes preeminent' in the modern interior, 'for we are aware that it, more than architectural form, acts strongly and directly, and creates an ambience.'[18]

The narrow convention observed by Emily Post still remains recognizable and legible today. The similarities between de Wolfe's library, Emily Post's 'Room for a Man,' and the room of *The International Style* exemplify the fully formed concept of modern color and finish in which simple, achromatic surfaces and natural materials are deemed masculine by virtue of their authenticity (or are they authentic by virtue of their masculinity?). That identity is remarkably independent of style, and it continues to characterize designers, occupants, and finishes to this day, warping and restricting design practices with its definitions. The opposition of natural finishes to applied colors derives its energy from resistance to the artificiality of 'taste,' which is affiliated with intuition, irrationality, and the feminine. The repeated efforts to develop a definitive science of color effects, either functionally, linguistically, or psychologically are all efforts to excise such subjectivities from architecture. The fear of taste also exacerbates the gap between the practical applications of color, which require the attention to arbitrary elements noted by Perrault, and the discourse which seeks to explain them. Colors are selected and applied in projects everywhere with little of the critical discussion received by the forms to which they are applied.

In a subsequent section of her book, Emily Post discussed the construction of 'Faked Bindings for Decoration' to artificially produce the *look* of masculine amenity.[19] This practice, and the decorative deployment of 'real' books too, operate not according to the logic by which formal architectural principles are explained, but according to the negotiation of identity and its discovery through representations. As illustrated in the bookcase collage by Max Ernst, that negotiation involves both the inspecting gaze of the occupant and the return look of the interior. A wall of books not only appears masculine, but reassures its occupant that he or she is conforming to the complex image of rationality, literacy, and authenticity that books convey. Again, the emphasis here is not on identities per se, but on the tension between the decorative urge to include a variety of color and the defensive exclusion of explicitly decorative practices. The logic of color conventions cannot be grasped by theories of identity without an equivalent consideration of decorative variety and the attention to occasion, both of which require narrative forms for their exploration.

The selection of colors and finishes is always an exercise of taste, and any such acknowledgment makes evident the deep affiliation of architecture with the other arts of convention – dressing, dining, dancing, or other activities. That perhaps is the deepest fear expressed by the privileging of natural over applied color: that acknowledgment of the arts of convention and the necessity of timeliness would undermine a profession dedicated defensively to timelessness. This is not an apology for individual tastes, but the observation that authenticity is simply a matter of appearances. It is through the discriminations of taste, shaped according to class and gender, as well as to form, material, and workmanship, that we discriminate among the qualities of materials and their finishes. The composition of material and color palettes is among the most demanding forms of discrimination required of architects and designers, and for which the wall of book filled shelves might serve as an apt reminder. (... p 13)

Notes

1 Henry-Russell Hitchcock and Philip Johnson, *The International Style* [1932], W W Norton & Company (New York), 1966, p 75.

2 For a history of the exhibition see Terence Riley, *The International Style: Exhibition 1 and the Museum of Modern Art*, Rizzoli (New York), 1992.

3 Edith Wharton and Ogden Codman, Jr, *The Decoration of Houses*, C Scribner's Sons (New York), 1897.

4 C Ray Smith, *Interior Design in 20th Century America: A History*, Harper & Row Publishers (New York), 1987. Margaret Milam Sharon, *Historical Perspectives on Interior Architecture/Design as a Developing Profession*, PhD diss, University of Kentucky, 1992.

5 This quotation is from a slightly different version of the lecture. Oscar Wilde, 'Art and the Handicraftsman', *The First Collected Edition of the Works of Oscar Wilde*, vol 14, Dawsons of Pall Mall [London], 1969, pp 292–308.

6 The concept of structural polychromy is examined at length in David Van Zanten, *The Architectural Polychromy of the 1830s*, Garland Publishing (New York), 1977; Robin Middleton, 'Colour and Cladding in the Nineteenth Century', *Daidalos*, 51, March, 1994, pp 78–89.

7 The question of authenticity in painting or cladding is taken up by a variety of authors. Gottfried Semper, *The Four Elements of Architecture*, Cambridge University Press (Cambridge), 1989, p 127. Owen Jones, *Grammar of Ornament* [1856], Van Nostrand Reinhold (New York), 1982, Proposition 35. Adolf Loos, 'The Principle of Cladding', *Spoken into the Void: Collected Essays, 1897–1900*, MIT Press (Cambridge), 1982, pp 66–9. Amédée Ozenfant, 'Colour in the Town', *The Architectural Review*, 82, July 1937, pp 41–4.

8 The concept of rhetorical topics in architecture is discussed in David Leatherbarrow, *The Roots of Architectural Invention: Site, Enclosure, Materials*, Cambridge University Press (Cambridge), 1993.

9 A distinction introduced in Carl Botticher, *Die Tektonik der Hellenen*, Ernst & Korn [Berlin], 1869. For a discussion, see Harry Francis Mallgrave, 'Introduction', *Empathy, Form and Space: Problems in German Aesthetics, 1873–1893*, Getty Center for Art and Humanities (Santa Monica), 1994, pp 45–6.

10 Heinrich Tessenow, 'Housebuilding and Such Things' [1916] 9H, *On Rigor*, 1989, p 27.

11 Hermann Muthesius, *The English House* [1904], Rizzoli (New York), 1987.

12 Muthesius, *The English House*, p 30.

13 Matei Calinescu, *Five Faces of Modernity: Modernism, Avant-Garde, Decadence, Kitsch, Postmodernism*, Duke University Press (Durham), 1987.

14 Hitchcock and Johnson, *The International Style*, p 75.

15 Emily Post, *The Personality of a House: The Blue Book of Home Design and Decoration*, Funk & Wagnalls Co. (New York), 1930.

16 Post, *The Personality of a House*, p 406. The reference to red books comes from an anecdote that she relates earlier in the book: 'This reminds me of a story that is true: The wife of an eminent author who had enlarged their library living-room was annoyed at the distressing emptiness of so many of the new bookshelves. So she went to a store that had advertised cheap editions and asked for 'lots of books.' Said the clerk: 'Which books may I get you?' To the horror of the clerk, she answered, 'Red ones!' She giggled afterwards at the clerk's obvious estimate of her literary taste,' p 188.

17 De Wolfe, *The House in Good Taste*, The Century Co (New York), 1913, p 78.

18 Hermann Muthesius, *Style-Architecture and Building-Art: Transformations of Architecture in the Nineteenth Century and Its Present Condition* [1902], Getty Center for the History of Art and Humanities (Santa Monica), 1994, p 86.

19 Post, *The Personality of a House*, p 438.

William W Braham, 'A Wall of Books: The Gender of Natural Colors in Modern Architecture', *Journal of Architectural Education*, vol 53, no 1, September 1999, pp 4–14.
(Excerpts pp 4–13)

A House for Josephine Baker

Karen Burns

Art historian and cultural theorist Karen Burns raises questions about the presence of race and gender in architectural design and how they are disclosed through criticism that attempts to 'read' architecture. Reviewing the work of several feminist theorists, she takes up the challenge of theorising racial difference in relation to both Josephine Baker and Adolf Loos' Josephine Baker House. These issues are unfolded through an examination of texts and images, but more importantly through Burns' observations about the conflation of Baker's body and house in writings about the house. Careful to avoid repeating colonialist operations, Burns reviews existing criticism and comment on the house and its inhabitant, noting that costume, skin and interior space are all described as surfaces supporting a point of difference and otherness.

The Unreadable Interior

The interior cannot be guessed at by looking at the outside.
Ludwig Münz and Gustav Künstler, 1966

In line with Loos's way of thinking, the exterior says nothing about the interior.
Benedetto Gravagnuolo, 1982

In this project for a house for Josephine Baker Loos uses a number of elements we find in his other work: the closed character of the facades.
Paul Groenendijk and Piet Vollaard, 1985

The compactness of the volume, the flat roof, the small, low openings, the vast blind surfaces and the bands of black and white marble created an exotic and mysterious image, vaguely evocative of African architecture, while providing no clues as to the interior.
Panayotis Tournikiotis, 1994[1]

If, as Beatriz Colomina has argued, writers have persisted in reading the architecture of the Baker House as attributes of Josephine Baker,[2] how might one understand these same writers' insistence that from the exterior the building's interior is unreadable, impenetrable by criticism?

Yet such a reading has been made. On the one hand the building's exterior veils the vision of the critic by sending the referent 'Africa' into a hazy and apparently unfocusable, imprecise reading (a smudge), and, on the other, the exterior presents a blankness, rather than a transparent path for criticism's line of sight. Vision fails criticism as insight.

Vision is often associated with mastery and assumed (but ultimately failed) distance.[3] However, these readings of the Baker House suggest a form of critical insight based on a protected and limited way of seeing. The Baker House seems to be a project that confronts (or is read as confronting) critics, again and again, with their own fallibility.

It eludes the project of 'interpretation' that nominally guides architectural criticism. Current modish strategies of reading might write the house as a triumphant excess that can never be recuperated by criticism, or as the moment when architectural theory and history touch the limits of their own knowledge.

However, as Loos's biographers always strive to remind the reader, the failure of a facade's transparency is ultimately decipherable as authorial origin: the author decided to reverse the tried-and-true terms of criticism (exterior must reveal interior) and build a blank or blind wall. Criticism itself opens again, and closes, the problem of reference.

Perhaps the puzzle of the Baker House can be solved by looking elsewhere, to another discourse, to the biography of Josephine Baker. Since architectural writing continually attributed features taken to belong to Josephine Baker as features of the house, were critics narrating a story about Baker's own interior?

Is it that Baker's house and body possess an unreadable interior, or is it that they provide a different model of the body, one that can be described as all surface, one that radically confounds the surface/depth binary.[4] Or does a conventional binary model operate in this text, against which Baker's house and body can be construed as lacking?

The figuration of the body as an inner/outer binary has featured in the recent reconceptualization of subjectivity. In Michel Foucault's analysis, the binary erases the social work of inscription. The interior is a privileged trope for the soul. Occupying the body's internal cavities, the soul is the interior space intrinsic to the substance of a particular body, the locale of that body's sovereign will.[5] Foucault's reading of the inscription of an internal space *on the body* displaces the spatial relations assumed by the inner/outer binary. Rewriting Foucault's theorization of the soul as something produced by social inscription *on* the body, Judith Butler observes that acts, gestures, and desire produce the semblance of an internal core or substance on the surface of the body.[6]

Neither Foucault nor Butler in the texts I am citing address the question of corporeal inscription as cultural difference, ethnicity, and race.[7] However, Foucault and Butler's location of the body's surface as the site for social inscription might assist in negotiating Spivak's criticism of the epidermal schema. Spivak argues against the ridiculously simple and singular nature of the epidermal schema's insistence on skin as *the* visible sign of difference. Locating all social inscription as a marking of surface, in the full complexity of that term (where does the body's surface begin and end?) places the skin, one organ, within a multiple network of corporeal organs, cells, and tissues. Reading, which is one form of social inscription, brings various parts of the corporeal to the surface. There is no natural, essential connection between skin and racial difference. But the intensity of focus on the epidermal schema conveniently ignores all the other work carried out by inscription on bodies.

Theorizing the importance of the fantasy of the internal, Butler explores the interior figure in psychoanalytic descriptions of the acquisition of a subject's identity. The structuring binary of surface/interior and its position in the description of psychic identity have a home, too, in architecture. While film and literary genres have rendered the domestic interior as an allegory of the psychic lives of its inhabitants, the architectural interior may be projected as a topography of the individual's own interior life. The inhabitants' sexual and psychic identities are worked by and within the spatial settings of the interior and its ritualized, sexual dramas.

Given these conventions, what are we to make of a house, interior, and inhabitant who are all surface? I do not believe that architectural commentaries rewrite the received terms of inner/outer body and subject as Judith Butler does. If the most commonplace meanings of these corporeal descriptions haunt the Baker House descriptions within this metaphysical binary, Baker cannot be the divided subject who is the subject of psychoanalytic inquiry. Without an interior, she has no possibility for an internal psychic space and no fantasized locale for the identity of self. This lack of interiority, or deferral, renders her not only as different from other inhabitants, but as someone whose interior is completely unknowable.

Ironically the Josephine Baker House was never built. All that remains is a model and plans whose interiors we are unable to inhabit. Within architecture, then, Baker's interiority is in one sense never realized; it is eternally deferred.[8]

These theoretical moves of forever pointing out exclusion and failure often leads to a dead end. It assumes a particular reading of the subject as a problem for criticism (and, similarly, for feminism). In the end it does not explain how the logic of criticism works in the Baker House commentaries: what tasks it performs, what actions it enables. To keep retrieving Baker as an exemplum of alterity is to keep pinning her back against the wall, to that place already assigned to her by criticism.

Thinking again of the unreadable interior, perhaps it has another function, apart from the invocation of certain myths of unreadable Africa in the logic of criticism. To produce the interior as a secretive place, one whose secrets cannot be *guessed*, at this stage of the story, creates narrative suspense. This is a function of critical writing. It sets the stage for the final drama of the interior. If the critic's dream of unimpeded visibility is blocked by the apparently mute surfaces of this place, it is recovered in the readings of the internal swimming pool, a place where criticism finds and flexes its own identity.   (... p 65)

Notes

1   Ludwig Münz and Gustav Künstler, *Adolf Loos: Pioneer of Modern Architecture*, trans Harold Meek, Thames and Hudson (London), 1966, p 195; Benedetto Gravagnuolo, *Adolf Loos*, trans CH Evans, Rizzoli (New York), 1982, p 191; Paul Groenendijk and Piet Vollaard, *Adolf Loos: House for Josephine Baker*, Uitgeverij 010 (Rotterdam), 1985, p 34; Panayotis Tournikiotis, *Adolf Loos*, trans Marguerite McGoldrick, Princeton Architectural Press (New York), 1994, p 95.

2   Beatriz Colomina, 'The Split Wall: Domestic Voyeurism', Beatriz Colomina (ed), *Sexuality & Space*, Princeton Architectural Press (New York), 1992, p 97.

3   See for example, Griselda Pollock's 'Modernity and the Spaces of Femininity', which is prefaced by a quote from Luce Irigaray: 'More than other senses, the eye objectifies and masters.' The essay is reprinted in Norma Broude and Mary D Garrard (eds), *The Expanding Discourse: Feminism and Art History*, Harper Collins (New York), 1992, p 245.

4   Theorists of the corporeal such as Vicky Kirby have argued (quoting Foucault's tracing of the workings of history as it is inscribed in the 'nervous system, in temperament, in the digestive apparatus'), 'The body's surfaces continue into the "interior". Paradoxically the surface is both the thing which supposedly divides and secures inside and outside and the thing that holds them together. Foucault's notion of inscription, which implies a surface to be written on, is an extraordinary surface that includes the bodies' depths and questions the division between interior and exterior.' Vicky Kirby, 'Corporeal Habits: Addressing Essentialism Differently', *Hypatia*, vol 6 no 3, Fall 1991, p 21, note 20.

5   Michel Foucault, *Discipline and Punish: The Birth of the Prison*, trans Alan Sheridan, Penguin (Harmondsworth, UK), 1982, pp 29–30.

6   Judith Butler, 'Gender Trouble, Feminist Theory, and Psychoanalytic Discourse', Linda J Nicholson (ed), *Feminism/Postmodernism*, Routledge (New York), 1990, p 136.

7   Judith Butler has written several essays addressing questions of ethnicized, raced corporeality in her book *Bodies That Matter*, Routledge (New York), 1993.

8   This reading was suggested by Rose Lucas at a presentation of an earlier incarnation of this paper to a Women's Studies symposium at Monash University in November 1993.

Karen Burns, 'A House for Josephine Baker', *Postcolonial Space(s)*, Gülsüm Baydar Nalbantoglu and Wong Chong Thai (eds), Princeton Architectural Press (New York) 1997. © 1997 Gülsüm Baydar Nalbantoglu, Wong Chong Thai and the authors. Reprinted by permission of Princeton Architectural Press.
(Excerpt pp 62–5)

Bodies and Mirrors

Ann C Colley

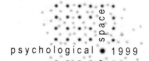

In this essay, Ann Colley discusses the correlation between physical bodies and their surroundings, particularly the space of nostalgia and recollection contained in Victorian literature. Working from the role memory plays in recalling our relationship to known environments, the particularities of the selected autobiographic accounts discuss the spaces of childhood through the invisible, aesthetic and ubiquitous body. This critical examination from an English literature academic proposes that the interior is not simply defined by the objects within it, but by our movement and inhabitation around and among them.

Years after they had left their childhood behind them, John Ruskin, Walter Horatio Pater and Robert Louis Stevenson continued to reflect upon the homes in which they had passed their early lives. In particular they thought about the rooms of their childhood. When they described these spaces, they did not simply re-present the contours and things that had composed the drawing-room of 28 Herne Hill in London, the interiors of the house in Enfield or the day nursery and bedrooms of 17 Heriot Row in Edinburgh. Instead, they considered how their physical being had related to the walls and windows of childhood.[1] Conscious of how this relationship defines the sense of one's surroundings, they let their memories resuscitate the dialogue their bodies had once had with these interiors. They understood that it is the child's being that shapes and illuminates the interiors of home. Articles do not define interiors; bodies that move and feel their way among these objects do.

Although Ruskin, Pater and Stevenson are all sensitive to the defining function of the body, each, not surprisingly, experiences the phenomenon in a different way. The result is that their autobiographical texts (*Praeterita*, 1885; 'The Child in the House,' 1878; *A Child's Garden of Verses*, 1885) offer three distinct models of how the consciousness of one's physical being illuminates the interiors of home. Ruskin's text speaks of the invisible body, Pater's of the aesthetic body and Stevenson's of the ubiquitous body.

The first model is Ruskin's. In his often grumbling, yet graceful, autobiography Ruskin describes the houses of his childhood: he writes briefly about 54 Hunter Street (London) and more extensively about the house at Herne Hill (four miles south of London). With a keen immediacy he describes the commanding views from their garret windows, the front and back gardens and the setting of the Herne Hill residence. But with their emphasis on 'prospect,' these passages do not represent Ruskin's experience of the interiors of home, for they belong more to the public Ruskin, the figure whose carefully selected words guided the British around Venice and directed readers' eyes to a more 'truthful' view of the Alps. Instead, the sections in *Praeterita* that reveal more intimate moments are those in which he once more steps inside his childhood surroundings and considers his relationship to them. No longer preoccupied by how a shadow falls on a cathedral's tracery or by the continuity of a building's structural lines, he dwells upon a few intimate moments of home and recalls how he had passed his days 'contentedly' inside rooms, comparing the colours in the carpet or gazing at the patterns in the bed covers. He remembers how he had once stood by the windows watching a wasp on the window-pane or repeatedly looking at the iron post out of which the water carts were filled.[2]

Paradoxically, in all these intimate spaces of home the presence of the body is virtually absent. In *Praeterita* Ruskin makes it clear that he had not occupied these comfortable recesses and corners with the fullness of his physical being but rather as an almost invisible entity. As if replacing metaphor with synecdoche, Ruskin describes his younger self by focusing exclusively upon his eyes that reach out as far as they can and leave the rest of his body behind, unobserved and unmolested. Throughout his work, the eyes replace the physical body by standing in for it.[3] To observe was enough. Ruskin moved through the rooms and interiors of home as inside a frame supporting a glass that hides the body in its dimness while allowing the eyes to peer through its dusk. When he sat observing, his eyes wandered into the patterns of the floors and walls; he travelled within the portchaise and stared out of its window; setting out on holidays, he took his position on a 'little box' between his mother and father and enjoyed the prospect appearing piece by piece before him.[4] Disappearing into the supporting brackets, his body released his eyes and gave him the freedom to stare, unnoticed, in 'rapturous and riveted' attention.[5] This granted him a protective invisibility that allowed him to observe without being engaged by anything other than himself. He existed as the spectator, not as the observed. Later in life he was always to value those moments when he could take note of his surroundings away from people's sight and consciousness. For instance, in 1842, alone in Champagnole, Ruskin recalls that his 'entire delight was in observing' without himself being 'noticed.'[6] Part of Ruskin's nostalgia for his childhood is to return to the monastic invisibility that allowed him the privacy of his visual ecstasy.

Pater's rendering of his childhood experiences in the semi-autobiographical portrait 'The Child in the House' is naturally different from Ruskin's. Although Pater's interiors, like Ruskin's, radiate an almost monastic aura, they by no means resemble Ruskin's, for the body that inhabits and forms them has a distinctly different effect. It is a sensuous presence. And although for Pater the visual experiences are just as essential as they are for Ruskin, these visual moments are not detached or bodiless. They emerge from and return to a body through which images move along the nerves and bring vitality to his being. In Pater's interiors, therefore, the child's body is just as significant as it is in Ruskin's, but not because of its inquisitive invisibility; it is conspicuous because of its willingness to be affected by what lies outside of it. Here the haptic and the visual conjoin to create an impressionistic body.

When Pater portrays Florian Deleal, the young boy in 'The Child in the House,' he dwells upon the boy's willing, though sometimes unconscious, acceptance of the visible, the tangible and the audible encircling him. Within, the winds from outside the house play on him and through the open windows the coming and going of travellers, the shadows of evening, the brightness of day, the perfumes from the neighbouring garden and the scent of the lime tree blossoms awaken his senses. The sensitive boy looks at the fallen acorn and the black crow's feathers that his sister has brought in from 'some distant forest' and discovers intimations of places beyond – these 'treasures' speak the 'rumour of its [the wood's] breezes, with the glossy blackbirds aslant and the branches lifted in them.'[7]

The outside and the inside come together in his body that risks being wounded by the tyranny of the senses and the surrendering of its boundaries – something the sheltered Ruskin could not expose himself to. From over the high garden wall, sentiments of beauty and pain float into Florian's consciousness and penetrate what Pater calls the 'actual body;'[8] the cry of his aunt on the stair when she announces his father's death strikes and quickens him; the wasp in the basket of yellow crab-apples stings him (Ruskin, recall, only watched the wasp at his window). The receptive Florian listens to the voices of people below speaking of the sick woman who 'had seen one of the dead sitting beside her' and then brings the ghostly figure into his own space so that the *revenant* sits 'beside him in the reveries of his broken sleep.'[9] Similarly he goes outside so that he may bring what is there inside. He passes through the garden gate, fills his arms with red hawthorn blossoms (the scent of which has already reached him) and returns to arrange these brilliant flowers in 'old blue china pots along the chimney piece.'[10]

Later, in two other imaginary and semi-autobiographical portraits, 'Emerald Uthwart'[11] and *Marius the Epicurean*,[12] Pater echoes many of the details describing Florian's experiences within his home. In these texts the children breathe, feel, touch, move and see with their bodies as Florian does. No eye, as in Ruskin's case, leaves the body to reside in the half-concealed recesses of a drawing room. The young and solitary Emerald is a child who, within the context of home, responds to the sights and sounds surrounding him – to the 'rippling note of the birds' and to the flowers in the garden that yield a sweetness when the 'loosening wind' unsettles them.[13] When flung open, the windows in the attic where he sleeps admit the scent of roses, and the faint sea-salt air envelops him as he sleeps under 'the fine old blankets.'[14] Similarly, the child Marius in the solitude of his early dwelling feels the sea wind that blows from the distant harbour, inhales the scent of the new-mown hay that the sea air sweeps into his room and takes pleasure in the view of the purple heath.

The affect of these children's sensuous bodies and consciousness is complemented by the interiors of home. Like Florian, who sees and touches what is outside the boundaries of his body, these interiors, as if they were bodies themselves, extend and incorporate what is beyond them – what is outside the windows or the enclosing walls. These interiors do not shut themselves off; they resist exclusiveness. Like a shuttle in a loom they move continuously inside and out of each other. In Florian's childhood home, for instance, the staircase moves the reader from floor to floor and up to a broad window, out to the swallow's nest that hangs beneath the sill and then back down into the house and out again on to the open, flat space of a roof that offers a view of the neighbouring steeples. Interiors and exteriors mingle. They pass through the intermediary spaces – the windows and gates left ajar – to meet and lie over and press against each other. In this manner the child's body and the rooms of home engage in an exchange. In a sense, each passes into the condition of the other.

The rooms of Stevenson's childhood reveal a third possibility, another way the body's effect converses with and gives shape to its surroundings. This time, though, it is neither Ruskin's curious invisibility nor Pater's receptive body that defines or intermingles with the interior; instead, it is the moat of sickness encircling the child's body that structures the spaces of home and creates the sense of the ubiquitous body.

Stevenson, who began writing his childhood poems during a particularly difficult time with his health, returns to those interior spaces in A Child's Garden of Verses.[15] He re-enters the rooms that recall the fevers, the severe bronchial infections, the earaches and, eventually, the haemorrhaging that from the age of two kept him for long periods in bed. Confined, the young Stevenson periodically missed school and passed his days 'exiled' from the company of other children. As his biographers have pointed out, Stevenson never forgot what he called the 'terrible long nights' through which he lay awake, in his words, 'troubled continuously by a hacking, exhausting cough, and praying for sleep or morning from the bottom of my shaken little body.'[16]

The interiors described in A Child's Garden of Verses recall the scenes of Stevenson's early confinement. The poems take place in the night nursery; they inhabit the land of the counterpane; they climb the stairs; they go into the walled garden and they look through the broad window of 17 Heriot Row. In a sense, each verse is a room shaped by the sick body's desire to escape from itself. The poems and the spaces they describe offer release from the enclosures of the body's frailty. Like the children in one of the verses, who break through a breach in the wall and go down to the mill ('Keepsake Mill'), or like the river that flows 'out past the mill, / Away down the valley, / Away down the hill' ('Where Go the Boats?'), out 'A hundred miles or more' into foreign lands – to Babylon, Malabar, Africa and Providence ('Pirate Story') – and like the swing that takes the child up high so he can look over the garden wall and 'see so wide' ('The Swing'), these poems reach beyond to places afar; they break through their limits and climb the cherry tree to look abroad ('Foreign Lands').[17]

In these poems the interiors of home do not isolate the convalescing child. Through his desire to be rid of what threatens to exile him, the ailing child shapes the rooms and enclosed gardens so that they carry him to places beyond. The young Stevenson convincingly substitutes one object for another; he transforms the chair, the stairs, the bedclothes, the windows and the flickering of the coals' embers into vessels of escape. The bedroom chairs stuffed with pillows become ships; a basket in the sun turns into a pirate's boat; the counterpane assumes its own topography of hills, dales and plains and the sheets merge into seas. These interiors liberate the sick body from itself.

Most of all, though, the desire of the sick child to find release from himself creates situations in which the child identifies with other children and, in that way, becomes part of a ubiquitous body so that he can for a while be less alone, excluded and strange. Within these rooms is a larger landscape that collapses the distant into the contiguous and, simultaneously, expands the immediate into the distant. The child senses, although he cannot see them, the presence of other children whose activities are similar to his. These children may live away in the far East or in the West beyond the foam of the Atlantic Sea ('The Sun Travels') and they may eat 'curious' food rather than 'proper meat' ('Foreign Children'); nevertheless, the sick child senses that they share a common physical rhythm: all 'dine at five' ('Foreign Lands'); like him, but in an inverted pattern, they go to bed and at dawn they awake and dress ('The Sun Travels').[18] These parallels form the larger, more inclusive body so that all children, even when confined and alone, belong to an unseen, unconscious, yet animated intertextuality of being that is theirs. Just as the sickly Stevenson once looked out of the nursery window, through the darkness of the night, to see the lit windows where other sick 'little boys' were also waiting for the morning, the child in the verses finds comfort in inclusiveness.[19] He knows there are others ready to receive and understand him, so that, for instance, when he launches his boats, he is aware that children 'A hundred miles or more' away will bring them into shore ('Where Go the Boats?').[20]

Because of this sense of ubiquitousness, the potentially lonely and isolated 'I' of the poems' interiors frequently joins the more inclusive 'We.' In 'A Good Play,' 'Pirate Story,' 'Farewell to the Farm,' 'Marching Song,' 'Happy Thought,' 'The Sun Travels,' 'The

Lamplighter,' 'My Bed is a Boat', 'Keepsake Mill' and 'Picture-Books in Winter,' the child attaches his being to others so that 'we' are afloat, 'we' swing upon the gate, 'we' march, 'we should all be as happy as kings,' 'we' play round the sunny gardens, 'we' are very lucky and 'we' see how all things are. It is, of course, this metamorphosis that empowers the child in *A Child's Garden of Verses*. Like the shadow that follows or jumps ahead of the child, his sick body is almost always a silent, threatening presence among the verses' lines. Yet, within the context of the poems' transfigured interiors, the child is able to reach beyond himself and connect with others and join the ubiquitous body of childhood. Through play and fantasy, the child alters the rooms of home and releases the suffering 'I' from the fragility of itself and thus realises the possibilities of a more encompassing and restorative 'we.' Stevenson's child, in a sense, brings to life one of the most vital experiences of interiority – the understanding that an interior does not exist for its own sake but, instead, for the desire of reaching something or going somewhere.[21]   (... p 46)

Notes

1 Their orientation anticipates those like Maurice Merleau-Ponty who argue that it is not through thought, absented from body, that one knows one's surroundings, but through one's 'bodily situation' – that one is conscious through the body's position in space. See M Merleau-Ponty, *The Primacy of Perception*, JM Edie (ed), Northwestern University Press (Evanston, Illinois), 1964, p 5. Their point of view also looks forward to twentieth-century architectural theorists such as Kent Bloomer, Charles Moore and Robert Yudell, who insist that one measures and orders the world from one's own body, that the body is in 'constant dialogue' with the buildings surrounding it. See K Bloomer, C Moore and R Yudell, *Body, Memory and Architecture*, Yale University Press (New Haven), 1977, p 57. Ruskin's, Pater's and Stevenson's sensitivity to the relationship of their bodies to their surroundings might, in some way, reflect the emphasis placed upon the child's body in nineteenth-century guides on raising a child. See 'Physiological Bodies', C Steedman, *Strange Dislocations: Childhood and the Idea of Human Interiority 1780–1930*, Harvard University Press (Cambridge, MA), 1995.

2 J Ruskin, *Praeterita: The Autobiography of John Ruskin* [1885], intro K Clark, Oxford University Press (Oxford), 1989, pp 12, 34, 7.

3 As if conscious of this substitution, Ruskin recalls the time he 'frightened' his mother 'out of her wits' by announcing that his eyes were coming 'out of his head'. See Ruskin, *Praeterita*, p 38. Many critics, of course, have remarked upon the importance that Ruskin attached to the act of seeing.

4 Ruskin, *Praeterita*, p 23.

5 Ruskin, *Praeterita*, p 50.

6 Ruskin, *Praeterita*, pp 155–6.

7 WH Pater, 'The Child in the House' [1878], WE Buckler (ed), *Walter Pater: Three Major Texts*, New York, University Press (New York), 1986, p 229.

8 Pater, 'The Child in the House', p 232.

9 Pater, 'The Child in the House', p 234.

10 Pater, 'The Child in the House', p 231.

11 WH Pater, 'Emerald Uthwart' [1892], WE Buckler (ed), *Walter Pater: Three Major Texts*, New York University Press (New York), 1986.

12 WH Pater, *Marius the Epicurean: His Sensations and Ideas* [1885], I Small (ed), Oxford University Press (Oxford), 1986.

13 Pater, 'Emerald Uthwart', p 344.

14 Pater, 'Emerald Uthwart', p 345.

15 RL Stevenson, *A Child's Garden of Verses* [1885], Airmont (New York), 1969.

16 D Daiches, *Robert Louis Stevenson and His World*, Thames and Hudson (London), 1973, p 10. Of all the photographs and paintings of Stevenson, none captures his fragility more than John Singer Sargent's 1885 portrait – painted the year *A Child's Garden of Verses* appeared – in which Stevenson's lank and almost transparent body moves through the shadows into darkness. His long thin fingers touch his face and his leg as if having to confirm their actuality.

17 Stevenson, *A Child's Garden of Verses*, pp 36, 28, 57.

18 Stevenson, *A Child's Garden of Verses*, p 29.

19 Daiches, *Robert Louis Stevenson and His World*, pp 10–11.

20 Stevenson, *A Child's Garden of Verses*, p 36.

21 For a discussion of this principle, see M Tafuri, *The Sphere and the Labyrinth: Avant-Gardes and Architecture from Piranesi to the 1970s*, trans P d'Acierno and R Connolly, MIT Press (Cambridge, MA), 1987.

Ann C Colley, 'Bodies and Mirrors: The Childhood Interiors of Ruskin, Pater and Stevenson', from *Domestic Space: Reading the Nineteenth-century Interior*, by Inga Bryden and Janet Floyd (eds), Manchester University Press (Manchester), 1999.

(Excerpt pp 40–6)

Movement and Myth: The Schröder House and Transformable Living

Catherine Croft

One of the promises of the Modern Movement in architecture was its ability to realise that once the plan was free and open, space could be demarked, reformed and reconfigured with the aid of kinetic architectural elements or mobile furniture units. Catherine Croft's text looks inside the social pragmatics of spatial transformability to see how, as a generator of form, it provokes the limit of what is acceptable and tolerable with regards to privacy, even within the social atmosphere between family members. Contextualised through the Rietveld–Schröder House, this issue is discussed through the realities of family life and how, over time, they change and force spatial issues of segregation and enclosure. While this house is discussed as the transformable object, the text reveals larger underlying transformations to do with living patterns, generational differences, cultural values and the re-edification of conventional spatial patterns critical to contemporary interior design.

Central to any analysis of the Schröder House is the nature of public/private space. Surveying the house in plan, the overall layout of the first floor is clear whether the partitions are open or closed. However, for the user, the realms created by the partitions must have been clearly delineated as private. This use of space is closer to the Arts and Crafts creation of spaces within spaces: the fireside alcove, the projecting oriel at Philip Webb's Red House (1859) encouraging separate activities within a companionable larger volume (although perhaps relegating female activity to marginal zones).

Ironically, however, by rejecting any clearly defined hierarchical space, the Schröder House becomes not more egalitarian but more dictatorial. For example, any conventional notions of privacy would have been dispensed with – one would actually have to make a bathroom by pulling out walls around the bath, the antithesis of a relaxing experience. The Schröder House's mythology might place an emphasis on a pioneering form of modern free living, but the reality is about control, not freedom. It could even be said to resemble life in prison, with its proscribed actions at proscribed times. The partitions, which are drawn at night to separate off the four corners of the space, providing separate sleeping areas for the children, do not make sense unless all are closed or all open. There is thus no scope for

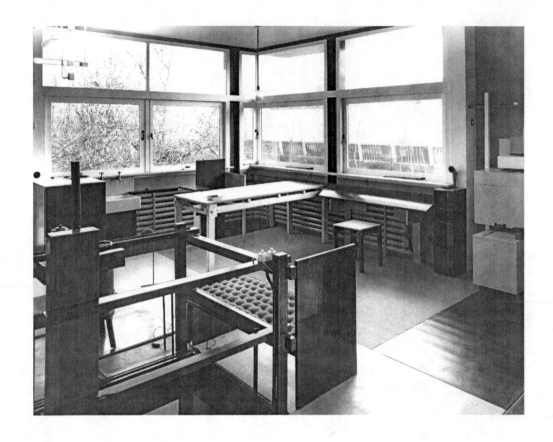

The Schröder House: interior c. 1987, after restoration. Photo courtesy of Hubert-Jan Henket, ©
Collectie Centraal Museum, Utrecht.

different time schedules – in contemporary terms, for a stroppy teenager to stay in bed until noon, or to leave filthy underwear strewn across the floor. This physical compression of family life must have placed strains on even the most unconventional set-up. Ultimately, Schröder craved greater privacy.   (... p 12)

Schröder's contemporaries were more impressed by the bold use of colour, sadly lost to us in the black and white photographs that record the house's original form. The elements of De Stijl – the unconventional elevations at the end of a conventional Utrecht street – were more controversial than the interior arrangements. However, from the beginning, reservations were raised about practicality. In 1925, J.G. Wattjes wrote:

> By rejecting the normal method of subdividing space – with fixed walls – and choosing a system of sliding partitions, an extremely flexible arrangement of the interior is achieved ... the intentions behind this 'machine for living in' is not that now and again you can change the arrangement of the interior, it is that each day you can alter it several times, as often as changing needs require. The question is, will such extreme flexibility in fact prove convenient in the long run? I very much doubt it.[1]

The house represents a form of intellectual alienation, from both conventional society and from conventional family arrangements.

More than any of the other buildings that make up the established modernist canon – the Villa Savoye, the Barcelona Pavilion, et al – the Schröder House combines a sense of pioneering architectural invention with close allegiance to a contemporary art movement; it is both a 'machine for living in' and an aesthetically composed work of the Dutch De Stijl movement. For many years, it was this relationship that formed the basis of critical appraisal, but the extent to which Rietveld himself saw the sliding screens and partitioning as ground breaking – something likely to have a lasting influence rather than being a highly idiosyncratic response to an individual client – is questionable.   (... p 14)

Note

1 JG Wattjes, 'Stories from Behind the Scenes of Dutch Moral Modernism', Crimson (with Michael Speaks and Gerard Hadders), *Mart Stam's Trousers*, 010 Publishers (Rotterdam), 1999.
Catherine Croft, 'Movement and Myth: The Schröder House and Transformable Living', *Architectural Design*, vol 70 no 4, 2000, pp 10–15.

Spatial Stories

Michel de Certeau

philosophical ● 1984

space

achronic

In his life as a scholar and Jesuit priest, Michel de Certeau traversed the disciplinary terrains of geography, phenomenology, psychoanalysis, philosophy and the social sciences. His work established 'spatial practice' as the proliferation of metaphors quantified only to the extent of distinct spatial experiences. In this text narration is explored as a negotiator between that which is seen, mapped and stable, and that which is experienced, toured and individuated. We are reminded that stories have the potential to define and describe legislatively as well as found a 'theatre of actions' that accumulates meaning and relevance over and through time. This text identifies the role narrative plays in both reading and acting in space, while acknowledging that spatial experiences are specific to each body, time and place.

In modern Athens, the vehicles of mass transportation are called *metaphorai*. To go to work or come home, one takes a 'metaphor' – a bus or a train. Stories could also take this noble name: every day, they traverse and organize places; they select and link them together; they make sentences and itineraries out of them. They are spatial trajectories.

In this respect, narrative structures have the status of spatial syntaxes. By means of a whole panoply of codes, ordered ways of proceeding and constraints, they regulate changes in space (or moves from one place to another) made by stories in the form of places put in linear or interlaced series: from here (Paris), one goes there (Montargis); this place (a room) includes another (a dream or a memory); etc. More than that, when they are represented in descriptions or acted out by actors (a foreigner, a city-dweller, a ghost), these places are linked together more or less tightly or easily by 'modalities' that specify the kind of passage leading from the one to the other: the transition can be given an 'epistemological' modality concerning knowledge (for example: 'it's not certain that this is the Place de la République'), an 'alethic' one concerning existence (for example, 'the land of milk and honey is an improbable end-point'), or a deontic one concerning obligation (for example: 'from this point, you have to go over to that one') ... These are only a few notations among many others, and serve only to indicate with what subtle complexity stories, whether everyday or literary, serve us as means of mass transportation, as *metaphorai*.

Every story is a travel story – a spatial practice. For this reason, spatial practices concern everyday tactics, are part of them, from the alphabet of spatial indication ('It's to the right,' 'Take a left'), the beginning of a story the rest of which is written by footsteps, to the daily 'news' ('Guess who I met at the bakery?'), television news reports ('Teheran: Khomeini is becoming increasingly isolated ...'), legends (Cinderellas living in hovels), and stories that are told (memories and fiction of foreign lands or more or less distant times in the past). These narrated adventures, simultaneously producing geographies of actions and drifting into the commonplaces of an order, do not merely constitute a 'supplement' to pedestrian enunciations and rhetorics. They are not satisfied with displacing the latter and transposing them into the field of language. In reality, they organize walks. They make the journey, before or during the time the feet perform it.

These proliferating metaphors – sayings and stories that organize places through the displacements they 'describe' (as a mobile point 'describes' a curve) – what kind of analysis can be applied to *them*? To mention only the studies concerning spatializing *operations* (and not spatial systems), there are numerous works that provide methods and categories for such an analysis. Among the most recent, particular attention can be drawn to those referring to a semantics of space (John Lyons on 'Locative Subjects' and 'Spatial Expressions'),[1] a psycholinguistics of perception (Miller and Johnson-Laird on 'the hypothesis of localization'),[2] a sociolinguistics of descriptions of places (for example, William Labov's),[3] a phenomenology of the behavior that organizes 'territories' (for example, the work of Albert E. Scheflen and Norman Ashcraft),[4] an 'ethnomethodology' of the indices of localization in conversation (for example, by Emanuel A. Schegloff),[5] or a semiotics viewing culture as a spatial metalanguage (for example, the work of the Tartu School, especially Y. M. Lotman, B. A. Ouspenski),[6] etc. Just as signifying practices, which concern the ways of putting language into effect, were taken into consideration after linguistic systems had been investigated, today spatializing practices are attracting attention now that the codes and taxonomies of the spatial order have been examined. Our investigation belongs to this 'second' moment of the analysis, which moves from structures to actions. But in this vast ensemble, I shall consider only *narrative actions*; this will allow us to specify a few elementary forms of practices organizing space: the bipolar distinction between 'map' and 'itinerary,' the procedures of delimitation or 'marking boundaries' ('*bornage*') and 'enunciative focalizations' (that is, the indication of the body within discourse).

At the outset, I shall make a distinction between space (*espace*) and place (*lieu*) that delimits a field. A place (*lieu*) is the order (of whatever kind) in accord with which elements are distributed in relationships of coexistence. It thus excludes the possibility of two things being in the same location (*place*). The law of the 'proper' rules in the place: the elements taken into consideration are *beside* one another, each situated in its own 'proper' and distinct location, a location it defines. A place is thus an instantaneous configuration of positions. It implies an indication of stability.

A *space* exists when one takes into consideration vectors of direction, velocities, and time variables. Thus space is composed of intersections of mobile elements. It is in a sense actuated by the ensemble of movements deployed within it. Space occurs as the effect produced by the operations that orient it, situate it, temporalize it, and make it function in a polyvalent unity of conflictual programs or contractual proximities. On this view, in relation to place, space is like the word when it is spoken, that is, when it is caught in the ambiguity of an actualization, transformed into a term dependent upon many different conventions, situated as the act of a present (or of a time), and modified by the transformations caused by successive contexts. In contradistinction to the place, it has thus none of the univocity or stability of a 'proper.'

In short, *space is a practiced place*. Thus the street geometrically defined by urban planning is transformed into a space by walkers. In the same way, an act of reading is the space produced by the practice of a particular place: a written text, i.e., a place constituted by a system of signs.

Merleau-Ponty distinguished a 'geometrical' space ('a homogeneous and isotropic spatiality,' analogous to our 'place') from another 'spatiality' which he called an 'anthropological space.' This distinction depended on a distinct problematic, which sought to distinguish from 'geometrical' univocity the experience of an 'outside' given in the form of space, and for which 'space is existential' and 'existence is spatial.' This experience is a relation to the world; in dreams and in perception, and because it probably precedes their differentiation, it expresses 'the same essential structure of our being as a being situated in relationship to a milieu' – being situated by a desire, indissociable from a 'direction of existence' and implanted in the space of a landscape. From this point of view 'there are as many spaces as there are distinct spatial experiences.'[7] The perspective is determined by a 'phenomenology' of existing in the world.

In our examination of the daily practices that articulate that experience, the opposition between 'place' and 'space' will rather refer to two sorts of determinations in stories: the first, a determination through objects that are ultimately reducible to the *being-there* of something dead, the law of a 'place' (from the pebble to the cadaver, an inert body always seems, in the West, to found a place and give it the appearance of a tomb); the second, a determination through *operations* which, when they are attributed to a stone, tree, or human being, specify 'spaces' by the actions of historical *subjects* (a movement always seems to condition the production of a space and to associate it with a history). Between these two determinations, there are passages back and forth, such as the putting to death (or putting into a landscape) of heroes who transgress frontiers and who, guilty of an offence against the law of the place, best provide its restoration with their tombs; or again, on the contrary, the awakening of inert objects (a table, a forest, a person that plays a certain role in the environment) which, emerging from their stability, transform the place where they lay motionless into the foreignness of their own space.

Stories thus carry out a labor that constantly transforms places into spaces or spaces into places. They also organize the play of changing relationships between places and spaces. The forms of this play are numberless, fanning out in a spectrum reaching from the putting in place of an immobile and stone-like order (in it, nothing moves except discourse itself, which, like a camera panning over a scene, moves over the whole panorama), to the accelerated succession of actions that multiply spaces (as in the detective novel or certain folktales, though this spatializing frenzy nevertheless remains circumscribed by the textual place). It would be possible to construct a typology of all these stories in terms of identification of places and actualization of spaces. But in order to discern in them the modes in which these distinct operations are combined, we need criteria and analytical categories – a necessity that leads us back to travel stories of the most elementary kind.   (... p 118)

Notes
1   John Lyons, *Semantics*, Cambridge University Press (Cambridge), 1977, II, pp 475–81, 690–703.
2   George A Miller and Philip N Johnson-Laird, *Language and Perception*, Harvard University Press (Cambridge, MA), 1976.
3   Charlotte Linde and William Labov, 'Spatial Networks as a Site for the Study of Language and Thought', *Language*, 51, 1975, pp 924–39. On the relation between practice (*le faire*) and space, see also Groupe 107, M Hammad et al, *Sémiotique de l'espace*, DGRST (Paris), 1973, p 28.
4   Albert E Scheflen and Norman Ashcraft, *Human Territories: How we Behave in Space Time*, Prentice-Hall (Englewood Cliffs, NJ), 1976.
5   Emanuel A Schegloff, 'Notes on a Conversational Practice: Formulating Place', David Sudnow (ed), *Studies in Social Interaction*, The Free Press (New York), 1972, pp 75–119.
6   See for example, École de tartu, *Travaux sur les systèmes de signes*, YM Lotman, BA Ouspenski (eds), PUF (Paris); Complexe (Bruxelles), 1976, pp 18–39, 77–93, etc.; Iouri Lotman, *La Structure du texte artistique*, Gallimard (Paris), 1973, p 309, etc.; Jüri Lotman, *The Structure of the Artistic Text*, trans R Vroon, Department of Slavic Languages and Literatures, The University of Michigan (Ann Arbor), 1977; BA Uspenski, *A Poetics of Composition*, trans V Zavarin and S Witting, University of California Press (Berkeley), 1973.
7   M Merleau-Ponty, *Phénoménologie de la perception*, Gallimard Tel (Paris), 1976, pp 324–44.

Michel de Certeau, *The Practice of Everyday Life*, ed and trans Steven Rendall, University of California Press (Berkeley), 1984.
© 1984 The Regents of the University of California. © Christian Bourgois Editeur. Reprinted by permission of the University of California Press.
(Excerpt pp 115–18)

Suitability, Simplicity and Proportion

Elsie de Wolfe

early 20th century decoration

social ● 1913

What appears in this text by Elsie de Wolfe as a call for use of common sense and practical design becomes the basis for good taste in early twentieth-century American domesticity. Claimed to be the concern of the woman of the household, comfort and decoration are not only the measure of a woman's skill and cleverness at establishing tranquillity but a political form of resistance towards patriarchy within the social and design spheres. Her message of what we would now recognise as modernism's aesthetic of the simple and unencumbered interior, was promoted as much through her popularity as a former stage actress as a designer for the wealthy and famous. De Wolfe's design principles of light-hued surfaces and mirrors to produce visually unified interiors helped to establish her as America's first female professional interior decorator.

When I am asked to decorate a new house, my first thought is suitability. My next thought is proportion. Always I keep in mind the importance of simplicity. First, I study the people who are to live in this house, and their needs, as thoroughly as I studied my parts in the days when I was an actress. For the time-being I really am the chatelaine of the house. When I have thoroughly familiarized myself with my 'part,' I let that go for the time, and consider the proportion of the house and its rooms. It is much more important that the wall openings, windows, doors, and fireplaces should be in the right place and should balance one another than that there should be expensive and extravagant hangings and carpets.

My first thought in laying out a room is the placing of the electric light openings. How rarely does one find the lights in the right place in our over-magnificent hotels and residences! One arrives from a journey tired out and travel-stained, only to find oneself facing a mirror as far removed from the daylight as possible, with the artificial lights directly behind one, or high in the ceiling in the center of the room. In my houses I always see that each room shall have its lights placed for the comfort of its occupants. There must be lights in sheltered corners of the fireplace, by the writing-desk, on each side of the dressing-table, and so on.

Then I consider the heating of the room. We Americans are slaves to steam heat. We ruin our furniture, our complexions, and our dispositions by this enervating atmosphere of too much heat. In my own houses I have a fireplace in each room, and I burn wood in it. There is a heating-system in the basement of my house, but it is under perfect control. I prefer the normal heat of sunshine and open fires. But, granted that open fires are impossible in all your rooms, do arrange in the beginning that the small rooms of your house may not be overheated. It is a distinct irritation to a person who loves clean air to go into a room where a flood of steam heat pours out of every corner. There is usually no way to control it unless you turn it off altogether. I once had the temerity to do this in a certain hotel room where there was a cold and cheerless empty fireplace. I summoned a reluctant chambermaid, only to be told that the chimney had never had a fire in it and the proprietor would rather not take such a risk!

Perhaps the guest in your house would not be so troublesome, but don't tempt her! If you have a fireplace, see that it is in working order.

We are sure to judge a woman in whose house we find ourselves for the first time, by her surroundings. We judge her temperament, her habits, her inclinations, by the interior of her home. We may talk of the weather, but we are looking at the furniture. We attribute vulgar qualities to those who are content to live in ugly surroundings. We endow with refinement and charm the person who welcomes us in a delightful room, where the colors blend and the proportions are as perfect as in a picture. After all, what surer guarantee can there be of a woman's character, natural and cultivated, inherent and inherited, than taste? It is a compass that never errs. If a woman has taste she may have faults, follies, fads, she may err, she may be as human and feminine as she pleases, but she will never cause a scandal!

How can we develop taste? Some of us, alas, can never develop it, because we can never let go of shams. We must learn to recognize suitability, simplicity and proportion, and apply our knowledge to our needs. I grant you we may never fully appreciate the full balance of proportion, but we can exert our common sense and decide whether a thing is suitable; we can consult our conscience as to whether an object is simple, and we can train our eyes to recognize good and bad proportion. A technical knowledge of architecture is not necessary to know that a huge stuffed leather chair in a tiny gold and cream room is unsuitable, is hideously complicated, and is as much out of proportion as the proverbial bull in the china-shop.

A woman's environment will speak for her life, whether she likes it or not. How can we believe that a woman of sincerity of purpose will bang fake 'works of art' on her walls, or satisfy herself with imitation velvets or silks? How can we attribute taste to a woman who permits paper floors and iron ceilings in her house? We are too afraid of the restful commonplaces, and yet if we live simple lives, why shouldn't we be glad our houses are comfortably commonplace? How much better to have plain furniture that is comfortable, simple chintzes printed from old blocks, a few good prints, than all the sham things in the world? A house is a dead-give-away, anyhow, so you should arrange it so that the person who sees your personality in it will be reassured, not disconcerted.

Too often, here in America, the most comfortable room in the house is given up to a sort of bastard collection of gilt chairs and tables, over-elaborate draperies shutting out both light and air, and huge and frightful paintings. This style of room, with its museum-like furnishings, has been dubbed 'Marie Antoinette,' *why*, no one but the American decorator can say. Heaven knows poor Marie Antoinette had enough follies to atone for, but certainly she has never been treated more shabbily than when they dub these mausoleums 'Marie Antoinette rooms.'

I remember taking a clever Englishwoman of much taste to see a woman who was very proud of her new house. We had seen most of the house when the hostess, who had evidently reserved what she considered the best for the last, threw open the doors of a large and gorgeous apartment and said, 'This is my Louis XVI ballroom.' My friend, who had been very patient up to that moment, said very quietly, 'What makes you think so?'   (... p 23)

Don't go about the furnishing of your house with the idea that you must select the furniture of some one period and stick to that. It isn't at all necessary. There are old English chairs and tables of the Sixteenth and Seventeenth Centuries that fit into our quiet, spacious Twentieth Century country homes. Lines and fabrics and woods are the things to be compared.

There are so many beautiful things that have come to us from other times that it should be easy to make our homes beautiful, but I have seen what I can best describe as apoplectic chairs whose legs were fashioned like aquatic plants; tables upheld by tortured naked women; lighting fixtures in the form of tassels, and such horrors, in many houses of to-day under the guise of being 'authentic period furniture.' Only a connoisseur can ever hope to know about the furniture of every period, but all of us can easily learn the ear-marks of the furniture that is suited to our homes. I shan't talk about ear-marks here, however, because dozens of collectors have compiled excellent books that tell you all about curves and lines and grain-of-wood and worm-holes. My business is to persuade you to use your graceful French sofas and your simple rush bottom New England chairs in different rooms – in other words, to preach to you the beauty of suitability. Suitability! *Suitability!* SUITABILITY!!

It is such a relief to return to the tranquil, simple forms of furniture, and to decorate our rooms by a process of elimination. How many rooms have I not cleared of junk – this heterogeneous mass of ornamental 'period' furniture and bric-a-brac bought to make a room 'look cozy.' Once cleared of these, the simplicity and dignity of the room comes back, the architectural spaces are freed and now stand in their proper relation to the furniture. In other words, the architecture of the room becomes its decoration.   (... p 26)

Elsie de Wolfe, *The House in Good Taste* [1913], Ayer Company Publishers (Stratford), 1998.
(Excerpts pp 17–23, 25–6)

On the Means by which Repose is Attainable in Decoration

Christopher Dresser

technological colour late 19th century 1876

After calling for all design work to be imprinted with the quality of repose, Victorian designer Christopher Dresser asserts that such value is directly related to the presence of knowledge and harmony. He outlines how to achieve this 'indispensable art quality' through subtle, neutral and sparing applications of colour, reflection and texture. Dresser's text is a testament to written discourse of the late nineteenth century where effect and experience were regulated by prescriptions of taste and decorum. It also situates interior design finishes and linings as significant contributors to spatial effect.

In my last chapter I insisted on the necessity for our achieving 'repose' in all our decorations, as repose is an indispensable art quality; but the means by which repose was to be attained was not clearly set forth.

In the absence of a manifestation of knowledge, and in the absence of harmony, there cannot be repose; but it does not follow that the reverse must be true, and that because knowledge and harmony are revealed in our works, that there must necessarily be the sense of repose. There is such a thing as a harmony of lights, of bright spots, of glitters, and all glitter is antagonistic to rest. In the manner of the combination of gems we often detect knowledge and harmony; but a room with its sides formed of glittering surfaces could scarcely yield repose, even were it formed of parts of such tints as produce, when combined, a true harmony.

Rooms having their walls largely formed of glazed tiles, or of varnished surfaces, are rarely satisfactory, for the reflections which they of necessity throw out are exciting, and excitement is antagonistic to rest. Excitement is endurable and even useful to the system, if sparingly indulged in; but the constant endurance of excitement is exhausting.

But how are we to achieve the necessary amount of repose in our rooms? We need not paint the walls of our apartments grey, nor of mud-colour, neither need we make them black; indeed, the highest sense of repose – *i.e.*, dreamy, soothing repose, may be realised where the brightest colours are employed. Repose is attained by the absence of any want. A plain wall of dingy colour reveals a want; it does not then supply all that is necessary to the production of a sense of quiet and rest. A wall may be covered with the richest decoration, and yet be of such a character that the eye will rest upon it and be satisfied.

If strong colours are used upon walls and ceilings, it is usually desirable that they be employed in very small masses; thus blue, red, and yellow may be used upon a wall (the three primary colours), either alone, or together with white, gold, or black, and be so mingled that the general effect will be perfectly neutral, and an effect so produced may induce the highest sense of repose. There will, however, be a glow, or radiance, about such a wall; yet this radiance will only give richness to neutrality, and this is desirable.

Those effects which are 'subtle' – which are not commonplace – which are attained by the expenditure of special skill or knowledge, are the best, provided that the end which is most desired is attained by them. A tertiary colour which is formed of two parts of yellow and one of red and one of blue – in fact, a citrine – is neutral. But a wall covered with a well-designed pattern of minute parts, with the separate members coloured red, blue, and yellow – the yellow being in relation to the blue and the red as two is to one[1] – would be neutral, yet it would be refined and glowing in effect, and thus it would exceed in merit the mere tertiary tint on the wall.

The white ceilings which we have in our rooms are almost fatal to the production of those qualities which yield the sense of repose or rest. A harmony between walls and a ceiling of cream tint[2] is much more easily attained than between walls and a white ceiling; but there is no reason whatever why a ceiling should not be blue, or any dark colour. No satisfactory room, of dark general aspect, can look well if the ceiling is white, and rooms which are somewhat dark in tone are often desirable. Furniture looks best on a dark ground, unless it be white and gold, when it is invariably execrable. Persons always look better against a somewhat dark background, and pictures on light strongly-figured walls are rarely sufficiently attractive to call to themselves the least attention. If it can be had, I like much window-space, to let in light, but the walls I prefer of darkish hue.

If the room is dark through lack of light, the walls may be light above, and have a dark dado – that is, the lower third, or any desired portion, may be dark, and the upper portion light. If this arrangement is adopted, and the upper part of the wall and the ceiling are each of cream tint, while in the cornice there is a rather broad line of deep blue, and one or more lines of pale blue, and perhaps a very fine line of red, these colours being all separated from each other by white – or, in the absence of a cornice, if the ceiling is surrounded by a border in blue and white – the effect will appear to be lighter and brighter than if the room were all white, and yet there will be a certain amount of repose about the general effect such as could not be easily attained were the ceiling white.

By our decorations we must ever seek to achieve repose, but we must always remember that repose is compatible with richness, subtlety, and radiance of effect.   (... p 12)

Notes

1   This is not rigidly correct, but for more exact information I must refer the reader to my *Principles of Decorative Design* (London), 1873, pp 40, 47, 48.

2   A tint formed by the admixture of a small portion of middle-chrome – that chrome which is half-way between the colour of a lemon and of a deep-coloured orange – with white.

Christopher Dresser, *Studies in Design*, Cassell, Petter and Galpin (London), 1876. (Excerpt pp 11–12)

Volatile Architectures

Jim Drobnick

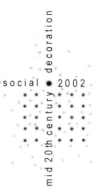

Artist, critic and curator, Jim Drobnick explores the potential for architectural thinking to engage with aesthetics via sensorial experience and olfaction. He suggests that the transcendent formality of the white cube gallery, in its pollution-free pristine state, relegates architecture to a purely visual state. Noting that the lack of aromatic smell provides less than full or lived body experience, he exposes a recent trend to include smell in contemporary postmodern museums. Their use of sensory saturation, assisted by diffusion technology and synthesised smells, is designed to engage the visitor on a physiological and psychological level. This process of opening the interior to the full range of the senses counters visual primacy and recognises that colour and smell have significant effect on our perception of space and objects.

'Volatile effects' is a phrase utilized by Walter Pater in his dismissal of architecture from the realm of the aesthetic.[1] He postulated that architecture, as the most concrete and utilitarian of arts, could not evoke the subtleties of the human spirit; rather, it could only present an artistic sensibility via oblique traces and ethereal suggestions:

> Architecture which begins in a practical need, can only express by vague hint or symbol the spirit or mind of the artist … [T]hese spiritualities, felt rather than seen, can but lurk about architectural form as volatile effects, to be gathered from it by reflection.[2]

Contrary to Pater's denial of architecture's artistic potential, I would like to appropriate and rehabilitate such 'lurking' sensations, 'vague hints' and 'volatile effects' as precisely the terms that can be employed to describe an olfactory approach to architecture. For Pater, these effects were more metaphorical than real, gathered as it were by reminiscence and reflection. In contrast, the volatile architectures I will discuss below are vividly sensorial and experiential – they are literally fragrant, pungent, or reeking. The aromatic dimension of buildings is one that has been for the most part neglected in architectural theory, yet the volatile effects created by odoriferous materials, ventilated scents, and other wafting perceptions can significantly influence one's experience of a structure. It would be simplistic to merely celebrate the inclusion of odours as some kind of corrective to the inodorate state of architectural thinking; I will instead outline a few of the issues and problematics of smell, art, and architecture.   (... p 263)

Museum Atmospheres

A curious development has been brewing recently regarding the inclusion of smell in the once-sterilized realm of the museum. Articles in the popular press not only note olfactory absence, but make demands for its inclusion. Witness a reviewer's disappointment at the display of 1960s costumes and music memorabilia at the Rock and Roll Hall of Fame and Museum:

> Does this exhibit 'capture the spirit of the psychedelic era?' Hell no. This is a collection of historical objects in a museum. There's not a whiff of patchouli oil in the place. It smells like school. If you want to get an idea of what the psychedelic era was like, find a copy of *Electric Music for the Mind and Body* by Country Joe and The Fish, put *Section 43* on that dusty turntable in the corner, light some incense, turn out all the lights and set your mind to 'wander.'[3]

And in a laudatory review of 'The American Lawn' at the Canadian Centre for Architecture, praises were heaped upon the innovative display technology, which engaged visitors by providing creative ways to see, touch, interact with, and move around the exhibition – but the absence of the smell of grass was mourned:

> Our suspicions that the museum experience can never truly simulate the real thing are confirmed, however: the fragrance that is so much a part of the 'lawn experience' is missing.[4]

How should these comments be interpreted? Are they evidence of a nostalgia for times past so excessive that objects without the requisite immediacy frustrate more than satisfy? Does today's audience expect the museum to provide a sensorially complete experience – to counteract the anaesthetized routine of everyday life? Is this the first intimation of a groundswell of support for something like a 'museum of smells' – as Andy Warhol (an enthusiastic perfume collector) envisioned thirty years ago?

Early in the twentieth century, Clive Bell derided the gloominess of a 'museum atmosphere' that enveloped works of art and asphyxiated visitors. 'Society,' he suggested, 'can do something for itself and for art by blowing out of the museums and galleries the dust of erudition and the stale incense of hero-worship.'[5] What Bell was advocating by means of olfactory reference was a revolution in museum philosophy, one that privileged the direct experience of emotion over that of scholarly sycophantism, that favoured inclusivity and democratization over mediation and intimidation by experts, that permitted visitors to make their own decisions and judgments rather than accepting the dogma of tradition. How literally Bell meant his comments about ventilating and reodorizing the museum is a matter of debate, but in the 1980s, institutions as diverse as amusement parks, living history sites, heritage centres, science museums, and other tourist attractions began to infuse their exhibitions with a wide variety of smells for reasons remarkably similar to the ones Bell articulated: to provide intense, immediate sensations, to make cultural experiences accessible to all, and to engage visitors in a personal, interactive manner.

Below are four perspectives on how postmodern museums utilize smell in their exhibitions: as heterogeneous stimulation, for sensory saturation, as an indicator of authenticity, and to engage with visitors on a more subtle perceptual level, one with implicit physiological or psychological effects.

1. Postmodern museums are defined against their modernist counterparts by virtue of their heterogeneity. That is, they participate in and exemplify the postmodern trend towards ambiguously defined spaces, ones that combine multiple functions and behaviours. The failure of the patrician class to preserve the museum as an elite, personal enclave has forced it to welcome a larger and more diverse public. Without abandoning the prestige of 'high' art, commercial, culinary, and entertainment factors have been intertwined with what is traditionally deemed the 'aesthetic.' Museums have appropriated elements from theme parks, malls, boutiques, food courts, and other types of cultural architectures. Given the indistinct boundaries and blurring of activities, aromas from in-house restaurants and cafés, perfumes from gift shops and other odours cross over the threshold and permeate the inner sanctum of artistic worship.

'Heterosmia,' a preponderance of smells from disparate sources, is my term to signify the condition of the postmodern museum. This is in contradistinction to the anosmic condition of the conventional museum. Heterosmia is not necessarily a condition sought out by postmodern art institutions; it is more an unintended result of the mixing and close juxtaposition of previously separated activities. Like the indoor mall, in which scents from a myriad of shops circulate and commingle, the heterosmic condition of the postmodern museum is one that has developed as a consequence of decisions about real estate, tourism, audience attendance, and the desire to transform a specialized institution into a one-stop, multiple-interest entertainment package.

2. Advances in aroma diffusion technology and the chemistry of synthetic compounds have led to scent being one of *the* most fashionable additions to the museum's repertoire of effects. Synthetic scents imply a certain power over nature, over history, over the limitations of visual artifacts; they demonstrate an institution's hipness towards multimedia and sensory-saturated viewing environments; they prove a vivid marketing tool; and serve as a quick fix for the image of the museum so that, despite the multiple crises challenging its credibility, it can avert self-scrutiny and structural change.

The use of smell as part of the 'five senses experience' – or what I call 'aromatopia' – gives the impression that an exhibition is a comprehensive, fully embodied encounter. Employed mostly by living museums and populist entertainments with a quasi-educational agenda, aromatopias draw upon the literary conception of the five senses (prevalent for the past two millennia) to convey the feeling of a complete, total, and all-encompassing nature. In some postmodern attractions, the rhetoric of total experience is nothing but a gimmick: a Madame Tussaud's exhibit supposedly featuring 'the smells of London' consists merely of theatrical smoke in the Chamber of Horrors. Other examples are better intentioned and more earnest. Living museums, for instance, purport to convey the full sensory experience of what it was like to live in a previous historical era:

> You can see and touch clothes as they were in the sixteenth century, you can eat Tudor food, you can listen to Tudor speech patterns, songs and music, use Tudor tools, walk around Tudor buildings, smell Tudor herbs.[6]

This multi-sensory strategy challenges the pedantry and dullness of the old-fashioned history museum, with its over-reliance on text, images, and decontextualized artefacts. Reliving the smells of a medieval town or pioneer homestead sets up expectations that require examination, as spectacle and myth collide with education and history. Like Foucault's 'heterotopia,' aromatopias are sites of polyvalency where orthodox behaviours are shed and alternative possibilities temporarily inhabited. The intensity and diversity of smells demarcates the museum's experience as decidedly 'other' – one olfactorily coded to be outside the routine of the ordinary and everyday.

3. Perhaps the most problematic employment of smells is their use to artificially heighten the 'realism' of the viewing experience, affirm the 'authenticity' of objects and secure the 'legitimacy' of the representations of other historical periods or cultures. Whether it is the Museum of the City of New York, where visitors experience facsimiles of historical documents, such as the Declaration of Independence, that are specially scented to smell 'old,' or the Smithsonian, where garbage and urine smells were diffused for an exhibit on the inner city, smells have been tactically employed to convey factuality, validity, the real.[7] Alexander Wilson provides, for example, the following description of a Disney ride where synthesized odours reinforce the realism of virtual environments:

> [W]e sail past simulated examples of biotic communities, whole underground rooms like display cases in a natural history museum, only here when you cross the desert region a hot wind blows in your face, and the jungle smells of water and decaying plants. Around another bend in the river we reach the Family Farm, which in turn smells faintly of hay and cowshit.[8]

While critiques of simulation and the hyperreal have proliferated in regards to audio and visual media, little attention has been devoted to the synthetic, postmodern uses of smell.[9] The discussion usually falls into two categories: the celebratory and the cynical. While glorifying rhetoric may be brought to task for its uncritical acceptance, negative readings of smell veer close to being backhanded apologies for visual dominance. For Kevin Walsh, the use of manufactured smells foregrounds a central problematic that, in essence, pertains to the use of smells to *represent* at all:

> The decontextualizing of smells from an historical period and placement in a twentieth-century tourist attraction seems highly dubious as each person visiting the centre will have a different perception or attitude towards a smell and it is quite likely that it will be very different from those held by the people who originally produced and lived with the smells. The problem is compounded by the fact that one begins to wonder if Victorian streets, Medieval universities and Viking villages were all steeped in the same, obviously-artificial, chemical-odour version of wet cats.[10]

One can certainly fault profit-oriented museums for recycling the same olfactory sensations in dissimilar contexts, but at what point does this critique emerge from a latent bias against the olfactory? And to what degree is it a circuitous defence of ocularcentrism? It is inconsistent to single out smells just because they are artificially produced (that is, mediated), or variable in interpretation, and not also critique other museum information that is mediated or variable; this would basically undermine the entire museological enterprise. The mutability of smell frustrates a quasi-authoritarian demand for the systematized deployment of 'correct' meanings and experiences. The distrust of the sensual has a long history in Western culture, a distrust which can be distilled into a contest between representational and presentational modes of information.

The argument against the use of synthesized rather than actual smells is stronger. Instead of confirming the authenticity of a certain experience, fake smells distort olfactory discrimination and sever the ability to connect odours to their natural sources.[11] In the search for predictable, cost-effective exhibit aromas, the disciplining and training of the senses (presumably one of the museum's goals) is sacrificed.

4. Smells, however, can still serve as a strategic intervention. In contrast to the highly mediated, homogenized, simplified, and commercialized use of artificial odours, the presentation of scent in a context-specific manner still holds a potential to reconfigure the museum experience. As museums shift away from basing their legitimation on master narratives and prescriptive interpretations, exhibits that include extra-visual sensory experiences grant heightened status to the subjective nature of knowledge production, and foreground experiences that are partial and uncertain. Authority and coherence are guaranteed not by collections and curatorial directives, but by each visitor's experience.[12]

Physical engagement, argues Tracy Davis, activates museum goers to 'perform' rather than 'consume' the content; that is, visitors are inserted into that indeterminate domain where they must individually negotiate the tension between the museum's framing ideology and the immediacy of personal experience.[13] Disparate sensory information may not easily coincide or harmonize, and indeed may foreground difference and contradiction – effecting a museum experience that is interrogative, temporal, pluralistic.

The featuring of smells and the full range of the senses in the museum undermines visual predominance not only on a perceptual level, but on a political one as well. Countering the primacy of the visual opens up the museum to behaviours, activities, and identities that are not necessarily Western, privileged, and masculine, and which fail to produce collectible artifacts. Marginalized, private, or everyday experiences, such as those typically associated with women's domestic labour, can be given distinction and value.[14]

Other kinds of olfactory presences, such as those at the Holocaust Museum in Washington, D.C., provide compelling evidence that no text, image, or audio guide is able to convey. As Davis writes of the museum's pungent 'Shoe Exhibit:'

> [I]ntellectual horror at an already familiar narrative of recent genocide is compounded by olfactory confirmation in a gallery where the odor of decomposing shoe leather cannot be obliterated by even the most energetic air conditioner ... [T]he shoes' odor invades visitors' bodies and in so doing cements concept to experience.[15]

This reinvigorated form of realism, whereby volatile particles of the exhibit literally bridge the gap between artifact and visitor, operates according to Davis 'on a micro-sensory level in order to trigger a cognitive appreciation for ideas way beyond the reach of mere historical verisimilitude.'[16] The fleshy smell of the shoe leather is a signifier in excess of language, one that is unexpected, unhyped. For exhibits to go beyond the visual presentation of objects, and engage with the other senses, is to venture into the dynamic realm of becoming rather than the static domain of being.   (... p 272)

Notes

1   Versions of this text were presented at the 'Universities Art Association Conference', 1998, and the conference 'Uncommon Senses', 2000. I would like to thank these audiences and, in particular, Jennifer Fisher, David Howes, Constance Classen, Kim Sawchuk, and Brian Foss for their constructive feedback. Research for this text was generously supported by a SSHRC grant.
2   Quoted in Anthony Vidler, *The Architectural Uncanny: Essays in the Modern Unhomely*, MIT Press (Cambridge, MA, and London), 1992, p 60.
3   Peter Feniak, 'What a short, odd trip it is', *Globe and Mail*, 10 May, 1997, A14.
4   Annmarie Adams and Helen Dyer, 'The Patch Where the Mower is King', *Montreal Gazette*, 27 June, 1998, J1-2. In fact, contrary to the reviewers' lament, the smell of grass was very much evident in a lawn sculpture by Mel Ziegler on the CCA's grounds.

94

5 Clive Bell, *Art* [1913], Capricorn Books [New York], 1958, pp 173, 185.

6 Kevin Walsh, *The Representation of the Past: Museums and Heritage in the Post-Modern World*, Routledge (London and New York), 1992, p 101.

7 Umberto Eco, *Travels in Hyperreality*, trans William Weaver, Harcourt Brace Jovanovich (San Diego, New York, London), 1986, p 11; Jillyn Smith, *Senses and Sensibilities*, John Wiley & Sons (New York), 1989, p 132.

8 Alexander Wilson, 'Technological Utopias', *The South Atlantic Quarterly*, vol 92 no 1, Winter 1993, p 169.

9 See Constance Classen, David Howes and Anthony Synnott, *Aroma: The Cultural History of Smell*, Routledge (London and New York), 1994, pp 203–5, for a discussion of smell as a postmodern sense.

10 Walsh, *The Representation of the Past*, pp 112–13.

11 Peter Damian and Kate Damian, *Aromatherapy: Scent and Psyche*, Healing Arts Press (Rochester, VT), 1995, p 130.

12 Sharon MacDonald and Roger Silverstone, 'Rewriting the Museums' Fictions: Taxonomies, Stories and Readers', *Cultural Studies*, vol 4 no 2, 1990, pp 176–91.

13 Tracy C Davis, 'Performing and the Real Thing in the Postmodern Museum', *The Drama Review*, 147, vol 39 no 3, Fall 1995, pp 15–40.

14 Gaby Porter, 'Seeing Through Solidity: A Feminist Perspective on Museums', Sharon MacDonald and Gordon Fyfe (eds), *Theorizing Museums*, Blackwell (Oxford, UK, and Cambridge, MA), 1996, pp 105–26.

15 Davis, 'Performing', *The Drama Review*, pp 35–6.

16 Davis, 'Performing', *The Drama Review*, pp 35–6.

Jim Drobnick, 'Volatile Architectures', *Crime and Ornament: The Arts and Popular Culture in the Shadow of Adolf Loos*, Bernie Miller and Melony Ward (eds), YYZ Books (Toronto), 2002.

Thing-Shapes

Winka Dubbeldam

Architect and academic Winka Dubbeldam postulates that while materials currently have the ability to trace memories through their surface, in the future they will have the potential to act as mnemonic interactive surfaces in literal and philosophic ways. She suggests that this proposition emanates from a collapse of the subject–object and interior–exterior dichotomies resulting in a set of intelligent layered responsive subjects and interiors. Informed by a generative and process-orientated design method and a desire to engage with Husserl's 'smooth' surfaces, boundaries are no longer barriers but are interactive; they are creases – a hard-soft space allowing for local conditions. The smoothness of the interior registers a relationship to the human body so that they are part of a system of 'thing-shapes.'

> *... A philosopher proceeding from the practical, finite surrounding world to the theoretical world-view and world-knowledge ... with his manifold finite shapes in their space-time [he] does not yet have geometrical shapes, the phoronomic shapes; [his shapes, as] formations developed out of praxis and thought of in terms of [gradual] perfection, clearly serve only as bases for a new sort of praxis out of which similarly named new constructions grow.*
> Edmund Husserl[1]

Architecture is by nature a 'slow' profession. Only through avant-garde movements and technological inventions has it challenged notions such as traditional craftsmanship, proportional systems and aesthetics. Now, in the 21st century, the computer has accelerated the mass media into digital electronic communication – whose tendency towards specialisation and individualisation has fragmented the mass society of the postwar period into a society of niche cultures (for example, hackers). Demassified niches, says Alvin Toffler, commandeer the space of the Internet.[2] The net operates not only on this microscale but also on a macroscale; increasing globalisation is transforming our cities into physical expressions of global economies in which only the traces of local cultures remain. Within this global network, a new hybrid condition proliferates in which the relationship between local and global is constantly adjusting. Situated precisely between the real and the virtual, architecture is challenged, yet it resists. As Gilles Deleuze states in his treatise *Bergsonism*, in developing new methodologies the first real challenge lies in the statement and creation of problems (the right problems); the second challenge lies in 'the discovery of genuine differences in kind; the third, [in] the apprehension of real time.'[3] The differentiation between the 'right' and 'wrong' problem and the introduction of real time is of interest here. The departure from a static perception of history (Husserl) and the proposition of a generative future (Deleuze) is where Deleuze and Husserl seem to overlap. In our present condition we find a collapse of the generative past and of the to-be-generated future, where the posing of probabilities and/or the right problems makes us active participants. For architects, this interactivity and the imperative to action necessitate an understanding of the scientific method as applied by mathematicians, and an engagement with the complex systems of the global network, thereby providing opportunities to develop the dynamic spatial constructs integral to this hybrid condition.

In mathematics there is a crucial difference between the 'thing' and the mathematical model of the thing. While geometry defines itself in absolute values, mathematicians study and define the state of the thing; this in turn defines the validity of the calculus applied, and thereby the definition of the thing itself. Mathematicians make assumptions about mathematical behaviour – such as the higher dimension (the manifold) – and research these hypotheses by using animated computer simulations. This overlap of the virtual and the real is where new propositions lie. The corporate world has adopted these behavioural studies, leaving the marketing structures of the 1980s behind. Studies of lifestyles and stock markets have replaced the innately too slow study of 'what the general public wants' and transferred it into a prognosis of probabilities: the flux and behaviour of global network economies, emerging immigration patterns and urban settlements. A space, unlike a place, is now an electronically created environment, subject to a multiplicity of real and virtual pressures, described by Kevin Kelly as possessing a 'different kind of bigness, rampant clusterings, peer authority and re-intermediation.'[4]

In this network economy, architecture has to become generative – not unlike phoronomic shapes as discussed by Husserl which imply the existence of generative structures out of which new similarly named constructions grow. Husserl's notion of 'horizon-exposition' refers to departures from the historical in which the activity of free variation runs through the conceivable possibilities of the life-world, giving rise to a general set of elements that go through all the variants of spatiotemporal shapes. This endless modulation, of which we can convince ourselves with apodictic certainty, implies the generation of a spatial construct not as a static device but as a set of inventions; not as literally moving objects but as surface registrations of force fields, smart systems and programmatic mappings. This generative, process-oriented approach is the basis and definition of the organismic paradigm – an organism is characterised by its immanent patterns of organisation. This is similar to spirit, which was also described by Leibniz as monads and by Hegel as *Begriff* or absolute ideas. These internal organising phenomena occur on all levels: in social interaction, in individual behavioural processes and in nature. Time and space relationships are inseparable; memory irreplaceable.

'Traditionally, we call body that part of substance that is caught in the sack of our skin' (Bernard Cache).[5] In Husserl's world of '"things," including the human beings themselves as subjects of this world ... all things necessarily [have] to have a bodily character.' He describes these pure bodies as 'spatiotemporal shapes [with] "material" qualities ... related to them' and names these 'thing-shapes.' Specific for these thing-shapes in their relationship to the human body are their 'surfaces – more or less "smooth," more or less perfect' – registrations that strive for gradual perfection. As he states, 'Here too, proceeding from the factual, an essential form becomes recognisable through a method of variation.'[6] The generative aspects of integral architecture activate these surfaces into a hybrid system of layering. Similar phenomena of collapse, inversion and negotiation characterise the concept of this architecture. The politics of layering, creasing and wrapping activate zones and environments where boundaries are negotiated and distinctions are blurred.

Industrial design with its speed of innovation in industrial-design technologies provides for a smoother and more intereffective relationship between design and the life it houses than does architecture. Imagine the following architecture: the first layer is a hard shiny shell, which protects against weather (rain, wind) and forces (traffic accidents, impact). Part of this outer hard shell is transparent and movable, a visor that can be slid open into different positions. Its form mimics the curvature of the hard shell, an active sun-filter adapts to the brightness of the sky. The second layer, an integral foam layer, negotiates between two systems: the shell's hardness and the biological frailty of the body. Its amorphic shape is configured by negotiating the imprint of these two systems. It is an informed, intelligent layer, constantly providing and adjusting, thus achieving ultimate efficiency and an optimisation of space. This smart layer adds comfort (softness) and impact protection, as it envelops and provides integrated amenities like communication, music and ventilation systems. The third and last layer is the animate body; or the animated body, the modulated void – a fragile unit, reflective of the soft body. It creates a space to be occupied, a free zone, undefined in use but specific to its environment. The human body – its other, its imprint – occupies, floating through, similar but not the same. The trace of efficiency of use, the memory of comfort allows for an organic formulation of space, thus negotiating desire with facility.

This description of an integral motorcycle helmet is an interesting example of interdependent layering, efficiency of use and negotiation of means. Here, behavioural aspects rule the state between two dynamics and architecture becomes a materially responsive expression, with its intelligence inciting efficiency of use, high performance,

Aida salon – Manhattan: 'Smart Wall fold out to accomodate programmatic pressures.'
Photo courtesy of Paul Warchol

smart controls and the resultant modulation of space. The form of the human body resembles this modulation and allows for a smooth transition between the layers.

Existing subject-object and interior-exterior dichotomies and hierarchies collapse, presenting us with a set of intelligent and layered objects, surfaces and skins, and a set of supple, responsive and connected subjects and interiors. With these sorts of collapses and inversions, we find ourselves in the midst of objects and subjects and exteriors and interiors that are constantly retooling and optimising each other. Nonhierarchical and boundaryless, it is along this labyrinthine smooth surface that we now constantly renegotiate and remake our contingent private and public architectures. Located in between at the incidence and co-incidence of modern life, we find the crease. The crease is malleable, soft, adaptable and multidimensional. Not unlike cartilage between spinal cord fragments, it allows for flexibility and precise adjustment. Disseminating the soft in the hard and the hard in the soft, and produced in collaboration with the complex exigencies of contemporary urbanism, the hard-soft space of the crease works between and conflates the requirements of the urban and the individual, demanding minimum space and providing maximum comfort and efficiency. It conflates mathematical behaviour with industrial precision into a set of smart layers, hybrid structures.

The crease as a hybrid construct was investigated as a set of 'smart' adaptable, supple walls in Aida's Hair Salon (2000), located on the Upper East Side of Manhattan. The design for this space was based on the concept of the wall as a smooth wrapper enveloping all functional requirements and leaving the space free of clutter; its creases create a sculpted void to be occupied by the clientele. The wrapper starts at the facade as a folded smooth stone surface; it transforms, softens and continues as it folds inside. Fade out the individual. Transgress the liminal space between the private and the public. Disavow the Internet's illusory Utopias of neutrality and democracy. Inhabit the slip between former dichotomies. Ride this slip until its surface creases from internal and external pressures, producing a space that is at once grotesquely beautiful, intimately public, urbanely private and tactilely cerebral. Penetrate the delicate surfaces of this crease, the unimagined depths of our fac(ad)es. Wander across these faces and keep moving. The soft zone, the wrapper, renegotiates both the urban landscape (hard space) and the private domain (soft space). Disseminating the soft in the hard and the hard in the soft, the smart wall encapsulates the human body while demanding minimum space and providing maximum comfort and efficiency. At the interior this wrapper encapsulates all of the programmatic requirements, such as storage, music, lighting, heating and cooling systems, as required for a modern urban work environment. All evenly distributed: a free zone. The result is a supple, smooth set of surfaces, where creases allow for local insertions of cutting stations, desks and seating elements. Bodies are seen not as objects in themselves but as integral parts of a system of thing-shapes with layered smooth surfaces, generating and regenerating space.   (... p 30)

Notes

1   Edmund Husserl, 'The Origin of Geometry', Jacques Derrida, *Edmund Husserl's Origin of Geometry: An Introduction*, University of Nebraska Press (Lincoln), 1989, pp 178–9.
2   Alvin Toffler, *The Third Wave*, Bantam Books (New York), 1981, pp 275–6.
3   Gilles Deleuze, *Bergsonism*, Zone Books (New York), 1991, p 14.
4   Kevin Kelly, *New Rules for the New Economy*, Penguin Books (New York), 1999, p 96.
5   Bernard Cache, *Earth Moves*, MIT Press (Cambridge, MA), 1995, p 130.
6   Husserl, Origin of Geometry, pp 177–8.

Winka Dubbeldam, 'Things-Shapes', *Architectural Design*, vol 72 no 2, 2002, pp 26–31.

The Dining Room

Charles L Eastlake

Inspiring a style to be named after him, Charles Eastlake's influential self-illustrated text sought a simpler cleaner style of furniture that could also be reflected in the decoration of the interior. In this excerpt his barbed attack upon upholsterers and the degradation of decorative art paves the way for the professional decorator as the arbiter of taste. In an effort to homogenise the interior, Eastlake sets a clear agenda by questioning conventional arrangements that seek room-to-room difference in both form and style.

Among the many fallacies engendered in the mind of the modern upholsterer, and delivered by him as wholesome doctrine to a credulous public, is the notion that all conditions of decorative art must necessarily vary with the situation in which that art is employed. It is not sufficient for him to tell us that the dining-room table and sideboard should, on account of the use to which they are put, be made after a more solid fashion than the drawing-room table and the cheffonier. He is not content with informing his customers (if, indeed, they need such information) that book-cases will be required for the library, and flower-stands are suitable for the boudoir, but he proceeds with great gravity to lay down a series of rules by which certain types of form and certain shades of colour are to be, for some mysterious reason best known to himself, for ever associated with certain apartments in the house. In obedience to this injunction we sit down to dine upon an oaken chair before an oaken table, with a Turkey carpet under our feet, and a red flock-paper staring us in the face. After dinner the ladies ascend into a green and gold-papered drawing-room, to perform on a walnut-wood piano, having first seated themselves on walnut-wood music-stools, while their friends are reclining on a walnut-wood sofa, protected from the heat of the fire by a walnut-wood screen. A few years ago, all these last-mentioned articles of household furniture were made of rosewood. In the early part of this century it was *de rigueur* that they should be mahogany; so the fashion of taste goes on changing from age to age; and I firmly believe that, if the West End upholsterers took it into their heads that staircases should be hung with *moire antique*, and that the drawing-room fender ought in summer time to be planted with mignonette, there are people who would repose implicit confidence in such advice. Take, for instance, the case of carpets. If the chaste and deftly associated colours which characterize the Oriental loom are right, and content us downstairs, why should we lapse into the vulgarity of garlands and bouquets for the design of our drawing-room carpet?

And so with regard to cabinet work. It is of course unnecessary to fit up a boudoir with furniture of the size and capacity which we require in a dining-room side-board. But though the shape of a cheffonier may differ from that of a buffet, there can be no reason whatever why the *style of design* in these respective articles of furniture should vary. We may require, in a modern reception-room, chairs of a lighter make and more easily moveable than those in a library, but why the former should necessarily have round seats and the latter square ones is a mystery which no one but an upholsterer could explain.

The truth is, there is an absurd conventionality about such points as these, to which most of us submit, under a vague impression that if we differ from our neighbours we shall be violating good taste. We pass from one principle of design for the ground floor, to another and completely distinct one when we have ascended two flights of stairs. We leave a solid, gloomy, and often cumbersome class of furniture below, to find a flimsy and extravagant one above. It may be a question which of these two extremes is the more objectionable. Judged by the standard of any recognised principles in decorative art, they would probably both be considered wrong. But it is obvious that they cannot both be right.

In the early part of the present century a fashionable conceit prevailed of fitting up separate apartments in large mansions each after a style of its own. Thus we had Gothic halls, Elizabethan chambers, Louis Quatorze drawing-rooms, &c., &c., all under one roof. It is scarcely possible to imagine any system of house-furnishing more absurd and mischievous in its effect upon uneducated taste than this. Indeed, it was the practical evidence that a healthy and genuine taste was altogether wanting. Choose what style of furniture we may, it should surely be adopted throughout the house we live in.   (... p 66)

Charles L Eastlake, *Hints on Household Taste in Furniture, Upholstery and Other Details*, Longmans, Green, and Co (London), 1868.
(Excerpt pp 63–6)

Men's Room

Lee Edelman

political 1996
late 20th century space

Lee Edelman's text examines the public men's room as an environment that is constructed (made/given rise to) by men's behaviour in the space, and at the same time cultural/social actions are conditioned by the space itself. He suggests that such spaces are far from a neutral, technological response to bodily necessities, but are designed by, and have designs on men. An analysis of one men's room where televisions have been installed above the urinal in an effort to make men feel 'at home', serves to reveal how architecture is being used to condition space when male sexuality is challenged by cultural norms of sexually specific behaviour. This post-structural reading conditioned by queer theory, suggests that for the men's room, architecture, masculinity and sexuality are interlinked.

The public men's room, architecturally speaking, is rarely a room with a view – or rarely, at least, a room that affords a view outside itself. Like the closet, to which it is near allied (both as 'water closet' and as site of bodily relations discursively tabooed), the men's room tends to lack windows. And on those occasions when windows do figure as part of its structural design, the glass, more often translucent than transparent, generally precludes any visual commerce between the areas without and within. Substituting mirrors for windows, satisfying the eye's desire for depth of field by returning its look to itself, the men's room, through a segmentation of space that can justly be called self-reflexive, gestures, despite the accessibility of that space to a subset of the 'public,' towards an idea of interiority, towards a principle of containment, implicit in the architectural imperative that shapes the subject – forming and informing him as the subject of ideology – in its own monumentalizing image, modeling the subject as container of space through the articulation of structural, because structuring, identities.

Closed in on itself as if to exemplify the very notion of constructed space, but always, of course, designed to permit exchanges between inside and outside analogous to those that would seem most successfully arrested by its circumscription of the visual, this locus of functional attention to culturally abjected bodily functions always necessarily functions in excess of a logic of mere functionality. The men's room, that is, though clearly conceived as a technological response to the hygienic concerns associated with bodily necessities, constitutes a social technology in itself to necessitate a certain relation between the male subject and his body. The design of the men's room, simply put, has palpable designs on men; it aspires, that is, to design them. As a site of representation, as a space intended to 'serve' the subject it collaborates to call into being, the men's room gives the male subject his body in its relation to symbolic space – effectively locating him within his body as he is located within space itself – by allowing him, before the only public, the male one, whose witness can matter, to enact, as if in a theater, the law of its mandatory closeting. I refer, with this, not only to the law of (heterosexual) masculinity as we know it – the law that reads the male body, in its potential to be seized, overwhelmed, by erotic stimuli not provoked by the 'proper' object (a woman) or centered in the 'proper' place (the genitals), as requiring consignment to a psychic space analogous to a closet – but also to the law whereby the straight male body becomes a closet itself: a spatial enclosure for an autonomous subject able to imagine inhabiting his body only by conceiving his body simultaneously as container and thing contained; as *being* and *needing* a closet; as bestowing upon him the social protection, the cultural shelter, it uniquely affords within our patriarchal sex-gender system, but only so long as he performatively shelters the structural flaw that opens his body, by way of its multiple openings (ocular, oral, anal, genital), to the various psychic vicissitudes able to generate illicit desires. As a prime arena for that performance, for that enactment of the body's compliance with the cultural regulation of desire, the men's room marks a critical stage both for and in the solicitation of masculine subjectivity.

But just as soliciting the subject can define the social project of the men's room, so it also names the threat against which the solicited subject must be sheltered. However much the men's room may prompt the performers within it to heed its own subjectifying call – the call it slyly assimilates to the irresistible call of nature itself – it allows for the possibility of error, for what the penal code calls soliciting for the purpose of committing unnatural acts. And the habitual structuring of the men's room to ensure the possibility of this error makes clear that whatever shelter it provides requires the presence of the threat its very design apparently solicits.

The men's room, set apart as it is to provide a culturally designated 'privacy' in which to respond to the body's demands, houses two highly differentiated spaces that re-establish within it the consequential distinction between public and private zones, mapping each of those attributes onto specified zones of the male subject's body. Thus, the genitals, though figured as the 'private parts,' acquire, through the openness of the urinal, a relatively 'public' status here, while the anus and its functional necessity bear weightier burdens of social embarrassment.[1] In the men's room the norms of male bodily display reverse the values that the laws of *pudeur* assign to the privatized portions of male anatomy in the world outside: you don't show your ass in the men's room, and you don't conceal your dick. The partition that distinguishes the privacy of the stalls from the exposure of the urinals and sinks, therefore, defines the men's room, like the U.S. Congress, as strategically bicameral, allowing each part of its legislative body to hold the other in check. As *camera lucida* and *camera obscura* at once, the men's room might simply come out and proclaim as its motto 'I am a camera' were it not that it operates more saliently as a factory for turning into cameras themselves all those who enter to confront, as if *in camera*, the unblinking eye of the law that keeps watch, through every patron's eye – including, signally, their own – to see that what is publicly displayed is never directly observed.

The law of the men's room decrees that men's dicks be available for public contemplation must never take place. The performative bravado, 'naturalized' only by virtue of cultural insistence, implicit in taking one's dick in one's hand in the presence of other men similarly engaged, depends upon one of two governing assumptions: either that such a display can occur because the space that permits it is consecrated, more or less explicitly, to the purposes of gay male sex, or that the display itself contemptuously – or apotropaically – declares its refusal to allow that such a space could possibly be one where gay men, or gay male desire, might appear. Oscillating between these two assumptions, the logic of the men's room compels the normative enactment of a vigilant nonchalance that responds to the disciplinary pressure that the men's room exerts upon visual relations. Though the open display of the glans at the urinal disavows its capacity to occasion desire, the vector of the gaze, however oblique, remains alert to observe the glance that exposes any interest at all in the glans thus exposed. Where better to discern the full force of aggression implicit in the question – 'Are you looking at *me*?' – that condenses our pervasive male cultural anxiety about the capacities of gay men to transform, or to queer, the consistency of the reality produced and assured by the gaze of the symbolic? And if, in response to that question as posed by a man at a urinal taking a leak, another patron, so occupied or not, should answer, unapologetically, 'yes,' or if he should urge his irate companion to seek out the cloistered protection of a stall if he so dislikes being looked at that way, then how could the first man respond to this blatant defiance of the law so cunningly built into the architectural disposition of this space but with what he must view as an *equivalent* violence, whether it be verbal – as in, for instance, the clarion-cry, 'Faggot!,' with which certain straight men imagine they display a triumphant acuity in unveiling what was staring them in the face all along – or physical – as in the numerous blows with which, in response to this discovery, they try to consign to oblivion all those of whose type they resent their inability to be, for so much as a moment, oblivious themselves.

At the urinal, then, the ritualistic indifference that must seem to accompany, and must seem to greet, each act of genital display aspires to conceal the constant scrutiny bestowed by every sidelong glance on every sidelong glance. Whereas women may retreat to the powder room alone or even, to the comically theatricalized befuddlement of heterosexual men, in pairs – to attend, as its very name suggests, to the question of how they look, men, upon entering the men's room, focus instead on how they are looking, or, more precisely, on how their looking may be looked upon in turn. If the men's room offers no windows through which the eye can escape its locale, and if it prohibits the eye from alighting on what the design of the urinal insists nonetheless on publicly drawing out, then its space might properly be interpreted as the very site of the symbolic gaze, as a space that monitors the circuitry of visual relations propping up a 'reality' in which each look of the subject is filtered through the gaze of a symbolic order that, in every sense of the word, solicits him. Consider, after all, that however much the men who stand shoulder to shoulder at the urinal may study the eyes of their neighbors through the corners of their own, the frontal force of their attention will fall, most often, upon their own member and the arc of what it voids. And what, in such a case, can the eye be looking for, or at, if not a look, if not a *way* of looking, that either will confirm the symbolic gaze that solicits the subject as heterosexual through the phallicization – which necessitates the ocularization – of the penis, or else will threaten, shake, solicit the coherence of the heterosexual subject through the recognition of another desire, another solicitation, superimposed upon the images that parade as solid social reality like distorting ghosts rudely conjured by interference in video reception when the signals from two adjoining channels are both displayed at once. His penis, that is, must be seen by the straight male subject as what sees him and hence, like the antenna of a television set, as what enables him to see: as the visible gaze of the symbolic, the part of his body least his own, that takes *his* measure and grants him a privileged place in the structure of social meaning as it justifies his place within the room set aside for men. But should its sublation into the phallic eye be put on the blink by the glance of a man who, seeming to meet what should be its gaze, seemingly gazes back only at meat, such justifications may vanish and, with them, the subject's own solidity, his place in the social architecture, as he and the images shaping his world themselves fade into ghostliness, unexpectedly picking up frequencies they had been programmed not to receive so as to keep their focus singularly fixed on the channel that common wisdom receives as the site of public access.

The following, written by Monique P. Yazigi, appeared under the title, 'What Do Men Want? Perhaps, Says a Restaurant, Private TV?,' in the 'City' section of the *New York Times* on 23 October 1994:

> *The American Renaissance Restaurant, at 260 West Broadway, has inset two 13-inch Mitsubishi television sets above the two black porcelain urinals in the men's bathroom. "You would have to be a man to understand why we did it," said John Aron, the manager of the restaurant, giggling. "Men usually have nothing to look at and they certainly don't want their eyes to wander."*

Tellingly, the entrance to the men's room here first passes, at least allusively, through Freud's interrogation of *female* desire – as famously expressed in his much cited query, '*Was will das Weib?*': 'What does woman want?' – as if to confirm a complementarity, like that of paired lavatory doors, that disavows any serious doubt about what men *really* want. Though the surety of that knowledge lets the title relax into the cultural stereotype, comically deployed, of the successfully domesticated heterosexual man whose desire has been channeled by – and toward – the channels on his TV, that humor can barely distract from the static introduced by conceiving the men's room as a place in which men's desires, susceptible to rechanneling as they thus appear to be, might plausibly find satisfaction. Indeed, when the restaurant's owner, accounting for the televisions in terms at a variance – strategically unremarked – from those of the manager cited above, explains that, 'We want people to feel like they're at home,' one might reasonably reflect on Freud's well-known analysis of the homelike and the unfamiliar, the *heimlich* and the *unheimlich*, which disconcertingly come together as the double-edged shadow of the uncanny cuts its way across the can to cancel any and every assurance about where men may feel at home.

For Freud, of course, the uncanny names the experience of derealization provoked by some threat to the ego's integrity that recalls the time before the ego had fully detached itself from the world. Bound up, therefore, with a sense of doubleness as the subject, in a vertiginous rupture of the ground on which he stands, senses himself unexpectedly observed and all at once starts to view himself through the eyes of another person or thing that seems, improperly and unnaturally, to usurp his subjectivity, the uncanny always manifests itself in a troubling, which can take specific form as a doubling, of the gaze. The subject, in *its* grip, will always feel that he is losing *his*, finding himself no longer at home in the world he thought he knew; for this alarming disappearance of the sense of 'at home-ness,' which occurs, however paradoxically, with a certain sickening familiarity, signals a toppling of the walls within which the subject has been constructed and through which he has realized the imaginary architecture of a self. The uncanny, then, might be understood as a distinctive type of 'home-sickness' that, like dwellings inadequately vented to allow air to circulate in and out, produces a sickness of and in the home that occasions a nostalgic longing for the sense of safety that 'home' once assured.

Only in such a context should one interpret the claim that TVs in the men's room help patrons to 'feel like they're at home.' Some men, to be sure, determined to catch every moment of excitement as they watch The Big Game, may leave the door to the bathroom ajar – or open – when they make their needful retreat to use the facilities at home, but very few would count among the tell-tale signs of 'homeliness' the luxury of having a television set available in the john. Although the 'meaning' of the television may be colored by its connection to the life men live in the living room, its association with the *heimlich* turns *unheimlich* in the bathroom, which is never to be conceptualized as a room wherein life could be lived. After all, as anyone who has ever placed or read a real-estate advertisement knows, bathrooms are not even numbered as rooms when describing the size of a home. Rather than make the space of the men's room as comfortable as one's own home, therefore, placing televisions above the urinals reflects an awareness that it only heightens in attempting to occlude: that the men's room is an uncanny space where the gaze of the symbolic order sees male bodies into social meaning, thereby establishing the men's room as a nodal point, ground zero, in the cultural compaction of masculinity into a logic of visual relations.

The manager of the restaurant comes closer to this truth in his mini-meditation on the customary misfortunes of the men's room and men's eyes. Just as the owner can only address the uncanniness that structures the men's room, however, through his representation of the television sets as making the space more like 'home,' so the manager can only identify the double vision the men's room induces by contradictorily insisting, on the one hand, that it offers those using it 'nothing to look at' while recognizing, on the other hand, a temptation within it fully capable of enticing their eyes 'to wander.' But this contradiction resolves into clarity once the visible dicks at the urinal, toward which their eyes might incautiously turn, are understood to carry, as if by legislative decree, a sort of Surgeon General's warning that labels them precisely *as* 'nothing to look at,' thus granting them all the power, and danger, of Yahweh rising up before Moses from out of another sort of bush. And just as the prohibition against glimpsing Yahweh's face coincided with a prohibition against speaking his name, so here, for the manager and owner both – as, indeed, for the culture they inhabit – the law that prohibits the gaze of a man from resting on his neighbor's dick suffers under prohibition itself as something that every man must know but none must ever pronounce, 'you'd have to be a man to understand,' as the manager rightly puts it, alluding to the homophobic commandment of the men's room that solicits the subject into manhood as unmistakably as the voice of Yahweh called Moses to his destiny before the Law.   (... p 157)

Note
1   These sentences condense an argument I have made at greater length in 'Tearooms and Sympathy; Or, The Epistemology of the Water Closet,' in my *Homographesis: Essays in Gay Literary and Cultural Theory*, Routledge (New York and London), 1994, pp 148–170. Since I will focus in this essay primarily on the significations informing the logic of the urinal, I cite here, by way of contextualization, a passage from 'Tearooms and Sympathy' that may help to trace the lineaments of my argument concerning the space of the stall:
       'I want to suggest that the men's room ... is the site of a particular heterosexual anxiety about the potential inscriptions of homosexual desire and about the possibility of knowing or recognizing whatever might constitute "homosexual difference".
       'This can be intuited more readily when the restroom is considered not, as it is by Lacan, in terms of "urinary segregation" – a context that establishes the phallus from the outset as the token of anatomical difference – but as the site of a loosening of sphincter control, evoking, therefore, an older eroticism, undifferentiated by gender, because anterior to the genital tyranny that raises the phallus to its privileged position. Precisely because the phallus marks the putative stability of the divide between "Ladies" and "Gentlemen", because it articulates the concept of sexual difference in terms of "visible

perception", the "urinary" function in the institutional men's room customarily takes place within view of others – as if to indicate its status as an act of definitional display; but the private enclosure of the toilet stall signals the potential anxiety at issue in the West when the men's room becomes the locus not of urinary but of intestinal relief. For the satisfaction that such relief affords abuts dangerously on homophobically abjectified desires, and because that satisfaction marks an opening onto difference that would challenge the phallic supremacy and coherence of the signifier on the men's room door, it must be isolated and kept in view at once lest its erotic potential come out' (pp 160–1).

Lee Edelman, 'Men's Room', Joel Sanders (ed), *Stud: Architectures of Masculinity*, Princeton Architectural Press (New York), 1996.
© 1996 Princeton University School of Architecture. Reprinteded by permission of Princeton Architectural Press.
(Excerpt pp 152–7)

'Decorators May be Compared to Doctors'

Emma Ferry

late 19th century decoration ● political 2003

Academic scholar Emma Ferry champions advice literature as both narrative discourse and historical documentation on design and taste. In this essay she provides a feminist recovery of the Garrett cousins' life and work recognising them as England's first female interior decorators. Critical to this position is their link to women's suffrage and late nineteenth-century feminist activity, paralleling their struggle to train and practise as decorators. Ferry notes that in their writing the Garretts appropriate the discourse of Charles Eastlake and relegate it to the past, while promoting the 'Queen Anne' style as the way forward.

Subverting Separate Spheres

In *House Decoration*, domestic ideology is subverted in two ways. First, the Garretts invert the gender identities created by Eastlake in *Hints on Household Taste*. Second, they use the text to demonstrate their professional status as trained 'house decorators' rather than domestic 'home-makers.'

In many ways, *House Decoration* is clearly imitative of Eastlake's *Hints on Household Taste*, though thankfully less verbose. Despite advocating different styles, the similarities remain clear. Compare, for example, the following comments about the front door, first by Eastlake:

> A good flat tint of olive green or chocolate colour will, however, answer all practical purposes, and besides being a more honest and artistic, is really a less expensive style of decoration. It is a great pity that the old-fashioned brass knocker has become obsolete ... The present cast-iron knocker is a frightful invention ... Good *wrought-iron* knockers of very fair design and manufacture, may be bought.[1]

and then by the Garretts:

> the bronzed front door and railing may be painted some good uniform shade of green or brown, and the cast-iron knocker and other door furniture exchanged for brass or wrought iron of simple design.[2]

Eastlake goes on to remark that 'Ladies are seldom called upon to choose between the merits of wrought and cast-iron for objects of domestic use,'[3] but clearly the Garretts were more than able to make such judgements. There are countless other examples of similarity between the two texts. Moreover, Eastlake is one of the few nineteenth-century writer-designers to whom the Garretts make reference:

> What is commonly sold as Gothic furniture, with gables and chamferings and gashes here and there to indicate carving, is for the most part a gross libel upon the sketches given by Mr. Eastlake, in his *Hints on Household Taste*, of a style of furniture which is simple and direct in its outline, and entirely free from those pretentious attempts at ornament with which even the simplest and cheapest furniture is now abundantly disfigured.[4]

While complimentary, it is notable that this comment, which appears in the chapter 'Houses As They Are,' links Eastlake with machine-made Gothic furniture.

Clearly the Garretts have appropriated the dominant discourse of Eastlake, but by reading between the lines it is possible to discern the muted discourse. Throughout, the reader of *House Decoration*, the aspiring purchaser of the services of a decorator or upholsterer is referred to as 'he' – a 'he' just as likely to be seduced by fashion as a 'she':

> In the foregoing principles it is hoped that a general idea has been given for a basis of operations which would prevent an amateur going very far wrong in the colouring of *his* rooms or the structure of *his* furniture. They may also enable *him* to speak with more authority to the upholsterer or the paper-hanger whom *he* employs, and may save *him* from being compelled to purchase furniture or to hang paper, not that they suit *his* rooms or *his* requirements, but because 'they are very tasty,' or because 'we are selling a great number of them' [my italics].[5]

This can be read as an ironic inversion of flustered female consumers succumbing – rather more melodramatically – to the persuasions of the upholsterer in Eastlake's *Hints on Household Taste* (1868):

> When Materfamilias enters an ordinary upholsterer's warehouse, how can she possibly decide on the pattern of her new carpet, when bale after bale of Brussels is unrolled by the indefatigable youth, who is equal in his praises of every piece in turn? … The shopman remarks of one piece of goods that it is 'elegant;' of another that it is 'striking;' of a third, that it is 'unique,' and so forth. The good lady looks from one carpet to another until her eyes are fairly dazzled by their hues. She is utterly unable to explain why she should, or why she should not like any of them.[6]

These inversions and gender references become more apparent when the Garretts consider the decoration and furnishing of the two most obviously gendered rooms in the house, the masculine Dining Room and the feminine Drawing Room.[7] In 'Houses As They Are,' a small ten-page section, they present a room-by-room analysis, examining the Hall, the Dining Room, the Drawing Room and the Bedroom exposing the horrors of the interior of an ordinary modern London house, and criticizing many of the 'unprincipled' decorative practices of the period. Significantly, the Garretts comment on the gendered nature of the principal rooms, particularly the Dining Room:

> the gloomy appearance of the rest of the room reminds one of the British boast that every Englishman's house is his castle, and that he wishes neither to observe nor to be observed when he retires into the dignified seclusion of this, the especially masculine department of the house-hold.[8]

In the feminine Drawing Room, the Garretts censure the work of 'some fashionable decorator and upholsterer'[9] who has been employed by the anxious ladies of the house, and describe with irony the inharmonious decorative scheme of this 'lamentably commonplace apartment.'[10] The following chapter, which also includes and refers to illustrations of their own furniture designs, is entitled 'Houses As They Might Be.' This is the most important section in *House Decoration* for appreciating the style the Garretts produced. Advocating neutral tones, harmonious drapery in soft velvets and simple, well-constructed furniture based on eighteenth century models, the Garretts return to the imaginary ordinary London house to redecorate it, creating a Utopian[11] vision of the 'Queen Anne' – style home.

In an inversion of Eastlake's flustered, novelty-driven *Materfamilias*, the Garretts present their readers with the *Paterfamilias* who is resistant to change:

> In the dingy and dreary solemnity of the modern London Dining Room we have but a melancholy survival of the stately hospitable-looking rooms of the last century. Yet there is no other room in the house where innovations are more grudgingly permitted, and an Englishman would suspect you of every other revolutionary tendency, if you proposed any radical changes in the colour of the walls, or in the forms and arrangements of the furniture.[12]

Women – at least women like the Garretts who have acquired the 'faculty of distinguishing good from bad design in the familiar objects of domestic life'[13] – are now positive agents of change and innovation. In spite of the glowering *Paterfamilias* – who seems to be their biggest problem, with perhaps the exception of the black marble chimneypiece – the Garretts redecorate the Dining Room and, having completed their refurbishment, 'leaving the master of the house to decide whether his digestion will be able to assimilate the novel treatment just proposed,'[14] they return to the Drawing Room. Whereas in 'Houses As They Are,' 'the ladies of the family are *told* that it is now their turn to have their tastes consulted,'[15] in 'Houses As They Might Be,' 'the ladies of the household *demand* the right of having their particular tastes consulted'[16] [my italics]. It seems, however, that the taste of these ladies is largely inspired by the decorative schemes of:

> Mrs A's beautiful Drawing Room 'in the dado style, I think they call it,' and Mrs B's charming idea of having flowers painted on the panels of the doors, 'so beautifully done they were exactly like real flowers.'[17]

Confident that the faults of these rooms can be explained, the Garretts go on to alter the Drawing Room 'in accordance with a more cultivated view of the principles of decorative art.'[18] Consequently, the Drawing Room is transformed into an affordably 'Queen Anne' style 'shrine.'[19] This section of 'Houses As They Might Be' concludes with a reminder of the need for aesthetic appreciation by the occupant of the re-decorated home. Here, like Eastlake, they argue that decorative art should be judged by the same standards applied to other forms of art; but, while Eastlake admonishes that 'class of *young ladies* who are in the habit of anticipating all differences of opinion in a picture-gallery or concert-room by saying that they "know what they like,"'[20] the Garretts advise *people* who claim to 'know what they like' to take care that their tastes 'are so far cultivated as to make it desirable to display them.'[21]

Perhaps the most intriguing chapter in *House Decoration* is devoted to draperies. Here the Garretts make their only explicit statement about the role of women:

> We hear a great deal nowadays of women's work and women's sphere. Here at any rate there can be no difference of opinion. Whether the arrangements of an ordinary household be sufficient, even if ordered with the greatest nicety, to occupy the whole of the housewife's time and thought, may be a disputed question, but everyone will agree that when a woman undertakes to guide a household, all these things should be of interest to her, and that the refinement and beauty of a house will, in the main, depend upon the trouble which she is willing to bestow upon small and comparatively insignificant details.[22]

One of these comparatively insignificant details seems to be household linen:

> Since the days of our grandmothers,[23] who spun their own linen, it seems that housewives and spinsters (now, properly speaking spinsters no longer) have neglected that important part of housekeeping, the household linen.[24]

Although a connection can be made between making and marking household linen and the Married Women's Property legislation of the period,[25] here the Garretts have returned to an idealized historical vision, seeing the home as a site of production rather than consumption:

> Surely the work of marking, wherein the cleverness of the worker might devise some fresh conceit on each article, would be more interesting than half the busy idleness with which the daughters of England now beguile their time.[26]

Considering the 'exhausting fight against the stream of prejudice, such as the Garretts had waged for many years,'[27] it is perhaps not surprising that they should express their impatience with the less politicised 'daughters of England' who waste their time in useless rather than 'useful and congenial' pursuits.[28]

The Garretts are not engaged in busy idleness. Rather than naturally gifted amateurs, they are trained professionals working in a male-dominated world. The clearest demonstration of their professional status occurs throughout their Introduction, which begins with a reference to a paper given by J. J. Stevenson upon 'the Queen Anne Style of Architecture' in 1874.[29] By defending and defining the style 'to the study of which the Miss Garretts have devoted their attention,'[30] they place themselves immediately in the context of their professional life. Demonstrating knowledge and understanding of one of the recent heated debates[31] of the architectural world, the merits of 'Queen Anne' style versus the Gothic Revival, they describe the rapid popularity of the new style and its suitability for new buildings:

> all we would urge is that for ordinary English houses, the style of house which was built during the eighteenth century, whose walls were of brick, and whose staircases were of wood (the houses, that is, which are now designated 'Queen Anne'), are more suitable than the so-called Gothic house.[32]

Clearly belonging to the 'Queen Anne' camp, the Garretts go on to explain the appeal of this style by comparing two London houses, one from Bloomsbury and one from South Kensington, 'each built originally for the same class.'[33] They invoke ideas of national identity, hoping that:

> The fashionable world of London may one day return and live in the houses which were built in the solid and unpretentious style so much in accordance with the best characteristics of the English people.[34]

Having thus established their stylistic approach, they return to the subject of their treatise, 'the internal fittings and decorations of houses.'[35] They begin by defining their profession, describing the skills of the consummate 'house decorator' who:

Should be able to design and arrange all the internal fittings of a house, the chimney-pieces, grates, and door-heads, as well as the wall-hangings, curtains, carpets, and furniture.[36]

They perceive the 'house decorator' (i.e. R. & A. Garrett) as a professional able to judge both the total effect and the minute details of the decorative scheme, and who aims to create a 'harmonious whole.'[37] The Garretts also underline their professional status by dealing at length with the relationship between client and decorator, no doubt speaking from experience when they comment, 'A great [deal] of trouble and vexation would often be saved if people would make up their minds beforehand how much they wish to spend.'[38]   (... p 29)

Notes

1 CL Eastlake, *Hints on Household Taste*, Longmans, Green & Co (London), 1868, 1878, pp 43–4.
2 R & A Garrett, *Suggestions for House Decoration in Painting, Woodwork and Furniture*, Macmillan & Co (London), 1876, p 36.
3 Eastlake, *Hints*, p 44.
4 R & A Garrett, *Suggestions*, p 32.
5 R & A Garrett, *Suggestions*, p 21.
6 Eastlake, *Hints*, p 11.
7 See J Kinchin, 'The Gendered Interior: Nineteenth Century Essays on the "Masculine" And The "Feminine" Room', P Kirkham (ed), *The Gendered Object*, Manchester University Press (Manchester), 1996, pp 12–29.
8 R & A Garrett, *Suggestions*, p 28.
9 R & A Garrett, *Suggestions*, pp 28–9.
10 R & A Garrett, *Suggestions*. In another volume of the 'Art at Home' series, Mrs Orrinsmith opens with a description of a very similar room, which she identifies as the 'ordinary lower middle-class Drawing Room of the Victorian era'. See Mrs Orrinsmith, *The Drawing-Room*, Macmillan & Co (London), 1877, p 1.
11 The inversion is a classic technique of Utopian fiction.
12 R & A Garrett, *Suggestions*, p 43.
13 Eastlake, *Hints*, pp 8–9.
14 R & A Garrett, *Suggestions*, p 55.
15 R & A Garrett, *Suggestions*, p 28.
16 R & A Garrett, *Suggestions*, p 55.
17 R & A Garrett, *Suggestions*, p 56.
18 R & A Garrett, *Suggestions*, p 56.
19 R & A Garrett, *Suggestions*, p 67.
20 Eastlake, *Hints*, pp 14–15.
21 R & A Garrett, *Suggestions*, p 68.
22 R & A Garrett, *Suggestions*, p 84.
23 *House Decoration* contains many references to 'the days of our grandmothers', a time when footstools were much bigger and ladies had far fewer dresses. This can be partially explained by Girouard's analysis of the English Aesthete and the development of 'Queen Anne' style: 'As an antidote to the present they recreated the past as an ideal world of pre-industrial simplicity, at once homely and Arcadian'. See M Girouard, *Sweetness and Light: The 'Queen Anne Movement' 1869–1900*, Yale University Press (Yale), 1984, p 5.
24 R & A Garrett, *Suggestions*, p 81.

25 See L Holcombe, *Wives & Property: Reform of the Married Women's Property Law in Nineteenth-Century England*, Martin Robertson (Oxford), 1983. See Lynn Walker's discussion of this legislation in her essay 'Women Architects', J Attfield and P Kirkham (eds), *A View from the Interior: Women and Design*, The Women's Press Ltd (London), 1995, in which she identifies the legal restrictions imposed on married women as an obstruction to their gaining access to the architectural profession, and suggests that the 'removal of the legal, ideological and psychological impediments by the Married Women's Property Acts therefore had great significance for all women, and it had particular importance for the entry of women into the architectural profession', p 96. The Garretts, however, were financially independent, unmarried women.

26 R & A Garrett, *Suggestions*, p 75.

27 E Smyth, *Impressions That Remained*, Longmans, Green & Co (London), 2 Vols 1919, Vol II, p 12.

28 *Englishwoman's Review*, 15 December 1882, p 548.

29 *Building News*, 26 June 1874, pp 689–92; *The Builder*, 27 June 1874, pp 537–8.

30 Rev WJ Loftie, 'Advertisement', in R & A Garrett, *Suggestions*, notes that the next volume of this series would be JJ Stevenson's *Domestic Architecture* which 'will apply the same principles to the exterior that are here applied to the interior of our houses', JJ Stevenson's *House Architecture*, although part of Loftie's original scheme, was not issued as part of the 'Art at Home' series, being published separately in two volumes by Macmillan in 1880.

31 See Girouard, *Sweetness and Light*, pp 57–63.

32 R & A Garrett, *Suggestions*, pp 3–4. The Garretts acknowledge the importance of Pugin, but reject Gothic Revival architecture as a suitable style for ordinary modern housing on the grounds of the inappropriate sham materials used by builders: 'When a large house or cathedral is to be built ... money will be forthcoming and the building will be of stone. But if a builder is "running up a street of Gothic houses", what happens? It is out of the question that he should use so costly a material as stone, and stucco therefore takes its place. It is we know, unreasonable to blame a pure and beautiful style for requiring a beautiful material.'

33 R & A Garrett, *Suggestions*, p 4.

34 R & A Garrett, *Suggestions*, p 5.

35 R & A Garrett, *Suggestions*, p 5.

36 R & A Garrett, *Suggestions*, pp 5–6.

37 R & A Garrett, *Suggestions*, p 6.

38 R & A Garrett, *Suggestions*, pp 88–9.

Emma Ferry, 'Decorators May be Compared to Doctors', *An Analysis of Rhoda and Agnes Garrett's Suggestions for House Decoration in Painting, Woodwork and Furniture (1876)*, *Journal of Design History*, vol 16 no 1, 2003, pp 15–33.

(Excerpt pp 26–29)

Berggasse 19: Inside Freud's Office

Diana Fuss and Joel Sanders

political ● 1996

mid 20th century furnish

Within this architectural study on the spatial configuration of Sigmund Freud's office, Diana Fuss and Joel Sanders offer a critical theoretical examination of surviving archival photographs to determine how vision, power and gender structure this scene of psychoanalysis. Recognising that the original photographs utilise techniques and strategies of street photography, Fuss and Sanders suggest that this private chamber of close and personal exchange, of intimate interiorities, is turned inside out for public display via the photographic images. Furthermore, objects collected within the space signal Freud's own obsession with power, and the positioning of furniture and mirrors is read in terms of the role body language plays as a spatial transaction.

The patient's entry into Freud's office initiates a series of complicated and subtle transactions of power, orchestrated largely by the very precise spatial arrangement of objects and furniture. Freud held initial consultations, between three and four every afternoon, in the study section of his office. Preferring a face-to-face encounter with prospective patients, Freud seated them approximately four feet away from himself, across the divide of a table adjacent to the writing desk. Located in the center of a square room, at the intersection of two axial lines, the patient would appear to occupy the spatial locus of power. As if to confirm the illusion of his centrality, the patient is immediately presented, when seated, with a reflection of his own image, in a small portrait-sized mirror, framed in gold filigree and hanging, at eye-level, on a facing window. As soon as Freud sits down at his desk, however, interposing himself between patient and mirror, the patient's reflection is blocked by Freud's head. Head substitutes for mirror in a metaphorical staging of the clinical role Freud seeks to assume. 'The doctor,' Freud pronounces in *Papers on Technique*, 'should be opaque to his patients and, like a mirror, should show them nothing but what is shown to him' (12: p 118).[1]

Freud's clinical assumption of the function of the mirror, and the substitution of other for self that it enacts, sets into motion the transferential dynamics that will structure all further doctor-patient encounters. In preparation for the laborious work of overcoming their unconscious resistances, patients are required to divest themselves of authority while seated in the very center of power. In a reverse panopticon, the most central location in Freud's study (the point from which the gaze normally issues) turns out to be the most vulnerable, as the patient suddenly finds himself exposed on all sides to a multitude of gazes. Viewed from both left and right by a phalanx of ancient figurines (all displayed at eye-level and arranged to face the patient), as well as from behind by a collection of detached antique heads and from in front by Freud's imposing visage, the patient is surveyed from every direction. Power in this transferential scene is exercised from the margins. From the protected vantage point of his desk chair, Freud studies his patient's face, fully illuminated by the afternoon light, while his own face remains barely visible, almost entirely eclipsed by backlighting from the window behind him.

'The process of psychoanalysis,' Freud goes on to remark in *Papers on Technique*, 'is retarded by the dread felt by the average observer of seeing himself in his own mirror' (12: p 210). The analogy of the mirror, used to describe the process of psychoanalytic self-reflection, makes its first appearance in Freud's work in his reading of the memoirs of Daniel Paul Schreber. Mirrors figure prominently in Schreber's transvestic identification: 'anyone who should happen to see me before the mirror with the upper portion of my torso bared – especially if the illusion is assisted by my wearing a little feminine finery – would receive an unmistakable impression of a *female bust*' (12: p 33). And what did Freud see when, alone in his office amongst his classical heads and ancient figurines, he turned to face his own image in the mirror? Freud, too, saw the unmistakable impression of a bust – head and shoulders severed from the body, torso-less and floating, like the Roman head overlooking his consulting room chair or the death mask displayed in his study. His head decapitated by the frame of the mirror, Freud is visually identified with one of his own classical sculptures, transformed into a statuary fragment.

Looking in the other direction Freud also saw only heads. A wooden statue of a Chinese sage sitting on the table between Freud and his patient severs the patient's head in the same way Freud's head is decapitated by the frame of the mirror. From the vantage point of the desk chair, the patient's disembodied head assumes the status of one of Freud's antiquities, homologous not only to the stone heads filling the table directly behind the patient (the only table in the office displaying almost exclusively heads) but also to the framed photographic portraits above them, hanging at the exact same level as the mirror.

For Freud, every self-reflection reveals a death mask, every mirror image a spectral double. In his meditation on the theme of doubling, Freud remarks in 'The "Uncanny"' that while the double first emerges in our psychical lives as a 'preservation against extinction,' this double (in typically duplicitous fashion) soon reverses itself: 'from having been an assurance of immortality, it becomes the uncanny harbinger of death' (17: p 235). By captivating our image, immobilizing and framing it, the mirror reveals a picture of our own unthinkable mortality.

Yet, as Freud notes elsewhere, it is finally impossible to visualize our own deaths, for 'whenever we attempt to do so we can perceive that we are in fact still present as spectators' (14: p 289). The mirror that memorializes also reincarnates, reconstituting us as phantom spectators, witnesses to our own irreplaceability. The mirror thus functions simultaneously like a window, assisting us in passing through the unrepresentable space of our violent eradication, and helping us, in effect, to survive our own deaths. This was indeed the function of Etruscan mirrors (so prominent in Freud's own private collection) on whose polished bronze surfaces mythological scenes were engraved. By differentiating between pictorial space and real space, the frame of the Etruscan mirror offers the illusion of a view onto another world. These mirrors, originally buried in tombs, assisted their owners in passing through their deaths: the Etruscan mirror opened a window onto immortality.

Lacan saw as much in his early reflections on the mirror stage. Radically dislocating the traditional opposition of transparency and reflectivity (window and mirror), Lacan instructs us to 'think of the mirror as a pane of glass, you'll see yourself in the glass and you'll see objects beyond it.'[2] In Freud's office, the placement of a mirror on a window frame further complicates this conflation of transparency and reflectivity by frustrating the possibility of opening up the space of looking that both crystalline surfaces appear to offer. Normally, when mirrors are placed against opaque walls, they have the capacity to act as windows; they dematerialize and dissolve architectural edges, creating the illusion of extension and expanding the spatial boundaries of the interior. But in this highly peculiar instance of a mirror superimposed on a window, visual access is obstructed rather than facilitated. Unlike the glass panes on Berggasse 19's rear entry doors, which allow the viewer's gaze to pass easily along a central axis from inside to outside, the composition of Freud's study window, with the mirror occupying the central vanishing point, redirects the gaze inward. By forcing the subject of reflection to confront an externalized gaze relayed back upon itself, the mirror on Freud's window interrupts the reassuring classical symmetries of self and other, inside and outside, and seeing and being seen that constitute the traditional humanist subject.[3]

The architectonics of the Freudian subject depends fundamentally upon a spatial dislocation, upon seeing the self exteriorized. It is not only that when we look in the mirror we see how others see us, but also that we see ourselves occupying a space where we are not. The statue that confronts us in the mirror permits us to look not only at but through ourselves to the 'object who knows himself to be seen.'[4] The domain delimited by Lacan's *imago*, "the statue in which man projects himself,"[5] is thus a strangely lifeless one. As Mikkel Borch-Jacobsen pictures it in 'The Statue Man,' this mirror world is 'a sort of immense museum peopled with immobile "statues," "images" of stone, and hieratic "forms".' It is 'the most inhuman of possible worlds, the most *unheimlich*.'[6]

What Freud sees in his mirror is a subject who is, first and foremost, an object, a statue, a bust. The 'dread' of self-reflection that Freud describes in *Papers on Technique* appears to issue from a fear of castration, of dramatic bodily disfigurement. If, as Freud insists in 'Medusa's Head,' the terror of castration is always linked to the sight of something, then it is the sight of *seeing oneself seeing* that possesses lethal consequences for the figure in the mirror. Like Medusa, who is slain by the fatal powers of her own gaze reflected back to her by Perseus's shield, Freud's narcissistic gaze makes him 'stiff with terror, turns him to stone' (18: p 273). Self-reflection petrifies. Perhaps this is the knowledge that so frightened, and so fascinated, Freud; the realization that the subject's 'optical erection' could only be achieved at the price of its castration, its instantaneous, fatal transformation into a broken relic.   (... p 124)

Notes
1 [Editors' note: Earlier in the essay Fuss and Sanders note: 'All citations from the *Standard Edition* hereafter cited in the text by volume and page number. *The Standard Edition of the Complete Works of Sigmund Freud*, trans and ed James Strachey, 24 vols, The Hogarth Press (London), 1953–1974.]
2 Jacques Lacan, *Seminar I: Freud's Papers on Technique*, Jacques-Alain Miller (ed), trans John Forrester, Norton (New York), 1988, p 141.
3 For an excellent discussion of challenges to the traditional humanism of the architectural window, see Thomas Keenan, 'Windows: of Vulnerability', in *The Phantom Public Sphere*, Bruce Robbins (ed), University of Minnesota Press (Minneapolis), 1994, pp 121–41. See also Beatriz Colomina, *Privacy and Publicity: Modern Architecture as Mass Media*, MIT Press (Cambridge), 1994, esp pp 80–2, 234–38 and 283 ff. An earlier discussion of windows and mirrors can be found in Diana Agrest, 'Architecture of Mirror/Mirror of Architecture', in *Architecture from Without: Theoretical Framings for a Critical Practice*, MIT Press (Cambridge), 1991, pp 139–55.
4 Lacan, *Seminar I*, p 215; see also p 78.
5 Jacques Lacan, 'The Mirror Stage as Formative of the Function of the I as Revealed in Psychoanalytic Experience', in *Écrits*, trans Alan Sheridan, Norton (New York), 1977, p 2.
6 Mikkel Borch-Jacobsen, *Lacan: The Absolute Master*, trans Douglas Brick, University Press (Stanford), 1991, p 59.

Diana Fuss and Joel Sanders, 'Berggasse 19: Inside Freud's Office', Joel Sanders (ed), *Stud: Architectures of Masculinity*, Princeton Architectural Press (New York), 1996.
© 1996 Princeton University School of Architecture. Reprinted by permission of Princeton Architectural Press.
(Excerpt pp 119–24)

Towards a Feminist Poetics: Infection in the Sentence

Sandra M Gilbert and Susan Gubar

psychological ● 1979

late 19th century space

English Literature academics Sandra Gilbert and Susan Gubar bring research on the interface of women and literature into the discourse on the interior and link it to gender politics. They use literary techniques to discuss the interior through the topography of one's innermost self, questioning the conflation between women, house and inner being. In this excerpt, their feminist reading of a literary work in which a woman writer narrates her experiences of textual /architectural confinement, is far from felicitous. Their essay demonstrates that women's writing is necessarily different from men's, and the gender (of the author's body) is inscribed in the text, and by implication, into the architectural surroundings under discussion.

While some male authors also use such imagery for implicitly or explicitly confessional projects, women seem forced to live more intimately with the metaphors they have created to solve the 'problem' of their fall. At least one critic does deal not only with such images but with their psychological meaning as they accrue around houses. Noting in *The Poetics of Space* that 'the house image would appear to have become the topography of our inmost being,' Gaston Bachelard shows the ways in which houses, nests, shells, and wardrobes are in us as much as we are in them.[1] What is significant from our point of view, however, is the extraordinary discrepancy between the almost consistently 'felicitous space' he discusses and the negative space we have found. Clearly, for Bachelard the protective asylum of the house is closely associated with its maternal features, and to this extent he is following the work done on dream symbolism by Freud and on female inner space by Erikson. It seems clear too, however, that such symbolism must inevitably have very different implications for male critics and for female authors.

Women themselves have often, of course, been described or imagined as houses. Most recently Erik Erikson advanced his controversial theory of female 'inner space' in an effort to account for little girls' interest in domestic enclosures. But in medieval times, as if to anticipate Erikson, statues of the Madonna were made to open up and reveal the holy family hidden in the Virgin's inner space. The female womb has certainly, always and everywhere, been a child's first and most satisfying house, a source of food and dark

121

security, and therefore a mythic paradise imaged over and over again in sacred caves, secret shrines, consecrated huts. Yet for many a woman writer these ancient associations of house and self seem mainly to have strengthened the anxiety about enclosure which she projected into her art. Disturbed by the real physiological prospect of enclosing an unknown part of herself that is somehow also not herself, the female artist may, like Mary Shelley, conflate anxieties about maternity with anxieties about literary creativity. Alternatively, troubled by the anatomical 'emptiness' of spinsterhood, she may, like Emily Dickinson, fear the inhabitations of nothingness and death, the transformation of womb into tomb. Moreover, conditioned to believe that as a house she is herself owned (and ought to be inhabited) by a man, she may once again but for yet another reason see herself as inescapably an object. In other words, even if she does not experience her womb as a kind of tomb or perceive her child's occupation of her house/body as depersonalizing, she may recognize that in an essential way she has been defined simply by her purely biological usefulness to her species.

To become literally a house, after all, is to be denied the hope of that spiritual transcendence of the body which, as Simone de Beauvoir has argued, is what makes humanity distinctively human. Thus, to be confined in childbirth (and significantly 'confinement' was the key nineteenth-century term for what we would now, just as significantly call 'delivery') is in a way just as problematical as to be confined in a house or prison. Indeed, it might well seem to the literary woman that, just as ontogeny may be said to recapitulate phylogeny, the confinement of pregnancy replicates the confinement of society. For even if she is only metaphorically denied transcendence, the woman writer who perceives the implications of the house/body equation must unconsciously realize that such a trope does not just 'place' her in a glass coffin, it transforms her into a version of the glass coffin herself. There is a sense, therefore, in which, confined in such a network of metaphors, what Adrienne Rich has called a 'thinking woman' might inevitably feel that now she has been imprisoned within her own alien and loathsome body.[2] Once again, in other words, she has become not only a prisoner but a monster.

As if to comment on the unity of all these points – on, that is, the anxiety-inducing connections between what women writers tend to see as their parallel confinements in texts, houses, and maternal female bodies – Charlotte Perkins Gilman brought them all together in 1890 in a striking story of female confinement and escape, a paradigmatic tale which (like *Jane Eyre*) seems to tell the story that all literary women would tell if they could speak their 'speechless woe.' *The Yellow Wallpaper*, which Gilman herself called 'a description of a case of nervous breakdown,' recounts in the first person the experiences of a woman who is evidently suffering from a severe postpartum psychosis.[3] Her husband, a censorious and paternalistic physician, is treating her according to methods by which S. Weir Mitchell, a famous 'nerve specialist,' treated Gilman herself for a similar problem. He has confined her to a large garret room in an 'ancestral hall' he has rented, and he has forbidden her to touch pen to paper until she is well again, for he feels, says the narrator, 'that with my imaginative power and habit of story-making, a nervous weakness like mine is sure to lead to all manner of excited fancies, and that I ought to use my will and good sense to check the tendency'.(pp 15–16)

The cure, of course, is worse than the disease, for the sick woman's mental condition deteriorates rapidly. 'I think sometimes that if I were only well enough to write a little it would relieve the press of ideas and rest me,' she remarks, but literally confined in a room she thinks is a one-time nursery because it has 'rings and things' in the walls, she is literally locked away from creativity. The 'rings and things,' although reminiscent of children's gymnastic equipment, are really the paraphernalia of confinement, like the gate at the head of the stairs, instruments that definitively indicate her imprisonment. Even more tormenting, however, is the room's wallpaper: a sulphurous yellow paper, torn off in spots, and patterned with 'lame uncertain curves' that 'plunge off at outrageous angles' and 'destroy themselves in unheard of contradictions.' Ancient, smoldering, 'unclean' as the oppressive structures of the society in which she finds herself, this paper surrounds the narrator like an inexplicable text, censorious and overwhelming as her physician husband, haunting as the 'hereditary estate' in which she is trying to survive. Inevitably she studies its suicidal implications – and inevitably, because of her 'imaginative power and habit of story-making,' she revises it, projecting her own passion for escape into its otherwise incomprehensible hieroglyphics. 'This wall-paper,' she decides, at a key point in her story,

> has a kind of sub-pattern in a different shade, a particularly irritating one, for you can only see it in certain lights, and not clearly then.
> But in the places where it isn't faded and where the sun is just so – I can see a strange, provoking, formless sort of figure, that seems to skulk about behind that silly and conspicuous front design. (p 18)

As time passes, this figure concealed behind what corresponds (in terms of what we have been discussing) to the facade of the patriarchal text becomes clearer and clearer. By moonlight the pattern of the wallpaper 'becomes bars! The outside pattern I mean, and the woman behind it is as plain as can be.' And eventually, as the narrator sinks more deeply into what the world calls madness, the terrifying implications of both the paper and the figure imprisoned behind the paper begin to permeate – that is, to *haunt* – the rented ancestral mansion in which she and her husband are immured. The 'yellow smell' of the paper 'creeps all over the house,' drenching every room in its subtle aroma of decay. And the woman creeps too – through the house, in the house, and out of the house, in the garden and 'on that long road under the trees.' Sometimes, indeed, the narrator confesses, 'I think there are a great many women' both behind the paper and creeping in the garden, and sometimes only one, and she crawls around fast, and her crawling shakes [the paper] all over ... And she is all the time trying to climb through. But nobody could climb through that pattern – it strangles so; I think that is why it has so many heads. (p 30)

Eventually it becomes obvious to both reader and narrator that the figure creeping through and behind the wallpaper is both the narrator and the narrator's double. By the end of the story, moreover, the narrator has enabled this double to escape from her textual/architectural confinement: 'I pulled and she shook, I shook and she pulled, and before morning we had peeled off yards of that paper.' Is the message of the tale's conclusion mere madness? Certainly the righteous Doctor John – whose name links him to the anti-hero of Charlotte Brontë's *Villette* – has been temporarily defeated, or at least momentarily stunned. 'Now why should that man have fainted?' the narrator ironically asks as she creeps around her attic. But John's unmasculine swoon of surprise is the least of the triumphs Gilman imagines for her madwoman. More significant are the madwoman's own imaginings and creations, mirages of health and freedom with which her author endows her like a fairy godmother showering gold on a sleeping heroine. The woman from behind the wallpaper creeps away, for instance, creeps fast and far on the long road, in broad daylight. 'I have watched her sometimes away off in the open country,' says the narrator, 'creeping as fast as a cloud shadow in a high wind.'

Indistinct and yet rapid, barely perceptible but inexorable, the progress of that cloud shadow is not unlike the progress of nineteenth-century literary women out of the texts defined by patriarchal poetics into the open spaces of their own authority. That such an escape from the numb world behind the patterned walls of the text was a flight from disease into health was quite clear to Gilman herself. When *The Yellow Wallpaper* was published she sent it to Weir Mitchell, whose strictures had kept her from attempting the pen during her own breakdown, thereby aggravating her illness, and she was delighted to learn, years later, that 'he had changed his treatment of nervous prostration since reading' her story. 'If that is a fact,' she declared, 'I have not lived in vain.'[4] Because she was a rebellious feminist besides being a medical iconoclast, we can be sure that Gilman did not think of this triumph of hers in narrowly therapeutic terms. Because she knew, with Emily Dickinson, that 'Infection in the sentence breeds,' she knew that the cure for female despair must be spiritual as well as physical, aesthetic as well as social. What *The Yellow Wallpaper* shows she knew, too, is that even when a supposedly 'mad' woman has been sentenced to imprisonment in the 'infected' house of her own body, she may discover that, as Sylvia Plath was to put it seventy years later, she has 'a self to recover, a queen.'[5]   (... p 92)

Notes

1 Gaston Bachelard, *The Poetics of Space*, trans Maria Jolas, Beacon (Boston), 1970, p xxxii.

2 Barbara Charlesworth Gelpi and Albert Gelpi (eds), *Adrienne Rich's Poetry*, Norton (New York), 1975, p 12: 'A thinking woman sleeps with monsters. The beak that grips her, she becomes' ('Snapshots of a Daughter-in-Law', #3).

3 Charlotte Perkins Gilman, *The Yellow Wallpaper*, The Feminist Press (Old Westbury), 1973. All references in the text will be to page numbers in this edition.

4 Charlotte Perkins Gilman, *The Living of Charlotte Perkins Gilman: An Autobiography*, Harper and Row (New York), 1975, p 121.

5 Sylvia Plath, 'Stings', *Ariel*, Harper and Row (New York), 1966, p 62.

Sandra M Gilbert and Susan Gubar, *The Madwoman in the Attic: The Woman Writer and the Nineteenth-Century Literary Imagination*, Yale University Press (New Haven and London), 1984.
©1979 Yale University ©1984 Sandra M Gilbert and Susan Gubar. Reprinted by permission of Yale University Press.
(Excerpt pp 87–92)

Woman's Domestic Body

Beverly Gordon

gender • 1996

late 20th century space

Looking at women's history through a material culture lens, Beverly Gordon investigates both physical and psychological associations between a woman's body and domestic interiors in the industrial age. This gendered reading of women's roles, home, fashion and decorative arts, discusses structural metaphoric relations between house and body and the impact of female character on a room. Home and body are shown to be inscribed upon each other so that space becomes an extension of the female inhabitant and an embodiment of home.

In her 1879 guide entitled *The Complete Home*, Julia McNair Wright told the story of a sickly, disabled girl named Margaret. As a form of therapy, the wise Aunt Sophronia had given her tasks related to fixing up the house, such as making wall pockets for display and decorating a room with plants. On surveying the results of her handiwork, Margaret 'lean[ed] back with a sigh of satisfaction,' saying, 'Don't I look nice! ... Why I feel almost well.'[1] Margaret identified completely with the room she had worked on – she literally became one with it. By 'fixing' her house, she had fixed herself.

Wright's moralistic story epitomizes the conceptual conflation between women's bodies and domestic interiors that was prevalent in the industrial age. Body and interior space were often seen and treated as if they were the same thing, so much so that they became almost interchangeable; symbolically, one could stand for the other. The following essay explores this conceptual overlay. It examines how the identification between self and interior became particularly linked with women and how far-reaching and pervasive it was. While the phenomenon was international in scope – it certainly was associated with bourgeois gender roles in Europe as well as North America – this discussion focuses for the sake of space primarily on American sources and images. Its close look at the interpenetration of the house and body brings together information and ideas that are typically treated separately, offering new insights about gender and women's roles and about the treatment of the house, fashion, and the decorative arts. It proposes a new theoretical framework from which to look at and understand their intersecting histories.

Vestiges of this conflationary metaphoric relationship remain today. Women are still primarily identified in our culture with the arrangement and outfitting of both the interior and the body. Tellingly, the 'women's pages' of daily newspapers, now typically packaged as the 'living' section, remain predominantly focused on home and fashion. Fashion itself is generally thought of almost exclusively in relation to women's clothes. Fashion shows and magazines draw predominantly female audiences, and, even in the academy, the study of fashion or dress is largely still a woman's endeavor. A similar situation prevails in relation to interiors. While males dominate the architectural profession and many men are interested in the exterior shell of the house, the domain still shifts to women once the attention is focused on the inside. The interior design profession is overwhelmingly female, and women form the primary audience for exhibits, advice literature, and even discussion of interior decoration. Sociological studies also indicate that the home is still primarily perceived as a female place, and we maintain practices that acknowledge this as our cultural norm. When newly married couples register for silverware, for example, it is the wives' initials that are typically imprinted, even though the silver is jointly owned.[2]

The modern gender conventions, however, pale in comparison with the conceptual conflation I am exploring. Roughly between the middle of the nineteenth and the middle of the twentieth centuries, and most strongly between about 1875 and 1925, the connection between women and their houses in Western middle-class culture was so strong that it helped shape the perception of both. In this period it seemed that a simile – women and interiors were like one another – was transformed into a synonym. The woman was seen as the embodiment of the home, and in turn the home was seen as an extension other – an extension of both her corporeal and spiritual self. The conflation functioned as what George Lakoff and Mark Johnson call a structural, or conventional metaphor, that is, a device for understanding or even experiencing one kind of thing as another. Such metaphors are not just a matter of language, Lakoff and Johnson maintain, but are part of our conceptual systems and thought processes. Metaphors are thus fully 'real,' because they help us define, make sense of, and even create reality. This structural metaphoric relationship between house and body was expressed in popular language and imagery throughout the industrial age and can be traced in everything from fiction to advice literature. As Harriet Beecher Stowe put it in her novel, *We and Our Neighbors* (1875), a married woman's character was made manifest in her home: '[Her] self begins to melt away into something higher … The *home* becomes [her] center and to her home passes the charm that once was thrown around her person … Her home is the new impersonation of herself.' *Impersonation* is a significant word in this context: the home did not just represent the woman, but became her, almost like another body. It was what the 'skilled corps of authorities' who contributed to the book *How to Make a Home Happy: A Housekeeper's Hand Book* (1884) termed 'part and parcel of one great whole.' They viewed the relationship of women and rooms as reciprocal: 'It is not we that make our surroundings merely, but our surroundings in turn make us … The very act of fashioning beautiful forms forms us into beautiful fashion.'[3]

Many writers emphasized the impact of female character on a room; over time, the space became more and more an extension of her. 'Have we not often remarked of a house or a room that it looks "just like her,"' asked Charles Warner in his 1911 treatise, *Home Decoration*, which proudly described a progressive public school project where principles of design were taught through such decoration. The boys built an actual house, while the girls designed its interior. The remark was included in a chapter directed to girls that focused specifically on dress and house decoration. Similar sentiments were expressed by others. Popular writer Helen Hunt Jackson remarked that rooms, like faces, have their own expressions, or 'countenances.' 'At the end of a few years of [living in a room] it is sure to be a pretty good reflection of our own,' she told her readers in *Making Home Life Attractive*.[4]

However, the reverse could also be true: a woman could reflect and even become a part of an interior. Edith Wharton frequently described fictional female characters who came to share physical traits with their houses, or who changed themselves to suit those houses more perfectly. Rooms took 'possession' of these women; a house had an 'almost human power to command.' Once the heroines had been so taken over by those spaces, Wharton implied, leaving them would be 'tantamount to self-annihilation.'[5]

In either case, women had to fit their houses. In 1878 Austrian museum director Jacob Von Falke insisted in *Art in the House* that a lady must be in harmony with her surroundings – 'she should be … the noblest ornament of her ornamented dwelling.' The idea was echoed more than forty years later by advice-giver Emily Burbank, who wrote on both costume and interiors. In *Woman as Decoration* (1920) she stressed that 'woman was herself an important factor in the decorating scheme of any setting,' so much a part of the room, in other words, that she was an actual piece of it.[6]

Turn-of-the-century paintings illustrating women in interiors routinely reflected this formulation. In Childe Hassam's 1918 painting, 'Tanagra,' for example, the woman literally blends into and almost becomes a part of the décor. The table so closely mirrors her dress that it functions as an extension of it, as does the Japanese screen behind her. The woman is shown among flowering plants – in contrast to the cityscape glimpsed out the window, she represents naturalness and fecundity – but like her, the plants are tamed, as they are cut or confined to a clay pot. The outside light shines on the woman, but she remains in the interior, completing it with her very presence (significantly, she glances at another female body). Other paintings played on many of the same ideas. Female figures matching and even merging into surrounding draperies were seen as early as the middle of the century in America – a well-known example is James Abbott McNeill Whistler's

'The White Girl' – but the convention is particularly associated with a group of impressionists that called itself 'Ten American Painters.' Playing on imagery from seventeenth-century Dutch masters such as Vermeer who also focused on women in interiors, Hassam and his colleagues often portrayed women sitting by windows or in front of mirrors, engaged in contemplative, domestic activities such as holding flowers, sewing, or reading. The women all appeared part of their surroundings.[7]

How did this conflation between animate woman and inanimate room come about, and why was it so strong in the decades surrounding the turn of the twentieth century? It was largely an outgrowth of women's ideal role in the culture that was created by industrial capitalism. An almost obsessive preoccupation with proper appearance was characteristic of the nineteenth century, a time of rapid and far-reaching social change fostered by unbridled industrialization and urbanization. Although upward social mobility was far from guaranteed, its success was apparently common enough by the middle of the century to support the popular belief that status was no longer ascribed as much as achieved. In a world of urban strangers, appearance became ever-more important as the outward sign of such achievement. This in itself was not new; wealthy individuals since the Renaissance had been very concerned with the impression created by what they wore. However, this preoccupation was now extended to whole new categories of people, comprising the majority of the population. Individuals on nearly every step of the social ladder had to be vigilantly concerned with and conscious of their presentation of self. Dress – the decoration of the body – and interior furnishings – the decoration of the home – together formed what in more contemporary terms has been called the *front* that projected the desired image to the world at large.[8]

Middle- and upper-class women bore the greatest burden of the necessary impression management in the nineteenth century. Men's ability to indicate their social status on their bodies was now considerably limited because their dress had became severely conscribed. This was related to changing economic and social patterns. Once men had moved their primary economic activities out of the home into an outside workplace, their clothing became highly codified; the dark and sober three-piece suit worn by every man who did not have to do physical labor has in fact been called the 'uniform of industrial capitalism.' The severe suit completely replaced the lavish clothing that had been worn by prosperous merchants and professional men before the French Revolution; lace, ruffles, embroidered waistcoats, tight-fitting silk breeches, and powdered wigs had all come to be associated with the excesses and irrationalities of the aristocracy and were no longer considered 'manly.' Women had no such restriction about advertising wealth and status; on the contrary, by their very economic idleness and concomitant elaborate dress, they now demonstrated the prosperity that the men they were associated with had achieved. Women thus became the primary consumers of fashion by the mid-nineteenth century, and keeping up with changing silhouettes and developments in woven fabric, lace, and

Childe Hassam, *Tanagra (The Builders, New York)*. Courtesy of Smithsonian American Art Museum, Gift of John Gellatly.

embroidery became an almost exclusively female concern. Men's relationship with fashion became primarily a matter of production. The first large-scale fashion business, in fact, was opened in Paris by designer/entrepreneur Charles Frederick Worth in 1858. Interestingly, given the fact that the product was women's dress and the clientele was female, the business was known as the '*House* of Worth' (author's emphasis).[9]

A similar situation developed with regard to domestic interiors. A prosperous and fashionable dwelling had long been important, as a social facade, but as middle-class men's sphere of economic activity moved almost completely out of the home, men typically became less and less directly involved with the appearance of the house itself. Again by about midcentury, the functioning and decoration of the house thus became the women's responsibility as well.[10] It is perhaps not surprising that body and dwelling came to be viewed together. Both bore the name, literally and legally, of the man who 'owned' them, and both were adorned to testify to his success.   (... p 285)

Notes

1   Julia McNair Wright, *The Complete Home: An Encyclopaedia of Domestic Life and Affairs*, JC McCurdy (Philadelphia), 1879, pp 167–8.

2   *Dress* is defined in the field as the total outward appearance of the body, including elements such as hairstyle, demeanor, and accessories. See Mary Ellen Roach and Kathleen Ellen Musa, *New Perspectives on the History of Western Dress: A Handbook*, NutriGuides (New York), 1980, p 11. An overwhelming majority of students in professional organizations related to costume and fashion are women, as are the students in university classes devoted to the subject. My own classes in this area draw only about 5 percent men. On interiors, see Jerome Togndi, 'The Flight from Domestic Space: Men's Roles in the Household', *The Family Coordinator*, vol 28 no 4, October 1979, pp 599–607; Jerome Togndi and John Ofrias, 'Women's and Men's Response toward the Home in Heterosexual and Same Sex Households: A Case Study', AD Seidel and S Danford (eds), *Environmental Design: Theory, Research, and Application*, EDRA (Washington, DC), 1979; Joan Kron, *Home Psych: Social-Psychology of Home and Decoration*, Clarkson Porter (New York), 1983, esp p 123. It is true that there are noted male designers in both fashion and interiors, but this in no way obviates the primary gender identification because the designers are engaged with these endeavors as businessmen. Furthermore, the clientele in both arenas remains female.

3   George Lakoff and Mark Johnson, *Metaphors We Live By*, University of Chicago Press (Chicago), 1980, pp 6, 147, 153. Stowe cited in Katherine C Grier, *Culture and Comfort: People, Parlors, and Upholstery, 1850–1930*, Strong Museum (Rochester, NY), 1988, p 6. *How to Make a Home Happy: A Housekeeper's Hand Book*, John Lovel (New York), 1884, p 117.

4   Charles Franklin Warner, *Home Decoration*, Doubleday Page for the Children's Library of Work and Play (Garden City, NY), 1911, p 122; Helen Hunt Jackson, *Making Home Life Attractive* [1879], reprint PF Collier and Son (New York), 1902, pp 47, 52–3. Jackson wrote novels, poetry, and nonfiction and was author of the much-reprinted novel *Ramona: A Story*, Roberts Brothers (Boston), 1884.

5   Susan Fehrenbacher Koprince, 'The Fictional Houses of Edith Wharton', PhD diss, University of Illinois, Champaign-Urbana, 1981, pp 50–2, 99, 119.

6   Jacob Von Falke, *Art in the House: Historical, Critical, and Aesthetic Studies on the Decorating and Furnishing of the Dwelling*, trans and with notes by Charles C Perkins, L Prang (Boston), 1878, p 333; Emily Burbank, *Woman as Decoration*, Dodd, Mead (New York), 1920, p xi.

7   Other painters and representative works include: Robert Reid, *The Violet Kimono* (1910) and *The Miniature* (1913); Edmund C Tarbell, *Girl Crocheting* (1904), *Three Girls Reading* (1907) and

Across the Room (ca. 1899); Joseph De Camp, *The Seamstress* (1916) and *Roses* (1909–10); and Thomas Wilmer Dewing, *The Necklace* (1907). Hassam's 1894 painting *The Room of Flowers*, which depicts Celia Laighton Thaxter in her summer house, is another excellent example of this phenomenon. Mrs Thaxter is so deeply buried in the interior that it is difficult to see her at all. See also Ulrich W Hiesinger, *Impressionism in America: The Ten American Painters*, Prestel-Verlag (Munich), 1991; Theodore E Stebbins, Jr, Carol Troyen, and Trevor J Fairbrother, *A New World: Master-pieces of American Painting, 1760–1910*, Museum of Fine Arts (Boston), 1983, esp pp 161, 321–22.

8 See especially Grier, *Culture and Comfort*; Kenneth Ames, *Death in the Dining Room and Other Tales of Victorian Culture*, Temple University Press (Philadelphia), 1992; Karen Lee Halttunen, *Confidence Men and Painted Women: The Problem of Hypocrisy in Sentimental America, 1830–1870*, Yale University Press (New Haven), 1982; John F Kasson, *Rudeness and Civility: Manners in Nineteenth-Century Urban America*, Hill and Wang (New York), 1990; Beverly Gordon, 'Meanings in Mid Nineteenth-Century Dress: Images from New England Women's Writings', *Clothing and Textiles Research Journal*, vol 10 no 3, Spring 1992, p 44–53; Simon J Bronner (ed), *Consuming Visions: Accumulation and Display of Goods in America, 1880–1920*, WW Norton for the Henry Francis du Pont Winterthur Museum (New York), 1989. The term front comes from the dramaturgical model of human interaction developed in Erving Goffman, *The Presentation of Self in Everyday Life*, Doubleday (Garden City, NY), 1959, pp 1, 36, 245. Goffman's model holds that individuals 'perform' 'on stage', are part of an audience 'offstage,', or operate 'backstage' or 'behind the scenes'. More recent theorists discuss much the same idea under the rubric of role theory; see Bruce Biddle, *Role Theory: Expectations, Identities, and Behaviors*, Academic Press (New York), 1979.

9 Jo Paoletti, 'Ridicule and Role Models as Factors in American Men's Fashion Change, 1880–1910', *Costume*, vol 19, 1985, p 132; Valerie Steele, 'Appearance and Identity', Claudia Brush Kidwell and Valerie Steele (eds), *Men and Women: Dressing the Part*, Smithsonian Institution Press (Washington, DC), 1989, p 16; Diana De Marly, *Worth: The Father of Haute Couture*, Elm Tree Books (London), 1980.

10 Witold Rybczynski, *Home: A Short History of an Idea*, Viking Press (New York), 1986, pp 70–1; Gail Caskey Winkler and Roger W Moss, *Victorian Interior Decoration: American Interiors, 1830–1900*, Henry Holt (New York), 1986, p 63; Clifford Edward Clark, Jr, *The American Family Home, 1800–1960*, University of North Carolina Press (Chapel Hill), 1986, p 104.

Beverly Gordon, 'Woman's Domestic Body: The Conceptual Conflation of Women and Interiors in the Industrial Age', *Winterthur Portfolio*, vol 31 no 4, 1996, pp 281–301.
(Excerpt pp 281–5)

Notes on Digital Nesting: A Poetics of Evolutionary Form

Mark Goulthorpe

philosophical • 2002
20th century space

Architect and academic Mark Goulthorpe discusses the poetic reverie of form generated by inner logic, and that emanating from digital scientific-rationale. Central to this discussion of the poetics of evolutionary form is Gaston Bachelard's concern for effect, and John Frazer's disinterest in the result. In the examples given he suggests both methods generate creative 'images' from internal and poetic imagination rather than through fabrication of an idealised external form. The implication for the interior when considered as an 'impulsion,' a force of egress trapped in form, is a malleable relationship between self and environment in which 'forms of absence' indicate the function of inhabitation. Critically, Goulthorpe projects a dream of imagination enhanced and actualised by digital generation that uncovers the need to address an 'image' adequate for inhabitation of a displaced spatial sense.

It seems to me that the power of certain projects by Lynn, Nox, Novac, etc (who I cite as examples of architects who develop their architecture through a phenomenologically rich creative discourse) may well lie in their capacity as 'images' rather than in their 'prudence' as actualisable architectural works, such images then seemingly legitimised by the *Poetics*. What would remain is for the onset of such 'images' to be accounted for, the thinking of the digital itself, and it is here that we might expect a quite marked shift in creative manner if we are attentive to the impact of digital technologies. Or rather, it remains to be seen how digital production, steeped in discourses of scientific rationalism of the type that Bachelard dismissed as inadequate for a poetics to emerge, yet which proffers entirely new genres of creative possibility, might offer sufficient scope for a genuine *cultural morphogenesis*.

Doubtless such an inquiry is an interminable and immense one, since it concerns the patterns of creativity latent in digital production, yet I share Bachelard's concern to interrogate the very manner of creative imagining. Here I restrict my interest to examination of a single text, John Frazer's *An Evolutionary Architecture*, through consideration of Bachelard's phenomenological 'opening.' Frazer's work is perhaps the preordinate expression of an emergent 'digital' discourse, and a pioneering attempt at the definition of a new architectural language as well as new patterns of creativity, which justifies the juxtaposition of two such apparently heterogeneous texts (both are accounts of evolving patterns of cultural imagination).

Yet Frazer's book is nakedly scientific-rational in its prescriptive manner, which Bachelard, attentive to the birthing of poetic imagination, repeatedly suggests as being inappropriate to *cultural* 'evolution.' Yet given the newness of the field, Frazer's text is not only one of the only ones that we have to consider, but seemingly exceeds its own scientificity in offering many points of departure for drifts into a *Bachelardian daydreaming*. Bachelard's reverie on *Shells* perhaps provides a counterpoint, where his interest 'to experience the image of the function of inhabiting' may be contrasted with the simple *will to shell-form*, which he derides. For Bachelard, the mesmeric geometries of shells, their outer appearance, actually defeat the imagination: 'The created object itself is highly intelligible; it is the formation, not the form, that remains mysterious.'[1] The essential force of the shell being that it is exuded from within, the secretion of an organism; it is not fabricated *from without* as an idealised form. The shell is left in the air *blindly* as the trace of a convulsive absence, the smooth and lustrous internal carapace then exfoliating in its depth of exposure to the air, a temporal crustation.

Such inversion of ideological tendency, an expansive mental *shell-emptiness*, Bachelard captures deliciously: 'The mollusc's motto would be: one must live to build one's house, and not build one's house to live in!'[2] Such inversion would seem to be a recipe for a *genetic architecture*, on condition that its secretions are unselfconscious and 'felicitous,' obeying an internal law. This describes the generative process outlined by Frazer in *An Evolutionary Architecture*, which becomes one of open-ended formulaic experimentation, Frazer deploying genetic algorithms to generate all manner of 'architectural' forms.[3]

However, Bachelard then dwells on the voluptuous inscrutability of the exposed inner shell which, born of an impalpable inner logic, provokes an imaginary dementia. Faced with the shell's indifferent beauty, poetic imagination involuntarily conjures endless series of grotesques, emergent forms that slide expansively in/out of the curvaceous yet inexpressive void. The shell seems to demand, that is, an appreciation of an *impulsion, a force of egress*, which is somehow trapped in the geology of the form, a latent trauma.[4] I have the sense, if only as a subtle shiver in Bachelard's phenomenological lyricism, that the *process of formation* is left as a mental material residue that then bends imagination to its logic; which would be the fully cultural wager, the *poetic*, of such improbable forms. Frazer's *grotesques*, by contrast, provoke no such traumatic impulsion, lacking a cultural qualification other than their technical feasibility. Certainly Frazer suggests that such genesis requires a 'natural selection,' but never offers sufficient parameters or process of selection, which Bachelard's processual sensibility would doubtless require to be fully developed, as a *poetics of evolutionary form*.

Yet if the empty shell conjures grotesques, by virtue of such implosion of determinism, the *Poetics* seems to carry an uncanny presentiment that as the shell-form becomes technically feasible such grotesqueness will not be generated by an impelled imagination, but simply as an abridged evolution, never attaining the *force of image*.[5] And it is here that an *evolutionary architecture*, if it is to crystallise a new 'function of inhabiting,' needs to cup its ear to the whispering shell, attaining in its creative imagining a felicity that separates it from an aborted genetic process, and the means of deploying its algorithmic and parametric (digital) propensity to material *effect*.

We might note, wryly, the dissimulating geometry of the Frazer Spiral, which is an optikinetic figure that impels a vortex-effect simply through the use of non-concentric circles. The figure is a well-known trompe l'oeil, exceeding the geometric closure of such simplistic generic form through its vertiginous disturbance of optic sense, stimulating an almost haptic mental experience. *Evolutionary architecture* might be seen to be deploying simplistic 'geometric' figures to similarly mesmeric effect, but nonetheless exhibiting a keen awareness that it is the *processual* capacity of a digital medium that is its most compelling attribute. And evidently in its prescription of an open-ended 'evolutionary' process it dreams of becoming *unabridged* in the potential richness of genetic algorithmic process.[6]

Yet if Frazer speaks as if from within the clam, dissimulating its genetic (processual) secrets, he nonetheless seems to spit out the pearl of subjectivity, dispersing the creative impulse throughout the body of the new medium, creativity and not simply receptivity becoming transsubjective. It is as if the phenomenological belief in substance (whether as word, act or gesture), in the essential *presence* of imaginative impulse, suddenly dissolves into a swirl of sedimentary digits. Henceforth cultural imagination sifts this informatic sea, bereft of a belief in any point of ultimate legitimacy.[7] Herein lies the struggle between intellect and sediment, which the ever-descending digital norms are apt to blanket.

Bachelard's chapter on *Nests* seems to similarly articulate forms that were predigitally imaginary but which now merit consideration in their actuality by architects. He muses on the nest as an intricate imprint of the inhabiting body, adjusted continually as a soft cocoon that outlines the aura of movement of the bird's rounded breast. This raises the spectre of an environment adapting to our bodies and continually recalibrated to suit the vulnerability of our relation to the environment. Such forms of 'dry modelling,' merging camouflage and comfort in a density of ambient 'stuff,' seem suggestive of an *alloplastic*[8] relation between self and environment, moderated by an endlessly redefined digital matrix. The empty nest, like the shell, carries an *unknowing impulsion, a trauma*, as if an interminable and complex three-dimensional weaving had been interrupted. Such *forms of absence*, as images of the function of habitation, offer a *cultural* correlative to the temporal generative processes of *evolutionary architecture*, outlined by Frazer in essentially rational terms.

Evolutionary architecture claims inspiration from natural processes (in fact from scientific-rational *models* of evolutionary process) by way of exploring the creative possibilities offered by a rapidly developing digital technology. It redeploys scientific models and patterns by considering digital systems as analogous to genetic ones, taking essentially analytical tools as opportunities for speculative creative endeavour. Bachelard, concerned as a philosopher of scientific rationalism to account for the *actual* evolution of creative process, is evidently unconvinced that any such analogy is adequate for the attainment of a 'poetic' image, highlighting the need for more profound forms of cultural imagining that his phenomenological reverie sets out to explore. In *The Poetics of Space* he outlines an expansive discourse that interrogates all manner of spatial conditions, concrete and imaginary, which he finds at work 'felicitously' in a wide range of poetic works. In this he also insists on accounting for the *effect* of the work, which is in marked contrast to Frazer's apparent disinterest in the result of an essentially automatic *praxis*.

However, Bachelard would be the first to dismiss 'intentionality' as offering any guide to cultural value, and would doubtless be intrigued by such 'unintentioned' and speculative technological experimentation. My interest in rereading Bachelard's 'natural' spatialities (the shell and the nest) then being to offer another reading on the general impulsion of *evolutionary architecture*, but from the perspective of a *discourse of bodily desire* (that of the *Poetics*). This is to neither legitimate nor denigrate Frazer's work, since although I find no 'image' in the book that is adequate to Bachelard's appellation, I nonetheless recognise the pertinence of such research and the inevitability of such 'creative' processes in a digital economy. Much rather, recognising less technically proficient but more poetically charged works emerging in Frazer's wake (some of which I have mentioned), I am eager to implicate the felicity of Bachelard's thought into an emergent digital *praxis*.   (... p 24)

Notes

1   Gaston Bachelard, 'Shells', *The Poetics of Space*, trans Marie Jolas, Beacon Press (Boston, MA), 1969, p 106.

2   Bachelard, 'Shells', *Poetics of Space*, p 106.

3   See, for instance, the section on 'Evolutionary Techniques' in John Frazer, *An Evolutionary Architecture*, Architectural Association (London), 1995, Section Two, p 68.

4   Following Henri Bergson, we might usefully separate *geological* from *geometric* form, where the geological manifests a temporal dimension, as if trapping time in its very materiality, sensed as such.

5   Bachelard's remark is starkly simple: 'In order to achieve grotesqueness, it suffices to abridge an evolution.' Bachelard, 'Shells', *Poetics of Space*, pp 108–9.

6   Consider comments such as 'The genetic code of the selected models is then used to breed further

populations in a cyclical manner ...' Frazer, 'Evolutionary Techniques', *Evolutionary Architecture*, Section Two, p 68, or 'We are inclined to think that this final transformation should be process-driven, and that one should code not the form but rather precise instructions for the formative process.' Frazer, 'Transforming the Output', *Evolutionary Architecture*, Section Two, p 69.

7   '"Imaginative use" in our case means using the computer – like the genie in the bottle – to compress evolutionary space and time so that complexity and emergent form are able to develop. The computers of our imagination are also a source of inspiration – an electronic muse.' Frazer, *Evolutionary Architecture*, Introduction, p 18.

8   Alloplastic is a term developed by Sandor Ferenczi and discussed at length in my essay dECOi Aegis Hyposurface: 'From Autoplastic to Alloplastic Space', 'Hypersurface Architecture II', *Architectural Design*, vol 69 no 9–10, 1999, pp 60–5. The terms articulate the difference between a rigid and static relationship between the environment and the self, an autoplastic rigidity, and a malleable and reciprocal alloplastic deformability.

Mark Goulthorpe, 'Notes on Digital Nesting: A Poetics of Evolutionary Form', *Architectural Design*, vol 72 no 2, 2002, pp 18–25.
(Excerpt pp 20–4)

Faith and Virtuality: A Brief History of Virtual Reality

Christian Groothuizen

technological light 2001

21st century

In this text, artist and designer Christian Groothuizen ignores the dualist divide between virtuality and actuality to position spatial experience within the context of affect and effect, sensation and imagination. In his emphasis on the performative aspect of materials in space over their visual surface depiction, Groothuizen places virtuality within the bounds of an immersive environment, dispelling any assumption that it is artificial, unrelated to lived space or dependent on computer technology to exist. Prompted by Paul Virilio's account of light occurring inside Chartres cathedral, he suggests the experience of special effects and lighting is a virtual experience critical to a new understanding of virtual space.

> Within a culture that is dominated by disembodied forms of knowledge, it becomes tempting to escape into mental fantasies. Hence virtual space becomes as much a refuge, into which we withdraw, as a space of freedom and exploration.[1]

The dualistic nature of modern Western culture's mindset suggests that conditions such as 'truth' and 'illusion,' 'virtual' and 'actual' are polarised in order to represent the fact that there can be no perceived common ground.[2] However, in terms of human experience, specifically feelings and sensations, we can see how the line between these terms becomes blurred. According to Damien Keown, 'There is no difference between reality and virtual reality. What one sees, hears and feels is identical in either case.'[3] In short, one does not see with the eyes but with the brain, and it is the way in which the brain interprets visual stimuli that is important here. 'We see through the eyes, [Plato] insisted, not with them.'[4] The 'world-as-seen' is constructed by the brain in the same sense as any virtual reality; in other words, virtual space is the only reality. In fact, 'virtual space' exists and has existed within what would commonly be considered the 'actual space' that we inhabit – that is, Euclidean space, topological space, Cartesian space and Newtonian space.

> The Gothic cathedral is a machine for bringing us to our knees.[5]
> All that is solid melts into information. All that is solid melts into hyperspace.[6]

The proposition put forward by Paul Virilio that 'Chartres cathedral is really a virtual work … a phenomenon of special effects and lighting'[7] calls for some investigation. The cathedral, in terms of a virtuality, exists as a virtual space of light and shade. This supposes that in response to the medieval obsession with divine light there was an effort to dematerialise the physical, structural presence of the cathedral. This was an attempt to produce a space that was 'literally divine, as immaterial and as luminous as possible,'[8] a virtual, light-filled space, and that 'light's primary role was performative … the medium was the message.'[9] The soaring, massive ranks of flying buttresses, so impressive from the exterior, become merely supporting characters from within. The literal bulk of the cathedral melts away, leaving the viewer within a theatre of light and shade. This bulk is dissolved away into tones of shade in order to give the light of the coloured glass, and the aureolic beams that come through them, their stage.

This perception of light should be interpreted in the context of the late medieval period in which these spaces were first built. At this time, there was a fascination with the metaphysical implications of light, which was commonly regarded as 'divine lux, rather than perceived lumen,'[10] and 'Scholastic metaphysics classified light as a substance, an "embodied spirit," which distributes divinity to all God's creation …'[11] It was therefore concluded, by St Bonaventure, that God was present in all things and, most notably, in objects that shone or allowed light to pass through them. There can be little doubt that the effect of vast 'backlit screens' of stained glass on the people of the Middle Ages who 'conceived of God in terms of light, and regarded it as the original metaphor for spiritual realities'[12] must have been numinous.

Further proof of the interest in the metaphysical properties of light as it was involved in the construction of cathedrals is evident in several texts, particularly Martin Jay's *Downcast Eyes*, which supports an ocularcentric view of medieval Christianity:

> In addition to the theological and scientific emphasis on sight, medieval religious practice also bore witness to its importance. The visionary tradition – based in part on a theatricalised interpretation of the injunction to imitate God (*imitatioDei*) and in part on the neo-platonic search for the colourless "white ecstasy" of divine illumination.

Jay also lists 'the brilliant light suffusing the great Gothic cathedrals (a light whose metaphysical importance was stressed from Abbot Suger on)' as an example of the medieval Church's knowledge of the 'power of visual stimulation.'[13]

The stained glass at Chartres has been described by both Henry Adams and Maurice Denis.[14] What is most revealing about their descriptions of the glass is that rather than describing the various biblical scenes, as one might expect, they instead speak of the effects of the coloured glass and the quality of light it produces, whereas Martin Pawley and others would label stained glass as 'the poor man's bible,'[15] simply a means of visually depicting a spiritual message for the masses. In the case of Chartres and many other Gothic cathedrals, it is the performative nature of light that most enthrals. The spiritual message is within the qualities of the glass rather than any iconography applied to its surface: 'Divinity radiated more through light as essence than through the images depicted on the windows.'[16]

More specifically, the stained-glass windows of Chartres cathedral have undergone close scrutiny and are described in terms that few other examples of Gothic cathedrals can match. In fact, Denis puts it best when he writes:

> In these windows, surely, it is neither the subject – which one sees only after a long look – nor the resemblance of the figures or objects represented that are deeply moving. It is the splendour of the windows that at first charms us like divine music: it is the play of colours, of light, in admirable proportions, that first incites us to prostrate ourselves.[17]

Henry Adams in his essay points out that the stained-glass artist had little interest in portraying scenes in any realistic sense.[18] In fact, it was the overall effect of colour and light when seen from a distance that the artist was attempting to achieve. Adams explains that individual details were often at the mercy of the 'big picture' and gives as examples the colour treatment of small figures amongst the stained glass; scenes that would often have a 'green camel or a pink lion [that] looked like a dog.'[19] It is this observation that encourages the view that Gothic stained glass was used for theatrical effect and not one of simple storytelling. Adams goes on to say that; 'The glass window was to him (the glass artist) a whole – a mass – and its details were his amusement ... they are above the level of all known art, in religious form; they are inspired; they are divine!'[20] An intriguing fact about the manufacture of the stained glass at Chartres is that the artisans who made the glass were inexperienced and produced overly colourful stock, which is what sets the experience of Chartres apart from other cathedral spaces, and would likely be a determining factor in Paul Virilio's statement that, 'it is a phenomenon of special effects and lighting.'[21] This concept of the experience of special effects and lighting as a virtual experience is fundamental to a new understanding of virtual space.

> The museum is the colossal mirror in which man finally contemplates himself in every aspect.'[22]

The architect Sir John Soane explored spatial ideas and ways of creating a spatial narrative through the use of 'spectacular effects and theatrical devices.'[23] He set about controlling the use and effect of natural and artificial light within his own dwelling, in order to elicit an emotional response from those who visited, thus creating a 'three-dimensional, inhabitable Spectacle,' an immersive environment created from special lighting effects.[24]

The Soane house is, like the cathedral, both a space of information and a space of light and shade. In a similar fashion to that used in the cathedral, Soane employed coloured glass in order to create an other-worldly and mysterious experience of the interior space of the house. He was interested in incorporating concepts such as the 'Picturesque' and the 'Gothic,' ideas prevalent at the time, and including them in his architecture and interior treatments. Towards this end, the predominant shade of glass is of a yellow hue that 'links itself to the poetic interest in twilight as the time of day most closely related to imagination and dream.'[25] This treatment is also in evidence in the Dulwich mausoleum (1811), where daylight is filtered through a lantern above the sarcophagi. Despite its diminutive size, the setting and the lighting create an effect as awesome as any cathedral. 'Soane was extremely sensitive to the essential role of light in creating a numinous architectural setting.'[26]

Soane collected objects of architectural interest on his travels, his 'grand tour,' and these can be found displayed throughout the house. It is, however, how these objects are displayed, and their setting, that is of most value to this study. The Soane Museum is an immersion space of condensed history, the 'collection' from Soane's travels being a 'mini grand tour' that compresses time both historically and experientially. It should be noted that the fragments of architectural salvage that make up part of the collection are in fact plaster copies of the originals, thus adding an extra layer of virtuality to the space. The convex mirrors found throughout the house in turn compress space and 'in its sheer repetition threatens to exceed its capacity to organise, confounding and confusing … dissolving, the spaces of the house into images.'[27] Mirrors of all types are used throughout the house as a means of illumination, but they also add an extra dimension 'they … provided, or amplified, poetic and picturesque effects of light and shade, expanded the spaces of the house, sometimes even providing the illusion of additional rooms.'[28] The Soane Museum as a whole is a series of 'spectacles;'[29] it is a theatrical space of special lighting effects.[30] This underlines Soane's well-documented interest in Romanticism as pure theatre.

> It is not about light, or a record of it, but it is light. Light is not so much something that reveals, as it is itself the revelation.'[31] 'Is there more to architecture than its reality?'[32] Something that has so far received much less attention, is the possibility of allowing the physical and virtual domains to merge. It is a matter of crossing the analogue and digital worlds of hybrid environments that can no longer be classified as one thing or another.[33]

The experience of an object or space whether actual or virtual is a construction of the brain which forms a conscious, and in some cases subconscious, reading of the object. Max Velmans explains that, 'the phenomenal world constructed by the mind or brain from information detected by the sense organs is, at once, psychological and physical.'[34] It is therefore reasonable to suggest that one's experience of a real-world VR space is likely to differ from that of another, especially if that space is as culturally and politically loaded as a religious or architectural spatial icon. This psychological spatial reading should be seen as an important factor in the understanding and experience of real-world VR.

The spaces that have been discussed in this study are, for the most part, formed around the experience of light within actual space. It is this use of light that, in the right circumstances, has the ability to disorientate the viewer to an extent that the experience cannot always be attributed to a 'measured' if this is at all possible, reading of the space. This is achieved through the manipulation of light by colouring, bending (in the case of reflection) or extraction, where the lack of light or the contrast between areas of light and shade conspire to confuse and disorientate. It is these states that allow for the possibility of being immersed in a real-world illusion to the point that one feels transported beyond the actual; transcending the physical. This is reiterated by Stacey Spiegel who states that, 'the traditional distinction between reality and virtuality disappears when one is in an immersive environment.'[35] This would then seem to confirm that the experience of virtual space within actual space is an achievable 'reality.'

The 'virtualities' within Chartres cathedral and the Soane house do differ in some respects from those of the computer-driven virtualities. Clearly, the latter are representational images resulting from the computational power of the computer. However, ultimately, they are virtual spaces created within the mind, which predominantly rely on the transcendent qualities of light as the medium on which the virtual experience rests. There is a longing and an ability within the human organism to reach such a transcendent state. This is, and has been throughout time, a major human preoccupation, whether through the use of meditation, drugs, art or religious ceremony. However, on the basis of the evidence presented here, it would seem that this transcendent state is often also achievable within the realm of actual space and can be considered to be an experience of virtual space. To appreciate this may necessitate a new understanding of the word 'virtual.'   (... p 55)

Notes

1   Victor Seidler, 'Embodied Knowledge and Virtual Space: Gender, Nature and History,' John Wood (ed), *The Virtual Embodied*, Routledge (London and New York), 1998, p 28.
2   Wood, *Virtual Embodied*, p 5.
3   Damien Keown, 'Embodying Virtue: a Buddhist Perspective on Virtual Reality', Wood, *Virtual Embodied*, p 85.
4   Martin Jay, *Downcast Eyes*, University of California Press (Berkeley, CA), 1993, p 27.

5 Neil Spiller, interview with the author, February 1999.

6 Marcos Novak, 'Next Babylon, Soft Babylon: (trans) Architecture is an Algorithm to Play', *Architectural Design*, vol 68 no 11/12, 1998, p 26.

7 Paul Virilio, 'We May Be Entering an Electronic Gothic Era', *Architectural Design*, vol 68 no 11/12, 1998, p 60.

8 Phil Tabor, 'Striking Home: The Telematic Assault on Identity', Jonathan Hill (ed), *Occupying Architecture: Between the Architect and the User*, Routledge (London and New York), 1998, p 227.

9 Tabor, 'Striking Home', Jonathan Hill, *Occupying Architecture*, p 227.

10 Lesley Lokko, 'The Ability to Provoke', Jonathan Hill, *Occupying Architecture*, p 52.

11 Tabor, 'Striking Home', Jonathan Hill, *Occupying Architecture*, p 226.

12 Lokko, 'The Ability to Provoke', Jonathan Hill, *Occupying Architecture*, p 52.

13 Jay, *Downcast Eyes*, p 39.

14 Maurice Denis, 'The Stained Glass', Robert Branner (ed), *Chartres Cathedral*, Norton (New York), 1969, p 233.

15 Tabor, 'Striking Home', Jonathan Hill, *Occupying Architecture*, p 226.

16 Tabor, 'Striking Home', Jonathan Hill, *Occupying Architecture*, p 227.

17 Denis, 'The Stained Glass', Robert Branner, *Chartres Cathedral*, p 234.

18 Henry Adams, 'The Twelfth-Century Glass', Robert Branner, *Chartres Cathedral*, pp 235–74.

19 Adams, 'Twelfth-Century Glass', Robert Branner, *Chartres Cathedral*, p 243.

20 Adams, 'Twelfth-Century Glass', Robert Branner, *Chartres Cathedral*, p 245.

21 Paul Virilio, 'We May Be Entering An Electronic Gothic Era', *Architectural Design*, vol 68 no 11/12, 1998, p 61.

22 Georges Bataille, *Essays: English Selections*, University of Minnesota Press (Minneapolis), 1985.

23 Helene Furjan, 'The Specular Spectacle of the House of the Collector', *Assemblage*, 34, 1998, pp 56–91.

24 Furjan, 'Specular Spectacle', pp 56–91.

25 Furjan, 'Specular Spectacle', p 79.

26 Brian Lukacher, 'Phantasmagoria and Emanations: Lighting Effects in the Architectural Fantasies of Joseph Michael Gandy', *AA Files*, 4, p 44.

27 Furjan, 'Specular Spectacle', p 60.

28 Furjan, 'Specular Spectacle', p 63.

29 Furjan, 'Specular Spectacle', p 63.

30 Furjan, 'Specular Spectacle', p 63.

31 James Turrell, as cited in Tabor, 'Striking Home', Hill, *Occupying Architecture*, p 228.

32 Jean Baudrillard, 'Truth or Radicality? The Future of Architecture', *Blueprint*, January 1999, p 30.

33 Ole Bouman, as cited in Neil Spiller, 'Split Sites and Smooth Aesthetics' (unpublished text).

34 Max Velmans, 'Physical, Psychological and Virtual Realities', Wood, *Virtual Embodied*, p 56.

35 Stacey Spiegel, 'Emerging Space', *Art and Design*, vol vii, May-June 1996, p 25.

Christian Groothuizen, 'Faith and Virtuality: A Brief History of Virtual Reality', *Architectural Design*, vol 71 no 1, 2001, pp50–5.

Thinking of Gadamer's Floor

Jacques Herzog

Jacques Herzog's text reveals design thinking related to his architectural practice, outlining attitudes towards the existing conditions of a building's constitution. Inspired by Hans-Georg Gadamer's recollections of his parents' waxed parquet floor, Herzog absorbs the reality of the occasion as a potential for a design strategy emphasising materiality informed by gravity. This process of extracting the intrinsic qualities of material and space directs the focus on the floor beyond the merely physical. His discussion of several projects, including the Tate Modern, highlights a process whereby interior renovation is a procedure of rigorous intervention, rather than the application of surface treatments.

A few years ago, the Centre Georges Pompidou in Paris invited a small group of architects to think about an exhibition on architecture that would feature new media rather than traditional architectural objects such as models, plans, and photographs. Despite the subsequent cancellation of the show due to a lack of funding, we had already started developing a concept based on the idea of interviewing four people from different fields and different generations, and asking them the very basic question, 'What is architecture?' Among the four, we wanted to ask a child; we wanted to ask an artist; and we also wanted to talk with a philosopher.

Our philosophical interview, which took place four years ago, was with the then 96-year-old Hans-Georg Gadamer, who studied under Martin Heidegger and became one of the greatest figures in German philosophy in the 20th century. The interview was especially interesting because Gadamer's words sounded as if from another time and world, a period when architecture had a kind of unbroken quality, and a now lost sense of the real. We asked Gadamer to describe what he saw architecture to be in the most general terms, and without reference to any specific architectural works. In his response he did not offer any theoretical explanations but instead told us a story from his childhood, growing up in the town of Breslau.

In the home of his parents, which was one of the Gründerzeit bourgeois villas in the town, there was a wonderful parquet floor in the formal reception room, into which the children (including the young Hans-Georg) were not allowed to enter except on special occasions like Christmas. Describing the piano and billiard table that stood on this bare floor, Gadamer spoke of this surface as something magical – a wonderful wooden floor, immaculately well-kept and polished so that it filled the space with the smell of wax. Every once in a while a friend of his father's would come to visit, and because it was often raining in Breslau, he would enter carrying his dripping raincoat and umbrella. The man, like his father a professor at the university, always appeared to be immersed in his own thoughts, and would, upon entering the forbidden room, always place his coat and soaking umbrella right down on the magical floor. As a child, Hans-Georg would be horrified that a friend of his father's would do such a thing. He still vividly remembers the image of the polished wooden floor decorated with water droplets from the sodden umbrella.

I often think of the Gadamer story because of its idea of the real. Gadamer's floor describes a concept of reality that does not exist anymore – the artisanal and traditional background of the floor itself has been lost for quite some time – but what makes this surface so interesting is its architectural potential for today. In this sense, Gadamer's floor can become an emblem for a very powerful design strategy in its emphasis on materiality, gravity, and maintenance, and its focus on the floor as a floor.

One of the most important architectural elements that makes the Tate Modern in London such a successful building with artists, curators, and the visiting public is the wooden floor that we introduced on almost all of its levels. Irregular and untreated, the oak floor planks are simply nailed down onto their joists. Brutal and beautiful at the same time, it is both rough like a piece of industrial architecture and soft like fashion designer Vivienne Westwood's hyper-sophisticated fabrics. We wanted to introduce a specific floor surface so as to ground or root people within this huge building, to exaggerate the sense they have in standing up vertically in front of the works of art. So, unlike Gadamer's parquet, the Tate Modern floor is an intellectual rather than an artisanal product. We were not interested in the nostalgia of revitalizing long gone methods of traditional production, but we were interested in the physical result, in the physical reality of traditional architecture. To achieve this sense of the real, we developed and tested full-scale mock-ups of almost every major detail in the building as part of a process driven by thinking, discussing, and trying, rather than rehearsing individually the necessary technical skills.

In this way, the Tate Modern floor became a prototype for our conceptual and strategic approach to architecture; an approach that is often masked with the traditional costume of architectural elements we all seem to have somehow seen before – comfortable and familiar. This wooden surface is, of course, not a single and isolated piece in that new museum. It is bound to the overall concept of the whole building, based on what we like to call aikido strategies. This is a system through which we try to take the pre-existing as a quality that, like in the techniques of the *aikido* martial art, you use for your own purposes, transforming it into your own energy. So what once seemed to be alien, hostile, and insurmountable, all of a sudden becomes a field where you can act and dictate the architectural and urbanistic scenarios.

The importance of these strategies became obvious to us when we were first faced with the huge brick mass of the existing Bankside power station. What could we possibly do? We could not propose tearing this huge brick mountain of a building down, or destroy any of its obvious architectural elements, such as the chimney (which initially we did not see as relevant to a museum of contemporary art). Another paradox of the existing structure was the obvious intention of its architect, Sir Giles Gilbert Scott, to connect the building to the brick tower of the cupola of Saint Paul's Cathedral immediately across the River Thames – a building that has a particularly strong urban and symbolic power in contrast to Bankside, which becomes more secluded and unpublic the closer one gets to it. Scott's design had been prominent and concealed at the same time; people had to be kept away from it. This was something we had to change, and in a way reverse, without destroying or losing the powerful energy of the existing structure. So we decided to drastically cut away the low-rise additions to the main body of the building that were literally masking the site. After these first operations we then added, piece by piece, elements such as the north entrance, the ramp, and the light beam, in a kind of genetic surgery that would incorporate the new pieces into an existing architectural family, all speaking the same language, almost as if they had been there all along.

Inside the building we decided to remove all of the machinery of the former power station, in order to reveal the structure in its most naked state. We became aware that the building was nothing but a huge envelope for that machinery: there was not a single space designed to be different from another; everything was filled with steel structures, platforms, boilers, valves, turbines, engines of every kind. With all of its generators removed, the turbine hall immediately struck us as a space of enormous potential; a volume that in an almost archaeological way could be dug out so as to become visible to an approaching public. People, we felt, should be able to reach the lowest point on the museum site, where all the existing structures could perform internally even more powerfully than the way they reveal themselves externally. At the same time, we wanted to achieve a nonhierarchical layout of the different levels in the museum, avoiding basement and main levels, and to suggest a more democratic treatment of space for a building that looked to become one of the leading museums of the 21st century.

Once we dug out the turbine hall we found the resulting space to be incredible and overwhelming, but it was almost too big and too industrial to serve as a public entrance to the new museum. In particular, we hated the domination of the vertical steel structural columns, and felt that we had to find something that both enhanced the power and logic of the churchlike interior while diluting its monumental impact. We tried many things until we found the light boxes, which, like the large glass piece on top of the building, seem to float, to be unstable in some way, and to cut through the steel columns. The fact that they are mounted in front of the steel structure (and not behind or in between) makes the columns appear less powerful than the light and glass. These light boxes have multiple functions, which are both dynamic and static: as quiet, more intimate spaces for visitors to rest; as windows that look both from the galleries into the turbine hall and from the hall into the galleries; as illuminating beacons for the main entrance; and, in a strange way, as almost cinematic monitors that project the movement of people.

In the gallery spaces we looked to continue to play with these various dichotomies, framed, the whole time, by the hard physicality of the wooden floor. Interestingly, a number of the artistic works that fill the completed galleries in the Tate Modem also allude to this overlapping of contradictory elements, notably Gary Hill's video installation, *Between Cinema and a Hard Place*, from 1991. As described by Sophie Howarth in the Tate exhibition catalogue, Hill uses video images to explore the metaphors, rhythms, and intonations of language. In a darkened room, 23 television monitors, both black-and-white and color, are stripped of their outer casing and arranged in lines like stones marking a boundary. Across the screens visual sequences unfold and fragment, moving from left to right. Initially it seems as if the images are triggered by a voice reading from 'The Nature of Language,' an essay by Heidegger. However, as the work continues, the precise correlation between sound and image becomes increasingly unclear. Monitors switch on and off; images flicker and blur. Scenes are transferred from screen to screen or extend across multiple monitors. The images explore the relationship between domesticity and landscape, and reflect on concepts of emotional and geographical closeness, which are the heart of Heidegger's text. Some were filmed from a moving car, and include houses, windows, bridges, fences, and signposts – the frontiers that define or delimit space. As its tide suggests, the work also questions the relationship between cinematic and real space. The physical presence of the hardware contrasts with the immateriality of the video imagery, the immediate gallery environment with the televised landscape. The spaces between the monitors insistently fragment the flow of images, underscoring the sense of dislocation expressed in the text.   (... p 116)

Jacques Herzog, 'Thinking of Gadamer's Floor', Cynthia C Davidson (ed), *Anything*, MIT Press (New York), 2001, pp 115–16.
(Excerpt pp 115–16)

Buildings and their Genotypes

Bill Hillier and Julienne Hanson

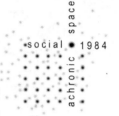

Bill Hillier, best known for his research on 'spatial syntax', and academic Julienne Hanson scrutinise the internal structure of cells using a method of gamma-analysis. They surmise that interior spaces are potentially separate events providing segregated spatial experience, a 'transpatial system' characterised by analogy and difference. For Hillier and Hanson, this system defines boundaries as distinct thresholds that sever the interior space from surrounding space. It differs from a system founded on spatial continuity between inside and outside. To overcome the duality of inside and outside, they suggest a shift from segregated interiors emblematic of social solidarity to encountering interiors suggestive of spatial solidarity, and contingent upon movement and interaction of inhabitants across the boundary.

Insides and Outsides: The Reversal Effect

A settlement, as we have seen, is at least an assemblage of primary cells, such that the exterior relations of those cells, by virtue of their spatial arrangement, generate and modulate a system of encounters. But this only accounts for a proportion of the total spatial order in the system, namely the proportion that lies between the boundary of the primary cell and the global structure of the settlement. No reference has yet been made to the internal structure of the primary cells, nor to how such structures would relate to the rest of the system. This section concerns the *internal* structures of cells: it introduces a method of syntactic analysis of interior structures, which we will call gamma-analysis; it develops a number of hypotheses about the relation between the principal syntactic parameters and social variables; and it offers a theory of the relations between the internal and external relations of the cell as part of a general theory of the social logic of space. Since the shape of the general theory is not at all obvious from what has gone before, some theoretical problems must be explored before questions of analysis and quantification can be opened.

One of the most common assumptions about space, sometimes explicit, more often implicit, is that human spatial organisation is the working out of common behavioural principles through a hierarchy of different levels. Thus from the domestic interior, or even

148

from the individual space, through to the city or region, it is assumed that similar social or psychological forces shape space, differing only in involving larger numbers of people and larger physical aggregates.[1] The assumption is so common that it deserves a name: we might call it the 'continuum' assumption. If the continuum assumption were true, the analysis of interiors would simply be a matter of taking the principles and techniques for the analysis of aggregates and applying them on smaller scale. Unfortunately, this would lead us to overlook a very fundamental fact, one which when taken account of adds a whole new dimension to the system. We might call it the fact of the boundary.

A settlement presents itself to our experience as a continuous object by virtue of the spatial relations connecting the outsides of boundaries. By moving about the settlement we build up knowledge of these exterior relations until we have a picture of some kind of the settlement structure. The spaces inside the boundaries have a quite contrary property: they are a series of – potentially at least – separate events, not a continuous system. The same drawing of boundaries that constructs a settlement as a continuous spatial aggregate with respect to the outsides of cells creates a set of discontinuous spaces on the insides of those cells, which do not normally present themselves to experience as a continuous spatial system with a global form, but as a series of discrete events, expressly and explicitly disconnected from the global system. They are experienced one by one as individuals, not as a single entity sustained by physical connections. This property lies in the very nature of a boundary, which is to create a disconnection between an interior space and the global system around, of which it would otherwise be a part.

By virtue of this fact of disconnection, the set of spaces interior to boundaries creates a different kind of system, one whose basic properties have already been discussed at some length: a transpatial system. A transpatial system, we may remember, is a class of spatially independent but comparable entities which have global affiliations, not by virtue of continuity and proximity but by virtue of *analogy* and *difference*. In such a system the nature of our spatial experience is different from our experience of a spatially continuous system. We enter a domain which is related to others not by virtue of spatial continuity, but of *structural comparability* to others of its type. We experience it as a member of a class of such interiors, and we comment on it accordingly. The relations between interiors are experienced as conceptual rather than as spatial entities, and the mode of organising global experience out of local observations is transpatial rather than spatial.

This is the fundamental fact of the boundary. There is no homogeneous continuum of spatial principles from the very large to the very small. In the transition from large to small there is a fundamental discontinuity where the system in effect reverses its mode of articulation of global experience out of local events. In moving from outside to inside, we move from the arena of encounter probabilities to a domain of social knowledge, in the sense that what is realised in every interior is already a certain mode

149

of organising experience, and a certain way of representing in space the idiosyncrasies of a cultural identity.

Even the continuous scale of spatial organisation is shown to be illusory by the reversal effect of the boundary. Behind the boundary, the reference points of space do not become correspondingly smaller. On the contrary they expand through their primarily transpatial reference. As a consequence of the nature of the boundary, the most localised scale of spatial organisation tends to become the most global in its reference. The boundary refers to the principles of a culture.

The duality of inside and outside adds a new dimension to the relation between social solidarity and space. A solidarity will be transpatial to the extent that it develops a stronger and more homogeneous interior structuring of space and, in parallel, emphasises the discreteness of the interior by strong control of the boundary. The emphasis in such a case will be on the internal reproduction of a relatively elaborate model. Words like ritualised and conformist might well be applied to such types of organisation. The essence of a transpatial solidarity lies in the local reproduction of a structure recognisably identical to that of other members of the group. The stronger and more complex the structure, therefore, and the more exactly it is adhered to, the stronger will be the solidarity. Such a solidarity requires the segregating effect of the boundary to preserve the interior structure from uncontrolled incursion. Solidarity means in this case the reproduction of an identical pattern by individuals who remain spatially separated from each other, as well as from the surrounding world. A transpatial solidarity is a solidarity of *analogy* and *isolation*: that is of analogous structures realised in controlled isolation by discrete individuals.

In contrast, a spatial solidarity works on the contrary principle. It builds links with other members of the group not by analogy and isolation, but by *contiguity* and *encounter*. To realise this it must stress not the separateness of the interior but the continuity of interior and exterior. Movement across the boundary, which would undermine a transpatial solidarity, is the fundamental condition of existence for a spatial solidarity. In such circumstances an elaborate and controlled interior cannot be sustained, but nor is it necessary. Encounters are to be generated, not limited, and this implies the weakening of restrictions at and within the boundary. A spatial solidarity will be undermined, not strengthened, by isolation. In a spatial solidarity, therefore, the weakening of the boundary is associated with a weaker structuring of the interior. Informality rather than ritual must prevail if the principles of the system are to be sustained.

Thus the reversal of space that occurs naturally at the boundary of the primary cell generates a dualism in the principles of solidarity that can relate society to space. An analysis of spatial patterns internal to the cell, and those relating the interior to the exterior, must therefore aim to capture the spatial correlates of these bifurcating principles. This will be possible because the dualism reflects only the dual nature of the boundary, which at one and the same time creates a category of space – the interior – and a form of control – the boundary itself. This dualism is invariably present in spatial patterns within buildings. The method of analysis to be outlined in this section on gamma-analysis will centre on these two dimensions and their interrelations. It will turn out that category and control are closely related to the basic parameters of alpha-analysis. Relative asymmetry in gamma-analysis will articulate the relations of the space, that is, of the category embodied by the space; and ringiness – i.e. distributedness – in gamma will articulate the relations of the boundary, that is the relations of control on the category.

A building is therefore at least a domain of knowledge, in the sense that it is a certain spatial ordering of categories, and a domain of control, in the sense that it is a certain ordering of boundaries. Sociologically speaking, a building relates this dualism to the universe of inhabitants and strangers by reversing the spatial and transpatial relations that were identified in alpha. Every building, even a single cell, identifies at least one 'inhabitant,' in the sense of a person with special access to and control of the category of space created by the boundary. An inhabitant is, if not a permanent occupant of the cell, at least an individual whose social existence is mapped into the category of space within that cell: more an inhabitant of the social knowledge defined by the cell than of the cell itself. Inhabitant is thus a categoric concept, and therefore a transpatial entity, and in that sense the inhabitant is part of a global categoric reality as a result of being mapped into the local bounded space of the cell, as well as being a member of a local spatial reality.

With strangers the effect is the opposite. Every building selects from the set of possible strangers a subset of 'visitors' who are persons who may enter the building temporarily, but may not control it. Pupils in a school, patients in a hospital, guests in a house, and prisoners in a prison all fall within this category of being more than strangers, in that they have a legitimate reason to cross the boundary of a building, but less than inhabitants, in that they have no control over that building and their social individuality is not mapped into the structure of space within that building. In this sense a building also localises the global world of strangers, by the same means as it globalises the local world of inhabitants. It realises a categoric order locally, then uses the boundary to interface this categoric order with the rest of the social world.

A building may therefore be defined abstractly as a certain ordering of categories, to which is added a certain system of controls, the two conjointly constructing an interface between the inhabitants of the social knowledge embedded in the categories and the visitors whose relations with them are controlled by the building. All buildings, of whatever kind, have this abstract structure in common; and each characteristic pattern that we would call a building type typically takes these fundamental relations and, by

151

varying the syntactic parameters and the interface between them, bends the fundamental model in one direction or another, depending on the nature of the categories and relations to be constructed by the ordering of space.

In the sense that it is some ordering of space, then, a building is at least some domain of unitary control, that 'unitariness' being expressed through two properties: a continuous outer boundary, such that all parts of the external world are subject to some form of control; and continuous internal permeability, such that every part of the building is accessible to every other part without going outside the boundary. To express this set of relations, and to avoid confusion with definitions of a building that depend on it being, for example, under a single roof, the term 'premises' will in future be used instead of 'building.' Premises are a domain of unitary control with the boundary and permeability properties given above, whose internal relations are developed by syntactic means into a certain kind of interface between inhabitant and visitors. Gamma-analysis is therefore the analysis of these spatial relations and controls realised though the permeability patterns of the subdivided cell.   (... p 147)

Note
1   See for example, Oscar Newman, Defensible Space; Crime Prevention Through Urban Design, Macmillan (New York), 1972; Christopher Alexander, et al., A Pattern Language: Towns, Buildings, Construction, Oxford University Press (New York), 1977. The most common form in which these ideas appear, however, is as assumptions, as for example in HMSO, Housing the Family, MTP Construction (Lancaster), 1974.

Bill Hillier and Julienne Hanson, 'Buildings and their Genotypes', *The Social Logic of Space*, Cambridge University Press (Cambridge), 1984.

(Excerpt pp 143–7)

Household Furniture and Interior Decoration

Thomas Hope

British art collector Thomas Hope published a volume of his own furniture sketches and interiors that ultimately proved to be influential in changing period perceptions of upholstery and interior decoration. In this excerpt, he attacks the loss of beauty and line, denouncing mechanical processes that result in furniture that is flimsy, lacking solidity and inelegant. Central to his argument is an appeal to recall the ways of the ancients, not only for their conceptions of beauty and utility, but as a search for form that is conducive to adapting contemporary modes of convenience. Exposing a now familiar argument, he implies that such forms would acquire a timeless quality, the expense of which outweighs the cheap but poorly made fashionable decorations prevalent at the time.

Under the general denomination of Household Furniture are comprised an infinite variety of different productions of human industry, wrought in wood, in stone, in metal, in composition of various descriptions, in silk, in wool, in cotton, and in other less usual materials. Each of these different articles, however simple be its texture, and however mean its destination, is capable of uniting to the more essential requisites of utility and comfort, for which it is most immediately framed, and with which it can consequently, on no account, dispense, a certain number of secondary attributes of elegance and beauty, which, without impeding the chief purpose of the object, may enable its shape and accessories to afford additional gratification, both to the eye and to the imagination.

Almost every one of these various articles however, abandoned, till very lately, in this country, to the taste of the sole upholder, entirely ignorant of the most familiar principles of visible beauty, wholly uninstructed in the simplest rudiments of drawing, or, at most, only fraught with a few wretched ideas and trivial conceits, borrowed from the worst models of the degraded French school of the middle of the last century, was left totally destitute of those attributes of true elegance and beauty, which, though secondary, are yet of such importance to the extension of our rational pleasures. Furniture of every description, wrought by the most mechanical processes only, either remained absolutely void of all ornament whatever, or, if made to exhibit any attempt at embellishment, offered in its decoration no approach towards that breadth and repose of surface, that distinctness and contrast of outline, that opposition of plain and of enriched parts, that harmony and significance of accessories, and that apt accord between the peculiar meaning of each imitative or significant detail, and the peculiar destination of the main object, to which these accessories belonged, which are calculated to afford to the eye and mind the most lively, most permanent, and most unfading enjoyment. The article only became, in consequence of its injudicious appendages, more expensive, without becoming more beautiful; and such remained the insipidity of the outline, and the unmeaningness of the embellishments, even in the most costly pieces, that generally, long even before the extreme insolidity and flimsiness of their texture could induce material injury in them from the effects of regular wear and tear, the inanity and tameness of their shapes and appendages already completely tired the eye and mind; and left these no other means to escape from the weariness and the disgust which they occasioned, than an instant change for other objects of a more recent date and a more novel construction.   (… p 2)

If thus great were the advantages which the adoption of the totally new style of decoration here described seemed to promise, the difficulties with which its execution was to be attended appeared not less considerable. The union of the different modifications of visible and intellectual beauty which were desirable, with the different attributes of utility and comfort which were essential; the association of all the elegancies of antique forms and ornaments, with all the requisites of modern customs and habits, having heretofore been so seldom attended to, in objects of common and daily use, I found no one professional man, at once possessed of sufficient intimacy with the stores of literature to suggest ideas, and of sufficient practice in the art of drawing to execute designs, that might be capable of ennobling, through means of their shape and their accessories, things so humble in their chief purpose and destination as a table and a chair, a footstool and a screen.   (… p 7)

In England much more attention is generally paid to the perishable implements of the stable than to the lasting decoration of the house; and it is therefore not impossible that many, even among those most disposed yearly to lavish enormous sums in the trifling and imperceptible changes which every season produces in the construction of the transient vehicle, may most strongly object to the expensiveness of the infinitely more important and more palpable improvements, of which is susceptible the more permanent fixture. To such it would be easy to prove, that the mode of decorating apartments, hitherto in vogue, which, through the paltriness of its materials, and the slightness of its texture, is subject to experience such speedy decay, and (what is worse) through the poverty of its forms, and the unmeaningness of its embellishments, is liable to occasion such rapid disgust; and which, consequently, is usually broken or discarded, long ere it has had leisure fairly to serve its time, though at first its cost be less, yet, by means of the incessant change of fashion which it stimulates and supports, on the whole, occasions a much greater expense than the style of furniture here set forth; which, little susceptible of experiencing premature destruction, for want of due solidity of form, and less liable, it is presumed, than the former, to suffer merited disgrace, while yet in all its freshness of youth, for want of intrinsic power to please, may be preserved in families, from generation to generation, as a valuable portion of the patrimonial estate.   (... p 16)

Thomas Hope, *Household Furniture and Interior Decoration: Executed from Designs by Thomas Hope*, Longman, Hurst, Rees and Orme (London), 1807. (Excerpts pp 1–16)

From *Wiener Kunst im Hause* to the Wiener Werkstätte

Rebecca Houze

Rebecca Houze provides a historical account of the link between design fashion and marketing most profoundly asserted by the Wiener Werkstätte. While the success of the Secessionist campaign is attributed to the fact that it was directed towards the feminine, it inadvertently moulded the woman of the house as a spatial artist and conflated that role with the endorsement of visual imagery from botany, youth and organic forms. Ornament and decorative motifs evolving from such imagery became the trademark for interior design which was regarded as a form of dressing. In this text, Houze points to the tension between resisting and exploiting issues of fashion with regard to the emergence of modern style and places interior design at the centre of the tussle between art, craft and design.

In an introductory article published in the first issue of the Secession-influenced design journal, *Das Interieur*, editor and architect Josef Folsenics described a 'true Viennese interior.' Its most significant characteristic, he writes, is '*Gemütlichkeit*,' a kind of cozy comfort. In the early nineteenth century, the *gemütlich* Viennese interior was epitomized by the Biedermeier style:

> Artist and housewife were united in a single person. Just as the young beauty could spend hours alone in front of the mirror, in deep, naive, contemplation of aesthetic questions – which hairstyle, which posture best suited her – so had she also, gradually, according to her aesthetic experience, turned her home into the charming garment of her intimate life.[1]

Modern architects such as Otto Wagner, and his students, Josef Hoffmann, Josef Olbrich, Josef Urban, and Otto Prutscher, embraced the Biedermeier style for its relatively simpler forms and clean lines, as well as for its association with a simpler domestic life. 'These men have outlined a new style,' Folsenics wrote, in the same article, 'and now women can return to their rightful role as interior designers.' Folsenics implied, however, that although women do possess an innate talent for home beautification, based on their intimate understanding of aesthetics through the perusal of their own beauty in the mirror, and of their talents in choosing their own wardrobes, they also possess the weakness to lose their aesthetic sensibility in times of artistic decline, specifically because of their tendency to follow fashion. Because of the recent infusion of artistic insight by (male) Secessionist designers, women, he believed, could once again make use of their decorating talents. This new style, in fact, Folsenics wrote, 'is much like a Viennese woman,' curvy and sensuous, yet intimate and ultimately more domestic than urban or cosmopolitan.[2] Folsenics's introduction reveals his strong ambivalence toward women, who, on the one hand, served as models of domestic artfulness yet, on the other, were incapable of true innovation, which must be accomplished by men. *Wiener Kunst im Hause* provided an interesting antidote to this conservative point of view, presenting interiors that were not only designed by women, but that creatively inspired the work of male teachers at the Kunstgewerbeschule. *Wiener Kunst im Hause* provided a new model for reconciling modern art and commerce, the domestic and the urbane.[3]

In 1900, an exhibition of student work from the Kunstgewerbeschule was sent to the *Paris Exhibition*. Works by talented female students, Else Unger and Gisela von Falke among others, were presented in a room designed by Josef Hoffmann. The decorative objects were displayed as if arranged in a private home, rather than for sale in a department store, or as permanent exhibits of an art museum. English art critic Gabriel Mourey wrote that the Kunstgewerbeschule, led by Josef Hoffmann, had presented the 'only truly modern and national style' at the *Paris Exhibition*. He attributed the successful fresh and cohesive quality of the designs to the school's rejection of all past and foreign influences, and to their peculiar mode of exhibiting complete 'interiors' rather than individual works.[4]

One of the favorite objects at the exhibition was a secretary desk designed by Else Unger in a carved wooden hydrangea motif.[5] This piece utilized the curvilinearity and botanical patterns that had come to be associated with the modern movement in Vienna, and with 'secessionist style' in particular. Vienna art critic Ludwig Hevesi described the feel of the new work as fresh and alive in contrast to the static, more historically based works of just a few years before. 'The motifs are taken from less frequently tread areas of botany,' he wrote. 'The plants are seen with freer eyes and depicted in a fresh, ornamental mood.'[6] This new era of modern art was exemplified by the work of the young, female designers.

This preoccupation with fresh new life was closely related to the artistic program of the Vienna Secession, which proclaimed youth, growth, and organic rejuvenation with their motto, 'Ver Sacrum,' (Sacred Spring), and with their visual imagery.[7]   (... p 6)

The most striking aspect of the room at the *Paris Exhibition* was its use of oversized ornamental motifs in appliqué textiles. The traditional appliqué embroidery technique of embellishing furniture coverings, cushions, upholstery, and drapery, by stitching cut pieces of cloth onto a cloth background, was extended to cover the walls as well. The modern Viennese interiors displayed at the *Paris Exhibition of 1900* revealed a growing interest in the use of textiles and traditional handwork not only as decorative objects to be incorporated into designed rooms, but as models for the organic, flexible dressing of an interior space. This application of textile 'dressings' to the walls of the pavilion directly relates to the German architect Gottfried Semper's influential 'Bekleidungsprinzip' (Principle of Dress), which was of theoretical significance to Otto Wagner and his students, including Josef Hoffmann. According to Semper, the textile arts represented the earliest form of man's art-making tendency, which would evolve into architecture. Woven mats, for example, which were originally hung to divide the space of a room, eventually became structural walls, which retained the woven texture of fiber in new materials, such as brick or stone.[8] Because textile arts such as lace, tapestry, and embroidery represented the seeds of artistic creativity, they took on a central role in programs for the reform of applied arts institutionalized at the Oesterreichisches Museum under the advice of Semper, who brought his ideas to Vienna in 1864.   (... p 7)

When the first Wiener Werkstätte showrooms opened in 1904, they adopted the model of the well-furnished home, which had been used by *Wiener Kunst im Hause*. These spaces included soft carpets and armchairs, upholstered in artistic textiles, for customers to relax in while gazing at the elegant glass cabinets displaying modern silver and porcelain wares. Walls were decorated with chic fashion illustrations. Ladies trying on clothing could walk around the shop barefoot comfortably on the soft, felt-covered floors. The stylishly outfitted interiors of the shop encouraged customers, such as Fredericke Maria Beer and Sonja Knips, wealthy patrons of the Secession, to mentally design their own aesthetically coordinated homes, furnished with products ranging from draperies, upholstery fabrics, and carpets to dishes, light fixtures, silverware, and shoes. Beer and Knips both had their portraits painted by Gustav Klimt, and commissioned apartments designed by Josef Hoffmann and outfitted by the Wiener Werkstätte. These patrons enacted the turn-of-the-century 'Gesamtkunstwerk,' in which the domestic living space became a theater of modern life. All spatial and visual elements including the structure of a building, its interior and furnishings, and the costume of its inhabitants were conceived as a single aesthetic statement. The best-known example of the secessionist *Gesamtkunstwerk* is Josef Hoffmann's mansion for the Stoclet family in Brussels, built between 1905 and 1911. The sumptuous dining and music rooms of the Palais Stoclet exemplified the theatrical spaces of the *Gesamtkunstwerk*, celebrating sight, sound, and taste in a symphony of sensual harmonies that paralleled the operas of Richard Wagner, from whom the concept originated. In his designs for the Palais Stoclet, Hoffmann was particularly attuned to fashion and to the Viennese identity of the new style of interior, even designing a dress for Madame Stoclet so that she would not clash with her living room décor as she had while wearing a French Paul Poiret gown.

The relationship between fashion and architecture in Vienna is well-documented, and has been of particular interest to scholars of the past decade whose work typically has focused on Adolf Loos.[9] Loos wrote a great deal about fashion, and was himself preoccupied with clothing in such a way that the concept of dress constantly informed his architectural designs. Loos's belief that understated dress was the most appropriate disguise for modern man extended to the stark, unconventional facades of his shops and private residences. The subtleties of Loos's interiors, however, reflect his more complicated understanding of architectural space as a garment that allows its inhabitants to psychologically negotiate their place in modern life. Loos's interiors simultaneously, as George Simmel suggests, allow one to display one's individuality, while assuming a degree of anonymity; they are both public and private; and domestic and urban.[10] Although Loos was extremely hostile towards the Secession and the Wiener Werkstätte, especially for the latter's reliance on excessive ornamentation, his understanding of the interior as a form of dress was quite similar to Josef Hoffmann's, and grew out of the same architectural theories of cladding introduced by Gottfried Semper in the mid-nineteenth century, and further developed by Otto Wagner in the early twentieth.

In his essay, 'The Principle of Cladding,' Loos, repeating Semper's theory, writes:

> The architect's general task is to provide a warm and livable space. Carpets are warm and livable. He decides for this reason to spread out one carpet on the floor and to hang up four to form the walls. But you cannot build a house out of carpets. Both the carpet on the floor and the tapestry on the wall require a structural frame to hold them in the correct place. To invent his frame is the architect's second task.[11]

Just as Josef Folsenics called for a '*gemütlich*' Viennese interior, Loos desired a 'warm and livable' interior space. This interior must be comforting and sensual, allowing the viewer or inhabitant to respond to it physically and psychologically. The interior also is a private, domestic, feminine space – a space for intimate conversation, sexual relations, and reproduction. It is a protective refuge from the public space of the modern city, yet it also mediates between the two realms. Different rooms served different purposes; while bedrooms were considered the most intimate and feminine spaces of a private residence, the social space of the dining room and the intellectual space of the library were coded masculine. The salon functioned as a space in which women would socialize while dressed in more relaxed and intimate garments, hovering on the boundary between public and private.

The Wiener Werkstätte's fashionability was the secret of its success. The close relationship between a specifically feminine dressing up in fancy clothes and dressing up the home in a splendid garment had its roots in the national Austrian decorative arts institutions, which fostered and promoted women's traditional textile arts, and recognized women's traditional role in home decoration.

Around 1908, *Wiener Mode* began to feature embroidery and textile designs for comprehensive room decorations on the back covers of the magazines. By this time, the Wiener Werkstätte was well established, and the room designs in *Wiener Mode* reflected the modern aesthetic in their choice of colorful or black and white geometric motifs. On the one hand, the popular interior designs in *Wiener Mode*, which usually were not attributed to a specific designer or design workshop, may be seen as a dilution of the modernist secession style of the Wiener Werkstätte. On the other hand, they cannot simply be understood as the last step in the decline of artistic idea to popular culture. Rather, the popular fashion magazine as a vehicle for perpetuating both commerce and culture already was well in place by the time the Secessionists began to market their new designs through the Wiener Werkstätte. Designers including Josef Hoffmann, Kolo Moser, and their students at the Kunstgewerbeschule responded to this mechanism as much as it responded to them. The design of artistic interiors and furnishings, and the marketing of fashionable goods, must be seen, rather, as a complementary process that allowed both ends to fuel one another creatively.

The modernist interest in textile arts and interior design in Vienna would not have emerged and blossomed as it did had it not been for the constant driving force of fashion, which provided a space for women to engage physically, either as designers or consumers, with the aestheticization of themselves and their living spaces through cloth and needlework. A domestic comfort was recovered in Vienna at the turn of the century by physically wrapping living spaces in pieces of embroidered cloth. The garment – especially the feminine garment – was a common metaphor for the interior living space at the turn of the century. It is important to recognize, however, that this form of feminine dress had as much to do with the idea of 'cladding' a space in cloth – a flexible, organic, fiber material – as it did with a particular style or fashion of clothing. Cloth itself has a long history of associations with the feminine, and as Semper interprets it, with our inherent creative tendencies. The textile-based style of interior decoration promoted by *Wiener Kunst im Hause* and perpetuated by the Wiener Werkstätte was derived from women's traditional handcrafts, which the Secessionists admired, imitated, relied upon, and fostered in their educational programs, publications, and exhibitions.   (... p 21)

Notes

1 'Künstler und Hausfrau waren in einer Person vereinigt. So wie die junge Schöne, wenn sie allein war, stundenlang vor dem Spiegel stehen konnte, um in naiver Vertiefung in ästhetische Fragen herauszubekommen, welche Frisur, welche Haltung, welche Bewegungsform ihr am besten steht, so hat sie auch auf dem Wege erfahrungsgemässer Aesthetik allmälig ihr Heim zum reizenden Kleide ihr es intimen Lebens ausgestaltet,' Josef Folsenics, 'Das Wiener Interieur', *Das Interieur* I, 1900, pp 3–6.

2 'Wer den Typus der echten Wienerin kennt, der weiss, dass im Glanze feuriger Augen, im Rosenschimmer blühender Wangen, in den wichen Wellenlinien des lachenden Mundes eine Seele schlummert, die mit der Innigkeit und Natürlichkeit ihres Empfindens allen Sinnenreiz der äusseren Erscheinung wie mit einem warmen milden Lichte überstrahlt. Diese persönliche Eigenart hatte stets die Tendenz, sich auf das ganze Leben zu übertragen, auf den gesellschaftlichen Verkehr, auf die

öffentlichen Vergnügungen und vor Allem auf das Familienleben und das echte Wiener Interieur,' Josef Folsenics, 'Das Wiener Interieur', *Das Interieur* 1, 1900, p 6.

3 Christopher Long, in his article, 'Wiener Wohnkultur: Interior Design in Vienna, 1910–1938', *Studies in the Decorative Arts*, Fall/Winter 1997–1998, pp 29–51, discusses the Viennese emphasis on domestic comfort, '*Gemütlichkeit*,' in the years between the wars as a reaction against the unified, hard-edged, functionalist style championed by the Bauhaus, as well as by Josef Hoffmann and the Wiener Werkstätte. Although the Wiener Werkstätte did embrace a model of interior design based upon unified rectilinear forms, I believe that the workshop's general interest in domestic design, stemmed from the same Viennese desire for *Gemütlichkeit* that Long suggests was at the root of the more popular and eclectic designs by Oskar Strnad and Josef Frank between the world wars.

4 Gabriel Mourey, 'Round the Exhibition-IV. Austrian Decorative Art', *The Studio* XXI, Oct 1900–Jan 1901, pp 112–13.

5 Ludwig Hevesi, 'Die Kunstgewerbeschule auf der Pariser Weltausstellung', *Kunst und Kunsthandwerk* III, 1900, p 117.

6 'In anderen aber ist der neue Stil schon lebendig. Die Motive warden aus weniger zertretenen Theilen der Botanik geholt, die Pflanzen mit freierem Auge angesehen und mit einer frischeren ornamantalen Laune verwendet,' Ludwig Hevesi, 'Die Kunstgewerbeschule auf der Pariser Weltausstellung', p 121.

7 By choosing the title 'Ver Sacrum' for their periodical, the Secessionists not only evoked the sacred rebirth of the world in springtime, but also recalled a Roman ritual in which the elders pledged their children to save society in times of national danger. By 'seceding' from the exhibiting society of the Academy of Fine Arts, the young artists pledged themselves to save culture from their elders. Their own Secession was based on the Roman model of the *secessio plebis*, in which the plebs defiantly withdrew from the republic, rejecting the misrule of the patricians. See Carl E Schorske, *Fin-de-Siècle Vienna: Politics and Culture* [1961], Vintage Books (New York), 1981, pp 214–15.

8 Gottfried Semper, *Der Stil in technischen und tektonischen Künsten, oder Praktische Aesthetik. Ein Handbuch für Techniker, Künstler und Kunstfreunde. Band I. Die Textile Kunst*, Verlag für Kunst und Wissenschaft (Frankfurt am Main), 1860–63.

9 Examples of recent work on Loos's relationship to fashion include: Janet Stewart, *Fashioning Vienna: Adolf Loos's Cultural Criticism*, Routledge (London and New York), 2000; Beatriz Colomina, *Privacy and Publicity: Modern Architecture as Mass Media*, MIT Press (Cambridge, MA and London), 1994; Mary MacLeod, 'Undressing Architecture: Fashion, Gender, and Modernity', Deborah Fausch, *et al*, (eds.), *Architecture: In Fashion*, Princeton Architectural Press (Princeton), 1994, p 38–123, and Mark Wigley, 'White Out: Fashioning the Modern', Deborah Fausch, *Architecture: In Fashion*, 1994.

10 The German sociologist Georg Simmel makes this point, for example, in his 1904 essay 'Fashion' in Donald N Levine (ed), *On Individuality and Social Forms*, The University of Chicago Press (Chicago and London), 1971, pp 294–323.

11 Adolf Loos, 'The Principle of Cladding', *Spoken into the Void: Collected Essays 1897–1900*, trans Jane O Newman and John H Smith, MIT Press (Cambridge, MA and London), 1982, pp 66–9. This passage also is quoted and remarked upon in Beatriz Colomina, 'Intimacy and Spectacle: The Interiors of Adolf Loos', *AA files*, 20, Autumn 1990, pp 5–15.

Rebecca Houze, 'From *Wiener Kunst im Hause* to the Wiener Werkstätte: Marketing Domesticity with Fashionable Interior Design', *Design Issues*, vol 18 no 1, Winter 2002, pp 3–23.
© 2002 by the Massachusetts Institute of Technology. Reprinted by permission of MIT Press Journals.
(Excerpts pp 4–23)

Wherever I Lay My Girlfriend, That's My Home

Lynda Johnston and Gill Valentine

gender ● 1995

late 20th century space

This essay by feminist geographers and academics Lynda Johnston and Gill Valentine suggests that 'home' takes on different and contradictory meanings for sexual dissidents as they share the home with heterosexual family members. The authors do not reify 'lesbian identity' or 'lesbian home' in a universal sense, but examine the performance of a lesbian identity in a family home where they have not 'come out'. The difficulty of communicating an identity via traditional means, including semi-fixed interior items such as pictures, books, curtains and so on, is inhibited by the hegemony of heterosexuality. For the subjects of Johnston and Valentine's focus group research, the home becomes a place of tension lacking ontological notion of 'home', 'place', 'privacy' and 'roots', as well as an 'unsafe' place lacking physical security.

The word 'home' has multiple meanings. In an attempt to clarify the concept, Somerville has picked out seven key dimensions: shelter, hearth (i.e. emotional and physical well-being), heart (loving and caring social relations), privacy, roots (source of identity and meaningfulness), abode and paradise ('ideal home' as distinct from everyday life).[1] This is, he claims, a classification that can be supported by Watson and Austerberry's empirical findings.[2] Of these seven meanings, it is the notions of privacy and heart that appear to have received most academic attention.

Being in a private space is at the heart of what it means to be 'at home' according to Graham Allan and Graham Crow. They argue that 'A home of one's own is … valued as a place in which members of a family can live in private, away from the scrutiny of others, and exercise control over outsiders' involvement in domestic affairs.'[3] This ability 'to relax' and 'to be yourself' away from the gaze of others, was also identified as one of the most important meanings of home by participants in Peter Saunders' research.[4] As one of his respondents explains:

> I can dress how I like and do what I like. The kids always brought home who they liked. It's not like other people's place where you have to take your shoes off when you go in.[5]

Peter Saunders summarises such sentiments when he states: 'The home is where people are offstage, free from surveillance, in control of their immediate environment. It is their castle. It is where they feel they belong.'[6]

But although the home may be a more or less private place for 'the family' it doesn't necessarily guarantee freedom for individuals from the watchful gaze of other household members: 'the public world does not begin and end at the front door.'[7] Rather, the ideology of 'the family' actually emphasises a form of togetherness, intimacy and interest in each others' business that can actually deny this privacy. Linda McDowell is one of many authors to have argued that women have little access to private space within the family home.[8] Likewise, children's space (usually a bedroom), is often subject to intrusion and violation by parents[9] and young people usually have less power than other members of the household to make decisions that determine the 'family lifestyle.'[10] The privacy of a place is not therefore necessarily the same as having privacy in a place. In this sense the distinction between public and private is complex and hard to draw, being simultaneously articulated at a multiplicity of levels.

Lesbians living in (or returning to) the 'family' house, who haven't 'come out' to their parents can find that a lack of privacy from the parental gaze constrains their freedom to perform a 'lesbian' identity 'at home.' Home is not for them, the place where they can, in Peter Saunders' words, establish the 'core' of their lives.[11] It does not, to use Somerville's classification, have any meaning as a source of identity or 'roots.'[12] Rather it is a location where their sexuality must often take a back seat. The most obvious expression of their identity – lesbian sex – is definitely off limits (at least when parents have them under surveillance) as Janice and Sharon, a New Zealand lesbian couple, explain:

> Well it makes me sad 'cos I can't take Sharon home, that's my problem 'cos I never came out to my parents.'
>
> Janice, New Zealand lesbian

> She took me home, and it was really uncomfortable. We didn't do anything. We slept in the same room but in separate, single beds. And your mother sounded confused 'cos Janice was going "Oh we'll just use the double bed, we'll just sleep in there, that's all right." Your mother [Janice's] was going "Um, are you sure? Look we've got the two single beds, how about you sleep in the single beds, come on Janice?"
>
> Sharon, New Zealand lesbian

(... p 102)

According to James Duncan, the home is a medium for the expression of individual identity; a site of creativity; a symbol of the self.[13] Such that Mary Douglas and Baron Isherwood describe the contents of the house and garden as 'the visible bit of the iceberg.'[14]

These semi-fixed domestic items, from curtains and wallpaper to pictures and books, are all supposed to help inhabitants to communicate an identity and outsiders to read it.[15] Many asymmetrical family homes are impregnated with 'heterosexuality.' Its overwhelming presence seeps out of everything from photograph albums to record collections. But the love that dare not speak its name in the family house can hardly cover the walls and smile down from the picture frames. And so lesbians restrict the performance of their sexual identity in their own physical surroundings, hiding pictures of lesbian icon kd lang under the mattress and gay fiction behind the bookcase, ever cautious that the privacy of their bedroom may be subject to the gaze of brothers, sisters and parents.

The constraints on the performance of a lesbian identity don't stop at the bedroom door. Judith Butler has critiqued gender, sex and the body as categories, suggesting that they are discursively produced by the effects of various institutional practices and discourses.[16] She argues that the body is not a ready surface awaiting signification but a set of boundaries, 'a surface whose permeability is politically regulated and established.'[17] As these women describe, the parental home can inscribe the lesbian body. While still 'being' a lesbian, for these women there is not the repetition or redoubling of the role that is necessary for the lesbian category to be expressed in a heterosexual environment.

> [I] cover my tattoos up when I go home, especially if mum and dad have company coming over. I do that, it doesn't worry me, that's it.
>
> Jackie, New Zealand lesbian

> [I dress more] conservatively ... kind of straight and less scruffy.
>
> Hayley, New Zealand lesbian

The home can therefore be a site of tension for women who identify as lesbians – a place where the ideal of the home as a place of security, freedom and control meets the reality of the home as site where heterosexual family relations act on and restrict the performance of a lesbian identity. Rather than being 'where above all one feels "in place,"'[18] 'at home' is where many lesbians feel 'out of place' and that they don't belong or fit in. In Somerville's terms, home may have meaning as a 'shelter' and an 'abode' but not as 'roots' or 'paradise.'[19]

> I mean, as much as I love my family I always feel I don't fit in. The only place I feel at ease is with gay people ... I feel I sit in a room full of my family and I feel I'm just not part of this, I don't fit in.   Jane,
> English lesbian

This lack of ontological security can also be accompanied by a lack of actual physical security. Research shows that whilst lesbians experience less abuse at the hands of

164

strangers than gay men, they are at the receiving end of more domestic violence perpetrated by family members 'disgusted' by their sexuality.[20] This violence, which can range from physical assault to verbal intimidation and harassment, contributes to shattering the myth of 'home as a haven.'   (... p 103)

Home is supposed to be where your heart is. It is supposed to provide a space for individuals to be themselves. The parental home may meet the needs of a 'daughter,' and most of the women interviewed did talk of their family home as 'loving and supportive,' but this was only when their lesbian identity was not being 'performed.' The parental home seems largely incapable of meeting the needs of the 'lesbian daughter' – except in a material sense. It may have the meanings 'shelter,' 'abode,' 'hearth,' but it doesn't appear to have the meanings 'privacy,' 'roots' (identity) and 'paradise' (ideal home). Rather the freedom to perform a lesbian identity, to relax, be in control and to enjoy the ontological security of being 'at home' appears to be best met when lesbians can create and manage their 'own homes.'   (... p 104)

We all have a multiplicity of subject positions and identities. 'Home' is one site where our identities are performed and come under surveillance and where we struggle to reconcile conflicting and contradictory performances of the self. 'Home' itself is also a term laden down with a baggage of multiple meanings: shelter, abode, hearth, heart, privacy, roots, paradise and so on. For women who identify as lesbians, the parental (or 'family') home is often a site where they have to manage the clash of their identity as a lesbian with their identity as 'daughter' from a heterosexual family. The struggle to control how their identity is read and received under the surveillance of vigilant parents can rob the parental home of its meaning as a place of 'privacy,' 'roots' and 'paradise.' Whilst being a place of material and emotional comfort ('shelter,' 'abode,' 'hearth' and even 'heart') that can meet the needs and desires of the 'daughter,' the parental home does not appear to meet the needs and desires of the 'lesbian.' It is a location where lesbianism and heterosexuality do battle. The heterosexuality of the home can inscribe the lesbian body by restricting the performative aspects of a lesbian identity but it can also be subverted itself by covert acts of resistance.

The 'lesbian home' is one site of lesbian identity construction and maintenance. Constituted to meet the needs and desires of lesbians, it appears to be a place of significance, of 'roots' and even 'paradise,' for many women. But despite the greater freedom to perform a lesbian identity within the boundaries of a 'lesbian home,' it is still a location where this identity comes under the surveillance of others, especially close family, friends and neighbours. It is not necessarily a place of 'privacy.' In some cases the physical site of the home is actually altered depending on the relationship of the visitor to the occupants so that a lesbian identity is not performed in the physical environment to the 'wrong audience,' thereby disguising the identity of the occupants. Alternatively, in an attempt to create the privacy necessary to conceal a lesbian relationship, couples can often withdraw from family, friends and the local neighbourhood and become isolated. This isolation can become stiflingly claustrophobic, smothering relationships and enabling abusive domestic situations to develop unnoticed under this cloak of privacy. Thus a lesbian home is not necessarily a place of emotional and physical well-being ('hearth' and 'heart'). Neither is it always a stable 'shelter' or 'abode' – domestic conflicts between women and their children and the usual ebb and flow of sexual relationships can all contribute to a fluidity in the membership and constitution of lesbian households.

The meanings of 'home' to the lesbians involved in this research are numerous and beset with contradictions. They are perhaps most neatly summed up by Massey when she writes about the home (in a different context): 'each home-place is itself ... a complex product of the ever-shifting geography of social relations present and past.'[21]   (... p 112)

Notes
1 P Somerville, 'Homelessness and the Meaning of Home: Rooflessness or Rootlessness?', *International Journal of Urban and Regional Research*, vol 16, 1992, pp 528–39.
2 Watson and H Austerberry, *Housing and Homelessness: A Feminist Perspective*, Routledge and Kegan Paul (London), 1986.
3 G Allan and G Crow (eds), *Home and Family: Creating the Domestic Sphere*, Macmillan (Basingstoke), 1989, p 4.
4 P Saunders, 'The Meaning of "Home" in Contemporary English Culture', *Housing Studies*, vol 4, 1989, pp 177–92.
5 Saunders, 'The Meaning of "Home" in Contemporary English Culture', p 181.
6 Saunders, 'The Meaning of "Home" in Contemporary English Culture', p 184.
7 Allan and Crow, *Home and Family*, p 5.
8 L McDowell, 'City and Home: Urban Housing and the Sexual Division of Space', M Evans and C Ungerson (eds), *Sexual Divisions: Patterns and Processes*, Tavistock (London), 1983.
9 P Hunt and R Frankenberg, 'Home: Castle or Cage?', *An Introduction to Sociology*, Open University Press (Milton Keynes), 1981.
10 R Madigan, M Munro, and SJ Smith, 'Gender and the Meaning of Home', *International Journal of Urban and Regional Research*, vol 14, 1990, pp 625–47.
11 Saunders, 'The Meaning of "Home" in Contemporary English Culture', p 187.
12 Somerville, 'Homelessness and the Meaning of Home', p 533.
13 JS Duncan, 'Introduction', JS Duncan (ed), *Housing and Identity*, Croom Helm (London), 1981, pp 2–4.

14 Quoted in Duncan, *Housing and Identity*, p 175.

15 A Rapoport, 'Identity and Environment: A Cross-cultural Perspective', JS Duncan (ed), *Housing and Identity*, Croom Helm (London), 1981.

16 J Butler, *Gender Trouble: Feminism and the Subversion of Identity*, Routledge (New York), 1990.

17 Butler, *Gender Trouble*, p 139.

18 J Eyles, *Senses of Place*, Silverbrook Press (Warrington), 1984, p 425.

19 Somerville, 'Homelessness and the Meaning of Home'.

20 See K Berrill, 'Anti-gay Violence and Victimisation in the United States: an Overview', GM Herek and KT Berrill (eds), *Hate Crimes: Confronting Violence Against Lesbians and Gay Men*, Sage (London), 1992; GD Comstock, 'Victims of Anti-gay/lesbian Violence', *Journal of Interpersonal Violence*, vol 4, 1989, pp 101–6.

21 D Massey, 'A Place Called Home?', *New Formations*, vol 17, 1992, p 15.

Lynda Johnston and Gill Valentine, 'Wherever I Lay My Girlfriend, That's My Home: The Performance and Surveillance of Lesbian Identities in Domestic Environments', *Mapping Desire: Geographies of Sexualities*, David Bell and Gill Valentine (eds), Routledge (London and New York), 1995.

© L Johnston and G Valentine. Reprinted by permission of L Johnston and G Valentine.

(Excerpts pp 100–12)

Interiors: Nineteenth-Century Essays on the 'Masculine' and the 'Feminine' Room

Juliet Kinchin

gender 1996

19th century furnish

This text by design historian Juliet Kinchen compares and contrasts what constitutes a 'masculine' and a 'feminine' room through material and social culture. As a gendered reading, it examines the domestic arena in which rooms codified against prevailing notions of 'dignity', 'gay', 'lightness' and 'massiveness', were equated with social and intellectual characteristics. Under this conception décor and furnishings are aligned with femininity including emotional and trivial sentiment, whereas massive monumental furnishings are associated with sombre masculinity and seriousness. Sexual identity and gender difference are rendered as social and spatial categories that transcend into the private sphere as factors in taste, morality, decency and virtue. Written with specific reference to the early nineteenth century, this text measures the degree to which aesthetic and social generalisations influence social circles and architectural interiors.

In the nineteenth century the private interior space of the middle-class home was increasingly defined as feminine territory, the antithesis of the public, external world of work peopled by men. Within the domestic arena, however, the key rooms tended to be further grouped to either side of a male-female divide, the most explicit contrast being between the 'masculine' dining room and 'feminine' drawing room. The male domain grew to encompass the hall, library, business, billiard and smoking rooms, whereas the boudoir, music room, morning room and bedroom were perceived as coming under the feminine sphere of influence. Each room-type was minutely codified in terms of its function, contents and decor. Within these formulae some variety was allowed but the keynote of the masculine rooms was serious, substantial, dignified (but not ostentatious) and dark-toned. By contrast, the more feminine spaces were characterised as lighter or colourful, refined, delicate and decorative.

When Thomas Sheraton's *Cabinet Dictionary* was published in 1803, this pattern of codifying interiors was firmly in place. The drawing room, being the apartment to which women withdrew after dinner, was identified as feminine. The most expensive and culturally refined of the public rooms, which 'showed off' the occupants to visitors, it provided an impressive backdrop for formal socialising, and a context in which unmarried daughters could be sized up by potential suitors. In Sheraton's words, the furnishings were 'to concentrate the elegance of the whole house.'[1] He recommended producing a lively, glittering atmosphere with expanses of mirror, bronzed fittings and extensive use of lighting, which would then be picked up in the 'gay style' and colourful upholstery of the music room.[2] The furnishing of a genteel bedroom was to be more restrained than either the drawing or music rooms but similarly 'light in appearance.'[3]

By contrast, the ideal dining room would exude 'a very august appearance' with hereditary credentials displayed in the form of family portraits. Size was all-important. The accommodating proportions of the space were to be amplified by the 'bold, substantial and magnificent furniture,' including a 'large' sideboard, a 'handsome and extensive' dining table, and chairs which were 'respectable and substantial looking.'[4] A 'bold, massive and simple' character was specified for the entrance hall which was to impress visitors from the outset with the male head of the family's 'dignity.'[5] Intellectual aspirations and classical brainwork were showcased in the gentleman's library, ideally furnished 'in imitation of the antiques' and presided over by portraits of appropriate role models ('men of science and erudition'). Nothing 'trifling' was to detract from the serious atmosphere of such masculine rooms, with 'little affairs' and 'innocent trifles' relegated to the more feminine tea room or dressing room.[6] By the same token, Sheraton specified the exclusion of books, globes and 'anything of a scientific nature' from the drawing room. There the accoutrements of artistic and less obviously intellectual accomplishments such as needlework, sketching and music-making were considered more appropriate.

The basic contrast drawn by Sheraton between the lightweight and the substantial – a contrast which resonated across different areas of sensory, intellectual, emotional and aesthetic experience – was fundamental to the elaboration of masculine and feminine furnishing schemes throughout the nineteenth century. Writing in 1864, Robert Kerr could advise that in the dining room,

> The style of finish, both for the apartment itself and the furniture, is always somewhat massive and simple ... the whole appearance of the room ought to be that of masculine importance.

Conversely,

> The character to be always aimed at in a Drawing-room is especial cheerfulness, refinement of elegance, and what is called lightness as opposed to massiveness. Decoration and furniture ought therefore to be comparatively delicate; in short the rule is this – if the expression may be used – to be entirely ladylike. The comparison of Dining-room and Drawing-room, therefore, is in almost every way one of contrast.[7]

The masculine conventions of the dining room were invariably constituted as an oppositional foil to those of the feminine preserves. Robert Edis echoed the male physique in his description of dining chairs in *The Decoration and Furniture of Town Houses* (1881); they were 'broad-seated and backed, and strong, compared to their 'light-waisted', curvaceous counterparts in the drawing room.[8] The contrast extended to the vexed question of sincere and 'authentic' expression. Away from the deceptive surfaces and ornamental distractions of the drawing room, it was easier to present 'masculine' furnishings as being what they seemed to be. The emphasis was on creating an impression of utilitarian durability. Whether in terms of the quantity of furnishings, the toughness of the materials, or the restrained use of colour and pattern, the decorative aspects of the dining room were to be deliberately understated: 'Few ornaments are requisite, beyond the display on the sideboard;' 'A turkey carpet is most suitable, and from its durability, economical.'[9] Edis expressed the generally held view that the furniture should be 'designed for use not show' and of serviceable and durable materials; 'good plain chairs of unpolished wainscot or American walnut are better than any highly polished surfaces' and upholstery was to be 'strong, serviceable leather, or morocco in preference to velvet.'[10] This restraint helped to lower the emotional temperature of the space, relegating the expression of aesthetic sensibilities, of sentiment and of trivial pursuits to the feminine preserve – just as Sheraton had done.

As a material, oak was ideal for representing notions of rugged masculinity, a link reinforced over centuries through the popular literary device of the sturdy-limbed oak wound round by the clinging vine. 'The oak is man, in firmness drest, / With strength of fondness in his breast, / Delighting in the lie:- / The ivy is the gentle wife' (*Scots Magazine*, March 1789). 'Heart of oak' also conjured up patriotic and martial overtones. More authentically national sentiment was invariably associated with masculinity. In Kerr's view the massive simplicity of both decor and furniture in the dining room reflected the 'substantial pretensions' of British character and food, and when it came to the selection of an appropriate historical treatment, this axis of meaning was expressed in the preference for hefty 'Elizabethan, Jacobean' and 'Baronial' styles, or the refinement of 'Adams' or 'Sheraton' ones.

> ... the English styles ... are expressive of a certain national sentiment which finds its strongest note in the family circle when gathered round the table at the evening meal. However popular the French styles may be for the drawing room or the boudoir they lack the distinct character which seems to be looked for in an English dining room.[11]

The 'distinct character' and the 'forcefully decided treatment' of the dining room was played off against the aura of indecisive or pallid 'confusion' apparently generated in the drawing room.[12] The construction of femininity in relation to predominantly French and Oriental styles had the effect of emphasising the clarity of the masculine core culture.

The peripheral nature of 'feminine' taste, and the link between manhood and national character was not new; it had featured in criticism of Thomas Hope's Frenchified *Household Furniture and Internal Decorations* published in 1807:

> At a time when we thought every male creature in the country was occupied with its politics and its dangers, an English gentleman of large fortune and good education has found leisure to compose a folio on household furniture ... There is in England we believe, a pretty general contempt for those who are seriously occupied with such paltry and fantastical luxuries; and at such a moment as the present, we confess we are not a little proud of this Roman spirit, which leaves the study of these *effeminate elegancies to slaves and foreigners* [emphasis added].[13]

Almost a century later the architect Reginald Blomfield expressed the same commonly held sentiments:

> Three great qualities stamped the English tradition in furniture ... steadfastness of purpose, reserve in design and thorough workmanship ... As a people we rather pride ourselves on the resolute suppression of any florid display of feeling.[14]

National sentiment, the life-style of the gentry, middle-class aspirations and the hierarchical pattern of familial relations were repeatedly reinforced, and literally internalised, through the daily ritual of the evening meal. The aura of hospitality, plenitude, 'cheery comfort and prosperity' was to be enhanced by 'full tones' and the 'rich juicy colouring' of the decorative schemes. References to dead animals in the use of leather upholstery, the full-blooded, meaty colour schemes, and the iconography of the hunt elaborated in carving, wall decoration or pictures, all insisted on the importance of a well-provided table and, by implication, a competent (male) provider. Clearly few men literally brought the supper home but the authority of the male head-of-house was signified by the ample 'carver' armchair from which, as chief carnivore, he could slice and apportion the meat for the day, a ritual ideally enacted against the theatrical backdrop of a sideboard groaning with food and laden with silver plate.

The basic formula for furnishing a dining room proved particularly resistant to change. Although a century separates Sheraton and the German design critic Hermann Muthesius, the language and conventions are instantly recognisable:

> By long tradition the English dining room is serious and dignified in character, its colour scheme dark rather than light, its furniture heavy and made of polished mahogany, it has a Turkish carpet on the floor and oil paintings, preferably family portraits, in heavy gilt frames on the walls.[15]   (... p 17)

Compared to the relatively stable formula for furnishing a dining room, the drawing room presented a minefield of possibilities; 'in no room of the house is there more latitude and a greater opportunity to show individual taste.'[16] There was a degree of tension between what needed to be there to make the room like those of one's peers, and the necessity to mark difference and individual (as opposed to class or public) taste. There was a plethora of styles and objects from which to choose, and no end of conflicting advice as to how to pick and mix them. The drawing room also elicited the most vitriolic criticism (usually, though not exclusively, from male critics), redolent of negative, moralising attitudes to women, which suggests either that the drawing room was a more sensitive barometer than the dining room in terms of taste and values, or that the construction of femininity was more hotly contested than notions of masculinity within the home, or both. (... p 18)

Notes
 1 Thomas Sheraton, *The Cabinet Dictionary* (London), 1803, p 218.
 2 Sheraton, *Cabinet Dictionary*, p 216.
 3 Sheraton, *Cabinet Dictionary*, p 219.
 4 Sheraton, *Cabinet Dictionary*, pp 194, 218.
 5 Sheraton, *Cabinet Dictionary*, p 216.
 6 Sheraton, *Cabinet Dictionary*, pp 218–9.
 7 Robert Kerr, *The Gentleman's House or How to Plan English Residences from the Parsonage to the Palace; with Tables of Accommodation and Cost, and a Series of Selected Plans*, John Murray (London), 1864, p 107.
 8 Robert Edis, *Decoration and Furniture of Town Houses: A Series of Cantor Lectures Delivered Before the Society Of Arts*, C Kegan Paul & Co (London), 1881, p 181.
 9 James Arrowsmith, *The Paper Hanger's and Upholsterer's Guide: A Treatise on Paper-Hanging and Upholstery, etc*, T Dean and Son (London), 1854.
10 Edis, *Decoration and Furniture of Town Houses*, p 181.
11 Kerr, *Gentleman's House*, p 94; HJ Jennings, *Our Homes and How to Beautify Them*, Harrison and Sons (London), 1902, p 152.
12 W Pearce, *Painting and Decoration* (London), 1878, p 76.
13 *Edinburgh Review*, 1807, Article XIV, pp 478–9.
14 C Holme (ed), *Modern British Domestic Architecture and Decoration*, Studio Special Number (London), 1901, p 18.
15 Hermann Muthesius, *Das Englische Haus* [Berlin, Wasmuth, 1904], English edn, Crosby Lockwood Staples (London), 1979, p 206.
16 Edward Gregory, *The Art and Craft of Home-Making* [1913], BT Batsford (London), 1925 p 43.

Juliet Kinchin, 'Interiors: Nineteenth-Century Essays on the "Masculine" and "Feminine" Room', Pat Kirkham (ed), *The Gendered Object*, Manchester University Press (Manchester and New York), 1996.
© 1996 Juliet Kinchin. Reprinted by permission of Juliet Kinchin.
(Excerpts pp 12–18)

Tables, Chairs, and Other Machines for Thinking

Mark Kingwell

philosophical ● 2002
20th century furnish

Philosopher and cultural theorist Mark Kingwell's excerpt addresses the interior from the perspective of furniture and its potential to operate beyond practical and functional concerns. Noting that the history of philosophy reveals little examination of these objects and declares no philosophy of furniture, he observes that for many philosophers furniture is a literal site of reflection, the location for thinking. To argue this he takes furniture beyond its aesthetic, functional and commodious history to its consideration as something that structures space, making space meaningful. Under this conception furniture becomes an invitation to think and to dream, exerting philosophic reflection or at the very least, facilitating philosophic inquiry.

The question in the background here, the unasked philosophical question, is really this one: what is furniture for? That may seem so obvious as to be not worth asking, but one of the things you learn as a philosopher is that the obvious-sounding questions are usually the most interesting ones.

Here is one kind of answer: furniture is for sitting on, lying on, sleeping on, and putting things on. We might call this answer *functionalism*, and it emerges as a common enough version of the Furniture Idea when we force the issue somewhat. Functionalism views furniture as, in effect, an extension of the human ability to complete physical tasks. Here, for example, is Marshall McLuhan talking about the relationship between furniture and the human body in his book *Counterblast*:

> A chair outers the human posterior. The squat position is 'translated' into a new matter, namely wood or stone or steel. The temporary tension of squatting is translated and fixed in a new matter. The fixing of the human posture in solid matter is a great saver of toil and tension. This is true of all media and tools and technologies. But chair at once causes something else to happen that would never occur without a chair.

A table is born. Table is a further outering or extension of body resulting from chair. The new fixed posture of chair calls forth a new inclination of body and new needs for the

173

placing of implements and stirring of food. But table also calls forth new arrangements of people at table. The fixing of a posture of the body in a chair initiates a whole series of consequences.

Or, as Burt Bacharach and Hal David more elegantly put it, 'A chair is still a chair, even when there's no one sitting there.' Notice how McLuhan speaks here of 'chair,' 'table,' and 'body' as if they were proper names or basic essences, categories rather than things. Notice, too, the causality implied in this kind of functionalism: we squat, therefore we need chairs; we have chairs, therefore we need tables; we have tables, therefore we need place settings.

That is not wrong. Once people began eating at tables, whole new vistas of social complexity opened up before them. Table manners became an issue, as did the ability to converse while at table. Carving meat in front of others was alone the subject of numerous Renaissance manuals for gentlemen – and still causes anxiety attacks among certain sons-in-law on their first holiday visit. In our own time, the art of throwing the perfect dinner party has become a bourgeois obsession which shows no signs of diminishing in this, the third decade of Martha Stewart's reign.

So functionalism makes a deep point. Furniture arises as the solution to certain problems, as a way of completing various human tasks – only to create, in the process of so doing, numerous new tasks. It also creates new kinds of aesthetic issues, as Poe reminds us. Any plane surface within a certain range of dimensions, and suspended or supported at a particular height off the floor, may be considered a table. This is the way in which, for example, a philosopher of kinds, natural or non-natural, nominal or real, would speak of tables and chairs. Individual instances are linked together by an articulable essence, consistency with a given design, or certain inductions that can be run, for good reasons, over the class of objects so styled – a good reason being, in this case, something like the combination of cultural and physical factors entailed by 'because you can sit in it.' But to leave the matter there is to fall into a mundane version of the furniture demolition of the Cartesian philosopher. Here all tables are equal because they are all merely extensions of our instrumental tasks and bodily dimensions. This misses a deep point about tables. A 'good' table, a table worth having, isn't just a handy surface or prop; it must also be striking, beautiful, elegant, or witty – or some combination thereof.

These are not functional virtues, they are *aesthetic* ones. But, as is so often the case when it comes to virtue, here aesthetic considerations are not entirely or easily separable from issues of functionality. Any good designer knows that a smooth, highly polished wood surface is both aesthetic and functional; so, depending on your taste, are tapered legs, pediment supports, S-curve lines, high straight backs, and reclining seats. Often enough to be remarkable, the more beautiful thing is also the more useful thing. Functionalism and aestheticism are often thought to be at war, but it would be more accurate to say that they are in creative tension. Rare is the piece of furniture that possesses no aesthetic sense whatsoever, however badly judged. More likely, but still rare, is the piece where aesthetic sense has entirely overwhelmed functionality – though many of us have probably had some near-miss experiences on that score, chairs so beautiful they threaten to pitch you onto the floor at any moment.

That is usually as far as most people get when it comes to thinking about the Furniture Idea, but of course there is much more still to say. Furniture is for doing things, and for being beautiful; but it is also for instantiating, and illuminating, certain kinds of *political* ideas. In *Das Kapital*, for instance, Marx introduces some insights about the nature of commodities by, as it were, putting a few things on the table. 'A commodity appears, at first sight, a very trivial thing and easily understood,' he says. And yet:

> Analysis shows that in reality it is a very queer thing, abounding in metaphysical subtleties and theological niceties. So far as it is a value in use, there is nothing mysterious about it ... The form of wood is altered by making a table out of it; nevertheless, the table remains wood, an ordinary material thing. As soon as it steps forth as commodity, however, it is transformed into a material immaterial thing. It not only stands with its feet on the ground, but, in the face of all other commodities, it stands on its head, and out of its wooden brain it evolves notions more whimsical than if it had suddenly begun to dance.

You might think Marx is evolving notions more whimsical than dance moves right there, but he means that the material thing is now a bearer of non-material significance, of ideological and social payload.

Commodity is not another word for *thing*, it is another word for *relationship*. That is why functionalism and aestheticism, even taken together, cannot tell us all there is to know about a table or chair. The plainest chair is still a product of someone's labour, and was acquired or made against a background of complex social relations determined in large part by money. Every table, from the humblest do-it-yourself kit to the finest handmade piece from Heidi Earnshaw, tells a tale of who owns what. For centuries, furniture has been, along with clothes, hairstyles, companions, leisure activities, and personal conveyances, a way of signalling one's place in a complex hierarchy of social relationships, key examples of Goffman's 'presentation of self in everyday life.' More specifically, it has functioned as what Veblen first labelled 'invidious comparison' through 'conspicuous consumption.'

In Veblen's jaundiced view, the messages are not always about what they seem to be about. On the surface, the furnishings of the country house or the high-rise apartment purport to send intricately coded messages of personal taste or sophistication or refinement – and indeed these semiotic codes may well be rooted in some degree of reality. But more basically these objects are purchased, placed, and displayed to indicate, sometimes quite precisely, one's average net worth and margin of disposable annual income. As the critic Adam Gopnik notes, 'Veblen is insistent – far more than Marx – on reducing aesthetics to economics.' Here is a typical sentence from the early master of consumerist analysis: 'The superior gratification derived from the use and contemplation of costly and supposedly beautiful products is,' Veblen writes, 'a gratification of our sense of costliness masquerading under the name of beauty.' Whatever bourgeois-bohemian rebels might like to believe, historically taste is most often just another name for status.

Furniture can also bear political messages in less obvious ways, plotting a new relationship to functionalism. Here, for example, is a passage from Don DeLillo's novel *White Noise*, a scene in which the narrator, a middle-aged Professor of Hitler Studies, catches sight of some undergraduate students scattered in the library of his university, and considers the value of the tuition – $14,000, in 1985 dollars – necessary to attend the elite institution:

> I sense there is a connection between this powerful number and the way the students arrange themselves physically in the reading areas of the library. They sit on broad cushioned seats in various kinds of ungainly posture, clearly calculated to be the identifying signs of some kinship group or secret organization. They are fetal, knock-kneed, arched, square-knotted, sometimes almost upside-down. The positions are so studied they amount to a classical mime. There is an element of over-refinement and inbreeding. Sometimes I feel I've wandered into a Far Eastern dream, too remote to be interpreted. But it is only the language of economic class they are speaking, in one of its allowable forms.

This studied casualness, this topsy-turvy disdain for the standard operating procedures demanded by chairs and tables, is more than youthful awkwardness. In fact, its outwardly awkward aspect actually hides a deep comfort level, a claim on understanding the way things work, a long acquaintance with the inner machinery of entitlement.

Only the truly privileged can lounge so unselfconsciously. Only they can drape themselves over furniture as if furniture has not been fashioned for the human body.

All of these points are part of what I called the Furniture Idea, but there is at least one further level of meaning alive in tables and chairs, and I want to end these reflections by saying something about it. Tables and chairs don't just make us think about function and form and politics. They don't just provide us with the handy platform for our own thoughts. They also make us think about *thinking*.

This happens only where tables and chairs take up their proper places, namely in rooms. And it happens because, as James Agee put it so movingly in *Let Us Now Praise Famous Men*, even the simplest room has the profound grace of human life and everyday aspiration. Writing of the desolate but beautiful homes of Southern sharecroppers that he and photographer Walker Evans examined with such compassion and wisdom, Agee said: 'There can be more beauty and more deep wonder in the standings and spacings of mute furnishings on a bare floor … than in any music ever made.'

Consider why this is so. Furniture structures space, making what is otherwise undifferentiated into something meaningful. I place a couch in an empty room and it acquires a new significance: the air now shimmers with the possibilities of conversation or napping or seduction. The absent protagonists of the various human stories that room has witnessed and will witness are instantly summoned, necromantically, by the couch's human dimensions, its constant invitation to sit or lie. More than this, though, the couch preserves in its placing the possibility of itself being placed somewhere else: every location of a piece of furniture thus calls attention to all the alternative locations which have, for the moment, been passed over. We are all attuned to this radiant aspect of furniture, though not all of us can tell immediately when or why a chair is placed oddly or suboptimally.

The cliché image of what I am getting at here is probably the fickle matron who, moving into a new space, has the exhausted movers try her massive oak-trim settee in every possible location, only to settle back on the very spot where they first dropped it. That image is outdated and maybe offensive, but I think we all share something of this impulse to rearrange the furniture. In Eugene Ionesco's play *The Chairs*, for example, characters enter the stage in order to add more chairs to the scene, each time rearranging and reordering the possibilities (and crises) of the existential situation. It seems to me that we are always doing this, physically or mentally, because we are looking for new ways to structure our allotted space, to make the most of it. We are, in effect, seeking new forms of meaning to create, new ways to think – and new thoughts to entertain. Naturally we can fail to do this well, and then our movements of furniture will be futile, superficial, merely distracting: as the adage has it, we will be rearranging the deck chairs on the *Titanic*. (A more disturbing contemporary echo of the idea can be found at a web site called www.furnitureporn.com, which features photographs of patio and office furniture arranged in various suggestive tableaux. You will never consider swivel chairs the same way again.)

Am I being fanciful? I don't think so. Furniture makes a room what it is, and rooms are where most of us spend most of our time. (Offices, after all, are rooms too.) How these rooms are furnished, what pieces inhabit them and give them shape, determines in large measure what kinds of thoughts are possible there. This is not just a matter of something like feng shui, though clearly that is one rigorous and ancient way of considering the matter. But consider something that is, for most of us, less exotic: rearranging the furniture in our own bedrooms, or even just watching the way the furniture changes as the light does.

In *À la recherche du temps perdu*, Proust speaks of the thoughts that come in hazy early morning, when we indulge, he says, 'the experimental rearrangement of the furniture in matinal half-slumber.' In *The Waves*, Virginia Woolf describes dawn light striking a tree outside her window, 'making one leaf transparent and then another.' At noon, she says, it 'made the hills grey as if shaved and singed in an explosion.' As afternoon fades, tables and chairs 'wavered and bent in uncertainty and ambiguity.' And in the evening, the same articles of furniture regain their solidity, so that they are 'lengthened, swollen and portentous.' Finally, as darkness fell, substance was drained from 'the solidity of the hills,' and the world was annihilated again.

The style of the furniture itself can be dreamy in this way, creating reverie-inducing tables and chairs. In *Le Spleen de Paris*, Baudelaire describes such a room as the ideal place to think. 'In a prefiguration of Jugendstil,' says Walter Benjamin of this project, 'Baudelaire sketches "a room that is like a dream, a truly *spiritual* room … Every piece of furniture is of an elongated form, languid and prostrate, and seems to be dreaming – endowed, one would say, with a somnambular existence, like minerals and plants."'

And as with style, so with a particular article of furniture. Gaston Bachelard, in *The Poetics of Space*, focuses on corners and nooks, the parts of a room where, he says, dreams may pool and gather. He likewise favours those items of furniture that enclose space or create inner reaches: 'Does there exist a single dreamer of words who does not respond to the word wardrobe?' he asks. 'Every poet of furniture – even if he be a poet in a garret, and therefore has no furniture – knows that the inner space of an old wardrobe is deep. A wardrobe's inner space is also *intimate space*, space that is not open to just anybody.' Not all intimate spaces are obvious. For instance, I used to take refuge in the improbable inner space of the family clothes hamper, where the dirty laundry was waiting to be taken to the washer. I used to think this strange until I discovered that my best friend also did it, and read Salman Rushdie's account, in *Midnight's Children*, of another child who, with perhaps better reason, sought the asylum of the hamper.

In such a space, with such vistas and dreams alive to our gaze, furniture is no longer something merely to sit upon; no longer the elevated surface where we lay our tools and our mealtime places. Here furniture is instead an invitation to think and to dream, a beckoning of possible ideas and half-formed notions. We all sit somewhere when we think, yes, and chairs hold us up while we work out our thoughts on desks and tables. But more importantly, what we sit upon or write upon are themselves thinking things;

not just tools that help us in chosen tasks, but aspects of humanity whose very presence is thought. The attempt of thought to think its own conditions is, as Kant reminds us, infinite and finally impossible: we cannot encompass ourselves within our own reflection. But we can, we must, begin this infinite task anyway, and furniture is one neglected but essential way to do so.   (...p 246)

Mark Kingwell, *Practical Judgments: Essays in Culture, Politics, and Interpretation*, University of Toronto Press (Toronto, Buffalo and London), 2002.
(Excerpt pp 238–46)

On the Loss of (Dark) Inside Space

Constanze Kreiser

technological 1990

achronic light

Questioning the way increased use of artificial lighting affects interiors, architectural designer and installation artist Constanze Kreiser opens a philosophical examination of the mediating effect of light. This author observes how an enclosure is gradually made lighter in the sense of weight and mass through the addition of openings that emit or filter light. This polemic on lightness and darkness raises questions of how light measures time, space and inhabitation and the temporal rhythms of everyday existence. But as Kreiser notes, when artificial light begins to imitate natural light it disturbs orientation, confusing window-effect with sky-effect. As such simulation technologies focus attention on recreating daylight or sunlight within, the tradition of limited brightness associated with the inside, night time and darkness is overturned.

Is inside space on the verge of disappearing? Is it being hindered by constantly improved light technology which is causing one of its fundamental qualities – darkness – to dissipate? And for what reason? Is it for the benefit of more outside space? Or for the benefit of a new spatial quality?

Light constitutes space in that it creates bright and dim zones, enabling the physical perception of a space.

Space does not originate with the construction of a building, but exists in the act of marking off a small unit from an infinite quantity. It is exactly this process which is achieved by sunlight: that which it illuminates is outside, shadowed surfaces forming inside.

Depending on whether lightness or darkness dominates, inside space is a dark space by day and a light space at night. Thus inside space is dependent on light, it is in constant contrast to the prevailing light conditions. Inside space at night has, however, existed only as of the invention of artificial means of lighting – from pine-torches to light bulbs. By day, inside space floats like a dark island in a sea of light.

The darkness to be found in inside space can be gradually brightened by breaking up light-absorbing matter (rock, tree trunks, etc.), by making openings and sending light rays on to leaves, water or stones.

Human manipulations of sunlight aim solely at creating inside space. They erect areas of darkness, which are then mitigated by openings in the confining surfaces. The manner by which light is supplied to inside is in its first phase an application of the observed relationship between light and matter in nature: i.e. absorption, transmission and reflection.

Light can only exert a mediating effect when there is a difference between the amount of light inside and outside. This difference is dependent on the membrane which is extended between inside and outside, light and dark. The more light it lets in, the more the inside loses of its specific inside spatial effect, until mediation between the outside and the 'almost-outside' is no longer necessary.

A sunray is enough to remind us of the existence of the surrounding outside. For it is with light that weather and time penetrate inside space. Light itself is not visible, hence it tells nothing of itself; nevertheless, it is the medium of messages. It tells – bolstered by its colours and mutability – of the respective seasons, the weather, the hour of the day.

In his buildings, Tadao Ando capitalizes on this quality of light to set measure and the relationship of objects to each other. These buildings are distinguished by a great clarity of almost sculptural impact. Daylight is let in from above as well as from the sides, and on the great part in such a manner that it does not coincide with the pathways through the interior, instead contributing to zoning it off.

Both internally and externally, Ando uses the same building and surface material, concrete, as well as the same means to invigorate the often large uniform surfaces: daylight. He allows daylight room to traverse the whole space, falling on undecorated surfaces, where light and shade reinforce each other, elucidating the building in the process. Ando's buildings stand firmly on the ground, timelessly, only light is in motion within them.

That it is possible for light and the fall of shadows to render the form of a building indistinct can be exemplified by another Japanese building. Yamamoto's Hamlet House in Tokyo exhibits an intricate form, rich surfaces on protruding and inset parts, the most diverse of materials, which, via the sunlight shining on it, appear to vibrate. The building's contours do not seem to be set, indeed, it is almost as if it were not anchored to the ground. Inside and outside merge. Transparent materials allow this merging to occur inconspicuously. The inside approaches the outside to such a degree that they no longer form opposites reconcilable by light.

Artificial light as a substitute for daylight represents – following the attempts made even up into the present to use daylight as a mediator and which are based primarily on absorption and transmission.

From the start, artificial lighting was conceived for inside. It was supposed to expel darkness from inside space. Yet it was not long until it was of greater significance to terminate the darkness of night, to prolong daytime. The goal became the imitation of sunlight which, however, with respect to sunlight's brightness, range and variability cannot in fact be achieved by artificial sources of light.

Artificial light is inherently limited in its brightness. Out of universal darkness it creates light inside spaces – outside as well – and it is as such the exact reverse of daylight. A nocturnal inside space is an individually brightened spot. Its brightness has a collective nature, and it is as a result that out of an accumulation of such single points of light, streets at night turn into inside space.

The transformation of streets into inside space is so powerful that its new appearance assaults the facades, taking over the ground floor windows originally belonging to the buildings' interiors in the process. As showcase windows they now contribute to lighting the street, their one-time function of letting light in is hereby totally abandoned, manifest in the erection of showcase-window backwalls.

Artificial light differs from sunlight in its having clearly distinct features. Quantity, colour, direction and constancy are easily describable – unlike daylight with its constant fluctuations.

In rooms having natural light sources during the day, there is no alternative: artificial light always plays a subordinate role! In the intention of substituting daylight, artificial light is best positioned where it can simulate the fall of sunlight. In this way the arrangement of the room, which was initially made with respect to the sources of sunlight, can remain unaltered. Such considerations led to so-called curtain light arrangements. Daylight and artificial light sources were given the same location directly at the window – neon tubes integrated into curtain rods. Just as common were electric wall-light installations of window-sized frosted glass, which were able to impart the illusion of diffuse daylight.

In any case, it was only with the advent of electric light that the desire to imitate natural light could be halfway satisfied, and at that only because the more easily imitated northern lights were chosen as the ideal. (Earlier means of lighting did not have the demanded steady brightness.)

All DIN-norms are based on this minimalized demand: artificial light should resemble diffusely radiating cloudy skies. These norms originated primarily in the fifties, when it was believed that by using neon lighting, a complete correlation between end and means had been achieved. Whole ceilings were construed of frosted glass, some constructionally partitioned, behind which light bulbs or neon tubes could be hidden in order to produce an even effect on the room below. Whether the lighting came from above or the sides, it was dealt with identically; whereby the illusive effect of light from above was decisively greater: for one because it was not within actual reach, and for the other because the eye did not have to do without the views it was used to having via windows.

With this application of artificial light, sunlight itself was not only imitated, but also the whole architectural arrangement of natural light sources. And such was the case even in spaces with actual windows. Nowadays, an unbroken walled-in space is given familiar structure, by merely calling forth vague memories of window-effect.

Totally unfamiliar and persiflaging all experience is the construction of a *Luminous Field* out of flower pollen as conceived by Wolfgang Laib in a church nave. It appears to reflect the sunlight falling through a window, without this window actually existing. Without employing auxiliary lighting, the luminous yellow succeeds in appearing as a materialization of light, a concentration, illuminated from within.

A helplessness can be found in dealing with the newer medium of electric light, which is different than all those preceding it; 'artificial lights' of earlier times, derived from fire, were based on a process of combustion, invariably had a flame, as well as a location of their own where the burning/shining took place. Originally situated on the floor (fire), light migrated to higher and higher locations in the room: oil and petroleum to the table, gas lamps still higher, on to walls. Electric light is predominantly installed on the ceiling, the earlier described window-like arrangements are the transition from the mere practical application to the artistic.

Electrically produced artificial light can thus be said to be under two-fold pressure towards imitation: lacking orientation, it imitates light as well as apertures. As familiarity with the 'new' medium increases, a separation of location and effect occurs, as demonstrated by Wolfgang Laib's *Luminous Fields*.

While the euphoria over the finally successful substitution of daylight by electric lights was still at its height, a counter-movement evolved which began to again experiment with daylight. Its followers did not find the quality of the man-made substitute all that convincing.

First to receive their attention was the window itself: the window with its unalterable determination of the room lying beyond it, which the user can only fit to his personal conception of lighting through secondary aids, such as window shutters, blinds or curtains.   (... p 94)

Constanze Kreiser, 'On the Loss of (Dark) Inside Space', *Daidalos*, no 36, 1990, pp 88–99. © 1990 Bertelsmann Fachzeitschriften GmbH, Gütersloh. (Excerpt pp 88–99)

Social, Spatial and Temporal Factors

Roderick J Lawrence

Housing and health expert Roderick Lawrence uses a historiographic and ethnographic method of inquiry to examine social variables relative to ordering domestic space, with particular emphasis on rooms for eating and preparing food in Australian and English households. Lawrence points out that although modernism brought aesthetic resolution to the kitchen and dining room, it failed to address a need for these rooms adapting to demographic shifts in family constitution and population. His text reminds us that while houses and their internal activities are ordered by long-standing habits in building and living patterns, they remain responsive to social influences in ways that have the potential to remake and reform them outside of a static framework of living standards. When such issues are considered within ecological reflection, house and housing designs that are attuned to the dynamic processes that occur within them may be produced.

Households possess a range of domestic and personal objects which serve a range of *manifest*, intentional and *latent* unintended functions in the sense used by Velben.[1] Any object may be attributed multiple functions, and a specific function may be fulfilled by different objects. A number of studies including Csikszentmihalyi and Rochberg-Halton, Douglas and Isherwood, Furby, Kron, Laumann and House, Lawrence, Pratt and Weisner and Weibel, show that, by themselves, manifest functions do not fully account for the prevailing pattern of domestic consumption, or the decoration and equipment of homes.[2] These studies therefore confirm Velben's statement that 'we must go on to consider the latent functions of acquisition, accumulation and consumption,' which are 'remote from manifest functions.'[3]

Many possessions do not serve only utilitarian purposes but are a means of communication with oneself, between members of the same household and with the public, including both friends and strangers. Csikszentmihalyi and Rochberg-Halton, for example, conclude from their study of 315 persons, who live in the metropolitan area of Chicago, that the respondents cherished personal possessions not only for monetary or use values, or the material comfort they provide, but primarily because they convey information about themselves and their relationships with other people.[4] In this respect, expected standards of living assume an important role as cues for non-verbal communication as Kron states:

> The furnishings of a home, the style of a house, and its landscape, are all part of a system – a system of symbols. And every item in the system has meaning. Some objects have personal meanings, some have social meanings which change over time! People understand this instinctively and they desire things, not for some mindless greed, but because things are necessary to communicate with ... And what is truly remarkable is that we are able to comprehend and manipulate all the elements in this rich symbol system.[5]

House forms, interior decoration and personal possessions are mediums enabling people to articulate their interpretation of their identity, how they relate to others in the same household and to friends and strangers. They are a means of self-expression, of role relationships, and also of the unequal power of individuals to attribute symbolic meanings to domestic space and objects, in order to express both private/personal and public/shared domains as shown by Bernard and Jambu, Hansen and Altman and Pratt.[6] Simultaneously, the house is attributed personal and social functions; as a haven for withdrawal from society and as a credential for esteem and the respect of others.

This discussion raises important questions about the meaning and use of personal possessions, home decoration and dwelling practices, of different socio-economic groups of people in the same society, as well as comparisons between people in different societies and cultures. Comparative studies of the cultural, social and psychological definitions of domestic objects and processes are overdue, because there is still a scarcity of research that identifies those objects which are more highly valued than others, by different groups of people in the same location, at the same or different times. In this respect, affluence is not merely an indicator that the wealthy own more possessions than the poor; it also implies that the former have a relatively greater degree of control and choice that can reflect and reinforce personal preferences and identity. Beyond the recognition of the pertinence of these questions there is still no comprehensive understanding of the functions of status claims. Moreover, what indicators enable us to measure these functions, and are there penalties for possessing household objects that are attributed contradictory social values? Such questions warrant extensive research in the immediate future.   (... p 118)

Notes

1 T Velben, *The Theory of the Leisure Class*, Macmillan (New York), 1912.

2 M Csikszentmihalyi and E Rochberg-Halton, *The Meaning of Things: Domestic Symbols and the Self*, Cambridge University Press (New York), 1981; M Douglas and B Isherwood, *The World of Goods*, Basic Books (New York), 1979; L Furby, 'Possessions: Towards a Theory of their Meaning and Function Throughout the Life-cycle', P Baltes (ed), *Lifespan Development and Behavior*, Academic Press (New York), 1978 pp 297–336; J Kron, *Home-Psych: The Social Psychology of Home and Decoration*, Clarkson and Potter (New York), 1983; E Laumann and J House, 'Living Room Styles and Social Attributes: The Patterning of Material Artifacts in a Modern Urban Community', *Sociology and Social Research*, vol 54 no 3, 1970, pp 321–42; R Lawrence, 'A More Humane History of Homes: Research Method and Application', I Altman and C Werner (eds), *Home Environments: Human Behavior and Environments, Advances in Theory and Research*, vol 8, Plenum Press (New York), 1985 pp 113–32; G Pratt, 'The House as an Expression of Social Worlds', J Duncan (ed), *Housing and Identity: Cross-Cultural Perspectives*, Croom Helm (London), 1981; and T Weisner and J Weibel, 'Home Environments and Family Lifestyles in California', *Environment and Behavior*, vol 13 no 4, 1981.

3 Velben, *Theory of the Leisure Class*, p 25.

4 Csikszentmihalyi and Rochberg-Halton, *Meaning of Things*.

5 Kron, *Home-Psych*, pp 19–20.

6 Y Bernard and M Jambu, 'Espace habité et modèles culturels', *Ethnologie française*, vol 8 no 1, 1978, pp 7–20; W Hansen and I Altman, 'Decorating Personal Places: A Descriptive Analysis', *Environment and Behavior*, vol 8 no 4, 1976, pp 491–504; and Pratt, 'The House as an Expression of Social Worlds', Duncan, *Housing and Identity*.

Roderick J Lawrence, *Housing, Dwellings and Homes: Design Theory, Research and Practice*, John Wiley and Sons (Chichester), 1987.

(Excerpt pp 116–18)

Wiener Wohnkultur: Interior Design in Vienna, 1910–1930

Christopher Long

early 20th century decoration political 1998

Architectural historian Christopher Long positions the values and work of the Wiener Wohnkultur group in light of emerging modernist design principles of the early twentieth century. The text covers the struggle between everyday inhabitation, historical tradition and craft against the ideals of the total work of art and industrialisation. However, the words and works of architects and designers such as Josef Frank, Oskar Strnad and Adolf Loos, active members of the group advocating 'living or dwelling culture', expose tendencies predating contemporary design attitudes and values towards functional aesthetics, the use of historical references and the sense of an unfinished evolving interior space as the site for living. 'Good', 'pleasing and 'practical' are shown to be attributes of responsible social design aligned with a market place saturated with new lines of furnishings designed to portray a progressive domestic interior.

The desire to merge the fine and applied arts – architecture, design, painting, sculpture, and the various crafts – and to weave together all of these various elements to make a coordinated whole was among the dominant features of Viennese interior design in the years just after the turn of the century. The search for this *Gesamtkunstwerk* ideal found its most complete expression in the work of Josef Hoffmann and the artists and craftsmen of the Wiener Werkstätte, who sought with their own special variant of the *Jugendstil* to forge a design language that would provide the basis for a new, unified modern culture. In the period after 1910, however, a reaction began to set in against such total work of art principles. The revolt was in large part the work of a group of young architects and designers, led by Oskar Strnad and Josef Frank, who emerged on the scene in the wake of two Kunstschau exhibitions in 1908–1909. (These international art exhibitions were organized by Gustav Klimt and his group to show the most recent tendencies in modern art, and they marked a watershed between art at the turn of the century and what followed.) In place of the carefully tuned 'harmonies' of the *fin-de-siècle*, Strnad, Frank, and the other members of their loosely conjoined circle substituted their own distinctive interpretation of the modern interior – a softened, cozy, eclectic look that drew both on historical forms and on more recent design directions such as the English Arts and Crafts movement. In the years between the two world wars, this new aesthetic, which came to be known as the *Wiener Wohnkultur* (literally, the Viennese living or dwelling culture), largely defined modern interior design in the Austrian capital. Perhaps more significantly, however, it also posed one of the main alternatives to the hard-edged, functionalist, and unified design style championed by Marcel Breuer, Ludwig Mies van der Rohe, and the other noted modernists of the time. Indeed, though it has been largely ignored by historians of modern design, the *Wiener Wohnkultur* represents one of the most ambitious and thoroughgoing attempts of those years to reconcile a modern form language with such everyday needs as physical and psychological comfort – precisely those aspects that many at the time found conspicuously lacking in the work of the avant-garde.   (... p 29)

Strnad and the others had been deeply influenced by König's teachings, especially his conviction that an authentic modern style could be based only on historical tradition. Although critical of those who used history as a 'model book,' charging that they 'denied the spirit of the old masters,' König rejected the notion that a modern expression could be forged *ex nihilo*. He assailed the attempts of Hoffmann and the other turn-of-the-century designers to invent a new design language, calling their ideas 'repulsive' and 'at best, empty whim.' In a speech König gave when he became rector of the Technische Hochschule in 1901, he declared: 'The assertion that the forms of architecture are pure products of fantasy is absurd; it is based on the erroneous notion that they exist apart from [their] empirical content.' History alone, he insisted, gives architectural forms their meaning: the 'arbitrary products of the imagination' are not only incomprehensible, but 'belong to the realm of the grotesque.' To abandon the past 'means the destruction of architecture.'[1]   (... p 30)

A living room that Strnad designed around 1912 already displays many of the rudiments of this new design direction. Although vestiges of the *Jugendstil* are still evident – in the geometricized carpet motifs and the rectilinear forms of the glass vitrine, for example – the room as a whole lacks any evidence of a single, unifying concept. The individual pieces exhibit varied treatments, materials, and finishes, and the appearance of the room as a whole is that of an assemblage of disparate parts. The various elements are intended to stand on their own, capable of being moved about at will without fundamentally altering the character of the room. Stylistically, the pieces bear the imprint of a variety of historical influences, but they represent no readily discernible period; their forms instead have been altered and reshaped so that although they seem familiar they are in fact 'new.'

In using historical forms in this way, Strnad departed from the approach of the conservatives as well as from that of the modernists; he neither rejected history nor attempted merely to reproduce it, but instead sought to apply its lessons to the design process. A ladder-back armchair that he also designed around 1912 provides a particularly clear illustration of his approach. The chair is obviously based on eighteenth century English and American models.[2] But Strnad has subtly 'redesigned' it, in the process both altering and slightly attenuating its forms. The result is a piece that is distinctive yet retains many of the characteristics of its historical predecessors.   (... p 32)

In their avoidance of *en suite* arrangements and stereometric detailing, both Frank's and Strnad's works represented a clear repudiation of the *Gesamtkunstwerk* ideals of the Secessionists. Frank wrote a few years later: 'Living spaces are not artworks, nor are they well-tuned harmonies in color and form, whose individual elements (wallpaper, carpets, furniture, pictures) constitute a completed whole. Rather they are spaces that must not only serve the immediate needs of their occupants, but also house both hand-crafted objects of art and machine-made objects of everyday life.' Modern living spaces, he continued, 'require a maximum of movement and brightness, a wealth of colors and forms, objects and materials.'[3] Frank insisted that interiors should present the impression of having evolved naturally over time, as a part of the process of living. It was the client, he maintained, not the architect or designer, who should ultimately decide what was to be included in the modern home. The architect 'can have no influence on what form these objects take.' He can only 'offer a framework or setting for a domicile. The home of an insensitive person, in which the architect has placed the most exquisite objects, tastefully and symmetrically ordered, placed, laid, and hung, will forever remain unfeeling and sober. The living space is never unfinished and never finished; it lives with those who live within.'[4] In rejecting the notion of the architect as supreme arbiter, Frank not only presented the client a new freedom but also redefined the modern interior. Rather than the product of a single aesthetic vision, the home in his view was a place where its inhabitants could live freely without being bound by strict aesthetic rules. The purpose of the home was not to project an image but to provide a genial environment where the events of daily life could unfold freely. By sanctioning the use of a wide range of different elements, both old and new, Frank was also making a plea for a modernism that was evolutionary rather than revolutionary, one that allowed for a new openness and expanded sense of its place within history. As long as objects from the past retained their usefulness and meaning, he insisted, they still had a place in the present.

This notion of using whatever was tenable from history owed much to Adolf Loos (1870–1933). Loos maintained that certain historical decorative art objects – Chippendale chairs, for example – represented a consummate blending of function and aesthetic appeal and could be used as 'ready-mades' in modern rooms.[5] In his domestic interiors, Loos combined various received objects – Oriental rugs, historical and contemporary furnishings, and other decorative pieces – with designs of his own to create arrangements that were familiar and comfortable yet still possessed a character in keeping with modern urban life. Loos's special brand of revivalism and his own strident repudiation of the *Gesamtkunstwerk* idea had a profound impact on Strnad, Frank, and the other members of their circle. In many ways, however, they went even further than Loos. Not only were they more willing to take historical forms and alter them to serve

Josef Frank (1885–1967), 'Living hall for a Country House', Room 13 at the Spring Exhibition Österreichisches Museum für Kunst und Industrie, Vienna, 1912. From *Deutsche Kunst und Dekoration*, v31, 1912, p 190. Photo courtesy of Christopher Long.

their own needs, but they also sought to break down the connection between architecture and interior decoration. While Loos typically still conceived of his furnishings in relation to their architectural surroundings (often arranging them formally or symmetrically to frame or accentuate various architectonic details), Strnad, Frank, and the others placed their pieces freely about the rooms. They also generally dispensed with larger built-in furnishings, preferring instead those that were light and freestanding, and they rejected the wainscoting and formal framing devices that Loos often employed, opting instead for minimal wall treatments – usually only white paint – which allowed the rooms to serve as more or less neutral containers.   (... p 34)

In an article that appeared in *Innen-Dekoration* in 1922, Strnad laid out the basic principles of the new design direction. Home furnishings, he wrote, should be light, movable, and carefully scaled to human dimensions. They should be placed independently of the room and arrayed so that the framing elements of the space – the walls, ceiling, corners, and floor – would remain visible: 'One should never attempt to make "architecture" with furniture,' he maintained, nor should it be used to divide or organize the room. The walls should be treated simply – in most instances merely painted white, which, he argued, would increase the feeling of spaciousness by suggesting the walls' immateriality. Rejecting axial arrangements and matched sets (*Garnituren*) of furnishings, he urged instead the use of casually placed individual pieces. Brightly colored Oriental rugs and fabrics could be added to 'dress' and accent the room, Strnad asserted, but industrially produced articles should be avoided because they engendered a sense of 'unease.' Above all, he cautioned, one should separate 'living and working:' 'a working space is not a living space (*Wohnraum*), and furnishings are not tools.'[6]

Strnad's explicit repudiation of the notion of the house as a reflection of the values and materials of the Machine Age underscored the commitment of the Viennese to preserving the nineteenth century bourgeois ideal of the home as a site of refinement and refuge. By the mid-1920s, however, this idea was increasingly coming to be anathema to the proponents of the modern movement, who argued that the domestic interior should be an extension of the world beyond. The Viennese adopted many of the other outward features of the progressive design of the time, however, especially the interest in greater simplicity and clarity and the emphasis on light and airy spaces. They also shared with more radical designers in Germany and elsewhere the move away from 'single-use' rooms in favor of spaces that provided for multiple activities.[7] Strnad and Frank were particularly concerned in their architectural work with creating spaces that were open, complex, and flowing, which they asserted heightened interest and livability – an idea that also found its way into the work of many other modernists.[8]   (... p 37)

In several articles published in the wake of the exhibition,[9] Frank countered these charges, arguing that while the 'functionalist' style of the radical modernists might be appropriate for the workplace, the home required a very different treatment. Modern man, he proclaimed, increasingly harried at work, needed spaces in which he could escape and relax. The home should not only offer comfortable areas for sitting and lounging but also provide an opportunity for psychological rest – a sense of the familiar and the 'sentimental.' To convert the home into a 'work of art' that excluded all references to the past or to those objects that give meaning to a person's life was to divorce the house from its true 'function.' Uniformity of style and color, which had become such an integral feature of modern design, Frank asserted, served only to foster a feeling of restlessness and unease. The alternative was to promote visual complexity through a myriad of colors, patterns, and forms. But because 'our time is not in the position to make decoration (*Schmuck*) and ornament,' Frank wrote, one had to rely on 'old textiles and patterns.'[10] This was possible because many old forms retained their usefulness despite the innumerable changes of industrialization; modern life, he declared, was rich enough to take over many of the things from former times: 'One can use everything that still can be used.'[11] (... p 42)

The *Wiener Wohnkultur* was neither a movement nor a coherent ideology, but rather an understanding of what people really wanted in their homes. In promoting this sort of 'mitigated' modernism, the Viennese had offered a middle path, an alternative to mere revivalism on the one extreme and a wholesale 'purification' and 'invention' on the other. In the fractious atmosphere of the interwar years, however, such attempts at compromise found few takers, and their message, whatever it merits, went unheeded. What gave the *Wiener Wohnkultur* and the later Swedish Modern their special appeal were not the specific stylistic lessons they offered but the vision of a 'way of life,' a set of general principles of how to dwell in the modern age without having to sacrifice comfort, convenience, pleasure, or a connection with the past. The special contribution of Strnad, Frank, and their followers was that they attempted to make room for these basic human requirements while still trying to speak a language that was consonant with modern life.   (... p 49)

Notes

1 Karl König, 'Die Wissenschaft von der Architektur und ihre praktische Bedeutung', repr in *Bauten und Entwürfe von Carl König herausgegeben von seinen Schülern* (Vienna), 1910, p 9.

2 Oskar Strnad was no doubt quite familiar with such pieces from visits to the Österreichisches Museum für Kunst und Industrie, which had numerous examples of Windsor and other seventeenth- and eighteenth-century English and American furnishings in its collections.

3 Josef Frank, 'Die Einrichtung des Wohnzimmers', *Innen-Dekoration* 30, December 1919, p 417.

4 Frank, 'Die Einrichtung des Wohnzimmers', p 417.

5 See Adolf Loos, 'Josef Veillich', *Frankfurter Zeitung*, 21 March 1929; repr in Adolf Loos, *Trotzdem 1900–1930*, Vienna, 1982, pp 213–18; also see Eva Ottillinger, *Adolf Loos: Wohnkonzepte und Möbelentwürfe* (Salzburg and Vienna), 1994, pp 26–8.

6 Oskar Strnad, 'Neue Wege in der Wohnraum-Einrichtung', *Innen-Dekoration* 33, October 1922, pp 323–4.

7 Christian Witt-Dörring, 'Wiener Innenraumgestaltung 1918–1938', Christian Witt-Dörring,

Eva Mang and Karl Mang (eds), *Neues Wohnen: Wiener Innenraumgestaltung 1918–1938*, exh cat, Österreichisches Museum für angewandte Kunst (Vienna), 1980, p 35.

8   See Oskar Strnad, 'Einiges Theoretische zur Raumgestaltung', *Deutsche Kunst und Dekoration* v31, 1912, pp 39–69; and Josef Frank, 'Das Haus als Weg und Platz', *Der Baumeister*, 29, 1931, pp 316–23. See also Christopher Long, 'Josef Frank and the Crisis of Modern Architecture', PhD diss, University of Texas at Austin, 1993; Christopher Long, 'Space for Living: The Architecture of Josef Frank', Nina Stritzler-Levine (ed), *Josef Frank, Architect and Designer: An Alternative Vision of the Modern Home*, exh cat, The Bard Graduate Center for Studies in the Decorative Arts/Yale University Press (New York and New Haven), 1996, pp 78–95; and Christian Witt-Dörring, 'Wiener Innenraumgestaltung 1918–1938', Witt-Dörring, Mang and Mang, *Neues Wohnen*, pp 31–5.

9   Josef Frank, 'Der Gschnas fürs G'müt und der Gschnas als Problem', Deutscher Werkbund, *Bau und Wohnung*, exh cat (Stuttgart), 1927, pp 49–55; and Josef Frank, 'Die moderne Einrichtung des Wohnhauses', Werner Gräff (ed), *Innenräume, Räume und Inneneinrichtungsgegenstände aus der Werkbundausstellung 'Die Wohnung'* (Stuttgart), 1928, pp 126–7. See also Josef Frank, 'Drei Behauptungen und ihre Folgen', *Die Form* 2, 1927, pp 289–91.

10 Frank, 'Die moderne Einrichtung des Wohnhauses', p 127.

11 Frank, 'Der Gschnas fürs G'müt und der Gschnas als Problem', p 55.

Christopher Long, '*Wiener Wohnkultur*: Interior Design in Vienna, 1910–1938', *Studies in the Decorative Arts*, vol V no 1, Fall-Winter 1997–1998, pp 29–51.
© Bard Graduate Center. Reprinted by permission of the Bard Graduate Center.
(Excerpts pp 116–18)

(Re)presenting Shopping Centres and Bodies: Questions of Pregnancy

Robyn Longhurst

Working within the discipline of geography, Robyn Longhurst's feminist reading examines the relationship between the shopping centre and maternal bodies as a means of unravelling the many ways bodies are socially, sexually and discursively produced, as they inhabit specific spaces. Feminist and post-structuralist theory is used to uncover moments of difference and exclusion, including the uneasiness of pregnant bodies (as markers of sexual activity), within an environment fashioned by a dominant culture that portrays female bodies as slim, attractive and sexy. As a critique on normative interior environments, this essay discloses ways in which gender and sexuality are inscribed on the material landscape of the shopping centre.

Many geographical knowledges tend to be premised on a dualism between mind and body.[1] What is more, the divisions between mind and body are gendered/sexed. The mind (reason and rationality) has long been associated with masculinity while the body (emotion and irrationality) has long been associated with femininity.[2] The discourses of geography in various and complex ways assert a division between abstract, rational Man and embodied, emotional Woman.[3] Of course, in 'reality,' both men and women 'have bodies' but the difference lies in that men are thought to be able to pursue and speak universal knowledge, unencumbered by the limitations of a body placed in a particular time and place, whereas women are thought to be closely bound to the particular instincts, rhythms and desires of their fleshly, located bodies.[4]

In this chapter I put bodies (bodies that are inseparable from minds[5]) centre-stage. Louise Johnson argues that feminist geographers have tended to employ a dichotomy between gender and sex and that there are a number of implications of employing this distinction.[6] One of these is 'the omission of the body as a vital element in the constitution of masculine and feminine identity and the consignment of those who argue for a "corporeal feminism" … into the nether world of biological essentialism.' Johnson goes on to explain that geographers, 'in their zeal to avoid the accusation of biologism and by embracing the logics of historical materialism and liberalism, have ignored the possibilities of examining the sexed body in space.'[7] Yet, as Johnson argues,[8] there are rich possibilities for feminist geographers in examining biology as a social construct rather than treating it as a natural given and/or ignoring it.[9]

One possibility for studying embodiment more closely in geography is to examine the relations between bodies and cities as constitutive and mutually defining. Feminist geographers to date have carried out substantial work on how (male) bodies make or create ('man-made') cities[10] but have focused little attention on how cities make or create bodies with certain desires and capacities. By that I mean, there is a 'complex feedback relation' between bodies and environments in which each produces the other.[11] Elizabeth Grosz argues: 'the city is one of the crucial factors in the social production of (sexed) corporeality.'[12] Examining the ways in which bodies are 'psychically, socially, sexually and discursively or representationally produced, and the ways, in turn, that bodies reinscribe and project themselves onto their sociocultural environment so that this environment both produces and reflects the form and interests of the body,' is a potentially rich area of research for geographers.[13]

I begin to examine some of the ways in which a specific space within a city might produce or create bodies with certain desires and capacities. This does not mean that essentialist accounts of the body have to give way to social constructionist accounts but rather that geographers and others could develop further some of the strategic possibilities for reconceptualising studies of people/environment relations by using a range of approaches in innovative ways. I focus on one distinctive mode of corporeality within a specific historical and geographical context. I examine some of the ways in which the corporeal can condition and mediate pregnant women's experiences of a specific place.

Studying pregnant women offers possibilities for disrupting masculinism in geography[14] in that pregnant women effectively illustrate the notion of Other being Self or Same. Pregnant women undergo a bodily process that transgresses the boundary between inside and outside, self and other, subject and object.[15] This serves to problematise the framework of binary opposition through which the authority of key concepts is established in geography. I focus on pregnant women's relationship not with cities *per se* but with one shopping centre – Centre Place – in Hamilton, Aotearoa/New Zealand.[16] More specifically, I examine how the discursive and material fields of Centre Place reinforce a notion of feminine beauty as slim and of pregnant women as unattractive and no longer sexually desirable.

This chapter is based on stories collected from thirty-one pregnant women, all of whom were pregnant for the first time and living in Hamilton. Sometimes I also spoke with pregnant women's husbands or partners. The data were collected over a period of approximately two years – May 1992 through to July 1994. I conducted focus groups with sixteen women, individual one-off interviews with eleven women and a series of

195

in-depth interviews and ethnographic work (which included visiting Centre Place) with four women for the duration of their pregnancy.

All of the women involved in the interviews and focus groups were near the end of their pregnancies. There was a large variation in the participants' personal and household income. Many had stopped full-time and part-time work. Over half the participants, that is, 61 per cent, were aged between 24 and 29 years old. Only one participant was aged over 35. There were no participants under the age of 15 years but five were aged under 19 years. In terms of ethnicity, twenty-seven participants defined themselves as Pakeha,[17] while four defined themselves as Maori.[18] The conversations with these women were not solely about Centre Place. Usually we talked more generally about their experiences of a variety of public places and activities. The agenda of questions that I used was as follows:

• What activities have you continued to carry out during pregnancy and what activities have you reduced or stopped carrying out during pregnancy?

• Which places have you continued to visit during pregnancy and which places have you reduced or stopped visiting during pregnancy?

• In what ways, if any, have your relationships with family, friends, colleagues and so on changed since you have been pregnant?

• Are there any activities that you have been advised (by family, friends, colleagues, strangers, doctor, midwife and so on) not to engage in during pregnancy?

• What could be done to help improve the quality of life (in terms of both the physical and social environment) for pregnant women who live in Hamilton?

In the course of addressing these questions many of the women discussed Centre Place maybe because it is one of Hamilton's most central shopping malls. I offer the stories in this chapter not as a way of securing 'true knowledge' but as a way of beginning to unravel some of the ways in which bodies are socially, sexually and discursively produced through inhabiting particular sociocultural environments.

Centre Place is situated in down-town Hamilton. Hamilton is a city of 102,000 people[19] located to the west in the northern half of the North Island of Aotearoa/New Zealand. The city grew as a service centre for the outlying rural Waikato dairy industry and has a reputation for being rather 'conservative.' Centre Place covers approximately five acres, contains large skylight windows in the roof and comprises two levels. Development of the centre started in 1984. When it opened in 1985, and for the next decade, it was heavily marketed as the 'Heart of the City' (a heart motif was used in its advertising) in an attempt to restore profitability to the city centre. Recently 'Heart of the City' was replaced with the slogan 'Your Complete Shopping and Entertainment Centre.' This coincided with a number of other changes. A second cinema complex – Village Showcase – opened in the Centre. The outside walls of the Centre were repainted pale mustard, trimmed with forest green. Yet another change was that the previous name, 'Centreplace,' was broken into two – 'Centre Place' – presumably in an attempt to emphasise its (physical and symbolic) central location. The heart motif was replaced with a spiral.

Facilities at Centre Place currently include a multi-storey car park, toilets, a 'lotto' (New Zealand Lotteries Commission) outlet, and a security and information centre. The major attractions include a Food Court, the Fox and Hounds English tavern, the Village 7 Cinema, the newly opened Village Showcase which contains three cinemas, and a range of shops (about ninety-five in total). These include boutiques, a fashion accessory shop, a swim and surf shop, a perfumery, a jeweller's, a florist, an art gallery, two appliance stores and a gift shop. Unlike most shopping centres Centre Place is not anchored by a supermarket or large department store. It is comprised solely of speciality shops many of which target their goods at (mainly Pakeha) women with access to middle/high incomes.[20] (... p 24)

Patrons at the Fox and Hounds tavern are supplied with high, backless bar stools rather than chairs. There are only eight chairs in the entire tavern. These stools were described by Mary Anne as: 'impossible – was sitting there thinking "where's a proper seat?" I was getting sore and so I'd rather not go any more' (individual interview).

It is perhaps no surprise that pregnant women's specific corporeal needs have not been considered by those who designed the tavern since such environments (long associated with alcohol and smoke) are not usually considered by society to be particularly 'appropriate' for pregnant women. It is widely believed that a pregnant woman's primary concern ought to be for her unborn child. The pregnancy in many ways does not belong to the woman herself. Rather, the 'mother' is simply thought to be 'the site of her proceedings.'[21]

Many of the pregnant women reported feeling discomfort in relation to the design and construction of Centre Place. To begin, the toilet facilities were reported as somewhat inadequate for pregnant women on two accounts: first, there are not enough toilets, leading to frequent queuing; and second, the cubicles themselves are small with one of them being positioned very close to a large structural pillar which makes it almost impossible for a visibly pregnant woman to enter. Given that the need to urinate with increased frequency is commonly met at the beginning and especially the end of pregnancy this is problematic.

Another point noted by pregnant women in regard to Centre Place was having to rely largely on stairs or escalators for access to the various levels. Climbing stairs can be tiring for pregnant women and mounting escalators can be problematic due to a change in their centre of balance. Although there are elevators in Centre Place these are small and there are often many people waiting to use them. Obviously there are many people who experience problems using stairs and/or escalators – people with strollers and prams, people with physical disabilities, elderly people, young children and so on.

Yet another problem identified by pregnant women who use Centre Place is that on wet days the flooring becomes slippery as water is tramped inside by users of the centre. Mats are laid out in some areas identified as particularly slippery (such as on ramps) in an attempt to improve the surface. For the pregnant women I spoke to, however, this did little to ease their worries about the possibility of falling and harming their unborn child.

Another problem that was identified for women in the advanced stages of pregnancy was 'fitting' into rows of seats in the Village 7 Cinema in Centre Place. Not only can it be difficult for pregnant women to sit comfortably for any period of time (there is no interval during movies screened at Village 7) in theatre seats but also it is often difficult for them to get to their seats. In the Village 7 Cinema complex four of the theatres have a reasonable amount of room between rows but the other three are cramped. Michelle, who was 33 weeks pregnant, commented: 'Trying to squeeze past people in the row in an attempt to get to your seat is difficult.' Joanne commented: 'People actually got up and moved into the aisle for me – it was really embarrassing.' Some pregnant women also mentioned these problems of uncomfortable seats and access to seats in relation to university lecture theatres and theatres used for live performance. For others, however, these were not considered problems.   (... p 30)

Notes
1   R Longhurst, 'Geography and the Body', *Gender, Place and Culture: A Journal of Feminist Geography*, vol 2 no 10, 1995, pp 97–105.
2   G Lloyd, *The Man of Reason: 'Male' and 'Female' in Western Philosophy*, London, Routledge (London), 1993.
3   See G Rose, *Feminism and Geography: The Limits of Geographical Knowledge*, Polity Press (Cambridge), 1993.
4   R Longhurst, '(Dis)embodied Geographies', *Progress in Human Geography*, vol 21 no 4, 1997, p 491.
5   L Johnson, 'Embodying Geography – Some Implications of Considering the Sexed Body in Space', *New Zealand Geographical Society Proceedings of the 15th New Zealand Geography Conference* (Dunedin), August 1989.
6   L Johnson, 'New Courses for a Gendered Geography: Teaching Feminist Geography at the University of Waikato', *Australian Geographical Studies*, vol 28 no 1, 1990, p 18.
7   Johnson, 'New Courses for a Gendered Geography', p 18.
8   Johnson, 'Embodying Geography', pp 134–8.

9 Longhurst, 'Geography and the Body'; Longhurst, (Dis)embodied Geographies'.

10 See Matrix Book Group (eds), *Making Space: Women and the Man-Made Environment*, Pluto (London), 1984; D Spain, *Gendered Spaces*, University of North Carolina Press (Chapel Hill and London), 1992; and LK Weisman, *Discrimination by Design: A Feminist Critique of the Man-made Environment*, University of Illinois Press (Urbana), 1992.

11 E Grosz, 'Bodies-cities', B Colomina (ed), *Sexuality and Space*, Princeton Architectural Press (Princeton, NJ), 1992, p 242.

12 Grosz, 'Bodies-cities', p 242.

13 Longhurst, (Dis)embodied Geographies', p 496.

14 See Rose, *Feminism and Geography*.

15 I Young, 'Pregnant Embodiment', I Young (ed), *Throwing Like a Girl and Other Essays in Feminist Philosophy and Social Thought*, Indiana University Press (Bloomington and Indianapolis), 1990.

16 Aotearoa is the Maori term for what is commonly known as New Zealand. Over the last decade, especially since 1987 when the Maori Language Act was passed making Maori an official language, the term Aotearoa has been used increasingly by various individuals and groups. For example, all government ministries and departments now have Maori names which are used, in conjunction with their English names, on all documents. Despite these moves, however, the naming of place is a contestatory process (see LD Berg and RA Kearns, 'Naming as Norming? Race, Gender and the Identity Politics of Naming Places in Aotearoa/New Zealand', *Environment and Planning D: Society and Space*, vol 14 no 1, 1996, pp 99–122) and I use the term Aotearoa/New Zealand in an attempt to highlight this.

17 'Pakeha' here refers to Aotearoa/New Zealand-born people of 'European' descent. Although the term 'Pakeha' has been (and at times still is) highly contested in Aotearoa/New Zealand (see P Spoonley, 'Constructing Ourselves: The Post-colonial Politics of European/Pakeha', M Wilson and A Yeatman, (eds), *Justice and Identity: Antipodean Practices*, Bridget Williams (Wellington), 1995) it is now used as a standard term of classification of ethnicity in the New Zealand Census.

18 'Maori' is the term commonly used to refer to the *tangata whenua* (literally 'people of the land') or indigenous peoples of Aotearoa/New Zealand. I use this term here, but wish to problematise such use. As Spoonley (1995) points out, the word 'Maori' is really a convenience for Pakeha/European to lump together divergent groups. The inverse of this, however, does not apply since Pakeha/European do not tend to identify themselves in terms of tribal affiliations.

19 Census of Population and Dwellings, *Waikato/Bay of Plenty Regional Report*, Department of Statistics New Zealand (Wellington), 1991.

20 S Fergusson, 'Myth and the Creation of Urban Landscapes: "Centre Place"', Research Project (unpublished), University of Waikato, 1991, p 23.

21 J Kristeva, 'Motherhood According to Giovanni Bellini', J Kristeva, *Desire in Language: A Semiotic Approach to Literature and Art*, trans Leon S Roudiez, Columbia University Press (New York), 1980, p 237.

Robyn Longhurst, '(Re)presenting Shopping Centres and Bodies: Questions of Pregnancy', Rosa Ainley (ed), *New Frontiers of Space, Bodies and Gender*, Routledge (London and New York), 1998.

© Robyn Longhurst. Reprinteded by permission of Taylor & Francis Books Ltd. (Excerpts pp 20–30)

The Tyranny of Taste

Jules Lubbock

As an expert on British architecture and town planning, Jules Lubbock conveys the degree to which architecture is implicated by politics, economics and morality. This selection focuses on early twentieth-century architecture and highlights modern architecture's intent to have the exterior form of a building determined by the interior. The qualities of the interior necessary to determine this plan included simplicity of form, absence of decoration, hygiene and personal cleanliness, efficiency and mass production. Lubbock demonstrates how British architects sought design changes in the home to reflect modern living and social change that rendered old pretentious house plans obsolete. Traditional spatial qualities of previous eras, especially the Victorian, yielded to spatial functionalism, the open plan and new technologies for heating and cooling.

With the Utility Scheme, the sacred divide between public and private had been breached, justifying fully the widespread fear that an Englishman's home, particularly if he were poor, was no longer his castle. But this was far from being the only effect of the Modern Movement on the previously honoured distinction between people's private and public affairs. The movement's ideology also resulted in radical changes to the ways in which both architecture and town planning were controlled.

In its very early days, with figures such as Loos and even with Gropius and Mies van der Rohe, Modernism had much in common with earlier architectural styles in that it worked within the established framework of the city. The 'Looshaus' in Michelerplatz in Vienna, for example, represented a way of placing a building on one corner of a square that differed from more traditional approaches only in the amount and type of decoration that Loos used. The same is true of Modernist buildings in London from between the wars, constrained by the London Building Act regulations governing height and street lines: the Daily Express building in Fleet Street; Simpsons in Piccadilly; Peter Jones in Sloane Square. Mature Modernism on the other hand declared that it had no truck with 'style,' that it was not a 'style' at all but a 'design method.'

The essential feature of this method was that the plan of a building must proceed 'from within to without,' that the exterior was 'the result of an interior' and neither a buffer between public and private nor something superimposed upon a building by the laws and conventions of the city.[1] One crucial rationale of modern architecture, for reasons given by Le Corbusier and others, was that nothing should impede the achievement of the most desirable domestic or commercial interior; hence the unparalleled attention that was given by architects to the design of furniture and everyday things. Any obstacle that did impede the creation of the new interior, such as the existing pattern of streets or skyline, or the ownership of building plots, or regulations that insisted upon the adherence of new buildings to the pre-existing pattern: all had to be swept away. In the interests of creating a new kind of private interior, the Modernists declared war upon the traditional townscape.

For these reasons one cannot discuss modern architecture properly without discussing modern town planning. As the writers of the 1930s reiterated: the true modern architecture could only flourish and its benefits could only be fully enjoyed if the old regulations were to go. Thus F. R. S. Yorke began his often-reprinted anthology *The Modern House*, first published in 1934, with an apology for the fact that he dealt only with the 'individual villa type house.' He did not pretend that 'the building of villas was a good, or even a possible, solution to the problem of housing the people.' But he accepted that people would continue to want to live in detached or semi-detached houses until the time when 'land is so controlled that flats can be planned in proper relationship to neighbourhoods and to open space.' The rules that were to govern the modern city, therefore, were to be determined to a considerable extent by the internal requirements of the modern home – or, rather, the interpretation of those needs by Modernist architects and their intellectual allies. In addition, the modern city needed to accommodate the motorcar. There was to be no let or hindrance, in the form of public regulations, upon the freedom of architects to work out ways of satisfying these requirements and express and realise their ideas. We shall therefore proceed in a Modernist manner, from inside out, discussing here the architecture of individual buildings before turning to town planning in the following chapter.[2]

So what were the qualities of the new interior that determined the plan of the modern building? Several features have already been mentioned. There was the evolution to a greater simplicity of form and absence of decoration, the cult of hygiene and personal cleanliness, the contribution of time-and-motion methods to the design of the house and particularly to the kitchen, the machine aesthetic and the cult of mass production. We have also referred to Le Corbusier's idea of the home as a machine for living in, a 'House-Tool.' Over and above was the feeling, expressed in the most vivid terms by Le Corbusier in the following passage, that the style of living had totally changed and that the home had to adapt to these new conditions, in exactly the same way as the factory and the office had done.

The Manual of the Dwelling

Demand a bathroom looking south, one of the largest rooms in the house or flat, the old drawing-room for instance. One wall to be entirely glazed, opening if possible on to a balcony for sun baths; the most up-to-date fittings with a shower-bath and gymnastic appliances.

An adjoining room to be a dressing-room in which you can dress and undress. Never undress in your bedroom. It is not a clean thing to do and makes the room horribly untidy. In this room demand fitments for your linen and clothing, not more than 5 feet in height, with drawers, hangers, etc.

Demand one really large living room instead of a number of small ones.

Demand bare walls in your bedroom, your living room and your dining-room. Built-in fittings to take the place of much of the furniture, which is expensive to buy, takes up too much room and needs looking after.

If you can, put the kitchen at the top of the house to avoid smells.

Demand concealed or diffused lighting.

Demand a vacuum cleaner.

Buy only practical furniture and never buy decorative 'pieces.' If you want to see bad taste, go into the houses of the rich. Put only a few pictures on your walls and none but good ones.

Keep your odds and ends in drawers or cabinets.

The gramophone or the pianola or wireless will give you exact interpretations of first-rate music, and you will avoid catching cold in the concert hall, and the frenzy of the virtuoso.[3]

This was taken up by the young British architects and writers of the 1930s who argued that the plan of a house had always been determined by its social functions. The mediaeval house centred around the hall while, in succeeding centuries, more and more private rooms were added for the purpose of display. But now, in the modern age of labour-saving devices, electricity, foreign travel, the disappearance of the dynastic family and the family home that went on for generations, out-of-door leisure pursuits, the cinema, dancing, motoring and motor-bikes, the old pretentious house plan had become obsolete. Boxy little rooms were unnecessary; modern people needed a large open-plan living apartment surrounded by smaller rationally planned service rooms such as the kitchen, bedrooms, bathroom.[4]

For the same reasons, the blazing Dickensian fire crackling in the hearth, standing for the very essence of English life and Cowper's ideal of 'the undisturbed retirement' of the family home, was out of tune with an age in which people went to the cinema, returning home to switch on an electric fire rather than facing the chore of relighting a heap of dead ashes. The living room no longer needed to be planned around the fireplace. With central heating and air-conditioning, the air could be heated, cooled, humidified, de-humidified and cleansed, and as a result the living room could be freely planned around different areas for different activities, removing internal congestion. Hence the importance of the flat roof which, unlike the pitched roof, did not dictate the shape of the house plan. With a flat roof the stairs could be top-lit and placed wherever it was convenient, instead of having to be next to an external wall for the purpose of lighting. Of course such an argument was absurd; for centuries in English terraced houses the stairs had indeed been tucked away in the centre of the house and, in grander examples, were top-lit as well.[5]

But over and above these functional arguments was the glamorous image, often reproduced, of the roof garden designed to echo the decks and sporting facilities of transatlantic liners: a new modern world of sunlight, hygiene and the breezy, unstuffy out-of-doors which Loos had celebrated, a little timidly perhaps, in his vignettes of the English sportsman riding his horse over heath and moor and madly peddling his bicycle. (... p 328)

Notes
1   Le Corbusier, *Towards a New Architecture* (London), 1965, pp 166–7.
2   FRS Yorke, *The Modern House* [1st ed 1934], Architectural Press (London), 1948, p 1. Hence the famous Parker-Morris standards for the internal specifications of *public* housing became the *only* standard to govern the design of a house, but they were standards for the interior in the absence of all statutory controls on the exterior.
3   Le Corbusier, *Towards a New Architecture*, pp 114–15.
4   Yorke, *Modern House*, pp 30–6; A Bertram, *Design*, Penguin Books (Harmondsworth), 1932, pp 71–3.
5   Yorke, *Modern House*, p 55.

Jules Lubbock, *The Tyranny of Taste: The Politics of Architecture and Design in Britain 1550–1960*, Yale University Press (New Haven and London), 1995.
© 1995 Jules Lubbock. Reprinted by permission of Yale University Press.
(Excerpt pp 326–8)

Streamlining: The Aesthetics of Waste

Ellen Lupton and J Abbott Miller

technological ● 1992

early 20th century furnish

Designers and writers Ellen Lupton and J Abbott Miller argue that the streamlined style of modernism emanated from the domestic landscape of the bathroom and kitchen, particularly the hygienic use of non-porous materials. They discuss the ramifications of streamline design as a reflection of mass production and consumption overlaid with the intention of suppressing or denying evidence of bodily waste. In this text Lupton and Miller highlight pivotal moments in the recent history of kitchen and bathroom furnishings as a function of form, economy and hygiene standards to reveal the body's implication with commodity. As such, the interior is constituted to be a site heavily linked to industrialised practices, economies and form-consciousness.

Between 1890 and 1940, America's culture of consumption took its modern form: products were mass produced and mass distributed, designed to be purchased and rapidly replaced by a vast buying public. The same period saw the rise of the modern bathroom and kitchen as newly equipped spaces for administering bodily care. The bathroom became a laboratory for the management of biological waste, from urine and feces to hair, perspiration, dead skin, bad breath, finger nails, and other bodily excretions. The kitchen became a site not only for preparing food but for directing household consumption at large; the kitchen door is the chief entryway for purchased goods, and the main exit point for vegetable parings, empty packages, outmoded appliances and other discarded products. By the phrase *process of elimination* we refer to the overlapping patterns of *biological* digestion, *economic* consumption, and *aesthetic* simplification. The streamlined style of modern design, which served the new ideals of bodily hygiene and the manufacturing policy of planned obsolescence, emanated from the domestic landscape of the bathroom and kitchen. The organically modeled yet machine-made forms of streamlined objects collapsed the natural and the artificial, the biological and the industrial, into *an aesthetic of waste*.

Towards the close of the nineteenth century, various consumer goods, from packaging, appliances, and furniture to interior architecture, began to acquire a vigorous new physique: the plush fabrics, carved moldings and intricate decorations of Victorian domestic objects were rejected as dangerous breeding grounds for germs and dust, giving way to non-porous materials, flush surfaces and rounded edges. This 'process of elimination' found its most extreme expression in the streamline styling of the 1930s, which borrowed the conical 'teardrop' from aerodynamics and applied it to countless immobile objects, from industrial equipment to electric waffle irons. Streamlining used bulbous forms with tapered ends and graphic 'speed whiskers' to invoke the rapid movement of an object through air or water. The mechanical devices of the industrial age, their elements assembled with visible nuts, bolts, belts and gears, surrendered to the new ideal of the object as a continuous, organic body, its moving parts hidden behind a seamless shell appearing to be molded out of a single piece of material.

We suggest that the fluid modeling of streamlined forms reflected the period's twin obsessions with *bodily* consumption and *economic* consumption. Streamlining was born of modern America's intensive focus on waste: on the one hand, its fascination with new products and regimes for managing the intimate processes of biological consumption, from food preparation to the disposal of human waste, and on the other hand, its euphoric celebration of planned obsolescence and an economy dependent on a cycle of continually discarded and replenished merchandise. Streamlining performed a surreal conflation of the organic and the mechanical: its seamless skins fluidly curved yet rigidly impervious to dirt and moisture. The molded form of streamlining yielded an excretory aesthetic, a material celebration of natural and cultural digestive cycles.

The flamboyant product designs of the 1930s were preceded by the more anonymous modernism of the bathroom and kitchen, which earlier had begun to replace heterogeneous collections of domestic equipment with continuous, coordinated ensembles, designed to administer a new technological regime of bodily care.

The bathroom as an architectural space did not exist prior to the late nineteenth century. In the pre-plumbing era, America's reluctant bathing customs revolved around portable containers – tubs, pails, chambers pots, and washstands – which were used in the kitchen or bedroom. As modern plumbing coordinated the delivery and removal of water and waste from the home, the toilet and tub assumed a necessarily fixed position in the home: they became *fixtures*. While early plumbed bathrooms maintained the decorative features of traditional domestic spaces – draperies, carpets, carved details – the 'modern' bathroom emerged at the turn of the century as an overtly industrial ensemble of porcelain-enameled equipment, with white, washable surfaces that reflected contemporary theories of hygiene.

The modernisation of the kitchen followed that of the bathroom, whose aesthetic of obsessive cleanliness resonates in the non-porous materials used for kitchen floors, walls and work surfaces in the 1910s and 20s, and in the gradual shift from free-standing appliances and storage units to boxy, built-in forms. Like the bathroom, the modern kitchen came to favor *fixtures* over furniture: the slender legs supporting individual units were absorbed into monolithic, built-in slabs which linked mechanical devices to work and storage cabinets. The modern kitchen emulated the unforgiving sparkle of the bathroom: it also reflected the production ideal of the modern factory, whose linear sequence of work stations enabled an unbroken flow of activity. This norm, which we call the *continuous kitchen*, was established by the end of the 1930s and still remains powerful today.

The changes in kitchen design were preceded by the rise of food packaging, a phenomenon which accelerated, in the 1880s, and soon dominated urban and suburban grocery sales across the US.[1] The food package encloses the product in a smooth, continuous skin, giving the organic, shapeless substance inside a clear geometric form. The package resists dirt, air and moisture, sealing off the product within, just as the shells of modern kitchen cabinetry and appliances would later enclose the tools and materials of the kitchen behind a seamless surface.

Packaging was a major force in the shift from locally-based agriculture to corporate food production around the turn of the century. By 1910, many brand names which remain 'household words' today were the trademarks of nationally distributed products, including Quaker Oats, Kellogg's Toasted Cornflakes, Heinz Ketchup and Campbell's Soup. Such manufactured personalities eased the transition between the traditional food store and the modern retail outlet, where packaging replaced the shopkeeper as the interface between consumer and product, endowing products with a graphic identity and a corporate address held accountable for defective goods.

Packaging provided a model for the early industrial design profession, whose pioneers extended the principles of advertising and packaging to the product itself.[2] The redesign of an object in the 1920s and 30s commonly involved its external package rather than its working parts. To 'streamline' a product often meant to enclose it with a hard new shell.

Streamlining metaphorically invoked a body gliding through fluid; it also served to accelerate a product through the cycle of purchase and disposal, stimulating sales and hastening the replacement of objects not yet worn out. The built-in disposability of food packaging became a paradigm for consumer goods more generally in the 1920s and 30s, extending a logic of digestion to durable objects. The policy of 'planned obsolescence' pictured the economy itself as a 'body,' whose good health depends on a continual cycle of production and waste, ingestion and excretion.

Advertising became a crucial lubricant for keeping this cycle regular, emerging as a powerful partner of mass distribution in the early twentieth century. Although it raised the cost of conducting business, advertising was defended as a laxative for hastening the flow of goods through the economy. Advertising created desire for new products and generated emotional differences between otherwise indistinguishable ones. It helped spread the emerging standards of hygiene, housekeeping, and nutrition by promoting new products that promised access to the rigorous ideals of modern bodily care.

A 'consumer economy' sells manufactured goods to a large populace through high-volume production, making individual items cheaper by selling a greater number.[3] American designers and advertisers in the 1920s and 30s used the term 'consumption' in reference to 'durables' such as radios, furniture and clothing; the term's more literal reference, however, is to the food cycle: to consume is to devour, to eat in a voracious, gluttonous manner. To 'consume' an object is to destroy it in the process of implementing it, as fire 'consumes' a forest. The advertising executive, Ernest Elmo Calkins, wrote in 1932 that an urgent task of marketing is to make people 'use up' products that they formerly 'used:' cars and safety razors must be consumed like tooth paste or soda biscuits.[4] Calkins thus compared the continual movement of goods through the economy with human digestion. To consume is to ingest and expel, to take in and lay waste. It is a *process of elimination.*

Giving voice to the ethos of disposal, the domestic theorist, Christine Frederick, employed the oxymoronic term 'creative waste' at the end of the 1920s to describe the housewife's moral obligation rhythmically to buy and discard products.[5] Her phrase 'creative waste' elevated the garbage of consumer culture into a form of positive production, valuing the destruction and replacement of objects as a pleasurable and socially instrumental act. Frederick and other promoters of consumerism conceived of 'waste' not merely as an incidental by-product, a final residue, of the consumption cycle, but as a generative, necessary force. In the consumer economy, 'production' finds a place inside the process of consumption, a cycle that reiterates the body's own form of 'creative waste,' excrement.

Reflecting and reinforcing the consumer culture's positive valuation of waste was the shift of cooking, bathing and defecating from positions of invisibility to dominance in the home. Formerly relegated to the cellar, exiled to the outhouse, or merged with the bedroom, these functions came to command the most expensive and technologically advanced features of the modern dwelling, their disciplined aesthetic radiating outward as a standard for the rest of the home and its inhabitants. The new governance of the house by the marginalized functions of the bathroom and kitchen reflected a shifting relationship between architecture and what Reyner Banham has called 'another culture,' comprising plumbers and consulting engineers – a culture 'so alien that most architects held it beneath contempt.' Banham describes a historical rupture in the discourse of design in the eighteenth century that divorced the 'art' of architecture from the making and operating of buildings.[6] We add to Banham's second culture the consumers – often female – who increasingly came to influence the shape of domestic space; the modern technologies of consumption directly address women's role in domestic life, a fact which both empowers and manipulates them.

In his essay on 'Infantile Sexuality,' Freud suggests that during a child's development, the sexual zones move from mouth to anus to genitals: the body is an open, relational field to be mapped and remapped into regions of desire.[7] Although the genitals commonly are viewed as the 'natural,' healthy focus of sexual life, the mouth and the anus are the initial sites of erotic pleasure. Desire, Freud argued, leans on the alimentary functions; desire always works in conjunction with – and in excess of – need, which lends it energy and justification. Desire latches on to the biologically vital functions of digestion; at the same time, physical needs are transformed by their collaboration with desire, and can never again be reduced to simple utility.

We suggest that twentieth-century design gradually articulated the bathroom and kitchen as the erotogenic zones of the domestic body. While the parlor or living room is the home's *symbolic* heart – its 'proper' architectural focus – this center was displaced by the utilitarian regions of the bathroom and kitchen, which became concentrated zones for built-in construction details, costly appliances and on-going maternal maintenance.

The new standards for personal and domestic hygiene, born out of scientifically-based health reforms, rapidly exceeded the demands of utility; the functional 'need' for clean bodies and clean houses has fed the culture of consumption, by mapping out the human and architectural body as a marketplace for an endlessly regenerating inventory of products. Just as sexual pleasure is propped on the utilitarian processes of digestion, the restless desire for new goods builds upon the fetishized routines surrounding biological consumption.

In her reading of Marx's *Capital*, Elaine Scarry describes the relation of manufactured goods to the human body as a relation of reciprocity; every artifact recreates and extends the body. In a zero degree state of production, human beings consume only enough fuel to regenerate their physical tissues. The body takes in food to build and maintain its own structure; the organism itself is the product, yielded through the process of consumption. Production at a more advanced state involves consuming a broader range of materials to further extend the body: chairs supplement the skeleton, tools append the hands, clothing augments the skin. Furniture and houses are neither more nor less interior to the human body than the food it absorbs, nor are they fundamentally different from such sophisticated prosthetics as artificial lungs, eyes and kidneys.[8] The consumption of manufactured things turns the body inside out, opening it up *to* and *as* the culture of objects.

For the product world of the early twentieth century, human digestion served as a metaphor for the economy as well as a territory to be colonized and rewritten by a wealth of new commodities. The consumerist body ingests and expels not only food – the prototypical object of consumption – but the full range of images and objects that pass through the cycle of manufacture, purchase, and disposal. In this *process of elimination*, the body itself is remade.   (... p 9)

During the 1920s and 30s, the modern bathroom and kitchen consolidated out of disparate collections of furniture and appliances into coordinated structures built-in to their surroundings. The bathroom became a compact organism lodged at the core of the home, while the kitchen became a miniaturized, open plan factory. The bathroom and kitchen formed twin temples to the processes of elimination, offering technological environments for the care of biological and economic consumption. We suggest that streamlining, the design style which enveloped innumerable American products in the 1930s, took shape out of the compelling ethos of bodily hygiene and domestic discipline embodied in the modern bathroom and kitchen. The industrially finished yet organically modeled forms of streamlining functioned, in part, as an excretory aesthetic, a plastic celebration of waste.

The technical term *streamline* refers to the path of a particle in fluid as it passes beyond a solid body. The study of streamlining began in the late nineteenth century as part of the new science of aerodynamics. The verb *to streamline*, dating from 1913, means to design or construct with a streamline: to modernize, to organize, to make more efficient and simple.[9]

Streamlining initially was applied to aircraft, ships, locomotives and automobiles in order to reduce the friction encountered as the vehicle passes through air or water. It quickly became a stylistic code evoking 'speed' and 'modernity,' applied to immobile objects for which aerodynamic engineering is more fictional than functional. Raymond Loewy's teardrop pencil sharpener of 1934 became a mythic object lesson in the misapplication of streamlining, cited by later critics as styling at its most absurdly theatrical.

The continuous, sculptural forms of streamlined objects seek to minimize mechanical joints and eliminate visible hinges, bolts and screws. This aspiration towards seamless construction was achieved by applying the processes of stamping, molding, and extrusion to metals and plastics such as steel, aluminum, bakelite and beetleware.[10] Each of these techniques depends on the existence of a 'body' from which the finished product will take its shape. In stamping, a sheet of material is struck against an exterior form; in molding, a formless substance replicates the interior contours of a vessel; in extrusion, a malleable material is forced through a shaped aperture. Stamping, molding, and extrusion each impart a clear, definitive form to a shapeless material.

Streamlining generalizes an object, enveloping its constituent parts inside a continuous body. The industrial designers of the 1920s and 30s sculpted shells to conceal the mechanical organs of objects, initiating a distinction between inside and outside, structure and skin. Numerous examples of product design primarily engage the outer casing of a device, not its working parts; many industrial designers began their careers in packaging, a medium whose built-in disposability offered a model for the planned obsolescence of so-called 'durable' goods. The continual stylistic update of consumer items such as refrigerators, toasters and cars shortened their life span and ensured their rapid replacement by new models.

By masking the machine's internal operation, the designer domesticated and humanized it. Raymond Loewy was certainly aware of the bodily, anthropomorphic quality of his design; in his autobiography he invokes the body of Betty Grable, 'whose liver and kidneys are no doubt adorable, though I would rather have her with skin than without.'[11] Loewy courts a coy Freudianism by titling a chapter of his book 'Sex and the Locomotive,' and he reveals that it was on a train that he was first kissed; such phallic innuendos resurface in publicity shots of Loewy astride his steam engines.

Within the literature on streamlining, phallic symbolism is an accepted subtext: for example, the first chapter of *The Streamlined Decade*, by Donald Bush, is titled 'The Science of Penetration.' Streamlining's evocation of movement, agency and progress, and its propensity for tapered, conical and cylindrical forms, makes it a susceptible carrier for masculine sexual connotations.[12] Yet the reduction of streamlined imagery to a phallic theme overlooks another bodily process: *the process of elimination*. Streamlining presents a surreal conflation of the man-made and the natural; it yields industrial objects whose complex curvature conforms to notions of the organic rather than the mechanical. By engaging the system of deliberate obsolescence with forms that are biologically curved yet industrially hard and incorruptible – and products that are aggressively 'clean' yet designed to be thrown away – streamlining embodied an aesthetic of waste, a material style for expressing the logic of consumption.

In his 1918 essay on anal eroticism, Ernest Jones described two possible reactions to excrement, carried into adult life from childhood experiences of pleasure and shame around the act of defecation.[13] One reaction, largely negative, results in disgust for all forms of waste, from dust, dirt, and soiled linen to wasted time. In behavior, the hatred of filth manifests itself in extreme stinginess, fastidiousness and organizational compulsiveness – a general 'withholding' or 'holding in.' This first reaction to dirt is expressed in modern design's imperative for cleanliness and enclosure, as evidenced, for example, in continuous kitchen cabinets, built-in bathtubs, seamless food packages, and streamlined office equipment. The modern obsession with dirt *affirms* filth even as its seeks to eradicate it: the attention to dust, sweat, bad breath, cooking odors, and the innumerable germs hiding in the cracks and crevices of the home was a process of *objectification* as well as elimination, making visible what had once been invisible, bringing to the surface impurities that once had passed unnoticed.

Jones describes a second response to anal eroticism, which acts upon symbols of waste in a *productive* manner: here, waste becomes the material of art, generosity and a general 'giving out.' Similarly, in the enthusiastic vocabulary of consumerism, phrases like Christine Frederick's 'creative waste' elevated the rhythmic disposal of goods to a form of positive *making*. The seemingly 'natural' life cycle of objects was propelled forward by streamlining, whose organic yet industrial forms marked the coexistence of a fetishized cleanliness with an economy that was dependent on waste.

As Stuart Ewen has pointed out, the marketing and advertising industry was familiar with Freud's manifesto of sublimation, *Civilization and its Discontents*. For example, Egmont Arens noted in his 1932 text, *Consumer Engineering* that *touch* is one of the 'sublimated' senses of modern culture – touch is a primitive faculty that has been culturally supplanted by the more intellectual, 'objective' senses of sight and sound. Arens encouraged designers of products and packages to appeal to the forgotten pleasures of tactility.[14] The sense of touch demands direct contact between body and product; like taste and smell, touch *incorporates* the object of perception – physically *consuming* it – rather than observing it from a neutral distance.

We argue that modern design's appeal to the sublimated sense of touch participated in a larger excretory aesthetic. As described by Sandor Ferenczi, tactility is part of a child's pleasure in handling his or her own feces. Excrement, a convenient but socially offensive toy, is displaced during the child's development by a series of progressively abstract substances: from clay, sand, and rubber to pebbles, marbles and coins.[15] The organically curved yet slick, impenetrable surfaces of streamlined merchandise embody a similar progression from soft to hard, dull to shiny, porous to non-porous, formless to formal. The prototypes for streamlined products typically were molded out of clay and then cast or stamped out of metal or plastic. Each object thus narrates a transformation from pliable, organic matter to a rigid, impenetrable form impervious to change and resistant to grime. The hard surface of the finished product retains the direct trace of its soft, globular origins, lodged in its contours like a childhood memory.

Raymond Loewy's much maligned pencil sharpener expresses a contradictory aesthetic of waste: its bulbous form reflects a pleasure in manipulating plastic matter, as well as a fastidious interest in hiding a messy interior behind the hard, clean physique of a 'streamlined' body. Loewy's pencil sharpener born out of soft, dull clay and then cast into a hard, shiny rigid, recalls the biological extrusions of feces, the child's first work of art; by engaging the policy of planned obsolescence, the pencil sharpener participated in the cycle of economic consumption as well. Streamlining conflates the life of the product with the life of the body, compacting into one form the *processes of elimination*: biological, economic, and stylistic.   (... p 69)

Notes

1 On the rise of corporate food industries, see Alfred D Chandler, *The Visible Hand: The Managerial Revolution in American Business*, The Belknap Press of Harvard University Press (Cambridge), 1977. On the American diet, see Harvey A Levenstein, *Revolution at the Table*, Oxford University Press (New York), 1988.

2 On the industrial design profession, see Arthur Pulos, *American Design Ethic*, MIT Press (Cambridge), 1983.

3 The ideology of consumerism is summarized and celebrated in Daniel J Boorstin, 'Welcome to the Consumption Community', *Fortune*, 76, 1967, pp 118–38. On social critiques of consumerism, see Daniel Horowitz, *The Morality of Spending: Attitudes Towards the Consumer Society in America, 1875–1940*, John Hopkins University Press (Baltimore), 1985. For essays on the development of American consumerism, see T Jackson Lears (ed), *The Culture of Consumption: Critical Essays in American History, 1880–1980*, Pantheon (New York), 1983. On scholarly approaches to the origins and interpretation of consumption, see Grant McCracken, *Culture and Consumption: New Approaches to the Symbolic Character of Goods and Activities*, Indiana University Press (Bloomington), 1988.

4 Roy Sheldon and Egmont Arens, *Consumer Engineering, A New Technique for Prosperity*, Harper Brothers (New York), 1932, p 32.

5 Christine Frederick, *Selling Mrs Consumer*, The Business Bourse (New York), 1929, p 81.

6 Reyner Banham, *The Architecture of the Well-tempered Environment* [1969], University of Chicago Press (Chicago), 1984, p 9.

7 Sigmund Freud, *Three Essays on the Theory of Sexuality*, Basic Books (New York), 1962, pp 39–72.

8 Elaine Scarry, *The Body in Pain: The Making and Unmaking of the World*, Oxford University Press (New York), 1985.

9 On the origins of streamlining, see Donald J Bush, *The Streamlined Decade*, George Braziller (New York), 1975, and Harold van Doren, *Industrial Design: A Practical Guide*, McGraw-Hill Book Company (New York), 1940, pp 137–52. On American industrial design, see Richard Guy Wilson, Dianne H Pilgrim and Dickran Tashjian, *The Machine Age in America, 1918–1941*, Brooklyn Museum (New York), 1986, and Jeffrey L Meikle, *Twentieth Century Limited: Industrial Design in America, 1925–1939*, Temple University Press (Philadelphia), 1979.

10 Clark N Robinson, *Meet the Plastics*, MacMillan Company (New York), 1949, and J Beresford-Evans, 'British Industrial Plastics Limited', *Design*, no 60, December 1953, pp 11–17.

11 Raymond Loewy, *Never Leave Well Enough Alone*, Simon and Schuster (New York), 1951, p 220.

12 Richard Pommer acknowledges the sexual, yet strictly phallic implications of streamlining in 'Loewy and the Industrial Skin Game', *Art in America*, March/April 1976, pp 46–7.

13 Ernest Jones, 'Anal-Erotic Character Traits', *Papers on Psycho-Analysis* [1918], Beacon (New York), 1961, pp 413–37.

14 Stuart Ewen, *All Consuming Images*, Basic Books (New York), 1988, p 49.

15 Sandor Ferenczi, 'The Ontogenesis of the Interest in Money', Sandor Ferenczi and Otto Rank, *Sex in Psycho-Analysis* [1914], Dover (New York), 1956, pp 269–77.

Ellen Lupton and J Abbott Miller, *The Bathroom, the Kitchen, and the Aesthetics of Waste: A Process of Elimination: MIT List Visual Arts Center*, The Center (Cambridge Mass). Distributed by Princeton Architectural Press (New York, NY), 1992.

© 1992 MIT List Visual Arts Center. Reprinted by permission of Ellen Lupton and J Abbott Miller.

(Excerpts pp 1–9, 65–9)

The Architecture of Manners: Henry James, Edith Wharton and The Mount

Sarah Luria

social ● 1999

late 19th century space

English literature scholar Sarah Luria probes domestic interior spaces in the works of two significant nineteenth-century authors in order to expose the extent to which manners, as a form of social order, impact upon inhabitation. She treats several fictional accounts as if they are historical moments, each one intricately unfolded in terms of how the interior is formed, furnished and lived. In these narratives supplemental descriptive background becomes the foreground for the period's role in forming design as a professional practice, and the interior's part in reflection and commentary upon broader gender, political and social issues.

[Edith] Wharton and [Henry] James believed that the home embodied and enforced a social, moral and economic order. Through their literary architecture they sought to redress two dominant domestic models of the Gilded Age – the agoraphobic Victorian town-houses of the old leisure class and the brazenly open mansions of the new Wall Street plutocracy. James and Wharton centred their domestic plan around an innermost room, a space of reflection and writing. The rest of the house served to provide a sequence of increasingly private spaces which led to and protected this sacred chamber. Wharton and James reproduced this climactic floor plan in their architectural criticism, their novels and, most concretely, at The Mount, the summer villa Wharton designed for herself in Lenox, Massachusetts.[1] I shall argue that, unlike the town-house's excessive restraint or the mansion's excessive consumption, the literary architecture of Wharton and James formulated a subtle social economics of restrained consumption. The chain of rooms both encouraged and deferred consumption by guardedly inviting the visitor to keep moving deeper into the house. Ultimately, however, the rooms led to restraint – to a space where one imagined but resisted the actual possession of one's innermost desires. They led, in other words, to the writing of fiction rather than the transgressing of social laws. The possibility of owning one's desires is traded for the more virtuous sublimation of those desires into an endless stream of possible stories for publication. In this way, the literary architecture of Wharton and James reconciled the breach between modern business and Victorian manners by combining positive features of both; their design renewed a tantalising commerce between public and private life, while nevertheless preserving a sacred innermost chamber.

That these two novelists of manners should have taken such a keen interest in domestic architecture has intrigued architectural and literary historians alike.[2] Amy Kaplan and Judith Fryer, in particular, have argued that Wharton's architectural expertise enabled her to redesign domestic space so that it released, rather than buried, her full creative powers.[3] Although they establish a link between domestic architecture and Wharton's identity as an author, both Fryer and Kaplan argue that Wharton's literary powers flourish mainly outside the home. Wharton's determination to join the male-dominated literary marketplace, Kaplan argues, 'pit[s] professional authorship against domesticity' and 'posits a creative realm outside of and antagonistic to the domestic domain.'[4] Fryer suggests that Wharton's creativity was most free in the 'secret garden' in which Wharton said she wrote. Ironically, this imagery of walled-in, outdoor space, Fryer concludes, is in conflict with the architecture Wharton so admired: 'Secret garden ... implies secret, blooming passion of a forbidden or illicit sort,' a 'mind-body fusion that [Wharton] negates in the rigidly controlled structures of her houses, gardens and novels of manners.'[5] In the end, both Fryer and Kaplan suggest that the interest of Wharton's architecture lies mainly in its role as an 'apprenticeship' a 'metaphor' or an analogy for her novels.[6]

In contrast, I contend that Wharton's domesticity is inseparable from her work. The house is essential because it physically realises the aesthetic of deferred and ultimately renounced gratification so prominent in Wharton's and James's work. It is a common literary ploy to postpone the reader's desired conclusion – the moment when the right woman finally gets the right man. In Wharton's and James's fiction, however, this deferred gratification typically leads to a non-event: hero and heroine must accept the social constraints that prevent their happiness and go their separate ways. Architecture, I argue, is instrumental to Wharton and James in bringing this impasse about. Through physical barriers – walls, doors, secluded chambers – literary architecture provides the tangible support needed to resist transgression; it reinforces manners and in that way leads to writing. Architecture, for Wharton and James, hence has the potential to be the space of writing – the buffer which keeps the storyless silence of possession safely at bay. Facing the barrier erected by moral convention, one invents rather than consumes.   (... p 190)

In *The Decoration of Houses*, Wharton warns against grand stairways or any stairway that is visible upon entering the house. To protect the sanctity of the home's private quarters, she recommends a staircase and by that she means a stair encased in its own room, protected by a door at the foot of the stairs and another one at the top.[7] Such a structure occurs at The Mount, as we shall see, and increases the barrier between public and private, between her entrance hall and her boudoir. Mrs Stevens's house must lack such a barrier, since the 'fast set' can shout upstairs. Significantly, this structural accessibility leads to or permits the social transgressions. In his account, Adams associates the fact that the young men 'go up' to the boudoirs with the 'clever game' that has been 'extemporised at the house.' It is as if the beauty contest grew out of the easy-going house and the lifestyle it promotes. The women's features are broken down and assigned a comparative numerical value; the vague, portentous question of a woman's beauty – and hence social value – is reduced to cold figures of commodification.

For Wharton and James, consumption is linked to transgression and they utilise this thrill as their own characters tread closer to the inner secrets of another character's life. But this thrill is only made palpable against a literary architecture of deferral and restraint. By contrast, the modern transgressive impulse makes itself unnarratable because it knows no limits. There is no poetry, no question and no possible story. Private spaces and thoughts have been made conspicuous, brought out to view and consumed for most effective publication.

The rebelliousness of the modern generation was a predictable and, in some senses, justifiable protest against the exaggerated and senseless layering of Victorian life. Wharton herself rebukes the Victorian estrangement of interior from exterior in *The Decoration of Houses*. She points, for example, to the window treatment religiously adhered to in the sitting-rooms of her mother's era:

> The windows in this kind of room are invariably supplied with two sets of muslin curtains, one hanging against the panes, the other fulfilling the supererogatory duty of hanging against the former; then come the heavy stuff curtains, so draped as to cut off the upper light of the windows by day, while it is impossible to drop them at night.[8]

Wharton depicts the Victorian home as a Poe-like setting where one is buried alive. She describes the debilitating effect of such a setting in a frequently-quoted early short story:

> I have sometimes thought that a woman's nature is like a great house full of rooms: there is the hall, through which everyone passes in going in and out; the drawing room, where one receives formal visits; the sitting room, where the members of the family come and go as they list; but beyond that, far beyond, are other rooms, the handles of whose doors are perhaps never turned; no one knows the way to them, no one knows whither they lead; and in the innermost room, the holy of holies, the soul sits alone and waits for a footstep that never comes.[9]

Wharton's psychological floor plan depicts an increasingly alienated course from most public to most private space. The soul is hopelessly removed from the house's business of everyday life. Wharton and James sought to bring the interior and exterior spaces of life back into a tense narratable relation that led from the vestibule all the way to the climactic 'holiest of holies.' Their power to do so stemmed from their understanding of manners. Wharton and James achieve spaces that 'do' a great deal, spaces that are at once conventional and surprising, even magical. The most concrete example of such a space is The Mount.

The Business of Going In

The Mount is also, like the house in the short story quoted above, a 'great house full of rooms' that leads from the outer rooms of Wharton's social life to her 'holiest of holies' – her bedroom. This is where, lying in bed, she wrote her stories. The path from the front door to Wharton's bedroom, essentially the last room in the house (with the exception of the servants' rooms upstairs), takes one through a series of rooms. At The Mount there are no open or vaguely-defined spaces – hallways are treated as enclosed rooms or 'galleries' joined by doors. Even the gardens were planned by Wharton as square 'rooms' connected by corridors or 'walks.' What Fryer terms the 'rigid' layout of The Mount has suggested to R.W.B. Lewis that Wharton had an 'obsession with enclosed as against unbounded spaces.'[10] But Wharton's home exhibits both the ceremony and containment of the old high society and the expansive circulation of the new bourgeoisie. Seven sets of doors lead to the drawing-room alone. The proliferation of doors draws one ever deeper into the house – there is always another door one can go through and a seemingly endless number of paths one can take.

The series of doors that led Wharton toward her inner life created precisely the 'inwardly projected' 'social ... domestic order' that James said manners required. The Mount serves as a gloss on James's curious phrase because the journey through the rooms of The Mount is indeed 'inwardly projected.' Its doors always open into a room, as Wharton says they must, in order to 'facilitat[e] entrance' and give 'the hospitable impression that everything is made easy to those who are coming in.' But at the same time Wharton positions her doors to 'screen that part of the room in which the occupants usually sit.'[11] Wharton's doors offer an invitation to enter and yet protect privacy through their controlled revelation of the house's interior. Like manners, the doors heighten intimacy while they also make social relations more formal. The opening door, for example, restores the key dramatic moment of entrance to its full intensity: it creates a prolonged moment of suspense during which neither the intruder nor the occupants can see each other – a moment of simultaneous revelation and concealment, as the occupants have time to stop what they were doing and turn to meet the new guest. Thus, an inwardly projected domestic order seems as determined to probe the inner life as it is to defend its sanctity. So, too, characters in the novels of Wharton and James rarely blurt out their feelings, but proceed through a discursive path of indirection.

'While the main purpose of a door is to admit,' Wharton writes in *The Decoration of Houses*, 'its secondary purpose is to exclude.'[12] Key doors in the house serve to separate outsiders from insiders, servants from residents and day visitors from overnight guests. Wharton's architectural creed reveals the extent to which doors themselves become a pivotal means of establishing a social order; it is they that do the including and excluding, with the result that they establish an inner elite by determining who is allowed in – and, crucially, how far in. The Mount establishes its subtle social order in large part through movement. Insiders have the greatest number of paths available, outsiders the fewest. Servants have access to the entire house but only through certain doors. While Wharton used The Mount for more general social entertaining, it provided, first and foremost, a retreat for her inner circle of literary friends, which, in addition to Henry James, included, among others, her literary mentor Walter Berry, writers Percy Lubbock and Gaillard Lapsley and the playwright Clyde Fitch. Wharton referred to this group as 'the Happy Few.'[13] Their elite status is registered by the fact that day visitors would have had a limited experience of the house while resident guests would have the privilege of knowing more of its inner mysteries.

One enters The Mount on the ground floor. The entrance hall is cave-like; Wharton conceived it as a grotto. At the south end of the hall is the door to the staircase which leads to the first floor and the principal rooms. At the top of the staircase one finds more doors. To the left is the first floor gallery, straight ahead lies the dining-room and, to the right, the door to the stairwell to the second floor. In the first floor gallery, one confronts more sets of doors. Two sets of double doors on the right lead to the drawing-room. At the far end of the gallery appears to be a set of double doors to Mr Wharton's den. And tucked in the corner, out of sight, lies the door to Edith Wharton's library. All of these principal rooms are also joined by doors between them – one can enter Mrs Wharton's library directly through a door from Mr Wharton's den or through the drawing-room, which in turn adjoins the dining-room. Each of these rooms also opens onto the terrace that wraps around the east elevation of the house, making for a second, outdoor hallway.

The way in which such a sequential floor plan might stimulate the production of fiction is demonstrated by a scene in James's *The Portrait of a Lady* (1881). At the start of the novel we find the main character, Isabel Archer, sitting, as is her habit, in the 'office' of her grandmother's house. The house is itself curious; once a double house, it has now been made into a single one. The office, which James describes as 'a mysterious apartment which lay beyond the library,' must have been the foyer to the old second house[14] ...

Once the foyer, the 'office' is now the last room on the first floor of the house. The old front door hence juxtaposes the public street with the most private room in the house. The bolted door leads not to the street but instead to Isabel's fantasies. This door that Isabel 'can't go into' again produces a richer environment than the drab brown stoop outside. The hope of ever actually possessing her vision – of getting up from the chair and walking through the door to the fulfilment of her innermost desires – is renounced for the ultimately more satisfying ability to wonder just what might be there.

In contrast with those of The Mount and Isabel's home, the floor plans of modern houses were aggressive models of consumption, where one could take in much in one glance or march straight upstairs and have one's fun. The literary counter-aesthetic of hindered pursuit and ultimate renunciation which I have been describing here is exhibited by what are essentially the last rooms in The Mount – the bedrooms on the second floor. These rooms are also, in an important sense, 'offices.' When shown to her guestroom, one of Wharton's guests exclaimed, 'What a perfect desk – everything conceivably needed for writing is there.'[15] When we consider Wharton's description of her writing process, we see that the bedrooms are perhaps spaces where one sublimates, rather than consummates, one's inner desires. (Both authors appear to have led largely celibate lives.[16]) Wharton describes her writing in bed as a rather dream-like erotic state. She 'waits breathlessly' for her characters to 'possess' her. She 'labors' and gives 'birth' to her novels.[17] Buried deep within her house, Wharton, like Isabel, embarks on endless paths of fiction.   (... p 198)

Rather than lead to some climactic event, the 'consecration' of their magnificence, the evening trails off inconsequentially into another American example of 'this struggle in the void – a constituted image of the upper social organism floundering there all helplessly.' The evening and the environment lack an overall narrative that leads, ultimately, to the attainment of a superior, interior space of production. The 'palace' is perfect, but in outward form only. James implies that the 'pitch' from the start is too high. One starts at the top and has no place left to go. There is no hierarchy of space, 'no sequence;' the evening does not connect or 'rhyme' with anything outside of itself. Only a 'great court-function' would have sufficed to 'crown the hour' and this the American 'upper social organism' of course cannot provide.[18]

The too high formality of the New York party missed not only the spatial but also the temporal development of a social evening. Where would a dinner-party at The Mount have 'gone on to' after eleven o'clock? The house's spaces provide a full range of scenarios for a productive evening. There is no need to go elsewhere, outside the estate, to an 'after-opera' party for instance, in order to achieve the evening's crowning moment. Depending upon how large or literary her company, Wharton would have led them to the drawing-room, the library or, if the evening and the company were fine, the terrace. Rather than a progression to increasing formality and ceremony, the rooms at The Mount suggest a course from formal relations to less formal, the intimacy increasing with the lateness of the hour.   (... p 199)

Wharton is careful not only to establish a climactic course between her rooms but also within each room itself. Each room at The Mount is preserved, in her words, as 'a small world by itself.'[19] Each retains, as James called it, 'that room-suggestion which is so indispensable not only to occupation and concentration, but to conversation itself.'[20] The library functions as a stage set that not only accommodates but also nurtures serious literary study. A chaise longue offers a comfortable place to immerse oneself in a novel; a table for periodicals suggests a browse through the contemporary literary scene; a cluster of seats around the fireplace invites focused literary discussion; and a fancy writing desk serves, since we know Wharton did not write fiction here, perhaps mainly as a symbol to remind the room's occupants of the final stage in the writer's absorption of great literature. Like the narrative structure of the rooms as a whole, the library furniture divides the preliminary work of writing fiction into several discrete tasks which together form the path described by Wharton in the artist's own development – from the study of 'the great literature of the past' and contemporary works, through reading and conversation, to the stage where the writer is ready to write her own work.[21] We move, in James's words, between 'concentration,' 'conversation' and 'occupation.' The careful arrangement of the room achieves and reunites both meanings of 'occupation.' The professional occupation which the library supports is one of spiritual fullness-of-being occupied by the deep and elusive meanings of human relations.   (... p 201)

Notes

1 For a wonderful description of Wharton's floor plan of The Mount and how that plan resonates in some of her novels, see J Fryer, *Felicitous Space: The Imaginative Structures of Edith Wharton and Willa Cather*, University of North Carolina Press (Chapel Hill), 1986 pp 65–75. The wide-ranging associations Fryer covers in her discussion of Wharton's architecture has opened up numerous paths of enquiry. I draw upon some of these in my analysis of Wharton's architecture as a specific social and economic order.

2 See for example, architectural historian RG Wilson's account of The Mount in 'Edith and Ogden: Writing, Decoration and Architecture', PC Metcalf (ed), *Ogden Codman and the Decoration of Houses*, David P Godine (Boston), 1988, pp 133–184. For a more theoretical study of James's use of architecture, see EE Frank, *Literary Architecture: Essays Towards a Tradition*, University of California Press (Berkeley), 1979, pp 167–216.

3 Fryer argues that it was not until Wharton escaped Newport and New York and built The Mount that her full creative powers were at last unleashed; see Fryer, *Felicitous Space*, pp 65–74. Kaplan contends that Wharton managed to escape the tradition of domestic, sentimental women's literature by writing *The Decoration*. Wharton's concept of 'interior architecture', set forth in *The Decoration*, provided an enabling 'metaphor' by which Wharton was able to get control of the home and enter the male-dominated marketplace as a 'professional' author; see A Kaplan, *The Social Construction of American Realism*, University of Chicago Press (Chicago), 1988, pp 77–80.

4 Kaplan, *Social Construction*, pp 70, 74.

5 Fryer, *Felicitous Space*, p 173.

6 Fryer discusses the structure of Wharton's first novel, *The House of Mirth*, as analogous to the floor plan of The Mount, see Fryer, *Felicitous Space*, p 75. For 'apprenticeship', see Kaplan, *Social Construction*, p 67.

7 E Wharton and O Codman, Jr, *The Decoration of Houses* [1897], Norton (New York), 1978, pp 112–17.

8 Wharton and Codman, *Decoration of Houses*, p 20.

9 E Wharton, 'The Fullness of Life', RWB Lewis (ed), *The Collected Stories of Edith Wharton* [1893], vol 1, Scribners (New York), 1968, p 14.

10 RWB Lewis, *Edith Wharton: A Biography*, Harper (New York), 1975, p 121.

11 Wharton and Codman, *Decoration of Houses*, p 61.

12 Wharton and Codman, *Decoration of Houses*, p 103.

13 Lewis, *Edith Wharton*, p 425.

14 H James, *The Portrait of a Lady* [1881], Penguin (New York), 1988.

15 P Lubbock, *Portrait of Edith Wharton*, Appleton Century Crofts (New York), 1947 p 28.

16 On Wharton's sex life with her husband, see Lewis, *Edith Wharton*, p 55. On James's celibacy, see L Edel, *Henry James: A Life*, Harper (New York), 1985, pp 166–7.

17 E Wharton, *A Backward Glance*, Scribners (New York), 1934, pp 198–204.

18 H James, *The American Scene* [1907], Scribners (New York), 1946, pp 162–3.

19 Wharton and Codman, *Decoration of Houses*, p 22.

20 James, *American Scene*, p 167.

21 E Wharton, *The Writing of Fiction* [1925], Octagon (New York), 1966, pp 18–22.

Sarah Luria, 'The Architecture of Manners: Henry James, Edith Wharton and The Mount', Inga Bryden and Janet Floyd (eds), *Domestic Space: Reading the Nineteenth Century Interior*, Manchester University Press (Manchester), 1999.
Reprinted by permission of Manchester University Press.
(Excerpts pp 188–201)

'House Beautiful': Style and Consumption in the Home

Ruth Madigan and Moira Munro

Ruth Madigan and Moira Munro's discussion of self-expression, personal style, and the constraints of social class and familial relations takes a social science approach to domestic consumption. Their qualitative interviews of working- and lower middle-class households suggest that 'good design' is not a condition of 'good taste'. Occupiers tended to reflect notions of homeliness, warmth and welcoming, in which consumer decisions are driven by use-value over style. For these consumers, judgements on their home are more concerned with respectability above style and visual presentation. Central to this work is a realisation that the domestic interior is constantly renegotiated in order to resolve the tension between identity and social role.

Twentieth-century changes in the technologies of heating, plumbing and refrigeration have had profound effects on the physical design of mass housing: the introduction of bathrooms, the disappearance of sculleries and the advent of the fitted kitchen.[1] More recent innovations in technology have focused on the home as a leisure centre, rather than the 'labour saving' devices for a place of (house) work. Deep-freezers, dishwashers and tumble dryers were first included in the General Household Survey in the 1970s, while video recorders, home computers and CD players were added in the 1980s, and wrought their impact primarily on the living-room or lounge. The central focus of the modern living-room has switched from the fire-place to the television. Televisions, which like radios[2] were initially disguised to look like pieces of furniture housed in wooden cabinets, have graduated from brown plastic teak-effect to a more obviously technological black casing, along with the video and sound system. The hi-tech look created a more masculine and industrial aesthetic. It is perhaps no coincidence that men rather than women were the target for home-based consumption in this area of leisure products, reflecting a gendered division of labour in which the home still functions as a place of rest, leisure and recuperation for men, but remains a place of work for women.[3]

The broad movements of contemporary design: Art deco, Moderne, Scandinavian modern, Hi-tech, only partially reflect popular preferences. If we look at what is actually available in modestly priced, mass-market stores (Landmark, MFI) we find a range of

221

choices which might be described as either traditional cottagey (flowers and pine); country house (flowers and mahogany); modern, hi-tech (plain colours and black ash); and postmodern (pastel colours and beech). There are many influences on the currents of popular taste. Adrian Forty has pointed out how different regimes of commercial management are reflected in different styles of office design.[4] The industrial efficiency of the hi-tech design was associated with Taylorist 'scientific' management regimes, only to be supplanted by a softer design (lighter colours and 'personal enclaves') to accompany the later human relations school of management. Office design has a real echo in home design where the starker contrasts of hi-tech are rapidly being replaced by pastel shades, lighter woods, and softer upholstery not unlike the 'customer friendly' refits which have transformed the public areas of building societies and banks over the last five years.

In practice, all these styles spill over into one another because few people buy all their furniture at the one time and because the styles themselves are hybrid. Lower income households are less likely to buy new furniture at all, relying on second hand purchases and hand-me-downs. Even when furniture is put together in room displays (as in mass-market mail order catalogues) the hi-tech style, for example, matches black ash units, black leather seating and plain floor coverings, with ruched bordello curtains and embossed velveteen wallpaper. It is these touches of plush which for most consumers rescues an otherwise sparse, Spartan style and imparts a feeling of comfort, luxury and indulgence which is important to many people's ideal of 'home,' but conflicts with a designer view of style, and no doubt 'good taste.' One can see both Hollywood and the country house providing images of what constitutes luxury in popular taste.

Change in the furniture industry has been a product of changes in retailing and distribution[5] rather than innovations in the production line. Production methods have on the whole remained rather traditional, relying on standardisation to make cost savings, batch production rather than mass production, power tools rather than automation. Ironically it is this which has enabled producers to continue to describe their products as 'made by the finest craftsmen,' 'upholstered by hand' with all the connotations of luxury hand-made objects and skilled crafts, when in fact most three-piece suites are constructed from the roughest of frames (hand made) and covered with foam and fabric using nothing more refined than a staple gun.[6]

This claim to craftsmanship is important in the iconography of furniture. It reinforces the familial values which are central to ideas of 'home:' solidity, continuity and honesty. But it also has important class overtones. As Bourdieu notes, the upper classes have always had a preference for antique products which may directly represent family continuity through inheritance, and may also be seen as investment.[7] These values have been reiterated by the professional and managerial middle classes' choice of reproduction furniture, old rather than antique, or real wood (the history of stripped pine would tell a

222

tale), though the language of craft production is also used to promote even cheaper ranges of furniture.

Despite these elements of conservatism in the furniture industry, there have been some important changes. The growth in out-of-town stores accessible to car owners[8] with lower rentals mean more space for display, with mock-up interiors including suggested colour schemes and accessories. The addition of cafés and children's play areas indicates a shift towards 'leisure shopping,' recognising that many people like to browse and absorb ideas without any immediate intention to buy. Ironically, DIY stores are an increasingly important outlet for furniture, particularly flat-pack furniture which perhaps represents the biggest single innovation in furniture production and marketing, overcoming many of the problems of storage and transport and substantially reducing labour costs in construction. Other mass-market stores remain relatively specialised however. Few have followed the Habitat/IKEA route, selling a 'total life-style concept' though these stores have undoubtedly had an impact on taste beyond their immediate range of customers.

Our own research begins to explore how far the aesthetics of the home are influenced by fashion (i.e. commercially-inspired styles designed to sell) and the extent to which these styles reflect other meanings derived from definitions of home in terms of familism or social class. These considerations were explored in two closely related pieces of empirical work: a postal questionnaire with 382 respondents, and twenty extended interviews, both carried out in 1991 …

It was immediately striking in our interviews that there was not generally a strong involvement with design as a way of expressing and demonstrating 'good taste.' Our sample of working-class and lower middle-class households did not appear to share the vocabulary of design and style promoted so strongly in the design-conscious 1980s. Responses to questions about how major items were chosen undermined the notion that respondents generally had a firm idea of the style they wanted to present. Instead, they pragmatically went out and bought what was available.

Mrs N: We just went to the shop. It was as simple as that. I didn't sit and plan it out or anything (aged 26, owner-occupier).

Such comments should not be taken to imply that there was no care or no interest in furnishing and decorating of the home, but the specifics of design were not uppermost. For most people such considerations were subordinated to other, related images of home, family and social class. When asked to describe what impression they hoped other people would have of their home, typically respondents expressed notions connected to familial ideology – homeliness, warmth and a welcoming feel:

Mrs G: That you can come in at any time, it's nice and homely (aged 28, owner-occupier).

Mrs R: You can come in and feel at ease, they don't have to feel that they have to watch what they are doing (aged 45, owner-occupier).

These expressions are also closely related to findings explored in our previous work which examined the meaning of privacy in the home. We argued that an important element of familial ideology was that the home should be a relaxed 'back-region' where material wealth and show is much less important than the human relationships sustained.

There is, however, a tension between the notion of home as a place in which to relax and the recognition that the home may also be revealing about the household. In the social groupings represented in this sample, the social standing of the household appears to be more strongly reflected in criteria of respectability, expressed as keeping up standards of cleanliness and tidiness, rather than overt striking for 'good taste' or a 'sense of distinction.'[9]   (... p 47)

The postmodern debate has rightly drawn attention to the pleasure people take in consumption. This is an important antidote to a rather one-sided view of consumers solely as 'victims' of aggressive marketing and manipulative advertising. However, the view of consumption as pleasurable leisure activity and a means of self-expression is easily overdrawn. 'Home' is an important expression of identity, yet it is an identity which is only partially achieved through appearances (furnishings and decor) and overt consumption. The social relations and 'etiquette' which dictate both relations within the household, and between the household and a wider public, are for most people much more important. The human relationships of being able to make people feel welcome, comfortable and relaxed, either as outsiders or as family members appear to be the dominant concern of the households in this study. They did not engage in discussions of style and design when expressing the way in which they hoped to achieve this effect. However, this apparent rejection of the centrality of consumption in shaping and expressing meanings of the home does not represent the full complexity of the relationship between the household and the home for the households in our study.

First, it is important to remember that this study contained households on relatively modest incomes. There is no doubt that participation in lifestyle shopping, careful co-ordination of style and detailed attention to 'taste' is severely restricted by considerations of cost and utility. The expense of buying major items militates against the development of a grand design and severely restricts the ability to respond to any new fashions in home furnishing. In the typical case things are acquired gradually and expected to last some time. It was evident that an important criterion for choosing furnishings and décor was their functionality, variously expressed as suitability for children, ease of keeping clean and the probable life of the item. Use value is a concept which gets neglected in the whole debate about the playfulness of signs and symbols.

Second, the judgements that these respondents typically believe are made about their houses are not to do with visual presentation and style, but to do with respectability. Standards of cleanliness and the efficiency of domestic organisation carry heavy moral overtones.[10] They are laden with judgements about social worth, as embodied in the division between the 'respectable' or decent poor and the 'feckless' or undeserving – though by no means confined to those who would consider themselves poor. These are issues which create anxiety not playfulness, particularly for women. Women typically take the responsibility for setting and maintaining standards of housekeeping and bear the brunt of unfavourable judgements. A common strategy of dealing with the potential conflict between the notion of home as a place of comfort and relaxation and the high standards of housekeeping required, is to reconcile the two in the notion that it is impossible to be relaxed or comfortable in a house that does not meet the high standard of cleanliness and tidiness desired. This, of course, implies a burden of constant effort to maintain these standards.

Third, advertising is designed to play on insecurities about being a good housewife/mother, and an attractive/fashionable wife or worker. The images that are presented create pressures to consume, underpinned both by the desire to have a clean and respectable house in which things are not worn or used, but also to be stylish. Shops and magazines often display fully coordinated sets of goods (furniture, carpets, fabrics, wallpapers, accessories) and design ranges with carefully matched and contrasting patterns and colours. The current style is arguably to present such displays as if they were an artful and individualistic assemblage, reflecting skill in interior design.

There was a considerable degree of anxiety expressed about an inability to reproduce such a harmonious effect through serendipity, suggesting both that people did feel it was important to achieve the right sort of look and also that a message that it is skill rather than money which achieves the effect is accepted.

We cannot forget that 'commodities' are designed for sale at profit. The creation of a postmodern aesthetic is just as much about selling as the mass marketing associated with Fordist production, even if it presents apparently more differentiated customised products. Differentiation may meet specialised needs and in that sense represents a response to the consumer, but it is also about creating 'needs' and amplifying social divisions. The evidence presented here suggests that people feel under increasing pressure to conform to a heightened consciousness of design and style in the home. For poorer households, this may not represent freedom to manipulate symbols and images in a way that enables self-expression, but may instead serve to re-emphasise their lack of resources.

We have tried here to get some insight into the way in which women, in particular, view their home and the items they have selected for it. We are very dependent on their own reporting; we did not, for example, participate in shopping trips or the process of decision making. We have to recognise that some responses are purely conventional. Everyone is scathing about the tactics used to sell double-glazing, but that does not mean they are immune to the hard sell. People can obviously be manipulated by advertising without realising, or despite their best intentions. Nonetheless, the apparent contradictions in an individual's responses are most revealing about the processes at work: the conflict between the home as a place to relax and make yourself comfortable, as against an ever-present sense that standards must be maintained; the idea that consumerism is something to be rejected and yet to be seen as out-of-date, or old-fashioned is a personal condemnation; the belief that things should be selected for utility and comfort competing with the desire for things which are new and look new.

Home and family are powerful concepts which shape not only the way in which we *perceive* our physical surroundings, but also the way in which we *construct* our surroundings. In some sense the physical can become an embodiment of these culturally dominant ideas. However, we must beware of simply 'reading off' meanings uncritically, without looking at how objects are used in practice. The 'family home' as presented by any of the major house-builders, for example, carries important symbolic meanings which are built-in to the very design of the house. This constrains but it does not determine the way in which the house is used, or the meanings which the consumers attribute to it. It is the complexity of this interaction between the physical and the intellectual, the objective and the subjective, which is emphasised in Bourdieu's concept of 'habitus.' As with other aspects of social life, style in the home is the subject of constant renegotiation. It is an important aspect of self-presentation and a statement about the social roles to which individuals aspire. It is constrained and circumscribed by the dominant and conventional meanings attributed to different patterns of consumption, and the material resources available to the consumer.   (... p 56)

Notes
1   WHE Dudley, *Design of Dwellings*, HMSO (CHAC, London), 1944.
2   A Forty, *Objects of Desire: Design and Society 1750–1980*, Thames and Hudson (London), 1986.
3   R Deem, *All Work and No Play: The Sociology of Women and Leisure*, Open University Press (Milton Keynes), 1986.
4   Forty, *Objects of Desire*.
5   L O'Brien and F Harris, *Retailing, Shopping, Society and Space*, Fulton Publishers (London), 1991.
6   Despite the relative expensiveness of furniture as a product compared with other household purchases, one-third of all furniture manufacturers have a turnover of £50,000 p.a. or less. Fifty-nine per cent of employees in the furniture industry are in enterprises which employ fewer than 100 people (compared with 18 per cent in the food industry, for example). (CSO Business Monitor 1990).

7 P Bourdieu, *Distinction: A Social Critique of the Judgement of Taste*, Routledge and Kegan Paul (London), 1984.

8 Q Lumsden, 'Take Some Comfort in Furniture', *The Independent on Sunday*, 25th July 1993.

9 Bourdieu, *Distinction*.

10 M Roberts, *Living in a Man-made World: Gender Assumptions in Modern Housing Design*, Routledge (London), 1991.

Ruth Madigan and Moira Munro, '"House Beautiful": Style and Consumption in the Home', *Sociology*, vol 30 no 1, 1996, pp 41–57.

© BSA Publications Ltd 1996. © Ruth Madigan and Moira Munro. Reprinted by permission of Ruth Madigan, Moira Munro and Sage Publications Ltd.

(Excerpts pp 43–56)

Living in Glass Houses

Kevin Melchionne

In this exposition on aesthetics and the interior, Kevin Melchionne proposes that Philip Johnson's Glass House *is a particularly hyper-organised interior environment that has a conception of order embodied in the arrangement of objects. Understood this way, domesticity becomes both an act of making and an art of living, implying that domestic practice is aesthetically and artistically significant. This notion is further expanded upon through the proposition that it implicates 'tidying' and labour in the art of domesticity.*

social ● 1998

mid 20th century material

In his *Philosophy of Interior Design*, Stanley Abercrombie writes that 'we can live happily with art – some cannot live happily without it – but we cannot live *in* art or even in a "white cube."'[1] This is a strange assertion by someone writing a book on interior design theory. Interior design is presumably an art and since we live in interiors, we must also live in art. Of course, what Abercrombie means is that we cannot live in interiors entirely given over to an aesthetic vision and, consequently, divorced from all consideration of what it might really mean to inhabit them. Abercrombie's examples include Piet Mondrian's *Salon de Madame B.* and Kurt Schwitter's *Merzbau*. I think we could add, by implication, a number of what are typically thought of as extreme examples of modern architecture, notably Philip Johnson's notorious *Glass House* in New Canaan, Connecticut.[2] The *Glass House* is a canonical example of high modernist architecture and interior design. The walls are made of plate glass, enclosing the structure while retaining a complete 360-degree view of the property outside. From the outside, one gets a free view into the interior as well. The interior itself is sparsely but carefully furnished in the characteristic high modernist mode.

Johnson's *Glass House* captured a great deal of attention when first built. It is still widely hailed as a high modernist masterpiece and is regularly included in surveys of modern architecture. At the same time that Johnson's house is celebrated as great architecture, it is sneered at for being unlivable. Despite its art-historical significance, the *Glass House* is thought by most to be unlivable not necessarily because it is aesthetically displeasing, but because it subordinates all other goals to this aesthetic pleasure. If the interior of the *Glass House* is thought of as ugly by many, it is perhaps because the attractiveness of an interior depends not just on visual spectacle but also perceived livability. The *Glass House* lacks what we judge today as livability: comfort, casualness, and a certain degree of dowdy familiarity. The building serves more to make an aesthetic point or an art-historical splash, and these motivations turn out here to be separate from the more mundane pleasures of domestic life.

At first glance, the *Glass House* seems to be very much a work of environmental art. Surrounded by glass walls, the occupant is immersed in, though not physically subject to, the shifting atmospheric conditions of the outdoors. Perhaps no other house allows the occupant a more intimate sense of its natural surroundings. But is this what is meant by an environmental aesthetic of domestic space? A basic precept of any introductory interior design course is that the role of interior design is to provide artistically satisfying and practically effective solutions to the organization of the environments in which we must do particular things, like cooking, entertaining, sleeping, bathing, and lounging. The art of domestic interior design would be to create an environment that facilitates domestic practice while at the same time making the environment worthy of aesthetic attention and admiration. On this view, the *Glass House* fails as full-fledged interior design (that is, as environmental art) because it never recedes into the background, never becomes an environment for the practices of everyday life.[3] The glass walls render the occupant perpetually self-conscious of being watched; the sparseness of the furnishings and the extreme orderliness of the house, where even table-top bric-a-brac are discreetly marked with indications of their correct location,[4] mean that one can never feel truly at home. The *Glass House* contradicts the long-standing Western association of dwelling with enclosure, privacy, and relaxation. As these tendencies are deeply entrenched, one can never get used to the *Glass House* and so can never truly inhabit it. But what a revealing failure it is! It is my contention that to genuinely understand what it takes to live in the *Glass House* will bring us a long way in understanding how it is that the *ordinary* process of inhabiting our homes is an artistic practice, a kind of environmental art.

On the conventional view of interior design sketched above, to truly inhabit the *Glass House* would require that one 'fix' it by adding some rooms off the back, walling in some of the plate glass, and introducing more furniture and clutter. But then, the building would no longer be the *Glass House*, the work of art designed by Philip Johnson. In order to live in a work of art, one must respect it as a designed product, that is, one must live according to its rules. This means not moving the furniture or adding objects, lest the composition be destroyed. It also means making sure that mess and clutter do not take over such that we can no longer see the original artistic creation. The respectful occupant must be a curator of sorts, preserving the house while living in it. This is clearly a difficult

229

way to live! Nonetheless, it is possible to inhabit the *Glass House*, but obviously one must be a special sort of person whom I shall term a 'radical aesthete.'

It is revealing that Johnson did not propose the house as a universal model of 'true living.' As he famously retorted to one visitor who expressed her aversion to living in it, Johnson did not design the house for anyone but himself. Johnson seems to embody this radical aestheticism; he gives to the search for aesthetic pleasure more importance than most people and is perfectly satisfied to live in ways that others perceive as dreadfully uncomfortable, even inhuman. In another of his famous quips, Johnson says that 'comfort is a function of whether you think a chair is good-looking or not.'[5] Thus, we can assume that Johnson does not experience the *Glass House* as uncomfortable. Rather, we should believe that Johnson inhabits the house in perfect harmony with its severe rules, which, after all, are presumably his own. Johnson never feels compelled to drag in a book case or a dumpy chair found at a tag sale, leave his clothes on the floor or let dishes pile up in the kitchen sink for days.

But perhaps Johnson does not really *live* in the *Glass House* as most people live in their houses. After all, the *Glass House* is not his primary residence. It has always been more of a weekend retreat from New York. There are numerous outbuildings on the property, probably serving to capture the predictable overflow of 'stuff' from the architectural masterpiece. Perhaps Johnson only pretended to live in the *Glass House* in order to make an aesthetic point or to promote himself as an architect. On this view, the *Glass House* remains half stage set, half hotel room. Were this an accurate representation of his intentions, Johnson's aestheticism would be posturing. For my purposes, it scarcely matters whether Johnson is really the radical aesthete that he makes himself out to be. It is possible to imagine how he would have to live were he to live in the house as it was supposed to be lived in, that is, to live in it in a way that respects it as art. We can still sketch out the domestic practice of this special person – a limit case of sorts – to help explain how living in a house on a daily basis can be seen as an environmental art.

Perhaps the *Glass House* is unlivable as a domestic space; but as a work of fine art, the *Glass House* does exactly what it is supposed to do, namely, to refine and intensify experiences already available to us in everyday life. Though the severity of the *Glass House* will strike many as perverse, I will argue that it is only an extremely refined version of what any sensitive homemaker creates. The *Glass House* helps us to see what I term the art of domesticity. The art of domesticity means not just that the house is art, but that the very way of living in it is also an art, made and remade on a daily basis. As we shall see, these two arts, making and living, are connected. Along with the important care-work that often characterizes domestic responsibilities, this is what I take to be the genuine meaning of the term *homemaking*.

The successful occupant of the *Glass House* or any other pristine, severe, and hyperorganized environment lives in the house in perfect harmony with its formal configuration and artistic meaning. On a daily basis, one achieves this harmony by developing a repertoire of habits that simultaneously achieves two things: first, it allows one to do everything one normally does in a home; second, our habits ensure that we always do these things in a way that respects and reflects the artistic integrity of the space.

In a hyperorganized environment, design leads and habit follows. The house is a spectacle to which the inhabitant must adjust. The practice of dwelling must respond to the conception of order embodied in the arrangement of objects. Johnson has created an ideal space, characterized by a clear exposition of formal principles like symmetry, unity, and harmony, in relative abstraction from conventional lifestyle patterns marked by privacy, informality, and comfort. As we have already noted, everything in the *Glass House* has a place. The space is a composition. To move (at least on a permanent basis) a piece of the composition is to destroy the work of art. Thus, the correct manner of inhabiting the *Glass House* must also be a form of protection of the original composition. To maintain the composition, the true occupant would have to return everything to its spot. Insofar as sustained domestic practice requires that household objects are used as a matter of unconscious habit, to correctly use them and return them would mean that one's habits are perfectly adjusted to the composition. Someone who habitually puts things back in their places has a habit-repertoire that is fully responsive to the organizational and aesthetic terms of inhabited space. Consequently, in order to successfully inhabit the *Glass House*, one would have to be extremely, perhaps perfectly neat and organized; neatness and organization would have to be perfectly habituated.

Rather than organizing the space around pre-existing habits, the body is implicated in the idealized order of the *Glass House*. Domestic practice becomes the art of maintaining the discipline of implication in the order, of more or less forcing habit to follow aesthetic conception. This explains why formal and hyperorganized spaces are felt to be 'uncomfortable' and their radical aestheticist occupants subject to the pop-Freudian epithet *anal*. The spaces demand too much. But the radical aesthete is less bothered than others by this imposition. The embodied experience – one might say, 'synaesthetic' – of being inside, indeed, part of the composition induces in the radical aesthete the greatest of pleasures. *Pleasure resides in the implication of the body in an aesthetically pleasing scheme, not just experience of space as an aesthetically pleasing visual field.*

This is admittedly an obscure kind of aesthetic experience. But I believe that it is very common. The fact that even nonradicals (who might still be aesthetes in some less extreme sense) are aware of the way spaces make aesthetic demands on the body can be seen in the discomfort felt by the nonradical in the formal environment. The sense that one cannot relax or slouch in a hyperorganized environment, that one must sit up straight, reveals that even the nonradical is aware of the way some spaces seem to require our bodies to aesthetically conform. Unlike the radical aesthete, the nonradical perceives the space as a nest of prohibitions. For the same reason, the fastidious feel uncomfortable in a dumpy room, where the dusty couch invites slouching and where 'good manners' come off as arrogance.

Unlike the radical aesthete, most people today tend to resent immensely the demands of formal rooms. While many are impressed by the strictly designed spaces of which Johnson's *Glass House* is the extreme example, few wish to live in them. Most of us lack the proper repertoire of habits. Even if we wanted to cultivate such a repertoire, our lives are simply too confusing and overloaded to do so. Not surprisingly, this radical aestheticism is usually practiced by single people living tranquil lives of autocratic self-indulgence or very wealthy families who can pay to have someone else maintain, that is, clean up, the rarefied design.   (... p 193)

Notes
1   Stanley Abercrombie, *A Philosophy of Interior Design*, Harper and Row (New York), 1990, p 135.
2   Philip Johnson, *The Glass House*, David Whitney and Jeffrey Kipnis (eds), Pantheon Books (New York), 1993.
3   With this definition of environmental aesthetics, I am relying upon Sparshott's now classic article on environmental aesthetics: FE Sparshott, 'Figuring the Ground: Notes on Some Theoretical Problems of the Aesthetic Environment', *The Journal of Aesthetic Education*, vol 6 no 1, 1972, pp 11–23.
4   As remarked by the designer, Ward Bennett, in Julie Iovine, 'Is There an Art to a Well-Placed Chair?', *The New York Times Magazine*, 12 March, 1995, p 72.
5   Philip Johnson, *Writings*, Oxford University Press (New York), 1979, p 138. Cited by Witold Rybczynski, *Home: A Short History of an Idea*, Viking (New York), 1986, p 211.

Kevin Melchionne, 'Living in Glass Houses: Domesticity, Interior Decoration, and Environmental Aesthetics', *The Journal of Aesthetics and Art Criticism*, vol 56 no 2, 1998, pp 191–200.
Reprinted by permission of Blackwell Publishing Ltd.
(Excerpt pp 191–3)

Dust

Celeste Olalquiaga

philosophical ● 1999

late 19th century material

Cultural historian Celeste Olalquiaga probes the ruins of modernity through Walter Benjamin's metaphor of dust (kitsch) as worthless detritus revealed by the loss of use value and aura. She discusses the collapsed, fragmented faded dreams of yesteryear relative to object appropriation in the Victorian interior where they are kept and protected for contemplation. Following this metaphor of dust, we note that the auretic value of pre-industrial objects, their exclusivity, is lost with mass production and greater accessibility, so that they can be copied, tampered with and traded.

The grey film of dust covering things has become their best part.

Walter Benjamin, '*Dreamkitsch*', 1927

While Rodney is metaphorically resurrected in the fantastic musings that make him a live component of my world, other hermit crabs collect the dust of forgetfulness on the once diaphanous bubbles that became their last homes. In the one short piece where he discusses kitsch, Walter Benjamin employs the metaphor of dust to describe the rundown state of dreams in modernity. Attuned to the fate of the aura, he says, dreams are no longer removed from concrete experience, but tangible and near. They have lost their romantic dimension, their 'blue distance,' fading into a sad grayness that figuratively represents the disintegration which befalls dreams when they cease being imaginary and enter the polluted atmosphere of everyday life.[1]

Benjamin associates this colorless state with the dust that accumulates on forgotten objects, establishing an analogy between what he calls the extinct world of things (things infused with aura, of course) and the worn-out condition of dreams: both are now in the realm of the banal, that is, of kitsch. What makes dreams and things kitsch, therefore, is their tangibility – the fact that they no longer stand 'two meters away from the body,' but have become instead familiar and accessible. The connection of kitsch and decay is underscored by their mutual susceptibility to physical touch. And, as is always the case with the aura, the loss of distance is occasioned by technology, which Benjamin likens to bills of currency, in other words, to exchange value: bills and technology stand for the exterior of things, as opposed to their essence. In this way, Benjamin seems to perpetuate the classic opposition between essence and appearance that implicitly underlies the official status of kitsch as a superficial phenomenon and art outcast.

Benjamin's apparent dichotomy between outside and inside, body and soul, assumes that once things have been touched by the deadly hands of commodity fetishism, they wilt like flowers. And truly, only in the faraway dimension of conceptual distance (or of memory) can things remain beyond the mortal trials of time and space, the wear and tear of age and use. This auretic distance is better understood with the help of what Benjamin distinguishes as 'cult value,' a traditional relationship to objects whereby these are infused with a sacred quality characteristic of cultures with a magic or theocentric view of the world. In turn, cult value is related to use value, where the worth of things is directly derived from their relationship to human activity, instead of subordinated to the laws of market exchange, or exchange value, as has been explained before.[2]

Although Benjamin longs for cult value, he recognizes its modern disintegration as the breaking down of old hierarchies (such as the one which places essence over appearance) and, consequently, believes technology has a revolutionary potential. Similarly, although for him the novel promotes an individualistic experience that is radically different from the communal one of oral and epic literary traditions, it enables for this very reason a creative understanding of the world (rather than an acceptance of handed-down beliefs) which can open the way for its transformation.

What is most relevant about Benjamin's kitsch essay, therefore, is that it describes the consequence of the shift from a mode of experience based on a sacred distance to a mode based on perceptual proximity. For Benjamin, modernity replaces the cyclic flow of traditional time with a mirage of movement constituted by sheer repetition: the new as the 'ever-always-the-same.'[3] This condition is exposed by dust, which can slowly accumulate on things given their ultimate immobility, since the proliferation in space does not grant things movement (that is, transformation) in time.

Ironically, or perhaps by some intuitive acknowledgment, stillness was feared by the pragmatic idealism of the nineteenth century, where everything had to have a reason, an explanation, or a function. Victorian interiors, apparently merely ornamental, had a practical purpose: to cover the emptiness left behind by the absence of tradition. Material proliferation was legitimized by the pretended usefulness of things that contained other things – albums, armoires, boxes, glass cases – often protecting them from this era's arch-enemy, dust. Interiors themselves, like the arcades of a few decades earlier, were created to protect objects from the outside, keeping them safe for contemplation.

The vast production of the late 1800s was geared to protecting, showing, holding – an obsession that accounts for this period's fastidious arrangements, where nothing is out of place and all the different elements participate in an obligatory meaningfulness. Dust is a cumbersome residue that taints what it touches and must be eradicated: dust is seen as dirt, a persistent contamination exuded by death onto the world of the living. Already the 1851 Crystal Palace featured two devices to combat dust: a structural feature whereby the wooden planks of the palace's floors were left slightly separate so that the dust could fall through them, and a bizarre 'vacuum coffin guaranteed to prevent decay.'[4]

Eventually, nineteenth-century production surpassed the spaces that so generously embraced it, overflowing them to such a degree that they almost drowned under the weight of their own culture. Satiated, this society then turned around and lashed out against its own abundance amidst self-accusations of superfluity and waste. After all, its objects were no longer connected to anything vital, but were the emblems of a cultural death perpetrated by commodification, the remnants of an aura (however mythical) whose brutal disintegration marked the end of an era. So, while Benjamin's dust metaphor states that dust – kitsch, the banal – is a worthless, extrinsic detritus, at the same time it exposes the cultural condition that made this metaphorical dust possible: the loss of use value and the disintegration of the aura.

This assertion can be extended to suggest that dust grants things a peculiarity that reconstitutes them as a new experience, validating instead of disqualifying them. To this effect, I would like to propose that even though dust – or boredom – settles on things that do not move, dust itself may also be seen as the last breath of tradition, and therefore different from the deadly repetition of modernity. The dust that falls on modern things is the decay of the aura, the decomposition of a previous era that, like the tons of shells and detritus that continuously sink to the ocean bottom, creates a new layer of sediment. The dust of modernity, a mix of boredom and death, is the most tangible aspect of the new historical time, a thin patina of shattered moments remaining after the frenzy of multiplication has subsided or moved away.

It should come as no surprise, then, that Benjamin equates dust with kitsch, since both are constituted by what I am distinguishing here as the debris of the aura. What is at stake for kitsch and dust is the transformation of reality from unitary to fragmented, from continuous to chaotic, along with a shift in the way we perceive, which goes from ritualistic to a pragmatic apprehension. The layer of dust makes things into opaque phantoms of themselves in the same way that kitsch is the distorted copy, or brilliant shadow, of a unique original that it transforms while replicating. And insofar as kitsch is like dust – a fragmented reminder of something now gone, a mundane proliferation that infiltrates homes at will, a bizarre form of object appropriation – then kitsch is liable to the same accusations and cleansing operations that dust must endure.

Dust is what connects the dreams of yesteryear with the touch of nowadays. It is the aftermath of the collapse of illusions, a powdery cloud that rises abruptly and then begins falling on things, gently covering their bright, polished surfaces. Dust is like a soft carpet of snow that gradually coats the city, quieting its noise until we feel like we are inside a snow globe, the urban exterior transmuted into a magical interior where all time is suspended and space contained. Dust makes the outside inside by calling attention to the surface of things, a surface formerly deemed untouchable or simply ignored as a conduit to what was considered real: that essence which supposedly lies inside people and things, waiting to be discovered. Dust turns things inside out by exposing their bodies as more than mere shells or carriers, for only after dust settles on an object do we begin to long for its lost splendor, realizing how much of this forgotten object's beauty lay in the more external, concrete aspect of its existence, rather than in its hidden, attributed meaning.

Dust brings a little of the world into the enclosed quarters of objects. Belonging to the outside, the exterior, the street, dust constantly creeps into the sacred arena of private spaces as a reminder that there are no impermeable boundaries between life and death. It is a transparent veil that seduces with the promise of what lies behind it, which is never as good as the titillating offer. Dust makes palpable the elusive passing of time, the infinite pulverized particles that constitute its volatile matter catching their prey in a surprise embrace whose clingy hands, like an invisible net, leave no other mark than a delicate sheen of faint glitter. As it sticks to our fingertips, dust propels a vague state of retrospection, carrying us on its supple wings. A messenger of death, dust is the signature of lost time.

Indeed, dust is where faded dreams and touch intersect, where the blue horizon fades to gray. Benjamin's distinction between dreams and touch reflects the aura's underlying hierarchy of value. In a time when the manufacturing of objects has given way to their mechanical and mass production, pre-industrial times are considered superior for representing a direct connection between producer/consumer and object; they are granted a transcendental dimension for seemingly bridging the gap between sensorial perception and symbolic apprehension. Within the parameters of use value the aura remains intact; the connotations of authenticity and uniqueness permeating process, object and subject.

Not so with mass production, which replaces use value with exchange value, where the emphasis is on accessibility and pragmatism. Having descended from the Mount Olympus of exclusivity, objects need no longer to surpass their immediate function on Earth, but can be relished instead for their corporeal existence. Like fallen angels, objects lose or rather ruin their auras upon descent, arriving with little more than a crumbling, dusty shadow of their once iridescent haloes. Deprived of supernatural immunity, the shaken-down aura falls prey to all the vicissitudes of earth-bound things: it can be touched, traded, copied and tampered with; it is but a fragment of its former existence. It is kitsch.   (... p 95)

Notes

1 Walter Benjamin, 'Traumkitsch [Dreamkitsch]', *Ausgewahlte Schriften*, Suhrkamp (Frankfurt am Main), 1966, vol 2, pp 158–60.

2 See Walter Benjamin, 'The Work of Art in the Age of Mechanical Reproduction' and 'The Storyteller', *Illuminations: Essays and Reflections*, Hanna Ahrendt (ed), trans Harry Zohn, Schocken Books (New York), 1969, pp 217–51 and pp 83–9, respectively. For the explanation of use value and exchange value, see footnote 6 on page 18. [Editors' note: Footnote 6 reprinted here. 'Use and exchange values were originally proposed by Karl Marx to describe the changes that modernization caused in modes of production and social conditions of labor. In use value, there is a direct connection between the workers who produce an artifact and the artifact itself, since the workers own, control or understand the process of production and can therefore benefit from their labor. By extension, use value implies a closeness between a society and the things it produces and consumes. This closeness is lost in late capitalism, where workers are not only disassociated from the process of production as a whole (they connect to it in a segmented and specialized way), but also alienated from the fruits of their labor, which no longer bears the traces of their work. In exchange value, the human connection to production is abstracted by the laws of market economy.']

3 Walter Benjamin, 'Central Park', *New German Critique* 34, Winter 1985, pp 42–3.

4 Patrick Beaver, *The Crystal Palace*, 1851–1936: *A Portrait of Victorian Enterprise*, Hugh Evelyn (London), 1970, p 54.

Celeste Olalquiaga, *The Artificial Kingdom: A Treasury of the Kitsch Experience*, Bloomsbury (London), 1999.
(Excerpt pp 87–95)

Colour and Method

Amédée Ozenfant

social ● 1937

early 20th century colour

Accredited with the founding developments in Purism in early twentieth-century architecture, Amédée Ozenfant wrote several essays in Architectural Review *on the topic of colour and its spatial and architectural application. The excerpt featured in this book addresses the specifics of colour theory from both a technical and observational/phenomenal view. Citing the beauty of the world and the miracle of things as his inspiration, Ozenfant figuratively opens up a pot of paint and unpacks its qualities as light-filtering substance. He abandons the notion of complementary colours to embrace a method of practice that binds light and colour into 'spectral absorption', This endeavour to offer an alternative theory of colour is discussed against colour effects on the interior and exterior.*

The architect is a poet. He must be a poet. Poet in form, colour and light. The three in one: the architect.

Only, through constantly seeing colour in the painter's pots, and also owing to the nasty tricks these coloured brews have often played on him, he sometimes ceases to realize and feel all that is marvellous in the physical phenomenon of colour. It is true to say that most of the world lives without noticing the extraordinary fairyland that the world is. And when man forgets the miracle of things, he ceases to be an artist.

That is why, even if a clear notion of the action of light and colour had no practical application to the architect's purpose, I would still draw a picture of these, so thrilling are their ways. This action is so astonishing that it is capable of raising us above stupid *habit* – this dangerous habit, which, according to the great Samuel Butler, and also Bergson, has contributed so much to the formation of our animal side, but which conceals from our mind and our heart the real and everlasting beauties of the world. Habit never allows us to discover, or even to do better than we already know how to do. And it is never a waste of time, whatever trade we are engaged in, to contemplate with careful regard the natural wonders, particularly when they have a bearing on our trades. Architecture is light, because it is through light that we see it. And light is colour.

Buying a pot of paint for sixpence at Woolworths is a gesture which does not greatly benefit our intelligence and our sensitiveness – but, what an insight into the universe, when we think that the brew which this pot contains, is a *filter* of light! Light is but a radiation of the same nature as X-rays. This light is the visible part of the stupendous electro-magnetic wave system, which 'explains' a great deal of the generality of appearances. Therefore, taking the job of painting a wall: it is no longer a vulgar occupation – it is to practice the alchemy of waves.

And furthermore, if the most delicate electrical phenomena can be registered in *figures*, there is no more need for respectful nervousness as regards colours; let us register them also in figures, instead of going on translating them into imprecise descriptions. Words are not made for that purpose.

But, first of all, we must define the terms which we will employ.

A colour is defined by:
First, its *hue*; that is to say, the *quality* which is its own, and which differentiates it from another colour.
Secondly, its *value*; that is to say, the *quantity* of light it transmits.

The sun, lamps, are *prime sources*. Colours may be considered as *secondary sources* of light.
Pigment is the powder of colour.
Binding is the substance which incorporates it, fixes it, and makes a usable colour of it.
According to the nature of its substance, the *pigment* transforms, *filters* the light it receives, before reflecting it.

Except in the case of a practically white body, bodies only reflect a portion of the light; and often a very small one. That is a very elementary truth! And is that the reason why too many architects forget this childish c-a-t – cat; in a country like this, where daylight is often rare? Many architects and decorators seem to take a mischievous pleasure in painting walls a dark colour, in providing prisons for the light. And, what is worse, these dark colours are chosen so neutral, that the *hue* cannot compensate, through the liveliness peculiar to bright shades (even if they are dark), for the loss of light by absorption.

And here is the opportunity to emphasize – and we will return to the point again – that smallness in quantity of light, can to a certain extent be remedied by the brightness of the hue of the colour; as bright hues, even dark ones, have the property of creating strong sensations, similar to those caused by a large luminous quantity.

Practical conclusions: one; in the case of lack of light (climate or architectural condition), bring in white and lively exciting colours.

Two; make it a habit, when observing or thinking of a colour, to distinguish between the *hue* and the *value*. It is well to acquire the habit of forming a clear idea – sufficiently clear to be retained in the memory – of the characteristic *hue* of colours, their irreducible personality, their *individuality*; and also of experimenting with the *values* of colours, by comparing them with a very white paper. This will make it easier to remember, and to take into account in designing, the factor of *quantity* of light in relation to white, that is to say, the effect that colours will produce with the white of the ceiling and the white portions of the rooms.

One easily assumes that the notion, *quality-hue* of colour, is proportionate to the *quantity-value* and also to the quality-hue of the light which illuminates the colour. Of course, under the yellowish light at the end of the day, or under that of ordinary lamps which are very rich in yellow, a green, for example, will appear more yellow than at noon, when sunlight is richer in blue rays. And these are facts to be remembered, because, according to the country, account must be taken of local conditions, when working out the architectural harmonies. But, when trying to take into account these local conditions, it is important not to err on the wrong side. For instance, how came this abundance of yellowish facades in London? Under the sun (rich in violet and blue rays – facades are hardly ever painted except in fine weather) they are cheerful enough; but during the dark days they appear dull, of a rancid butter yellow; whereas the whites sing gaily, because they generously reflect practically the whole of the light; and these whites appear all the brighter when their surroundings are darker: and the sombre colours, by contrast, become beautiful and telling. *London requires linen collars.*

The old London architects provided whites. Why have they been almost totally abandoned? The new architects intended to fight against foggy greys, and give a sense of sunlight by yellowing the whites. But in the sun yellows sing; in the shadow they are silent.

These errors are also due to the fact that people do not generally think of the manner in which light acts, in order to produce colour. Everyone knows that the so-called white light is composed of a very great quantity of waves of various hues, vibrating at different frequencies. The number of vibrations per second characterizes each pure light-hue. The sum of all these vibrations, that is, of the various-coloured elementary lights, constitutes what is called white light.

But few people are accustomed to think of any material colour as a *filter* retaining all the coloured vibrations, with the exception of those which it reflects, and the hue of which characterizes the particular colour. It is important to keep this law well in mind when colours are ordered and mixed. An example: a corn-poppy and a poppy-colour powder appear poppy-red, because the texture of the petals of the poppy, and the poppy powder, absorb all the other colours of the spectrum of so-called white light, and only reflect the red and the yellow, the combination of which creates the impression of poppy-red.

The leaves on the trees appear to be green, because they retain all the radiations from the sun, with the exception of the green. Magnificent lawns enliven England with green, because the chlorophyll sets its traps for the sun rays. The same applies to all coloured bodies. Material colours, therefore, are wave filters.

Now, we are all taught at school that if you mix a green with a red (so-called complementary colours), you will obtain a black, or at least a blackish colour. The 'complementary' red and green, orange and blue, yellow and violet, are supposed to delight in comradeship but to kill each other in marriage … (which, as we sometimes discover, is a slander). In reality, if you mix a light vermilion with a certain light green, you will obtain, not the expected dirty shade promised by this theory, but a very true yellow, which seems absurd and contrary to the theory. But the theory of complementary colours, such as it has been for a long time propounded in schools, did not take *realities* sufficiently into account: in this case, the complicated phenomena of spectral absorption by coloured powders.

Taken alone, orange vermilion absorbs all the coloured radiations constituting the light, with the exception of the yellow rays and the red rays, the mixture of which appears orange colour when it is alone; yellow-green absorbs all the rays, with the exception of yellow rays and certain blue rays, which it leaves free and reflects in a green mixture. But, when combined the two colours – orange and green – act as follows:

The orange pigment catches the blue rays which the green pigment allows to escape; only yellow and red, therefore, are reflected by this pigment; but green pigment absorbs the red rays which the orange allowed to go free, and thus, by the action of the two pigments, light, after striking their mixture, is reflected in yellow.

This is only a simplified outline of the phenomenon. It is in fact even more entertaining, because the eye is subject to aberrations: for instance, one hue sometimes affects nerves which specialize in other hues. But this summary is sufficient to reason with: and anyhow, this way of looking at it is already far less faulty than the usual theory.

Few architects, however, have spent the necessary time in acquiring the habit, by reasoning and experience, of foreseeing more or less the colour which will result from the mixing of different powders. Therefore, at the moment when he is endeavouring to 'materialize' his colour scheme (assuming that he has a clear idea, which is rare, of what he wants) he witnesses the most disappointing results. Everyone has noticed, with astonishment, the strange magics, the paradoxical colours, disclosed at the bottom of the painter's pot, when he has been asked to prepare a colour: 'You know, a green something like tins;' a rose 'like that,' 'a yellow not too yellow.'

And the architect waves his hand in the air, his eyes half closed, in a dream.

The poor devil of a painter would have to be a medium to be able to guess what is going on within you. Generally, he is nothing more than an honest workman who endeavours to understand you. So, the colour is never what it was desired to obtain. And weariness overtakes you, before you have obtained the desired colour; a colour which is sometimes felt, but hardly ever defined, even in the mind of the architect.

Much worse: it will happen sometimes that, while making absurd mixtures (that may sound like practical jokes) a pleasant tone is produced by miracle; in reality quite different from that which it was intended to obtain. And as the tone is an appealing one, it is eagerly accepted. The original idea has been abandoned and architecture is again the result of chance. And this was the moment when the utmost precision was necessary. Yes, the architecture is the outcome of miracles. Do you believe in miracles in architecture?

We have just said 'precision.' Though the form of architecture needs to be precise, we must admit that, in the matter of dimension, a certain allowance can be made in the precision of form; for instance, in a large room. A difference of two or three centimetres is not a very serious matter. In spite of the tremendous progress of modern architecture, the latter is still far from having reached the decree of perfection of the temples of the Acropolis, in which the precision in measurements is of the order of one millimetre. But, as regards colour, our modern eye is very precise and exacting. No doubt, it has been much refined by certain kinds of painting in the nineteenth and twentieth centuries, which have played an important part in the development of modern sensitiveness, and by the fact that modern painting is based on colour refinement. The tremendous progress of colour printing, of posters, the high level of fabric dyeing, the expert selections of dress-making, have made the modern eye extremely sensitive; our eyes are perhaps even more sensitive to colour than those of the ancients. As a result, the least departure from the exactness of a colour is noticed and can compromise the whole architecture of a building.

Therefore, our eye has very precise requirements – but the means of satisfying them are left to the most complete absence of precision.

During the past thousands of years means of measurement have been evolved, such as the metric system (from one centimetre to one millimicron) enabling any measurement to be taken with the utmost precision. But, for colour, we still do without any 'scale.' It is true, paradoxically, that it is precisely for the study of light that the most admirably accurate instruments, spectroscopes, have been invented. They have helped in discovering the structure of the universe and the composition of the stars; their speed and the speed of light … But these instruments, so ideally accurate, have been hardly used at all in connection with the questions we are discussing here; that is, those relating to material colours. The spectroscope, though it has been employed to study in the most accurate fashion the composition of coloured light; though it has enabled us to give a characteristic number to each of the very numerous pure colours, of which light is composed; though it enables us to check the composition of the light reflected by material colours, is of no practical use in the hands of architects. It is an instrument for verification, for identification; it is not a constructive instrument.

It must be emphasized that its function is entirely different when dealing with spectral light, from when it deals with light transformed by material pigmentary colours. Example: the mixing of pure hues from luminous sources has a tendency to produce white, whereas the mixing of the same hues, but of coloured powders, has a tendency to produce black. This is natural, since in the case of direct light the effect comes from addition, whereas in the case of lights reflected by pigments, it comes from subtraction.

A great scientist, who was also a great practical man, the physicist Chevreul, Director of the Gobelins tapestry works in Paris, recognized, nearly a century ago, the necessity of preparing a chart, composed of samples of lines, answering the needs of those who use colours.

Until the eighteenth century, the Gobelins tapestry makers dyed the yarns from a range of 115 hues (each one bearing a descriptive name). Some of these names are charming: for example, the range of blues consisted of the following: '*blue-white, nascent blue, pale blue, fading blue, darling blue, celestial blue, Queen's blue, deep blue, Royal blue, woad flower, dark blue, Aldego, hell blue.*'

Chevreul writes in one of his works: '*If the colours used at the Royal Manufacture of Gobelins formerly formed constant ranges, since 1825 these ranges tend to disappear.*' But, at that time, a real decadence of the art of tapestry was apparent. The artists were working by chance, plunged in the *infinity* of colour. The most admirable tapestries of the Middle Ages, such as those which may be seen at South Kensington, and particularly the incomparable tapestry to be seen in one of the churches in Brandenburg, in Prussia, were composed of about a dozen shades, not more! So, the artist could easily *think out* the colours, and the tapestry maker apply them.

If we recall these details, it is not as an historical note, but, since our aim here is to arrive at practical methods, because they embody a whole teaching, now generally lost. The ancients perfectly understood that it is only possible to play in tune on an instrument which is itself in tune, and *not too complicated*. The admirable piano only has 96 keys, and that is already a great deal. What would be the good of a piano with an *infinity* of keys?

Chevreul established a *Chromatic Circle*. He selected from the solar spectrum the hues then reputed to be 'complementary,' opposed two by two to each other; that is to say, the mixture of which should theoretically produce black. Then he systematically added to each of them and to their mixtures, a progressive quantity of black; that is to say, of obscurity. Unfortunately, he committed the error of relying too much on the spectroscope. And again, the limited range of printing colours at his disposal a hundred years ago did not enable him to prepare a truly practical chart; that is, a sufficiently exact one. But Chevreul was, to our knowledge, the first one who tried to create a *practical* working method.

And still today, the architect is content to be, from the point of view of colour, in a comparable position to that of an architect who has no scale for measuring form.

But, happily, it is only through ignorance that he remains in this inconvenient, and dangerous situation, because, at present, *there exists a colour chart – not a perfect one to be sure – but one which has at least the merit of being relatively true.* It is the first practically usable working tool for colour.   (… p 92)

Amédée Ozenfant, 'Colour and Method', *Architectural Review*, vol 81, February 1937, pp 89–92.
© The Architectural Review. Reprinted by permission of EMAP Construct.
(Excerpt pp 89–92)

Ordering the World: Perceptions of Architecture, Space and Time

Michael Parker Pearson and Colin Richards

Building upon the notion that reciprocity occurs between thinking and acting, Michael Parker Pearson and Colin Richards propose that inhabitation and the built environment also have mutual and overlapping bonds. Stemming from a social and archaeological perspective, these excerpts investigate how a house expresses and maintains social order while also embodying personal meaning. They first demonstrate how symbolism and function are not mutually exclusive and then proceed to open a discussion about the coherence and difference between various modes of inhabitation. Under this conception, values and concepts of domestic inhabitation are shown to be culturally specific and further suggest, through an analysis of space syntax, that symbolic meaning needs to be considered alongside historical and social context.

The house not only embodies personal meanings but also expresses and maintains the ideology of prevailing social orders.[1] We will look later at how prehistoric and early historic societies organized their space as symbolic creations of cosmic order, but various commentators have pointed out that contemporary space also expresses a cosmic order. Writing of modern America, Constance Perin suggests that the cosmic Order expressed is 'of the American heaven and hell in the suburban pull towards salvation and the urban push of social pollution.'[2] She also shows that principles of social order are translated into settlement patterns by the practices of everyday life, relating to physical proximity, social homogeneity, race relations, form of tenure, housing styles, income levels, privacy and community.[3] Others have shown how the ideology of housing as private ownership of dwellings in separate, individualized space according to wealth has fragmented household units within the workings of modern capitalism and its accompanying processes of individualism and privatization.[4] The places of work and leisure have become separated and where people live is determined more by their place of employment than by their family roots.

It may be difficult for us to see symbolism and function (or utility) as commingled and conjoined. When we designate an artefact as symbolic, there is often the assumption that it serves no other purpose. We might also consider ourselves 'utilitarian' or 'pragmatic' in outlook, as though our world view had no symbolic principles. Yet the two are linked inextricably. We take concepts, such as utility or comfort, and consider them to be universal principles although they are culturally specific, relative values. In his influential book *House Form and Culture*, Amos Rapoport explained how western notions of comfort, adequate lighting, heating, pleasant smells, absence of smoke, privacy, bathroom hygiene and orientation to the view, beach or sun might not be shared by other cultures.[5] As Nigel Barley has observed, the British have an obsession with explaining everything in utilitarian terms.[6] He goes on to say that a Toradjan rice farmer would find our own attitudes to houses totally impractical and incomprehensible since, having bought a house, through the loan of an extraordinary sum of money, we then spend most of our time elsewhere, trying to earn the money for repayment.[7]

The average English house may be analysed in terms of these, and other, structuring principles. Many people like to consider that their taste or way of living is unique to them, that individuality is a concept that enables each of us to have the freedom to express ourselves uniquely. Yet our uniformity in structuring our domestic shells is predicated by age, gender, class, ethnicity and other aspects of social context. In England, patterns of domestic space have been consistent since the Industrial Revolution.[8] Most houses have been independent dwellings with a 'withdrawing' room or parlour at the front and a kitchen (or scullery until the mid-twentieth century) at the back. The living room was likewise toward the rear of the house. Bedrooms are normally located upstairs (if there is an upstairs), with separate lavatory and bath at the back and upstairs (after World War I). Rooms and spaces within the house are strongly demarcated according to use and objects contained. Rooms for daytime living and for night-time sleeping are rigidly differentiated. Traditionally, the parlour or drawing room was a shrine-like room which contained ancestral furniture and ornaments, photographs and heirlooms. This 'public' room was used for those special occasions – the rites of passage such as christenings, marriage and funeral gatherings or Sunday tea when formality in behaviour and dress were to be observed. The pragmatist might account for the siting of kitchen, bathroom and toilet at the rear in terms of utility of plumbing, and explain the demarcation of rooms as stemming from the need to prevent messy practices such as food preparation from ruining smart furniture and carpets. Viewed from within the structuring principles of comfort, utility and hygiene, these are no doubt sensible and practical strategies. But when we stand back and ask why the plumbing is not at the front of the house (nearer to the sewer and mains supply running under the street) or why we need smart furniture, we begin to grasp the cultural particularity of the situation.

Roderick Lawrence has taken the approach of the social anthropologist and shown that the vast majority of English dwellings conform to a set of codes or rules which are articulated by a series of oppositions. These are front/back, clean/dirty, day/night, public/private, male/female and symbolic/secular or sacred/profane.[9] Space within the house is organized as a gradient or hierarchy of rooms within each opposition. For example, as one proceeds through the house from front to back or from downstairs to upstairs, one moves along a 'privacy gradient' from most public to most private spaces.

Lawrence shows how sets of oppositions may be articulated.[10] For example:

$$\frac{\text{Front}}{\text{Back}} = \frac{\text{Symbolic}}{\text{Secular}} = \frac{\text{Parlour}}{\text{Kitchen}} = \frac{\text{Special occasion}}{\text{Daily routines}}$$

He also demonstrates that the internal organization of domestic space is different in England and Australia. While both apply similar oppositional principles, the configurations are slightly different. For example, Australians are more likely to have their dining rooms at the front of the house. Sub-cultures make the situation more complex. In northern English cities, such as Sheffield, the traditions of working-class community dictate that visitors approach the back, and not the front, door. In total contrast, the apartments of the Swiss and French do not utilize these binary oppositions but are based on very different notions of organizing domestic space.[11]

Lawrence is also interested in the boundedness, conceptual and physical, of the house. He observes that the space around dwelling units is treated in particular ways. Likewise, boundaries between rooms might be important. For example, he found gender role differentiation far stronger in English than in Australian homes, and many of his English interviewees were concerned to screen off from the living room the smells and sights of dirty utensils and food in preparation.

We have come a long way from medieval conceptions of the house as a large semi-public structure, with its central and large hall for receiving visitors, for feasting and other commonly shared activities. During the late medieval and post-medieval periods, private space expanded at the expense of such areas[12] until today we end up with the vestigial, obligatory 'hall' – a tiny room or passageway just inside the front door, where visitors are received, boots removed and coats hung up. Now only a boundary zone with the outside world, such space seems ludicrous when we consider its medieval origins. Yet its transformation encapsulates the increasing privacy of the domestic house and the erosion of communal and semi-public space. As a result, we now inhabit small islands, isolated and secured, within a great void.[13]

As cultural gastropods we should be very much in control of our domestic domains, particularly when many feel that it is the one setting for relationships that we feel we can manipulate. And yet a small but growing number of people have considerable problems living normal lives in such surroundings, or spend many hours in rituals and routines of domestic purification or the instilling of a sense of order in their homes. The disabling obsessive behaviours that may result[14] can prevent people even from entering their own homes for fear of rendering them impure. People may also have considerable trouble negotiating boundaries (such as moving from sitting down to standing up, crossing thresholds or stepping off a kerb) and become helplessly enthralled by elaborate private rituals. The link between sacredness and cleanliness was touched on by Lord Raglan, who interpreted the cleaning and tidying of western homes as a modern version of preserving the sanctity of the house by keeping it free from symbolic pollution, a concept explored by Mary Douglas.[15]

Houses in western society are also status symbols and the hierarchical social order is encapsulated in their variety. The ranking of 'detached,' 'semi-detached,' 'terrace' and 'flat' in Britain indicates the amount of space, garden area and privacy which are indicators of social position.[16] In Britain the ideology of house-ownership is stronger than in other countries in Europe, and the distinction between owned and rented accommodation (the latter typified by council housing) is another feature of the class hierarchy. The match between social classes and house types may not be absolute, but the hierarchical classification of dwellings acts as a totemic system of moral and social taxonomies for the British class structure, both exemplifying and reinforcing it. (... p 9)

In many societies the east, the direction of the rising sun, is considered auspicious and often the most significant of the cardinal points. Among most of the ethnic groups of Madagascar, the house is traditionally aligned north – south. West is profane in relation to the sacred east, north is high status and south is low. For the highland Betsileo and Merina,[17] the Sakalava[18] and the Bara,[19] the doorway is located on the west side towards the south. In the seating arrangements at formal occasions the male head of the household is seated in the north-east corner (which may have a small shrine) with men of lesser seniority ranged along the east wall towards the south. In the south part of the house sit the women and children. As one enters the house through the door one moves towards the auspicious domain. Traditionally this house layout also functioned as a zodiacal calendar, using Arabic-derived notation. The layout of the house is also mirrored by the organization of the settlement. The senior households are to the north-east. New houses are built in the south-west so, over time, the village gradually migrates from north-east to south-west. In other parts of Madagascar the system is different. Amongst the Antandroy of the south, the doorway is on the north side and the men sit towards the south end, away from the hearth which is located just inside the door. Equally, status within the settlement declines from the south to the north.

The importance of east as a cardinal point for us is evident in the very word 'orientation' – a looking to the rising sun[20] – which we use today to express the general notion of 'direction.' Some cultures, however, are 'occidented.' For example, the ancient Tarascan state religion in Central America employed a concept of four quarters of the earth

248

associated with the four cardinal directions emerging from the centre. North was equated with right and south with left – seen from the vantage of the rising sun.[21] Cunningham's classic study of the Atoni house in Indonesian Timor – south of the equator – illustrates an interesting variant on orientation (that is 'facing east').[22] Whilst the Atoni are 'oriented' – making prayers towards the east which is their direction of origin – it is forbidden to 'orient' the door, since the sun must not enter the house. The direction of the door is called *ne'u* (meaning south and right). This might seem reasonably straightforward, except that Cunningham observed that houses might be aligned in various directions though rarely directly east-west.[23] Whether this incongruence, between the actual position of a door and the conceptual naming of that position, had developed over time or had been apparent for centuries, we do not know. An alternative dislocation between meaning and building can be found in situations where the traditional orientation of buildings is maintained yet the discursive and apparent meaning for this is lost.

The Atoni house, as a model of the cosmos, expresses explicitly the order of the human, natural and supernatural world[24] and its organizational principles are invoked in politics and other aspects of daily life. Moreover, it is not simply analogous to the cosmos, but is integrated within it. It is constructed according to concentric and diametric principles. The four cardinal points organize the locations of the key internal features: sleeping platform, main platform and water jar. The door is at the south. The north or left side is the interior and associated with female space, while the right side includes the outer area, inside the door and the front yard, a male domain. The house's corner posts and the interior posts that support the rafters form two other axes, north-east to south-west and south-east to north-west. The roof, with its upper regions associated with the spiritual and male spheres, may also be contrasted with the lower, female and secular. Concentric order moves out from the hearth to the interior posts, to the door, to sleeping platforms at the east and west, and the fixed water jar at the north, and to the corner posts. An outside area beyond them is further defined, not only as the front yard but also as a further 'outside.' Order in the Atoni house expresses the twin concerns of unity and difference, and their continual interpretation. The wall and roof represent the unity of the house and its social group, while the internal divisions symbolize and articulate the structured social groupings which are pervaded by the premise of inequality.[25]   (... p 17)

The approaches outlined so far constitute an exploration of meaning in architectural symbolism. Such an approach is concerned with semantic architectural codes.[26] These involve denotative and connotative meanings, such as denotative functions (roof, window), and connotative functions (triumphal arch, tympanum, palace) and connotative ideologies (dining room, menstruation hut). Syntactic codes involve spatial types such as circular plan, high-rise and panopticon. Eco considered that the study of syntax and semantics should be pursued jointly but conceded that the study of purely syntactic codifications was an appropriate pursuit as well.

Finding such codifications and defining them with precision, we might be in a better position to understand and classify, at least from the point of view of semiotics, objects whose once denoted functions can no longer be ascertained, such as the menhir, the dolmen, the Stonehenge construction.[27]

Similarly pessimistic observations on the difficulties of recovering the semantic codes, as discussed so far, were made by Mary Douglas:

> The organization of thought and of social relations is imprinted on the landscape. But, if only the physical aspect is susceptible of study, how to interpret this pattern would seem to be an insoluble problem.[28]

The study of space syntax, along with other approaches such as architectural semiology, formal analysis, EBS (environment-building studies) and 'architectronics' have been developed[29] and applied to archaeological situations, often with some success. Foster's application of network analysis to Iron Age broch settlements in Orkney,[30] Chapman's study of evolving social hierarchy in south-eastern Europe in the Copper Age[31] and Fairclough's[32] study of the medieval castle's development are all excellent examples.[33] Preziosi's study of Minoan architectural design identifies the components and significative units which form the larger entities of the palace settlements.[34] From a modular analysis of ground plans, he identifies the rules of Minoan spatial syntax. Glassie's study of Middle Virginian folk housing similarly identifies the rule sets for house design and their transformations over time.[35]

Formal analysis of space syntax, however, has come in for strong criticism.[36] By ignoring symbolic meanings we overlook the possibility that design structures have different meanings in different cultural contexts. The approach may also ignore differing cultural strategies of privacy regulation. Unwarranted assumptions about relative depth of space as equivalent to ease of access are implicitly made, while it rarely yields any information on the meaning and uses of specific spaces. Moreover, such analysis has been described as highly codified and mechanistic involving the systematic extraction of symbols from their historical and social context.[37]

Despite these reservations, there is no doubt that space syntax will continue to serve as a useful device in the archaeologist's toolkit. Recent studies (notably Fairclough's and Chapman's) indicate that, when linked to the study of meaning and context, such approaches may be very fruitful. However, it is not our concern in this volume to integrate the two approaches. Instead we will concentrate on the study of symbolism and meaning, since this approach has been regarded as nigh impossible for the archaeologist and because we consider that it is a critical area of study for understanding past architectural schemes and their transformations.   (... p 30)

Notes

1 JS Duncan, 'Introduction', JS Duncan (ed), *Housing and Identity: Cross-cultural Perspectives*, Croom Helm (London), 1981, p 1.

2 C Perin, *Everything in its Place: Social Order and Land Use in America*, Princeton Architectural Press (Princeton), 1977, p 216.

3 Perin, *Everything in its Place*, p 210.

4 AD King, *The Bungalow: the Production of a Global Culture*, Routledge and Kegan Paul (London), 1984, p 254.

5 A Rapoport, *House Form and Culture*, Prentice-Hall (Eaglewood Cliffs), 1969, pp 60–2, 131–32.

6 N Barley, *Native Land*, Viking Press (London), 1989, p 47.

7 Barley, *Native Land*, p 51.

8 RJ Lawrence, *Housing, Dwellings and Homes: Design Theory, Research and Practice*, John Wiley (Chichester), 1987, p 90.

9 Lawrence, *Housing, Dwellings and Homes*, pp 103–7.

10 Lawrence, *Housing, Dwellings and Homes*, p 90.

11 RJ Lawrence, 'Public Collective and Private Space: A Study of Urban Housing in Switzerland', S Kent (ed), *Domestic Architecture and the use of Space: An Interdisciplinary Cross-cultural Study*, Cambridge University Press (Cambridge), 1990.

12 G Fairclough, 'Meaningful Constructions – Spatial and Functional Analysis of Medieval Buildings', *Antiquity*, vol 66, 1992.

13 K Dovey, 'Home and Homelessness', I Altman and CM Werner (eds), *Home Environments. Human Behavior and Environment: Advances in Theory and Research*, vol 8, Plenum (New York), 1985, p 57.

14 See Annie EA Bartlett, 'Spatial Order and Psychiatric Disorder', Michael Parker Pearson and Colin Richards (eds), *Architecture and Order: Approaches to Social Space*, Routledge (London and New York), 1993.

15 A Raglan, *The Temple and the House*, Routledge and Kegan Paul (London), 1964, p 42; M Douglas, *Purity and Danger: An Analysis of the Concepts of Pollution and Taboo*, Routledge and Kegan Paul (London), 1966.

16 K Sircar, 'The House as a Symbol of Identity', DW Ingersoll and G Bronitsky (eds), *Mirror and Metaphor: Material and Social Constructions of Reality*, University Press of America (Latham, Maryland), 1987.

17 S Kus and V Raharijaona, 'Domestic Space and the Tenacity of Tradition among some Betsileo of Madagascar', S Kent (ed), *Domestic Architecture and the use of Space: An Interdisciplinary Cross-cultural Study*, Cambridge University Press (Cambridge), 1990.

18 G Feeley-Harnik, 'The Sakalava House (Madagascar)', *Anthropos*, vol 75, 1980, pp 559–85.

19 R Huntington, *Gender and Social Structures in Madagascar*, Indiana University Press (Bloomington), 1988.

20 W Lethaby, *Architecture, Mysticism and Myth* [1891], Architectural Press (London), 1974, p 53.

21 HP Pollard, 'The Construction of Ideology in the Emergence of the Prehispanic Tarascan State', *Ancient Mesoamerica*, vol 2, 1991, p 168.

22 CE Cunningham, 'Order in the Atoni House', R Needham (ed), *Right and Left: Essays on Dual Symbolic Classification*, University of Chicago Press (Chicago), 1973.

23 Cunningham, 'Order in the Atoni House', pp 206–7.

24 Cunningham, 'Order in the Atoni House', pp 234–5.

25 Cunningham, 'Order in the Atoni House', p 232.

26 U Eco, 'Function and sign: The Semiotics of Architecture', G Broadbent, R Bunt and C Jencks (eds), *Signs Symbols and Architecture*, Wiley (Chichester), 1980, pp 38–9.

27 Eco, 'Function and sign', pp 35–6.

28 M Douglas, 'Symbolic Orders in the use of Domestic Space', PJ Ucko, R Tringham and GW Dimbleby (eds), *Man, Settlement and Urbanism*, Duckworth (London), 1972, p 513.

29 B Hillier, A Leaman, P Stansall and M Bedford, 'Space Syntax', *Environment and Planning Series B*, vol 3, 1976, pp 147–85; R Fletcher, 'Settlement Studies (Micro and Semi-micro', D Clark (ed), *Spatial*

Archaeology, Academic Press (New York), 1977; B Hillier and J Hanson, *The Social Logic of Space*, Cambridge University Press (Cambridge), 1984; A Rapoport, *History and Precedent in Architectural Design*, Plenum (New York), 1990.

30 S Foster, 'Transformation in Social Space: The Iron Age of Orkney and Caithness', *Scottish Archaeological Review*, vol 6, 1989, pp 34–55; S Foster, 'Analysis of Spatial Patterns in Buildings (Access Analysis) as an Insight into Social Structure: Examples from the Scottish Atlantic Iron Age', *Antiquity*, vol 63, 1989, pp 40–50.

31 J Chapman, 'The Creation of Social Arenas in the Neolithic and Copper Ages of SE Europe: The Case of Varna', P Garwood, D Jennings, R Skeats and J Toms, (eds), *Sacred and Profane: Proceedings of a Conference on Archaeology, Ritual and Religion*, Oxford 1989, Oxford University Committee for Archaeology (Oxford), 1991.

32 G Fairclough, 'Meaningful Constructions – Spatial and Functional Analysis of Medieval Buildings', *Antiquity*, vol 66, 1992.

33 Many other applications may be found in R Samson, *The Social Archaeology of Houses*, Edinburgh University Press (Edinburgh), 1990; S Kent (ed), *Domestic Architecture and the Use of Space – an Interdisciplinary Cross-cultural Study*, Cambridge University Press (Cambridge), 1990; O Grøn, E Engelstad and I Lindblom, *Social Space: Human Spatial Behaviour in Dwellings and Settlements*, Odense University Press (Odense), 1991; J Gero and M Conkey (eds), *Engendering Archaeology: Women and Prehistory*, Blackwell (Oxford), 1991; and in a special issue of the journal *Environment and Planning B* – renamed *Design and Planning* – R Boast and P Steadman (eds), 'Guest editorial: Analysis of Building Plans in History and Prehistory,' *Environment and Planning B: Design and Planning*, vol 14, 1987, pp 359–484.

34 D Preziosi, *Minoan Architectural Design: Formation and Signification*, Mouton (Berlin), 1983.

35 H Glassie, *Folk Housing in Middle Virginia*, University of Tennessee Press (Knoxville), 1975.

36 E Leach, 'Does Space Syntax Really "Constitute the Social"?', D Green, C Haselgrove and M Spriggs, (eds), *Social Organisation and Settlement: Contributions from Anthropology, Archaeology and Geography*, BAR Int Series (Suppl) (Oxford), vol 47, 1978; I Hodder, *Reading the Past: Current Approaches to Interpretation in Archaeology*, Cambridge University Press (Cambridge), 1986, pp 39–41; Lawrence, *Housing, Dwellings and Homes*, pp 52–3.

37 Lawrence, *Housing, Dwellings and Homes*, p 48, citing P Knox, 'Symbolism, Styles and Settings: the Built Environment and the Imperatives of Urbanised Capitalism', *Architecture and Behavior*, vol 2 no 2, 1984, pp 107–22.

Michael Parker Pearson and Colin Richards, 'Ordering the World: Perceptions of Architecture, Space and Time', Michael Parker Pearson and Colin Richards (eds), *Architecture and Order: Approaches to Social Space*, Routledge (London and New York), 1993.

A World of Unmentionable Suffering

Barbara Penner

political ● 2001

late 19th century ● furnish

Barbara Penner's social and cultural analysis of the debate surrounding women's public lavatories operates as a critical theorised historical account of the way an everyday object is implicated in patriarchal power structures. She demonstrates that this space is predicated on male-centred views of the female body, ablution and 'public' space. By suggesting that interior spaces are conditioned by gender and class this text indicates that interior arrangements are far from neutral. In addition, Penner offers a feminist geographical perspective that regards space as active agent in producing social relations and identities, particularly as this building type, the convenience, became a public and urban sign of women's visibility. Such visibility, she argues, was also a threat which necessitated an elaborate spatial sequence to eliminate the publicity of a street entrance and control women's occupation of the interior.

This paper proposes to investigate the various manifestations of the Park Street lavatory debate, drawing on the sometimes conflicting evidence of the *St. Pancras Vestry Minutes*, the accounts of Vestry meetings in the *St. Pancras Gazette* and the writings of George Bernard Shaw. Its aim is not to reconstruct one true version of the controversy; rather, it is to provide a detailed account of how the decision to build an everyday object such as a public lavatory for women was implicated in producing, maintaining and contesting the patriarchal power structure.

Underlying this project are two central propositions. The first is that a lavatory is not simply a technological response to a physical need but a cultural product shaped by complex and often competing discourses on the body, sexuality, morality and hygiene. In other words, far from being neutral or self-evident, the planning of conveniences is informed by a set of historically and culturally specific notions that are loaded in gender and class terms. To cite an obvious example: prior to the modern industrial period, toilets were frequently communal and mixed. It was only in the nineteenth century, with increasingly strict prohibitions on bodily display and the emergence of a rigid ideology of gender, that visual privacy and the spatial segregation of the sexes were introduced into lavatory design, and they continue to be its dominant features today.[1]

The second proposition follows on from the first and takes its cue from the work of feminist geographers such as Gillian Rose and Doreen Massey, and architectural historians like Beatriz Colomina; everyday spaces such as public lavatories do not merely passively reflect existing social relations and identities but are involved in actively producing and re-producing them.[2] According to this view, users do not have a universal response to spaces but experience them differently according to factors such as their sexuality, gender, race, class and age. Daily encounters with the built environment continually position people in relation to the dominant power structure, enforcing and reinforcing their differences. (Rose likens everyday space to 'an arena' where power relations are '(re)created and contested.')[3] While power relations most obviously operate in everyday space through physical barriers and various forms of exclusion, as we will see, they can also work more subtly, creating invisible boundaries that shape experience in equally powerful ways.

If we accept the role of everyday space in shaping personal and collective experience, then the fight over the construction, location and visibility of the Park Street lavatory does not appear marginal or unimportant. Instead, we see such a debate as being necessarily political, invoking issues such as access and mobility, as well as a more complex set of social relations. On a basic level, as the Vestrymen well knew, the presence or absence of a female lavatory on Park Street sent local women a powerful message about their right to occupy and move through the streets of Camden Town. Moreover, by its very nature, the debate over the lavatory's construction contested prevailing cultural notions of privacy, decency and femininity, concepts which are not stable but are open to redefinition within certain, historically specific limits.

Although it did not represent a dramatic break with convention, this paper will argue that small struggles like the Park Street debate pushed against the boundaries of existing social concepts, allowing for a subtle, sometimes subversive, renegotiation of their terms. As such, what seems at first to be little more than a local political clash over an everyday space deserves to be recognized as, in the words of Lisa Tickner, 'an integral part of the fabric of social conflict with its own contradictions and ironies and its own power to shape thought, focus debates and stimulate action.'[4]   (... p 37)

As Davis and Dye's comments indicate, the reason why ladies' conveniences were notorious financial duds, was not simply because poorer women could not afford to use them. The reality was that, far from being universally put to use by women, public lavatories were often shunned by them, whether out of fear, distaste or, as Davis and Dye put it, with no small degree of impatience, a 'peculiar excess of modesty' which often forced their closure.[5] The degree to which women had internalized the patriarchal system of representation, particularly the discourse of decency and femininity, can be roughly gauged by the sheer number of times this observation recurs. Their widely acknowledged embarrassment was why the St. Pancras Vestrymen could argue with some confidence that, if built, the Park Street lavatory would occupy 'too public a position and ladies would not care to use it for this reason.'[6]

There is something profoundly ironic about a public amenity being condemned for being 'too public.' However, the sense of transgression roused by this excess of publicity must be understood in light of the lavatory's intimate association with the female body, as the container of its natural functions: urinating, defecating and menstruating. Owing to its provocative corporeal associations, a female lavatory evoked the spectre of sexuality which, as Walkowitz has observed, encompassed a nebulous constellation of issues above and beyond sexual conduct itself: 'dangerous sexualities [for the Victorians] had as much to do with work, life-style, reproductive strategies, fashion and self-display … as with nonprocreative sexual activity.'[7]

Sexuality was explicitly invoked when, after the Park Street site was abandoned, Mr McGregor promised to find a 'suitable house for use of ladies' as an alternative; the laughter which accompanied his remark makes clear what type of house the Vestrymen had in mind (a joke given extra *frisson* owing to the proximity of several 'houses of ill-fame').[8] The easy slip from lavatory to brothel betrays the most extreme prejudice of the concerned citizens, the Vestry and of women themselves: that, in using a public convenience, women would be little better than 'public' women, prostitutes, who exposed their bodies in the streets.

Certainly, as the condemnation of the convenience as an 'indecent' object or an 'abomination' signals, the objections to its construction had an unmistakable moral dimension. They implied that providing a lavatory would encourage a gradual loosening of the tightly maintained mechanisms of control which circumscribed women's movements and behaviour – with potentially disastrous consequences for standards of decency and the ideal of femininity. It was not only sexuality and gender but class which underlay such fears. The complaints about the 'promiscuous' mixing of working- and middle-class female bodies which occurred in such facilities indicates that decency and femininity were defined primarily as middle-class attributes: mixing in the lavatories threatened the moral contagion of the 'ladies' by the factory and flower girls, auguring the former's descent into vulgarity and corruption.

When lavatories were provided, the desire to reduce an overt connection with women's bodies and prevent mixing affected discussions not only about the conveniences' location but their design as well. Often located underground without windows, protected from the 'public' gaze and, by means of internal partitions, from the eyes and ears of other women, the conveniences were meant to seal off and contain the 'unmentionable' secrets of the female body. Other strategies of concealment focused on reducing the prominence of the lavatory's entrance, as it was in negotiating its threshold that women were most compromised.

Davis and Dye, for instance, enthusiastically approved of one design which obscured the entrance to the ladies' facilities, praising it as an ideal scheme for avoiding 'the publicity which is such a barrier to the use of those places by the opposite sex.'[9] This proposed building, while providing a street entrance to the men's facilities, eliminated the street entrance for the women's. Instead, the women's conveniences could only be reached through the ladies' waiting room, located at the end of a sequence of spaces which moved from the most visible and public (the general waiting room, lobby and parcels office), to the semi-private (the ladies' waiting room), to the most invisible and private (the ladies' lavatories). This hierarchical distribution of rooms according to degrees of privacy, gender and class was not uncommon but was a well-established convention of late Victorian planning. Deployed in domestic, public and commercial interiors from country houses to schools to hotels, it perhaps reached its apotheosis in the elaborate sequence of ladies-only Club and Retiring Rooms which developed in department stores like Harrods and Debenhams a decade later.

In considering tactics aimed at containing the female presence, we are now treading on familiar academic ground. As feminist historians such as Elizabeth Wilson and Judith Walkowitz have convincingly demonstrated, by the mid-to-late Victorian era, increasing female (working-class) mobility was widely regarded as a potential threat to patriarchal order and a wide variety of strategies were deployed to check it: from the production of an ideology of separate spheres which aimed to confine 'respectable' women to the home, to the creation of laws aimed at regulating prostitutes (i.e. the 1864 Contagious Diseases Act), which made all women in the city streets an object of speculation.[10]

Yet like most of these strategies and in spite of their careful design, lavatories were only ever partially successful at containing the secrets of the female body. At the edges, a reminder of things buried or concealed continually threatened to break through. For a women's convenience exposed female bodies at the same time as it hid them, amplifying their presence in the public mind. In addition to the conveniences' physical presence in the street, medical reports about their necessity, campaigns and political struggles for their provision and the press coverage of those struggles had the effect of making the female body the legitimate subject of popular scrutiny. Far from suppressing the female body, debates such as that in St. Pancras gave it greater symbolic force, pushing it from the sidelines to an increasingly public and central position.

As this movement was not one that sat easily with the Vestrymen, local tradesmen and property-owners, or even with a large proportion of women, it did not go unchallenged. Indeed, this sense of discomfort and anxiety lay behind the passionate objections to the

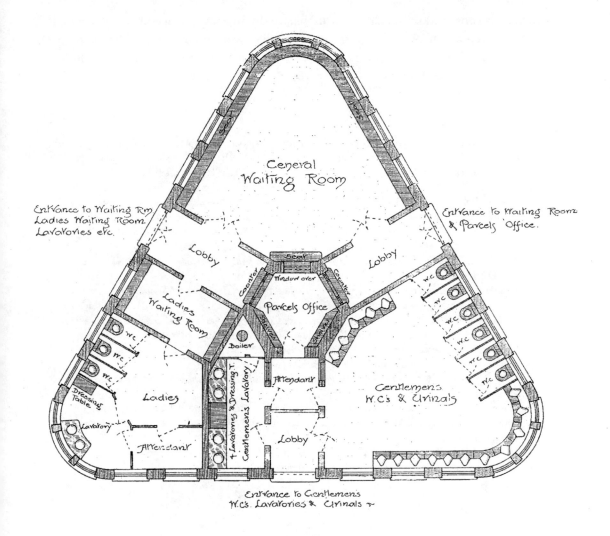

Central
Waiting Room

Entrance to Waiting Rm
Ladies Waiting Room
Lavatories etc.

Entrance to Waiting Room
& Parcels Office.

Lobby

Lobby

Ladies
Waiting Room

Seat

Window over

Counter

Counter

Parcels Office

Boiler

WC

WC

WC

Dressing
Table

Ladies

Attendant

Lavatories & Dressing T.

Gentlemens Lavatory

Attendant

WC

WC

WC

WC

WC

WC

Gentlemens
W.C's & Urinals

Lavatory

Attendant

Lobby

Entrance to Gentlemens
W.C's. Lavatories & Urinals

⚘ PLAN ⚘

Proposed Waiting Rooms and Convenience at Bristol by R. Stephen Ayling, Architect, c. 1898. Courtesy
of Barbara Penner.

lavatory's construction and ultimately mobilized the attack on the wooden obstruction in Park Street – a symbol of the future lavatory and of women's presence in the metropolis – an aggressive reminder, to the disorderly women who forgot their place, of who ultimately controlled the streets.   (... p 48)

Notes

1 For an account of the increasingly strict rules guiding conduct and displays of the body, see Norbert Elias, *The Civilizing Process* [1934], trans E Jephcott, Blackwell, 1994; and Richard Sennett, *Flesh and Stone: The Body and the City in Western Civilization*, Faber & Faber, 1994.

2 The relationship between space, identity and gender is elaborated in Doreen Massey, *Space, Place and Gender*, Polity Press, 1994; Gillian Rose, *Feminism and Geography: The Limits of Geographical Knowledge*, Polity Press, 1993; and Beatriz Colomina, 'The Split Wall: Domestic Voyeurism', Beatriz Colomina (ed), *Sexuality and Space*, Princeton Architectural Press, 1992, pp 73–130.

3 Rose, *Feminism and Geography*, p 17.

4 Lisa Tickner, *The Spectacle of Women: Imagery of the Suffrage Campaign, 1907–1914*, Chatto & Windus, 1987, p ix.

5 George B Davis and Frederick Dye, *A Complete and Practical Treatise on Plumbing and Sanitation Embracing Drainage and Plumbing Practice etc*, E and F Spon, 1898, pp 171, 185. Their statements are borne out by the fact that the Ladies' Lavatory Company at Oxford Circus failed because 'ladies feared to be seen entering' it. Alison Adburgham, *Shopping in Style: From the Restoration to Edwardian Elegance*, Thames and Hudson, 1979, p 141.

6 *St. Pancras Vestry Minutes*, vol 22, July–December 1900, p 282.

7 Judith Walkowitz, *City of Dreadful Delight: Narratives of Sexual Danger in Late Victorian London*, Virago Press, 1992, p 6.

8 These houses of ill-fame were located just a mile away, clustered in streets like Warren Street off Tottenham Court Road. Michael Holroyd, *Bernard Shaw: Volume 1, 1856–1898*, Penguin Books, 1990, p 413.

9 Davis and Dye, *Complete and Practical Treatise*, p 182.

10 Elizabeth Wilson, *The Sphinx in the City*, University of California Press, 1991.

Barbara Penner, 'A World of Unmentionable Suffering: Women's Public Conveniences in Victorian London', *Journal of Design History*, vol 14 no 1, 2001, pp 35–51.
© 2001 The Design History Society. Reprinted by permission of B Penner and the Design History Society.
(Excerpts 36–48)

The Apartment

Georges Perec

philosophical 1999

mid 20th century furnish

Georges Perec, renowned for his literary work, takes time to question the banal and mundane activities occurring in the spaces of our inhabitation. In this excerpt he discloses the ordinariness of space when considered alongside functionality of room requirements, particularly when mapped through a slice of time. Against this method of narration, Perec proposes several other spatial layouts generated by either functional relationships between rooms, or the functioning of senses, or days of the week, or thematic arrangements.

A bedroom is a room in which there is a bed; a dining-room is a room in which there are a table and chairs, and often a sideboard; a sitting-room is a room in which there are armchairs and a couch; a kitchen is a room in which there is a cooker and a water inlet; a bathroom is a room in which there is a water inlet above a bathtub; when there is only a shower, it is known as a shower-room; when there is only a wash-basin it is known as a cloakroom; an entrance-hall is a room in which at least one of the doors leads outside the apartment; in addition, you may find a coat-rack in there; a child's bedroom is a room into which you put a child; a broom closet is a room into which you put brooms and the vacuum cleaner; a maid's bedroom is a room that you let to a student.

From this list, which might easily be extended, two elementary conclusions may be drawn that I offer by way of definitions:

1. Every apartment consists of a variable, but finite, number of rooms.
2. Each room has a particular function.

It would seem difficult, or rather it would seem derisory, to question these self-evident facts. Apartments are built by architects who have very precise ideas of what an entrance-hall, a sitting-room (living-room, reception room), a parents' bedroom, a child's room, a maid's room, a box-room, a kitchen, and a bathroom ought to be like. To start with,

259

however, all rooms are alike, more or less, and it is no good their trying to impress us with stuff about modules and other nonsense: they're never anything more than a sort of cube, or let's say rectangular parallelepiped. They always have at least one door and also, quite often, a window. They're heated, let's say by a radiator, and fitted with one or two power points (very rarely more, but if I start in on the niggardliness of building contractors, I shall never stop). In sum, a room is a fairly malleable space.

I don't know, and don't want to know, where functionality begins or ends. It seems to me, in any case, that in the ideal dividing-up of today's apartments functionality functions in accordance with a procedure that is unequivocal, sequential and nycthemeral.[1] The activities of the day correspond to slices of time, and to each slice of time there corresponds one room of the apartment. The following model is hardly a caricature:

07.00	The mother gets up and goes to get breakfast in the	KITCHEN
07.15	The child gets up and goes into the	BATHROOM
07.30	The father gets up and goes into the	BATHROOM
07.45	The father and the child have their breakfast in the	KITCHEN
08.00	The child takes his coat from the and goes off to school	ENTRANCE-HALL
08.15	The father takes his coat from the and goes off to his office	ENTRANCE-HALL
08.30	The mother performs her toilet in the	BATHROOM
08.45	The mother takes the vacuum cleaner from the and does the housework (she then goes through all the rooms of the apartment but I forbear from listing them)	BROOM CLOSET
09.30	The mother fetches her shopping basket from the and her coat from the and goes to do the shopping	KITCHEN ENTRANCE-HALL
10.30	The mother returns from shopping and puts her coat	

	back in the	ENTRANCE-HALL
10.45	The mother prepares lunch in the	KITCHEN
12.15	The father returns from the office and hangs his coat up in the	ENTRANCE-HALL
12.30	The father and the mother have lunch in the (the child is a day boarder)	DINING-ROOM
13.15	The father takes his coat from the and leaves again for his office	ENTRANCE-HALL
13.30	The mother does the dishes in the	KITCHEN
14.00	The mother takes her coat from the and goes out for a walk or to run some errands before going to fetch the child from school	ENTRANCE-HALL
16.15	The mother and the child return and put their coats back in the	ENTRANCE-HALL
16.30	The child has his tea in the	KITCHEN
16.45	The child goes to do his homework in the	CHILD'S ROOM
18.30	The mother gets supper ready in the	KITCHEN
18.45	The father returns from his office and puts his coat back in the	ENTRANCE-HALL
18.50	The father goes to wash his hands in the	BATHROOM
19.00	The whole small family has supper in the	DINING-ROOM
20.00	The child goes to brush his teeth in the	BATHROOM
20.15	The child goes to bed in the	CHILD'S ROOM
20.30	The father and the mother go into the they watch television, or	SITTING-ROOM

                   else they listen to the radio,
                   or else they play cards, or
                   else the father reads the
                   newspaper while the
                   mother does some sewing,
                   in short they while away the time
21.45   The father and the mother
             go and brush their teeth in the   BATHROOM
22.00   The father and the mother
             go to bed in their   BEDROOM

You will notice that in this model, which, I would stress, is both fictional and problematic, though I'm convinced of its elementary rightness (no one lives exactly like that, of course, but it is nevertheless like that, and not otherwise, that architects and town planners see us as living or want us to live), you will notice then, that, on the one hand, the sitting-room and bedroom are of hardly any more importance than the broom closet (the vacuum cleaner goes into the broom closet; exhausted bodies into the bedroom: the two functions are the same, of recuperation and maintenance) and, on the other hand, that my model would not be modified in any practical way if, instead of having, as here, spaces separated by partitions delimiting a bedroom, a sitting-room, a dining-room, a kitchen, etc., we envisaged, as is often done these days, a purportedly single, pseudo-modular space (living-room, sitting-room, etc.). We would then have, not a kitchen but a cooking-area, not a bedroom but a sleeping-area, not a dining-room but an eating-area.

It's not hard to imagine an apartment whose layout would depend, no longer on the activities of the day, but on functional relationships between the rooms. That after all was how the so-called reception rooms were divided up ideally in the large town houses of the eighteenth century or the great bourgeois apartments of the *fin de siècle*: a sequence of drawing-rooms en suite, leading off a large vestibule, whose specification rested on minimal variations all revolving around the notion of reception: large drawing-room, small drawing-room, Monsieur's study, Madame's boudoir, smoking-room, library, billiard-room, etc.

It takes a little more imagination no doubt to picture an apartment whose layout was based on the functioning of the senses. We can imagine well enough what a gustatorium might be, or an auditory, but one might wonder what a seeery might look like, or an smellery or a feelery.

It is hardly any more transgressive to conceive of a division based, no longer on circadian, but on heptadian rhythms.[2] This would give us apartments of seven rooms, known respectively as the Mondayery, Tuesdayery, Wednesdayery, Thursdayery, Fridayery,

Saturdayery, and Sundayery. These two last rooms, it should be observed, already exist in abundance, commercialized under the name of 'second' or 'weekend homes'. It's no more foolish to conceive of a room exclusively devoted to Mondays than to build villas that are only *used* for sixty days in the year. The Mondayery could ideally be a laundry-room (our country forebears did their washing on Mondays) and the Tuesdayery a drawing-room (our urban forebears were happy to receive visitors on Tuesdays). This, obviously, would hardly be a departure from the functional. It would be better, while we're at it, to imagine a thematic arrangement, roughly analogous to that which used to exist in brothels (after they were shut down, and until the fifties, they were turned into student hostels; several of my friends thus lived in a former *'maison'* in the Rue de l'Arcade, one in the 'torture chamber', another in the 'aeroplane' [bed shaped like a cockpit, fake portholes, etc.], a third in the 'trapper's cabin' [walls papered with fake logs, etc.]). The Mondayery, for example, would imitate a boat: you would sleep in hammocks, swab down the floor and eat fish. The Tuesdayery, why not, would commemorate one of Man's great victories over Nature, the discovery of the Pole (North or South, to choice), or the ascent of Everest: the room wouldn't be heated, you would sleep under thick furs, the diet would be based on pemmican (corned beef at the end of the month, dried beef when you're flush). The Wednesdayery would glorify children, obviously, being the day on which, for a long time now, they haven't had to go to school; it could be a sort of Dame Tartine's Palace,[3] gingerbread walls, furniture made from plasticine, etc.   (... p 33)

Notes
1   This is the best phrase in the whole book!
2   A habitat based on a circa-annual rhythm exists among a few of the 'happy few' who are sufficiently well endowed with residences to be able to attempt to reconcile their sense of values, their liking for travel, climatic conditions and cultural imperatives. They are to be found, for example, in Mexico in January, in Switzerland in February, in Venice in March, in Marrakesh in April, in Paris in May, in Cyprus in June, in Bayreuth in July, in the Dordogne in August, in Scotland in September, in Rome in October, on the Côte d'Azur in November, and in London in December.
3   The reference is to a well-known French *comptine*, or nursery rhyme.

Georges Perec, *Species of Spaces and Other Pieces*, trans John Sturrock, Penguin Books (London), 1999.
© 1997 John Sturrock. Reprinted by permission of Penguin Press.
(Excerpt pp 27–33)

The Kitchen as a Place to Be

Norman Potter

technological ● 1990

late 20th century furnish

As a designer, Norman Potter writes about the basic and simple issues of kitchen design as a form of resistance to the proliferation of industrialised time- and labour-saving devices and appliances in contemporary kitchens. This critique also questions standardised commercial storage units with worktops, arguing that they have an economic basis antithetical to kitchen design. While he speaks of this space as an instrument and a workshop, Potter uses his writing and built projects to advocate placing greater value upon preparing and eating meals as ritualistic social gatherings.

Kitchen design is usually impoverished, and its terms of reference falsified, as much by consumer fantasy as by the commercial pressures that incidentally nourish it; but the High Street retail store is the more obvious culprit. Properly speaking, there are people and places – equally individual – and there is the 'kitchen situation' to be variously interpreted and made actual. Ideally, there should be nothing else, though kitchen requirements can be generalised-out, within limits, in a modern building design for an unknown user. Such kitchens will generally be minimal but in their own terms none the worse for that – one thinks immediately of Wells Coates in London NW3 and Le Corbusier in Zürich. The more individual kitchen becomes a workshop job (but first find your workshop, and then afford it). The usual alternative, from any furniture shop, is a permutation of the familiar storage units with worktops, distinguished in price, but little else, by surface finish, detail, and material. Such assemblies have little to do with kitchen design: their essential uniformity reflects the production and marketing feasibilities of their commercial origin.

One has to start somewhere in considering the nature of a kitchen, the 'hub of the house,' and where better than with the exemplary minimal example illustrated here. Its weight is four ounces, its form is a model of clarity and intelligence, and no product designer has yet reached near enough to design the life out of it (nor would it pay him, at this cheaper end of the trade). It has to be said that the fuel – meta tablets – is also in use as a slug killer, and so is environmentally suspect. Even without this handicap, I don't see this kitchen winning a Design Award. It should do, of course, if only to remind us how much junk there is around with allegedly better credentials. Every household should have one.

Kitchen designers are obliged to design with, and to integrate in various ways, a certain amount of technical equipment that is industrially produced – taps, sinks, cookers, etc, apart from portable items – and there, of course, is the rub. Much diligent catalogue searching is entailed, often in out-of-the-way trade sources, discontinued lines, etc; some products may need to be de-styled or practically modified; and a few may even require visual isolation as the only acceptable price of their inclusion at all. I have spent too many hours in my life dismantling junky pseudo-high-tech plastic assemblies, stripping the surplus dials and insignia off them, and replacing, or relocating, their indifferently designed finger controls. However, the ready and recent wide availability of divided oven, grill, and counter-top insert has been welcome.

I do not propose to discuss the full range of kitchen options, all the way from the traditional farmhouse living room – the Aga option – to the rail or airplane snack-servery. Much can be studied and learned from such solutions, and not only in terms of their ergonomics. There are also (in this area as in others) many special cases to which satisfactory answers have never been developed; as, for instance, in the bed-sitting-room and for people with physical handicap. I began work on a mobile kitchen but had to abandon it. Far less comprehensively, the mobile trolley is interesting to compare in the two examples illustrated. The Canella trolley holds its liquor better than the well-known Aalto alternative, and is in other and more detailed respects a more practical answer. On the other hand, the Aalto is so beautifully generalised (and so beautiful to look at) that it can be used for almost anything that fits. Such inspired simplicity bespeaks a natural survivor, as might be said of other Aalto pieces which seem, at first acquaintance, imperfectly realised in the organic impress of their use.

Returning to more ordinary kitchen situations, they should reflect the values people attach to preparing food and eating together. Obviously this has something to do with the time, money, and space available. I have known personally only one true artist of the cookbook – Patience Gray – and she made do, I noticed, with no more than a few (good) pots and pans in a far corner of her studio. Sharing the delight of a meal with her, it occurred to me that Schnabel's advice for the food of the spirit – that music is to be experienced, not consumed – is also something to try for in kitchen design; a guiding principle in search of formal and material equivalence. At least the feel of a kitchen might militate in that direction.   (... p 137)

Confronting the more ambitious structure for the Penton kitchen, 'simple' is not perhaps the first word that comes to mind; though I believe there is a necessary and rational clarity in the way the elements come together, without which the approach would seem arbitrary and over-structured. The work was commissioned by an architect (Richard Penton) mainly for the use of his mother and her housekeeper/companion, who greatly enjoyed cooking and wanted a kitchen environment of some distinctive identity. The requirements and various alternative ways of meeting them were analysed in considerable detail in a job report extending to other matters of use and layout in the house; the report was in fact (as of course all reports should be) a fully consultative instrument. This kitchen occupied the centre of a former ground-floor drawing room, which was opened out into a room adjoining to form one continuous space between north and south windows. The kitchen, with dining space adjoining, touching and noting all its perimeters – was by its physical nature distinguished from loose furniture elsewhere in the large room, a consideration that appealed to its users (which was just as well). The job was workshop-built but for London, which required some unit-prefabrication and other standardised details, in order to keep within a fairly tight budget. This degree of generality, meeting requirements highly idiosyncratic in all other respects, gave the job its special character – half-way between joinery and simplified cabinetmaking.

As far as possible the whole kitchen was considered in the round, i.e. as seen and used in movement: there are no 'backs' in the accepted sense, except where a (required) partial screen faces the related south end of the room. There is next-to-no gadgetry: this is the opposite extreme to the highly generalised and frictionless modern kitchen in which time and labour saving comes first. The Penton kitchen is efficient to the extent that it gives pleasure, and a positive sense of location to its concerns – of being in and with them. A definite circulation pattern is imposed by the usual sequences of preparation, cooking, clearing, followed through obviously enough by the placing of parts, but the structure interpenetrates quite freely with the rest of the room-space. Since one complex is therefore entered within another, the kitchen parts are closely grouped, almost within reaching distance from a central working position, to offset a possible ambiguity in relationship. Help with various operations, such as washing-up or clearing from the dining table, or table setting, therefore takes place across the relevant work-surfaces rather than side-on to them. There is distinctively an 'inside' and an 'outside' to this kitchen (therefore) – given added definition by the shallow platform or podium from which the structure rises, but between the in and the out there is active functional (and random) discourse.

The job was done mostly with mahogany and parana pine, plywood where used being faced with white, blue or black formica. The sink working surface, mahogany, is used for food preparation and has (apart from the fixed chopping board) a catalyst-acting bar finish, heat and moisture resistant ('Phenopol'). A small standard silent refrigerator is located at optimum height for sight and reach; the cooker is isolated and vented through a former chimney breast. Waste is taken from the end of the sink surface into a vented cupboard-bin immediately beneath.

It is interesting that this kitchen is difficult to discuss in terms of 'description' and 'detail' because in fact it was all detail, and the classical task of subordinating components to elements (a preoccupation of mine) without losing their ready and natural availability, was here a special interest in the job. For instance, the client wanted certain items – mainly glassware – displayed and lit and on view from the dining area. This occurs in the two-sided upper storage cupboard – distinguished by screening in clear plate glass (wired glass below) – which is fluorescent lit from below, but the horizontal trough had also to accommodate a sliding cutlery tray at one level, and a bread board at another.

There are two support systems, the primary one in softwood grooved for lighting cable, the secondary being a run of mahogany horizontals which locate, and hold, containing storage boxes in the required places, but also locate switches and socket outlets (the switches therefore appear in the nearest thing to an apron frame beneath work surfaces). The doors to all cupboards (other than the standard fridge) are treated as separate applied flat screens projecting forward and above the bottom edge of these mahogany horizontals, the extent of projection forming the handle (some doors therefore open downwards). A cupboard opening only one way – towards the dining table – does duty for what is usually called a 'sideboard;' that is to say, it houses items such as table napkins and cereals which simply go backwards and forwards to the table without any more interior kitchen circulation. Otherwise there is a through-circulation of items to and from the table – clearing to the outside of the sink surface, washing, drying, storage into the two-sided glass fronted cupboard, table-laying from the other side of it. The relatively small surface under the fridge to one side of it is free of this circulation. The small cupboard above – hesitating in its orientation – is for items (preserves, etc) used partly within the kitchen and partly on the table. (From the angle of inclination, the kitchen interior is seen to win, but some items (condiments, etc) might be duplicated in the two cupboards, whereas marmalade, as an instance, might store in the table cupboard. The logic of this would depend partly on familiarity of use.)

The triangulated unit above the sink, supporting a bleakly exposed but on the whole direct and acceptable water heater, has provision for a loudspeaker extension from hi-fi at the south end of the room, not fitted in the photograph. The sink unit derives direct daylight from the north-facing windows. The cooker was the plainest and simplest then available with the door opening the right way round, but even then all the controls were reorganised onto a panel at its rear. There is cookbook stowage just round the corner as part of the screen, with provision for bills, and nearby there is hanging space for kitchen aprons and the like.

Shown here is the kitchen landscape as seen from the dining table: visible here are the sliding cutlery box, the white painted end-grain of a fixed chopping board, the colour-coded switch plates on the frame below the sink surface, and the clearance gap to wastebin below.

The way this job is handled owed much to a general standpoint on conversions, namely, to enter history into them, and to expose the meeting of old and new expressively – the usual alternative being to modify or screen an existing situation (as with a false ceiling) and use it merely as a weight-carrying discarded shell. I repeat here what must be said of several jobs – and they did have to me an added investigative interest in spatial terms – because I think the approach did add not only a situational clarity to what was going on, but also a valid sense of continuity; the taking of food being a prime agent of precisely that. There is nothing really instant about food; although meals are pretty basic, there is process, ritual, and continuity involved, and I think this kitchen had the feel of that.

In a later job with the same distance problem from the workshop – a small bookshop also described here – I took a quite different approach to the way the job was built, but then bookshelves are not fully screened containers. Here the distinction was stressed, though partly, I think, as a manufacturing and assembly convenience. As to the construction of these containers, if the workshop had owned a heavy spindle, I would have preferred a comb/finger corner jointing system for its through-and-through character – dovetails would have been quite wrong. The joint used was natural to the Dominion, gave under test an adequately spread glue area, and allowed through-machining of grooves (i.e. without stopping) top and bottom – for, in this case, the sliding glass. Normally such a joint is protected from racking stress by a glued and planted back panel – which I now find worrying looking at the two-sided cupboards which of course lack that benefit, though in fact the construction seems to have held up over many years without trouble.

It so happens that this kitchen was rated a success. When the owner eventually moved elsewhere, it seems she was so attached to the structure that joiners were employed to dismantle the whole thing and re-erect it on an entirely different site. The results of this I have never dared to explore. The design was, of course, distinctively a one-off – so much for 'place and occasion in design' (but at least a continuing one-off for its user). Since the considered alternative was apparently to present the kitchen to the V&A, I can hardly complain on either count.   (... p 151)

Kitchen 'as became.' Photo © Estate of Norman Potter, 1990. Reproduced from Norman Potter, Models & Constructs, Hyphen Press, (London), 1990, p150.

Making Charleston (1916–17)

Christopher Reed

Whether regarded as a refuge for wartime conscientious objectors or a retreat from urban life, it is clear that Charleston served as an experiment in social and domestic living and a place for the expression of Bloomsbury modernism. Christopher Reed links two vital aspects of this group's project through an analysis of individual room decorations. He also notes that the different techniques and use of colour, texture and pattern for ornamental painting were transposed from object to painting-of-object. The practice of painting surfaces and furnishings as a mode of self-expression altered rooms beyond recognition, resisting the period's dominant social and political culture.

The facts of Charleston's discovery are worth rehearsing as a corrective to both journalistic fantasies that [Vanessa] Bell, inspired by her sister's 'weekend retreat,' was just 'looking for her own quiet place in the country to paint,' and more purposeful mis-representations of Bloomsbury whiling away the war in the comfort of its country seat.[1] Facing legal persecution and popular prejudice, Bell moved her children and companions to a dilapidated farmhouse, where the men worked six days a week as manual laborers on food rations so insufficient that [Duncan] Grant grew thin and rheumatic.[2] Charleston was unfurnished and [David] Garnett and Grant initially slept on the floor. Even after furniture arrived, the house lacked electricity, central heating, and hot water, while cold water had to be pumped by hand – except when the pump froze altogether during the winter. Visitors were asked to bring their own blankets and hot water bottles. Adding to the logistical complications, Bell, in order to school her children in such an isolated locale, accepted two little girls as boarders and, with her housemaid, taught classes. Leonard Woolf's memoirs stress the rigors of rural living during the war: 'our daily life was probably nearer that of Chaucer's than of the modern man,' he explained, describing how to reach Asheham from the train station, 'more often than not, wet or dry, we walked the four miles along the river bank and across the fields with knapsacks on our backs. All the water we used in the house we had to pump from the well. Sanitation consisted of an earth closet.'[3] Virginia's promotion of Charleston to her sister reveals what would be taken today as the extraordinary isolation Bell faced: 'it only takes half an hour to walk to Glynde Station ... and you have Firle, with its telephone, quite near.'[4] First reactions to Charleston from others in Bloomsbury tempered appreciation of its beauty with dismay at the work it entailed. 'Because the bloody government has made slaves of Duncan and Bunny, need it make one of you?' Clive demanded of Vanessa, offering to sell some of their art so she could hire help.[5] Walking to Charleston on a rainy day, a visiting Molly MacCarthy claimed the prospect of the lonely house and fields looked so much like Wuthering Heights that she burst into tears.[6]

Despite Charleston's drawbacks, the new residents approached it optimistically. Garnett, who preceded Grant from Wissett, reported with delight on Charleston's spaciousness: 'I am fond of Wissett – but it is so cramped ... Charleston is splended. Easy, roomy. I am quite sure my temper will be infinitely better.'[7] Bell's letters about Charleston invoke Bloomsbury houses freely chosen before the war: the walled garden compares to Asheham's; there is a tennis court like those in Bloomsbury squares or the badminton green at Durbins. Describing the interior, Bell emphasized its suitability to her aesthetic and social ideals. 'The rooms are very light and good proportions,' she told Grant, while to [Roger] Fry she made the best of the sparseness, writing, 'I hope to carry out the idea I have always had of bedrooms with the minimum of furniture.'[8] As at Wissett, Bell and Grant immediately began to remake the look of the house. By December, Woolf reported that Charleston was 'covered with various bright shades of Distemper' (recent discoveries of old layers of vibrant blue and green paint, often applied directly over the existing wallpapers, bear out this claim).[9] The decorations created at and for Charleston during the war years offer a remarkable record of its artists' determination to create a place where Bloomsbury's social and aesthetic ideals could be preserved.

Probably the first decoration that, in Quentin Bell's words, 'brought Charleston into the Post-Impressionist world,' was his mother's painted window embrasure in the sitting room where the household gathered during that first cold winter to eat around a makeshift hearth constructed from firebricks following Fry's instructions.[10] Bell borrowed from her earlier abstract paintings to decorate the narrow panels flanking the window with rectilinear compositions in mottled ochers with blue accents. Another rectilinear decoration, this one in red and mottled shades of gray, also dating to the first months of Bloomsbury's inhabitation, filled one wall of an upstairs room Bell first used as her studio (and which doubled as her sons' bedroom).[11] These early abstract decorations linked Charleston to the decorating schemes being promoted by the Omega at this period. By 1917 the Omega was promoting wall decorations based on 'the contrast of two or three pure colours applied in simple rectangular shapes, to transform a room completely, giving it a new feeling of space or dignity or richness,' as Fry described them in *Colour* magazine. Despite their simplicity, Fry insisted, these decorations revealed the sensibility of their artist-creators, because of their 'peculiar moiré effect' realized by applying fast-drying paint with small brushes: 'only the artist has the necessary free elegance of handling which will render such a transparent quality agreeable.' Such marks were not the signature of just any artists, of course but of modernists. Fry explained, 'it is only of late years, and among the more modern artists, that all this interest in the decorative possibilities of paint and of architectural design has grown up. It is all part of the reaction against the photographic vision of the academic schools and of the new interest in pure design.'[12] Although she was no longer participating in Omega commissions herself, Bell's first decorations at Charleston reveal her continuing allegiance to the workshops' changing aesthetic. Arrangements of color and texture deployed as expressions of individual sensibility began the work of claiming Charleston for modernism.

Over the subsequent months, as with the arrival of pieces of Omega furniture and pottery, Charleston came increasingly to embody Bloomsbury's ideals for modern domesticity. Fry's semi-rural Durbins was a particularly important model and source. Fry sent flowers and artichokes from Durbins's garden. The latter, which were not commonly grown in England, were particularly significant emblems of Bloomsbury's francophile modernism, both for their culinary uses and for their cubistic appearance, which, Fry claimed, made them ideal ornamental plantings – the patterns of overlapping chevrons in several of his Omega designs have been seen as allusions to artichokes.[13] The closest echo of Durbins in Charleston's garden, however, was what Bell described as a 'small cemented place to sit out in,' which she proposed to decorate with 'a small inlaid piece of mosaic of odd bits of china, glass, etc. in the centre and also a narrow border round the edge,' soliciting from Fry the left-over tesserae from his unfinished badminton mosaic.[14]

Through the years, as many commentators have noted, Charleston's interior and exterior were depicted in pictures that blur the boundaries between art and decoration, image and reality, in a cycle where domestic existence and aesthetic creativity reinforce one another in a complex but coherent whole.[15] This reflexivity began in the downstairs room the family used most. Across from Bell's rectilinear designs on the window frame, Grant, during their first year in the house, painted the upper panel of the door with an image that is both a still life – a genre of easel painting with claims to the status of fine art – and a depiction of the window the door faces (including since-removed wallpaper inherited from previous tenants). This fusion of art and decoration is emphasized by the existence of an oil-on-canvas version of the same composition (minus the wallpaper) that Grant exhibited at the London Association of Artists in 1927, where – in yet another demonstration of reflexivity – it was purchased by Keynes, a part-time resident of Charleston.[16] Both versions of the motif link interior with exterior and art with nature: the flowers (possibly the artificial blooms produced at the Omega) and pot on the inside window sill blend with the forms and colors of the trees seen through the panes, while the flanking columnar forms may be seen equally well as representations of curtains – brilliant orange in the version on the door – or as decorative frame for the image.[17]

A similar analysis applies to Bell's decorations on the upper panels of two doors in Grant's bedroom. Bell reported that she began decorating this room because it was the only one upstairs with a hearth and hovering over the fire allowed her to stay warm.[18] Perhaps inhibited by the cold, she said, 'I'm not doing anything very startling – only pots of flowers and marbled circles.'[19] Despite this self-deprecation, Bell's bouquets – given the season, these are almost certainly the Omega's dramatic fabric flowers that Vanessa pronounced 'more beautiful than God's attempts' – swirl in complicated patterns within frames of bright red, purple, and orange.[20] The stippled and sponged panels of the 'marbled' rectangles and circles contrast the free play of modernist mark-making to the neat symmetry of the geometrical forms, with both playing against the swirling brush strokes of the flowers. The brilliant shades of these decorations would have glowed against the dark green paint the artists originally used to obliterate the busy wallpaper, turning this room in the cold farmhouse into a Post-Impressionist environment, where rooms look like paintings, and nature and artifice fuse in an exuberant expression of a modern sensibility.

As these bouquets on doors suggest, much of the decoration at Charleston returned to the garden imagery of early Omega interiors and before. In Bell's bedroom, Grant, apparently reciprocating for her decorations in his bedroom, painted the four-paneled door with a catalog of his favorite symbols of sensuality and abundance. The two narrow upper panels depict the same kind of nearly-nude figures bearing funnel-shaped baskets on their heads that Grant had put in his first Post-Impressionist decorations for Keynes's Cambridge rooms seven years earlier. Each of the smaller lower panels presents another of these distinctive baskets, brimming with multi-colored fruit. Grant updated these allusions to earlier Bloomsbury dwellings by bracketing Bell's window with images of their dog and a farm-yard bird, he recalled, 'to guard her at night and wake her up in the morning.'[21] The iconography of Grant's decorations in this room, ranging from the family dog to Mediterranean fantasies, reflects an aspiration – consistent since Eleanor and Wissett – to redeem rural exile in England by recasting it in terms of the pleasures associated with Post-Impressionism, now conceived not simply as a modern style of aesthetic self-expression, but also as the stuff of recent memory. This redemptive fantasy is reflected in Garnett's language describing the early years at Charleston, where, he reports, 'one after another the rooms were decorated and altered almost out of recognition as the bodies of the saved are said to be glorified after the resurrection.'[22]

Furniture painted by Bell and Grant amplifies tendencies evident in their treatment of walls and woodwork. Cupboards painted by Bell during her first year at the house enliven symmetrical arrangements of circles and curves with the occasional floral still life, with all these elements deployed – as in her decorations for the door and mantel in Grant's room – to emphasize the panels and moldings of the carpentry, exaggerating the forms of conventional design. Grant, on the other hand, embellished carpentered surfaces with fanciful imagery. The chair-shaped ends of a wooden bench, for instance, he filled with figures of naked, kneeling angels, one male and one female, their wings sticking up onto the back support.[23] Similarly, each of the four sides of a simple logbox displays a naked male angel dancing or making music in a style that alludes equally to Piero della Francesca and to Grant's own painted shutters at Brunswick Square.

That these differences were self-conscious is suggested by a bed that Grant painted for Bell, which wittily blends their two styles. Bell's characteristic centralized 'marbled' circle dominates the back of the headboard, embellished with her initials but illusionistically tied to the panel's corners by red ribbons, so that her impulse toward pure geometry is turned into a modernist version of a rococo medallion. On the front of the headboard, overlooking the pillow, Grant painted a mask backed by iridescent wings, a figure he identified as Morpheus, the god of sleep and dreaming. Flaunting Bloomsbury's preference for intuitive expressiveness over laborious craftsmanship, Grant roughly nailed two unpainted scraps of wood to the face to create a three-dimensional headdress and nose for an effect that has been compared to both Romanesque stone carvings and Brancusi's sculpture, but that also summons the spirit of Picasso's avant-garde assemblages.[24]

This play with characteristic style, with form and figuration, as well as with allusions to art histories recent and otherwise, characterizes another well-preserved example of painted furniture from this era: a simple wooden chest. This piece, too, uses Bell's marbled circles in rectilinear panels, one on a short side, and three lined up along the back. On close inspection, however, the marbling on the central circle on the back resolves into a Post-Impressionist still life in Grant's style, while on the other short end of the trunk a similar still life expands to fill more fully the square panel – though small rounded wedges of marbling intruding on the corners recall the abstract circular format. The long front panel of the trunk, in contrast, is treated as a picture plane with an image of a languorous male swimmer reminiscent of Grant's Borough Polytechnic mural filling the space from corner to corner. The trunk's play with figuration and form combines with iconographic allusions to the tradition of the *cassone* (Italian proto-Renaissance painted trunks, which often juxtapose personal heraldic emblems with a sprawling nude Venus), though the *cassone's* usual depictions of travel and adventure in landscape are pointedly replaced by the still lifes of domestic objects. This fusion of the mundane and local with the Italianate and erotic is clearest in an image revealed only by opening the lid of the trunk. Here Grant's version of the classical nude Leda, instead of being forcibly impregnated by Zeus in his guise as a magnificent swan, welcomes into her curving arms a homely duck of the kind that lived on Charleston's pond. Framed under a proscenium curtain, this Leda reads as a larger-than-life theatrical figure, or, perhaps, as a backdrop to a play in which the duck is the actor. In either case, the image links farm life at Charleston with a fantastical access to the legacy of Italian culture and modern art.

Grant's satisfaction with this image is evidenced by its repetition as a more finished painting, which was coveted by several visitors to Charleston.[25]   (... p 187)

Notes

1 M Panter-Downes, 'Charleston, Sussex', *New Yorker*, 18 August 1986, p 60. Jill Johnston incorrectly reported, 'During the war, half the year was spent at Charleston, the other half at Gordon Square in London', *Secret Lives in Art: Essays on Art, Literature, Performance*, Chicago Review Press (Chicago), 1994, p 75; compare Gertrude Himmelfarb: 'Charleston became the wartime center of the clan – "Bloomsbury by the Sea"', *Marriage and Morals Among the Victorians*, Alfred A Knopf (New York), 1986, p 38.

2 D Garnett, *Flowers of the Forest*, Chatto & Windus (London), 1955, pp 130–41.

3 L Woolf, *Beginning Again: An Autobiography of the Years 1911–1918*, Hogarth Press (London), 1963, p 60.

4 V Woolf to V Bell, 14 May 1916, *The Letters of Virginia Woolf*, Nigel Nicolson and Joanne Trautmann (ed), Harcourt Brace Jovanovich (New York), 1975–1981 vol 2, 1995; compare Q Bell, *Elders and Betters*, John Murray (London), 1995, p 5.

5 C Bell to V Bell, winter 1916 and October 1916, Charleston Papers, Tate Gallery Archives. Compare V Woolf to V Bell 22 January, 1917, *Letters*, vol 2, p 137. The Bells sold one of Thackeray's manuscripts, which Vanessa had inherited from her father, to pay for the move to Charleston.

6 R Shone, *Bloomsbury Portraits: Vanessa Bell, Duncan Grant, and Their Circle*, Phaidon (Oxford), 1976, p 164.

7 D Garnett to D Grant, September/October 1916, in F Spalding, *Duncan Grant: A Biography*, Chatto & Windus (London), 1997, pp 191–2.

8 V Bell to D Grant, September 1916, in F Spalding, *Duncan Grant*, pp 191–2. V Bell to R Fry, October/November 1916, Charleston Papers, Tate Gallery Archives.

9 V Woolf to M Llewelyn Davies, 29 December 1916, *Letters*, vol 3, p 133. Grant's 1917 still life, *Paper Flowers*, depicting a corner of the mantel in the sitting room at Charleston, also records this brilliant wall color; see R Shone, *The Art of Bloomsbury: Roger Fry, Vanessa Bell and Duncan Grant*, Tate Gallery (London), pp 131–2.

10 Q Bell and V Nicholson, *Charleston: A Bloomsbury House and Garden*, Henry Holt (New York), 1997, p 24.

11 Italian wallpapers were later collaged into this composition, which is documented in its first state in a photograph.

12 R Fry, 'The Artist as Decorator', *Colour*, April 1917, rpt in Christopher Reed (ed), *A Roger Fry Reader*, University of Chicago Press (Chicago), pp 208–9. An example of this Omega work is on the wall behind the bed commissioned by Lalla Vandervelde in 1916.

13 Crafts Council, *Omega Workshops 1913–1919*, Crafts Council (London), 1984, p 48.

14 V Bell to R Fry, 3 August 1917, Charleston Papers, Tate Gallery Archives. A subsequent letter from Fry refers to this as 'D's mosaic,' suggesting that Grant was primarily responsible. This is not the same patio as the 'piazza,' designed by Quentin Bell in 1946 and also decorated with bits of broken china and glass, in Charleston's garden today.

15 Simon Watney's *The Art of Duncan Grant*, John Murray (London), 1990, pp 51–4, is especially eloquent on this point.

16 Grant's *Through a Window* is no 35 in D Scrase and P Croft, *Maynard Keynes: Collector of Pictures, Books, and Manuscripts*, Fitzwilliam Museum (Cambridge), 1983. Keynes also bought *The Kitchen*, another image evocative of Charleston.

17 No visual record remains of the decoration on the lower panel of the door, which was accidentally broken in 1918; its current decoration dates from 1958; see Q Bell and V Nicholson, *Charleston*, pp 23, 29. Grant's still life is similar to Bell's *Charleston Pond*, in which an Omega vase and a painted box, probably from the Omega, share colors with the pond seen through the window.

18 V Bell to R Fry, Winter 1917, Charleston Papers, Tate Gallery Archives. Bell here calls this room 'the studio,' a purpose it served only briefly; see V Bell, *Selected Letters of Vanessa Bell*, Regina Marler, (ed), Pantheon (New York), 1993, pp 200–1.

19 V Bell to R Fry, 22 February 1917, in Q Bell and V Nicholson, *Charleston*, p 112.

20 V Bell to R Fry, July 1915, in R Tranter, *Vanessa Bell: A Life of Painting*, Cecil Woolf (London), 1998, p 17.

21 In Q Bell and V Nicholson, *Charleston*, p 96.

22 D Garnett, *Flowers of the Forest*, p 175.

23 The bench, much weathered in existing photographs, is no longer extant, but a pen sketch of the figures remains in a private collection. My thanks to Simon Watney for bringing this to my attention.

24 S Watney, *Art of Duncan Grant*.

25 This oil on board painting is now in the collection of Wolfgang Kuhl, London.

Christopher Reed, *Bloomsbury Rooms: Modernism, Subculture, and Domesticity*, Yale University Press (New Haven and London), 2004.
© 2004 by Yale University. Reprinted by permission of Penguin Press.
(Excerpt pp 183–7)

The Clubs of St. James's: Places of Public Patriarchy

Jane Rendell

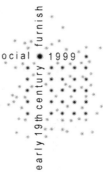

Jane Rendell uses theoretical discussions of gender difference to explore the architectural space of eighteenth-century male only clubs. She suggests that such spaces differentiate between men and women through forms of patriarchy and furthermore, men from other men through fratriarchy. From established notions that men's clubs operate as segregated private and social places for relaxing, Rendell outlines a case for their consideration as refuges to rival the familial home. They offer alternatives to domestic intimacy situated within the confines and security of a male-centred public realm. Club rules and elaborate interior planning are shown to codify space and monitor behaviour between proprietor, members, servants and strangers of both sexes.

the basement of a clubhouse [...] is usually sunk to a good depth so as to contain an additional floor within it, that is, an entresol between the lower most or kitchen floor and the apparent external ground floor. This economy of plan – which may be said to be particularly English – provides a complete habitation for the domestic and official part of the establishment, and an invisible one also [...][1]

From a liberal rights perspective, clubs offer the right to be alone, the right to confidentiality and the safe-guarding of individuality.[2] The club is a space of civil society, free from the coercive state and political constraints of the public realm – public morality, legal constraint and corporate interest; and at the same time, set aside from the emotional pressures and social demands of the private familial realm. Lying between the political public and the social private, I argue in this section that the club, by offering all the comforts of a private environment without the stresses of family life and all the freedom of the public realm without its political responsibilities, represents the domestic space of public patriarchy.[3]

Clubs are seen alternatively as the place in which bachelors might prepare for domestic life, and as a married man's refuge from family life.[4] As in the home, day-to-day routines were important to the functioning of the clubs, and times for meals, for supper and dinner, were set out in the club rules.[5] 'Club life' involved a large amount of time spent indulging in routinised behaviour with no purpose but leisure. A typical day was described as a long breakfast at eleven, a walk down Bond Street, a look into a club on Pall Mall at four o'clock, a four-course meal and a dessert at seven o'clock, and two rubbers of cards from midnight until two o'clock.[6]

Early club-houses were initially conversions of family homes and many of the new buildings at first modelled themselves on domestic dwellings. The design for the Savoir Vivre's club-house, consisting of a north section for the members and a southern one for 'a single man of fashion,' resembled that of a town house, a private rather than a public building, both in terms of its elevation, a 'modest and domesticated front,' and its asymmetric plan, the main staircase placed to one side and a series of rooms arranged in linear sequence from front to back.[7] The internal layout of Brooks's, with its rooms on two floors distributed around a central staircase, is more formal and public than Boodle's, but also follows a model adopted by domestic buildings, in this case the Palladian country villa. Only in the early nineteenth century, as clubs grew larger and their role changed from gathering places for the upper classes to drink and gamble to centres of a public and more institutional nature did they require different kinds of buildings. It has been argued that the first club to break the 'domestic' tradition was Charles Barry's Travellers' Club of 1819. Based, however, on the Italian palazzo, the design still takes a domestic, if not also civic, architectural typology as its model.[8] Subsequent club designs did move, however, towards the erection of large free-standing buildings with plenty of space around them externally. The rooms arranged internally around a central double height space housing the staircase, gave each room equal status and access from a public hallway, rather than the sequential arrangement of earlier clubs where one room had to be entered to reach another.

Particularly in the proprietor-managed eighteenth century club-house, based on a small and exclusive membership, the social hierarchy can be compared to the domestic household.[9] While the relationship between members might be considered 'fraternal,' that of the proprietor (owner and/or manager) and the members to the servants, operated on a 'patriarchal' or hierarchical basis, where the dominant role of the members and the subservient role of servants was observed within the spatial organisation of the club. Domestic activities associated with the running of the club, such as cooking, cleaning, storage were subjugated to the places of the least importance, considered unsightly and where possible kept hidden from view. Staff were confined to distinct service zones within the club building, to basement kitchens, attic sleeping quarters and various places at the rear of the building.

Extreme lengths were taken to provide separate internal circulation, staircases and different routes, for staff and members, to avoid contact unless for serving purposes. For example, when Boodle's added a new dining room in 1834, a new staircase connecting kitchen and dining room was built to avoid members seeing staff carrying food.[10] Club rules also codified the social relations between occupants of the club, members and servants, proprietor and members, strangers and members. Certain groups were allocated particular times, places and specified activities.[11] Decisions about who could do what where were important in distinguishing members from non-members, for example, Jewish money lenders who came to the clubs could not enter but had to wait in the stranger's room on the ground floor near the entrance.[12] In both Brooks's and Boodle's, the most exclusive club activities; drinking alcohol, eating and gaming, took place in the members' suite of rooms upstairs, visitors were entertained in the ground floor coffee or morning room:

A Member may admit a Friend or Friends on the ground Floor where they may have Tea or Coffee but no Wine. No Cards or Gaming to be allowed except in the rooms upstairs.[13]

The streets around St. James's also offered domestic places for men in the form of chambers and hotels. Some were men returning to England from military or diplomatic service abroad, others were young bachelors, just moved to London from their family homes, who did not wish the financial burden of buying a large house and were not ready to marry.[14] The bachelor chamber is represented as the most important domestic space for men outside the family home at this time. This was the place where men dressed and groomed, met for breakfast and prepared themselves for a day in the city.[15] The Albany, a series of seventy bachelor chambers intended for men of the nobility and gentry, was built off Piccadilly in 1803-4 by Alexander Copland to Henry Holland's designs. Each flat was self contained, but a dining room, bar and hot and cold communal baths were also provided. Despite the rule concerning the limitation of the use of apartments for residential purposes, Henry Angelo had a fencing school in the Albany in 1804, and Gentleman Jackson held his pugilistic training rooms there in 1807.[16]

Hotels, such as Clarendon's, Limmer's, Ibbetson's, Fladong's, Stephen's and Grillon's, also provided spaces of male domesticity and intimacy in the city, where the only activities were everyday ones, such as eating, drinking and sleeping.[17] Some hotels were known for their special features, for example, Fenton's medicinal baths, Parsloe's chess club, the Smyrna Coffee House's billiards and for members of the sporting world, Limmer's, a 'midnight Tattersall's.'[18] Taverns too provided men with a social place for relaxing outside the home,[19] and even public spaces such as streets, were described as places for men to relax. Bond Street, for example, was described as a 'fashionable lounge,'[20] and men were 'at home' on St. James's Street.[21]

A number of sites in St. James's were the foci of male urban routine, from mid-day rising and leisurely dressing; to a late afternoon promenade around Bond Street, St. James's

Street and Pall Mall purchasing commodities and displaying self, dress, horse and carriage; to evening activities including suppers, card parties and routs held at family homes and visits to assembly rooms, theatre or opera; followed finally by the club for gambling and drinking till dawn:[22]

> Such was the costume in which he was destined to show off, and thus equipped, after a few minutes they emerged from the house in Piccadilly on the proposed ramble, and proceeded towards Bond Street.[23]

The large amount of traffic on streets, both vehicular and pedestrian, created a need for individuals to adopt distinctive styles of public urban behaviour, such as walking on certain sides of the street or fast and aggressive driving of wheeled vehicles.[24] Coaching clubs, for example the Whip club, the Benson and the Four-in-Hand, were very popular in the early nineteenth century. Members would meet at regular intervals and display themselves in certain London Squares before setting off on a cross-country ride to dine:[25]

> [...] on such days the windows in that neighbourhood displayed a brilliant assemblage of fine ladies, and carriages of every description crowded the avenues adjoining.[26]

Specific modes of dressing, talking and walking reflected men's intense pre-occupation with self-presentation and public display. Bond Street and St. James's Street, with their gun shops, booksellers, theatre ticket agents, sporting prints exhibitions, hatters, tailors, cravat makers, hairdressers, perfumers, jewellers and other expensive tradesmen, catered solely for the male consumer.[27] Fashion and sporting shops, like chambers, hotels, sporting venues, coffee houses, clubs and taverns, provided places to display public masculinity through the exclusion of women. Establishing the correct aspects of gendered identities was critical to the representation of public patriarchy, young men on St. James's Street were considered to be street nuisances either for their effeminacy, 'ladies men who scent thy mawkish way' or for their roughness.[28]

Centres for sport in the vicinity, such as Manton's shooting gallery on Davies Street,[29] were important for establishing male bonds through shared activities. Gentleman Jackson's training rooms for young pugilists located at 13, Bond Street was a place where men met to train and watched each other display physique and sporting skills.[30] Although major pugilistic fights took place outside towns, or at the 'manly venue' of Fives Court, St. Martin's Street, Leicester-Fields,[31] on occasion the London homes of the nobility, domestic space usually associated with the family, would be used to stage special fights for an élite crowd.[32] With the exception of the Jockey Club and the Marylebone Cricket Club,[33] sporting clubs all met in taverns often owned by members of the sporting fraternity, for example Tom Cribb's (ex-Champion of England) tavern on Panton Street.[34]

Such taverns, frequented by both working-class professional boxers and the upper-class patrons, were the social centres of sport.

The basis for such shared male pursuits as drinking, sporting and gambling, originated at male-only education institutions, first at schools, such as Eton, and later at universities, such as Cambridge and Oxford.[35] Clubs formalised these male upper class bonds in the form of cultural institutions,[36] which linked specific sports to particular clubs, for example, fox hunting at Boodle's and the Turf at White's. As ways of communicating and exchanging information, clubs as well as magazines, maps, sporting calendars, were places from which to organise out-of-town activities and make bets.[37] As commercial forms of entertainment, sporting activities were characterised by competition and scale, and did not only create bonds between men but were used to establish dominance and determine hierarchies.[38] Clubs provided mechanisms for privileged groups to establish and control sporting legislation.[39] (... p 176)

Notes

1 JM Scott, *The Book of Pall Mall*, Heinemann (London), 1965, p 102.

2 Judith Squires, 'Private Lives, Secluded Places, Privacy as Political Possibility', *Environment and Planning D: Society and Space*, vol 12, 1994, p 393.

3 Scott, *Book of Pall Mall*, p 100.

4 See Edward Walford, *Old and New London*, Cassell, Petter and Galpin (London), 1873, p 140 and Scott, *Book of Pall Mall*, p 61.

5 See 'Subscription Book for 1764–1774' and 'Subscription Book for 1779–1782', Brooks's Club Archives, n p, rules 7, 22 and 23; 'Subscription Book for 1794–1798', 'Subscription Book for 1799–1805', 'Subscription Book for 1806–1813' and 'Subscription Book for 1814–1821', Brooks's Club Archives, n p, rules 7, 21 and 22. See 'Original Rules and List of Members & C, Boodle's Club 1857–1880', Boodle's Club Archives, n p, rule 10.

6 Felix MacDonogh, 'Vacant Hours', *The Hermit in London*, Henry Colburn (London), vol 2, 1819, pp 143–53. This account describes the Oriental, founded in 1824 by members of the East India Club who found they did not fit in well to English society. The Oriental Club was built at the west end of Hanover Square by Benjamin Wyatt in 1828. See Denys Forrest, *The Oriental, Life Story of a West End Club*, Batsford (London), 1979, p 23. Another account describes the Nabob club. See MacDonogh, 'The Nabob Club', *Hermit*, pp 211–6.

7 'Particulars of a Valuable Leasehold Estate Called the Savoir Vivre, St. James's Street', November, 1802.

8 Peter Fleetwood-Hesketh, 'The Travellers' Club, London', *Country Life*, 17 November 1966, pp 1270–1274.

9 Walford, *Old and New London*, p 143.

10 The drawings for this addition are interesting in that they colour code the separate circulation of members and staff, clearly indicating their social separation in the mind of the architect. See JB Papworth, 'Addition of a Kitchen and Dining Room, Boodle's Club, 28 St. James's St., London', 1834, ref PAP 93 (33), 17–21, Royal Institute of British Architects Drawings Collection, London.

11 'Original Rules and List of Members & ç, Boodle's Club 1787–1791', Boodle's Club Archives, n p, rules 5 and 10.

12 See for example, Percy Rudolph Broemel, *Paris and London in 1815*, Murray and Co (London), 1929, p 114; Captain Gronow, *Reminiscences of Captain Gronow Formerly of the Grenadier Guards*

and M.P. for Stafford Being Anecdotes of the Camp, the Court and the Clubs at the Close of the Last War with France Related by Himself, Smith Elder and Co (London), 1862, pp 78 and 183–6 and WM Weare, The Fatal Effects of Gambling, T Kelly (London), 1824, p 269.

13 'Original Rules and List of Members & C, Boodle's Club 1787–1791', Boodle's Club Archives, n p, rule 6.

14 John Feltham, Picture for London for 1818, 19th edition, Longman, Hurst, Rees, Orme and Brown (London), 1818, pp 412–16.

15 William Heath, Fashion and Folly: or the Buck's Pilgrimage, William Sams (London), 1822, plate 3; Amateur, Real life in London, or the Rambles and Adventures of Bob Tallyho, Esq. And his Cousin the Hon. Tom Dashall, Through the Metropolis; Exhibiting a Living Picture of Fashionable Characters, Manners and Amusements in High and Low Life, Jones and Co (London), vol 1, 1821–1822, pp 101–2; Pierce Egan, Life in London, or, the Day and Night Scenes of Jerry Hawthorn. Esq. and his Elegant Friend Corinthian Tom, Accompanied by Bob Logic, the Oxonian, in their Rambles and Sprees Through the Metropolis, Sherwood, Neely and Jones (London), 1820–1821, pp 145–8, and MacDonogh, Hermit, vol 2, pp 35–8; 'An Exquisite's Diary', vol 3, pp 79–86.

16 See for example, FHW Sheppard (ed), The Survey of London, Athlone Press (London), University of London, vol 32, 1960, pp 44–5, 98–9, 111–20, 258–9 and 367–89 and Dorothy Stroud, Henry Holland: His Life and Architecture, Country Life (London), 1966.

17 Feltham, Picture, 1818, pp 286, 412.

18 Gronow, Reminiscences, 1862, pp 74–5.

19 Brian Harrison, Drink and the Victorians: The Temperance Question in England 1815–1872, Faber & Faber (London), 1971, pp 39–40.

20 Amateur, Real, vol 2, p 365.

21 Egan, Life, p 8.

22 See for example, Amateur, Real, vol 1, p 102; Bernard Blackmantle, The English Spy, Sherwood, Jones and Co (London), vol 2, 1825, p 253; Egan, Life, p 213; Gronow, Reminiscences, 1862, pp 74–9; and MacDonogh, 'A Morning Ride in a Noble-Man's Curricle', Hermit, vol 2, pp 35–42, especially pp 40–1.

23 Amateur, Real, vol 1, p 102.

24 John Badcock, A Living Picture of London, for 1823, and Strangers Guide Shewing the Frauds and Wiles of all Descriptions of Rogues, W Clarke (London), 1828, pp 47–8. See also Penelope Corfield, 'Walking the City Streets, an Eighteenth Century Odyssey', Historical Perspectives, vol 16, 1990, pp 132–74, p 147; Thomas Burke, The Streets of London, BT Batsford (London), 1940, p 107; Johnson, Eighteen and AE Richardson, Georgian England, BT Batsford (London), 1931, p 81.

25 See Captain Gronow, Captain Gronow's Last Recollections Being the Fourth and Final Series of the Reminiscences and Anecdotes with a Portrait, Smith, Elder and Co (London), 1866, p 97; and Derek Birley, Sport and the Making of Britain, Manchester University Press (Manchester), 1993, p 31.

26 Jacob Larwood, The Story of the London Parks, Francis Harvey (London), vol 8, 1872, pp 283–4.

27 Captain Gronow describes the bootmaker, Hoby, next to the Guards' Club, and the fashionable 'coiffeur,' Rowland next to the Thatched House in St. James's Street. See Captain Gronow, Recollections and Anecdotes being a Second Series of Reminiscences of the Camp, the Court and the Clubs by Captain R. H. Gronow (Formerly of the Grenadier Guards and M. P. for Stafford), Smith, Elder and Co (London), 1863, pp 136–7. See also Alison Adburgham, Shopping in Style, Thames and Hudson (London), 1979, pp 76–7; Alison Adburgham, Shops and Shopping 1800–1914, George Allen and Unwin (London), 1981, p 7 and Burke, Streets, p 109.

28 A plate from William Heath features St. James's Street and some associated verses. William Heath, Fashion and Folly Illustrated in a Series, 1822, plate 14; and MacDonogh, Hermit, vol 5, 1819, pp 36–8.

29 Gronow, Reminiscences, 1862, pp 210–11.

30 Gentleman Jackson was a figure central to early nineteenth century boxing. Jackson's Rooms were formerly D'Angelo's Rooms, a family who had been running a riding school and fencing academy for

30 years. See Pierce Egan, *Boxiana* (*Boximania, or Sketches of Ancient and Modern Pugilism*), G Smeeton (London), 1812, p 289; Pierce Egan, *Boxiana*, Sherwood, Neely and Jones (London), 1818 and Pierce Egan, *Boxiana*, Sherwood, Neely and Jones (London), 1821, p 13. See also Dennis Brailsford, *Bareknuckles: a Social History of Prize Fighting*, Lutterworth Press (Cambridge), 1988, pp 70–1. See George and Robert Cruikshank, 'Art of Self-Defence: Tom and Jerry receiving Instructions from Mr. Jackson, at his Rooms, in Bond-Street', Egan, *Life*, p 217.

31 A typical journey to get to a fight is described, the type of transport used to get there, the role of the patrons and nobility, and the placing of bets. See Amateur, *Real*, vol 1, pp 604–20. Including two plates showing the road to a fight and the mixture of people of all classes. See also Pierce Egan and Robert Cruikshank, *The Road to a Fight or Going to a Fight at Musley Hurst or a Picture of the Fancy*, 1814. This is a continuous strip of pictures, 14 ft by 2.5 inches, wound on a spindle and enclosed in a cylindrical box, with an illustration of a boxing match on the lid. See also Egan, *Boxiana*, 1818, pp 14–15.

32 H Alken, 'A Private Turn-up in the Drawing Room of a Noble Marquis', Jones and Co (London), 21 July 1821; Amateur, *Real*, vol 1, p 620.

33 James E Marlow, 'Popular Culture, Pugilism and Pickwick', *Journal of Popular Culture*, vol 15 no 4, 1982, pp 16–30, p 18.

34 See George and Robert Cruikshank, 'Cribb's Parlour: Tom introducing Jerry and Logic to the Champion of England', Egan, Life, p 220. Boxiana listed houses kept by pugilists and other people connected with the sporting world around the country and in London. See Egan, Boxiana, 1821, p 20. Tom Cribb was a retired Champion of England, beating Tom Molineaux at Thistleton Gap on 28 September 1811. See Egan, *Life*, p 219.

35 See for example, Blackmantle, *Spy*, vol 1, p 57. The links between private male-only education and sporting rituals have been explored by Derek Birley; see Derek Birley, 'Bonaparte and the Squire: Chauvinism, Virility and Sport in the Period of the French Wars', Derek Birley (ed), *Pleasure, Profit and Proselytism*, Frank Cass (London), 1988, pp 21–41.

36 See Sheppard (ed), *Survey*, vol 29, pp 334–5 and 419–24.

37 Dennis Brailsford, *British Sport: A Social History*, The Lutterworth Press (Cambridge), 1992, p 53. See for example, E and J Weatherby, *The Racing Calendar*, 1794–1830; *The Sporting Magazine or Monthly Calendar of the Transactions of the Turf, The Chase, and every other Pleasure Interesting to the Man of Pleasure and Enterprise*, 1793; John Lawrence, *The Sportsman's Repository*, 1820 and Yorkshire Gentleman, *The Sporting Almanack and Olympic Ephemeris*, Knight and Lacey and C Stocking (London), 1826.

38 Dennis Brailsford, *Sport, Time and Society*, Routledge (London), 1991, p xi and Derek Birley, *Sport and the Making of Britain*, Manchester University Press (Manchester), 1993, pp 2 and 4–6.

39 Interview with Mr Edmunds, Secretary of Boodle's Club, July 1995.

Jane Rendell, 'The Clubs of St. James's: Places of Public Patriarchy – Exclusivity, Domesticity and Secrecy, *The Journal of Architecture*, vol 4 no 2, 1999, pp 167–89.
© 1999 The Journal of Architecture. Reprinted by permission of Taylor & Francis Ltd.
http://www.tandf.co.uk/journals
(Excerpt pp 173–6)

Rethinking Histories of the Interior

Charles Rice

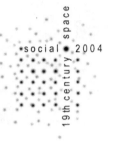

Architectural historian Charles Rice examines the relationship between an image of the domestic interior (media) and the domestic environment (setting) through the historical emergence of the bourgeois domestic interior. To expose a problematic between the spatial and imagistic sense of the interior, Rice notes that for both Walter Benjamin and Charles Baudelaire this doubled experience is held within material and immaterial registers, producing de-realised experiences. The specificity of the interior view and specific spatial practices of inhabitation are used to criticise interior histories that pronounce an essentialised view of the domestic interior. This criticism is generated in light of the established texts by Mario Praz, Peter Thornton and Charlotte Gere.

The word 'interior' has undergone several shifts in meaning. It had come into use in English from the late fifteenth century to mean basic divisions between inside and outside, and to describe the spiritual and inner nature of the soul. From the early eighteenth century, interiority was used to designate inner character and a sense of individual subjectivity, and from the middle of the eighteenth century the interior came to designate the domestic affairs of a state, as well as the interior sense of territory that belongs to a country or region. It was only from the beginning of the nineteenth century, however, that the interior came to designate what the *Oxford English Dictionary (OED)* records as: 'The inside of a building or room, esp. in reference to the artistic effect; also, a picture or representation of the inside of a building or room. Also, in a theatre, a "set" consisting of the inside of a building or room.'

The first use of the word in this domestic sense is dated 1829 from a publication entitled *Companion To Theatres*: 'A few interiors, two or three streets, and about the same number of country views, would last as stock scenery for several seasons.' An entry from George Eliot's diary of 1858 has a use in the sense of a genre of representation: 'The two interiors of Westminster Abbey by Ainmueller admirable.' The *OED* entry for interior decoration suggests a usage for interior which is more specifically domestic: 'The planned co-ordination for artistic effect of colours and furniture, etc., in a room or building.'[1] The first use given is *Household Furniture and Interior Decoration*, the title of Thomas

Hope's 1807 publication, which, along with Charles Percier and Pierre Fontaine's *Recueil de décorations intérieurs* of 1801, marked the newly emergent interior as a site of professional struggle between architects and upholsterers. Through the nineteenth century, interior decoration began to articulate itself separately from architecture.[2]

In this way, the interior emerges with conceptual specificity in the context of bourgeois domesticity. It is not simply architectural, but it borrows on the enclosure provided by architecture to be articulated through decoration, the literal covering of the inside of an architectural 'shell.' In this sense the interior is also not simply spatial, but is equally an image-based phenomenon.

There are further doubled conditions of the interior that consolidate the significance of its historical emergence. A sense of doubled experience, the way in which an inhabitation of the interior is caught between material and immaterial registers, is captured in 'The Twofold Room,' a prose poem of 1862 by Charles Baudelaire. It begins with a description of 'A room just like a daydream, a truly spiritual room, in which the air is tinged with rosiness and blue.'

> The furniture takes on elongated shapes, prostate and languorous. Each piece seems to be dreaming, as if living in a state of trance, like vegetable and mineral things. The draperies speak an unvoiced language, like flowers and skies and setting suns.[3]

In a similar vein to this poetic evocation, Walter Benjamin's 1939 exposé of the bourgeois domestic interior describes it as a material space which produces de-realised experiences.[4] For the bourgeoisie, the interior emerges as a space separated from sites of work and productive labour, and becomes a place of refuge from the city and its new, alienating forms of experience. In the interior, subjects confront themselves in psychologically charged ways through the medium of objects and furnishings. Benjamin writes of the private individual inhabiting the interior by 'taking possession' of things in divesting them of their character as commodities: 'The collector proves to be the true resident of the interior.' By bestowing a 'connoisseur's value,' rather than a 'use value' on objects, the collector 'delights in evoking a world that is not just distant and long gone but also better – a world in which, to be sure, human beings are no better provided with what they need than in the real world, but in which things are freed from the drudgery of being useful.'[5] These things become what Benjamin calls the traces of inhabitation.

Yet Baudelaire's interior is sealed off from the everyday world only in reverie. The internal coherence of his animate, nature-like room changes with the intrusion of reality into the room and its interiorised world. This intrusion comes with 'a terrible, heavy thump' on the door, at which point he remembers:

285

Yes, this hovel, this home of everlasting boredom, is indeed my own. Look, there are the fatuous bits of junk, my dusty and chipped furniture; the fireless hearth with not even a glowing ember in the grate all fouled with spit; the dingy windows down which the rain has scrawled runnels in the grime; the manuscripts riddled with cross-outs or left half done; the calendar on which the evil days of reckoning are underlined in pencil.[6]

A space of immaterial, de-realised experience, Baudelaire's interior is also the space of his work, and of his relation to the productive cycle. His plight figures the way in which the increased awareness of the bourgeois interior as a space removed from the everyday world also produced a measure for assessing the living conditions of the working classes, those for whom the domestic and the productive spheres were not necessarily separated.[7] More broadly, this relation between reverie and the reality of the onward march of time gives a context for understanding the bourgeoisie's relation to the world of objects as commodities, to the industrialising city, and to their social and political identity through the nineteenth century.

Baudelaire and Benjamin's immaterial experience occurs in relation to a space for and of the psyche, a space that borrows on the material attributes of the everyday domestic interior – its furnishings – and imbues them with a transformed, psychological significance. In his introductory lectures on psychoanalysis from the beginning of the twentieth century, Sigmund Freud delineates a further doubled condition of the interior when he describes a suite of rooms to explain the structure of the unconscious:

> Let us therefore compare the system of the unconscious to a large entrance hall, in which the mental impulses jostle one another like separate individuals. Adjoining this entrance hall is a separate, narrower, room – a kind of drawing-room – in which consciousness, too, resides. But on the threshold between these two rooms a watchman performs his function: he examines the different mental impulses, acts as a censor, and will not admit them into the drawing-room if they displease him.[8]

Historically, Freud was a collector of antique statuary which adorned and, in Benjamin's terms, made his consulting rooms, which were attached to his apartment in Vienna, into a domestic interior.[9] This interior provided the setting for the scene of transference taking place between Freud and his patients. And much of the force of the Oedipus Complex as a model for how Freud delineated the complex of attachments between subjects comes from the consolidated, and in some ways overdetermined place of the family in bourgeois life from the nineteenth century.[10]

The bourgeois domestic interior emerges historically in the nineteenth century through an accumulation of traces, and in relation to occluded meanings. At one level, we can understand these aspects of its historical emergence as intrinsic to the bourgeoisie's experience of domesticity in the nineteenth century. But what does the doubleness of the interior, and the idea that the interior is historically emergent in this way, mean for how we might write a history of this domestic experience? In other words, how can we gain access to and evaluate an historical experience which is complicated by a condition of doubleness?

The primary complicating factor is the idea that the interior's spatial and imagistic senses do not map directly onto each other. As we learn from Baudelaire, the imagistic sense of the interior is not simply transparent to its spatial sense. This presents problems for conventional ways in which the evidence of the interior is gathered to reconstruct and interpret historical conditions of domesticity.   (... p 278)

It was from the beginning of the nineteenth century that interior views were painted and drawn as ends in themselves, as a specific genre. Charlotte Gere has argued that practices of interior decoration were directly linked to the emergence of this genre: 'That this interest in interior decoration (prompted by the publications from Percier and Fontaine, and Hope) had a direct bearing on the taste for interior views is evidenced by the fact that so many of them show rooms that must just have been decorated and newly arranged.'[11] Gere's album of interior water colours provides a history of the decoration of the nineteenth-century interior evidenced through its representation, but this project hides an essentialist view of the interior which betrays the historical specificity of the bourgeois interior doubled between representational and spatial practices. In the following passage, Gere shifts from describing the historical conditions for the emergence of the genre of the interior view, to describing how these representations become evidence for a much broader conception of the history of the interior:

> The depiction of rooms for their own sake, rather than as a background to a narrative, anecdotal or portrait painting, germinated, reached its fullest flowering and died within the space of one century. It was not unusual for such interiors to form a group, representing different aspects of several rooms. They were intended to be placed in albums rather than to be framed and hung, and remained an almost secret possession. ... When the interior view went out of fashion in the second half of the nineteenth century, their very existence seems to have been forgotten. They were rendered obsolete by the development of a photographic camera capable of focusing on a great depth of field and thus able to do the job of the interior view-painter much more quickly and no less efficiently. Some of these [photographic] albums survive, giving an invaluable picture of decorating taste in the period 1880–1910, before they too were forgotten, like the albums of paintings they had superseded. Mario Praz's rediscovery of this minor but fascinating art barely thirty years ago (his pioneering *Illustrated History of Interior Decoration* was published in 1964) was a revelation, and the

historic no less than aesthetic importance of the subject is now recognised by a group of informed collectors.[12]

While Perrot realised the ultimately private nature of the evidence of privacy, Gere is signalling the shift of visual representations of the interior from being familial possessions to becoming historical, and therefore public, documents. The implications of this shift can be seen most clearly in relation to Mario Praz's seminal work. His *Illustrated History of Interior Decoration* provides a selection of visual representations of domesticity from ancient Greece through to Art Nouveau, and a commentary upon them.[13] The introduction to Praz's book muses on the literary and representational evocation of furniture, the home and the interior. Praz sees the house and its interior as a continuum, which is always in need of furnishing. In witnessing the destruction of houses after the second world war, their interiors laid open with 'some still furnished corner, dangling above the rubble, surrounded by ruin,'[14] Praz sees that:

> The houses will rise again, and men will furnish houses as long as there is breath in them. Just as our primitive ancestor built a shapeless chair with hastily-chopped branches, so the last man will save from the rubble a stool or a tree stump on which to rest from his labours; and if his spirit is freed a while from his woes, he will linger another moment and decorate his room.[15]

Such an observation of the timeless qualities of 'human nature' is the platform upon which Praz launches his history of the interior. He writes quite directly of the interior and its furnishing as reflecting the 'character' or 'personality' of the occupant, working from a basic division of human nature between those who 'care about their house, and those who care not at all about it.'[16] Based on his reading of decorative tendencies from visual representations, Praz sees that:

> perhaps even more than painting or sculpture, perhaps even more than architecture itself, furniture reveals the spirit of the age. And there is nothing like a retrospective exhibition of furnished rooms in a chronological sequence to declare to us, at first glance, the varying personalities of the rooms' occupants.[17]

Praz's book aims to provide the published equivalent of this 'retrospective exhibition,' taking the idea of the inhabiting subject, and the interior and its decoration, as pre-given concepts for the construction of this history, not ones that have emerged out of particular historical conditions. Referring to Benjamin, whose exposé on the interior he cites at length,[18] Praz collects traces of the inhabitant through their visibility in the interior. Yet he generalises this bourgeois condition as one obtaining across all history. He ignores the historical specificity of the genre of the interior view, and how it might relate to specific spatial practices of inhabitation, by rendering the idea of visual representation across many genres transparent to spatial conditions of domesticity. What has been tacitly recognised as a particular historical emergence has been used to authorise a transhistorical and essentialised view of the domestic interior.

We must ask: what is the impetus behind this sort of essentialised historiography? An answer may be found in another history of the interior, Peter Thornton's *Authentic Décor: The Domestic Interior 1620–1920*. Thornton takes the cue for his investigation from this quotation from Macaulay's 1848 *History of England*:

> Readers who take an interest in the progress of civilisation and of the useful arts will be grateful to the humble topographer who has recorded these facts [about the meanness of the lodgings of those taking the waters at Bath, early in the eighteenth century], and will perhaps wish that historians of far higher pretensions had sometimes spared a few pages from military evolutions and political intrigues, for the purpose of letting us know how the parlours and bedchambers of our ancestors looked.[19]

In these terms, a history of the interior supplements traditional grand historical narratives, whereby one's supposed innate appreciation of domesticity would colour the background of past events. What is common in all of these histories of privacy, domesticity and the interior is that they attest to a post-nineteenth-century way of seeing. This way of seeing authorises a general historical retrospection which is itself not appreciated within an historical context. This situation approaches what Michel Foucault terms traditional history:

> We believe in the dull constancy of instinctual life and imagine that it continues to exert its force indiscriminately in the present as it did in the past. But a knowledge of history easily disintegrates this unity, depicts its wavering course, locates its moments of strength and weakness, and defines its oscillating reign.[20]

A 'knowledge of history' relates to what Foucault terms effective history. It is a history of discontinuity, for the sake of breaking tendencies for recognition and 'rediscovery of ourselves'[21] in acts of constructing narrative-driven traditional histories. In Foucault's terms, the emergence of the interior, in its doubleness, can be cast as an event in the schema of effective history, an event that, when perceived as such, enables a 'reversal of a relationship of forces.'[22] By returning to Benjamin's exposé of the bourgeois domestic interior, we shall see the importance of understanding the historical emergence of the interior within this schema of effective history. And far from providing an increased consciousness of everyday domesticity within the continuum of history, we shall see that essentialised histories of the interior, privacy and domesticity have produced a sleep of historical consciousness.   (... p 282)

Notes

1 *Oxford English Dictionary*, 2nd ed, Clarendon Press (Oxford), 1989.

2 Peter Thornton, *Authentic Décor: The Domestic Interior, 1620–1920*, Viking (New York), 1984, pp 10–12.

3 Charles Baudelaire, 'The Twofold Room', Francis Scarfe ed and trans *The Poems in Prose, with La Fanfarlo*, Anvil Press (London), 1989, p 37.

4 Walter Benjamin, 'Paris: Capital of the Nineteenth Century (exposé of 1939)', in Rolf Tiedemann, (ed), *The Arcades Project*, trans Howard Eiland and Kevin McLaughlin, The Belknap Press of Harvard University Press (Cambridge, MA and London), 1999, pp 19–20.

5 Benjamin, 'Paris', p 19.

6 Baudelaire, 'The Twofold Room', p 39.

7 Important here is the sociological research conducted by Henry Mayhew into slums in London in the middle of the nineteenth century. Against a bourgeois consciousness of domestic comfort, Mayhew's research points to where basic standards of comfort in dwellings are not achieved amongst the working classes. See Henry Mayhew, 'Home is Home, be it Never so Homely', in Viscount Ingestre (ed), *Meliora, or Better Times to Come* (London), 1851, pp 258–80. See also Martin Hewitt, 'District Visiting and the Constitution of Domestic Space in the Mid-Nineteenth Century', Inga Bryden and Janet Floyd (eds), *Domestic Space: Reading the Nineteenth-Century Interior*, Manchester University Press (Manchester and New York), 1999, pp 121–41, for an account of the surveillance of the working class by the middle classes in Britain.

8 Sigmund Freud 'Introductory Lectures on Psychoanalysis, Lecture XIX: Resistance and Repression [1916-1917]', in James Strachey ed and trans *The Standard Edition of the Complete Psychological Works of Sigmund Freud*, 24 vols, The Hogarth Press (London), 1953–1974, vol 16, pp 295–6.

9 See Joel Sanders and Diana Fuss, 'Berggasse 19: Inside Freud's Office', Joel Sanders (ed), *Stud: Architectures of Masculinity*, Princeton Architectural Press (New York), 1996, pp 112–39.

10 See Jacques Donzelot, *The Policing of Families*, trans Robert Hurley, Hutchinson (London), 1980; Nikolas Rose, *Governing the Soul: The Shaping of the Private Self*, Free Association Books (London), 1990.

11 Charlotte Gere, *Nineteenth Century Interiors: An Album of Watercolours*, Thames and Hudson (London), 1992, p 13.

12 Gere, *Nineteenth Century*, p 14. Peter Thornton puts this argument thus: 'It was fashionable, from about 1815 to about 1840, to draw and paint views of interiors. Grand people instructed a draughtsman to make pictures of their favourite rooms; the less grand did it themselves', Thornton, *Authentic Décor*, p 217. Gere recognises that there are precedents for interior view-painting in examples from the eighteenth century. She suggests that these earlier examples were either isolated representations that were informational sources in relation to the rooms they depicted (rather than having 'artistic' merit, which would define a genre in Gere's terms), were representations of well-known houses in periodicals and other publications, or were representations produced to accompany visits to well-known buildings. Thornton argues that the practice of allowing visits to well-known houses, and the attendant publications, ceased around 1840, when the interior shifted from being a space for the display of taste and wealth, to being the space of familial privacy and the cultivation of domestic virtues. See Thornton, *Authentic Décor*, p 210. For an in-depth discussion of one particular eighteenth century drawing type, see Robin Evans, 'The Developed Surface', *Translations from Drawing to Building and Other Essays*, Architectural Association (London), 1997, pp 55–91.

13 Mario Praz, *An Illustrated History of Interior Decoration from Pompeii to Art Nouveau*, trans William Weaver, Thames and Hudson (London), 1964. Alternative edition: An *Illustrated History of Interior Furnishing from the Renaissance to the 20th Century*, trans William Weaver, George Braziller (New York), 1964. The two editions are identical, and despite the supposed 'Renaissance' beginning of the American edition, it still includes the plates 'from Pompeii.'

14 Praz, *Illustrated History*, p 17.

15 Praz, *Illustrated History*, p 18.

16 Praz, *Illustrated History*, p 19.
17 Praz, *Illustrated History*, p 25.
18 Praz, *Illustrated History*, pp 25–9.
19 TB Macaulay, *History of England from the Accession of James II* (London), 1848, vol 1, Ch III. Quoted in Thornton, *Authentic Décor*, p 8.
20 Michel Foucault, 'Nietzsche, Genealogy, History', Paul Rabinow ed and trans *The Foucault Reader*, Penguin (London), 1984, p 87.
21 Foucault, 'Nietzsche', p 88.
22 Foucault, 'Nietzsche', p 88.

Charles Rice, 'Rethinking Histories of the Interior', *The Journal of Architecture*, vol 9 no 3, 2004, pp 275–87.

© 2004 The Journal of Architecture. Reprinted by permission of Taylor & Francis Ltd. http://www.tandf.co.uk/journals

(Excerpts pp 276–82)

Designing the Dinner Party

Rachel Rich

Rachel Rich targets the social history of the late nineteenth-century dining room in terms of architecture, furniture and table decorations, alongside the bourgeois love of order and specialisation. She discusses the dining room as a place where the bourgeoisie exercised spatial and decorative design informed by domestic advice literature, advice that transformed the physical environment of the English and French interior. The dining room was characterised as having masculine identity through its furniture and decorations, and Rich observes that the female mark was reserved for flowers and place settings. Reflecting a middle-class ideology, such spaces provided a venue for displaying good taste, manners and social rank, and above all reputation.

The period 1860–1914 saw the publication of a wide range of sources on domestic architecture in both London and Paris.[1] The ideas put forth in these publications were not new or radical, but instead reflected changes in the theory and practice of domestic architecture that had been emerging gradually since the eighteenth century. The publication of such a large body of advice literature at this period, however, indicates the wider dissemination of ideas that were once restricted to an elite minority. There are other reasons why this period is suitable for a study of bourgeois ideals of the domestic interior. For one thing, it was a period of middle-class identity consolidation. A second factor is that it was a period in which new social and cultural practices led to shifts in gender identity. Recent work on the department store has shown that women were increasingly inhabiting the commercial sphere in the second half of the nineteenth century, and that their identity as guardians of the home was being expanded to include their role as shoppers and consumers, as well as beings capable of enjoying the pleasures of urban life, such as eating out.[2] In part, because of women's greater ability to move through the city, the boundaries between private and public spheres, never a clearly demarcated line, were becoming increasingly blurred. The emphasis in decorating advice manuals on the presentation of the dining room to outsiders reveals a perceived need from readers for guidelines on how to create a home that was both public and private. The dining room needed to be a space in which a family shared meals and created bonds of affection, while at the same time presenting the public face of the family to the outside world, which was increasingly perceived to be encroaching on the inner sanctum of the home. Examining bourgeois ideals about domestic design in the period 1860–1914 reveals one way in which contemporary arbiters of taste were attempting to consolidate bourgeois ideology by incorporating it into the physical world of the middle-class home. At the same time, it reveals how advice literature was used to normalize gender identities in a period of rapid change and redefinition.   (... p 50)

The way that space was organized and negotiated was crucial to middle-class perceptions of the role of dining both in everyday life and for special occasions. Though fashions changed, certain basic ideas about the space and design of this room, the role of which was simultaneously public and private, decorative and functional, remained constant throughout the period. Table settings differed between private family meals and more formal dinner parties, and at every occasion important messages were conveyed by the physical appearance of the room in which meals were consumed. The imposition of a set of standards of spatial and decorative ideals was a key feature of how the bourgeoisie placed their stamp on the environments they inhabited. Ethnologists Frykman and Löfgren argue that an understanding of middle-class ideology can best be achieved through the study of the trivialities of everyday life, such as the organization of the home.[3] Looking at the intersection of design and domestic ideology is one place to begin to attempt to address these issues.[4]   (... p 51)

Dining room furniture, it was generally agreed, had to be solid and masculine. As we have seen, a dining room/kitchen dichotomy existed to separate the production and consumption areas of food within the home. At the same time, a similar opposition existed between the dining room and the drawing room, which were conceived of as representing the masculine and feminine spheres of domestic activity. The English drawing room, or French *salon*, was intended to be the feminine reception room, and was designed accordingly.[5] In the dining room, the master of the house was supposed to rule, and this was reflected in the choice of furniture. Wheeler described the drawing room as an area of the house devoted to the use of the ladies, and insisted for this reason that any woodwork in it should not be treated as woodwork, since 'there always seems an incongruity and rudeness about grained doors or polished maple.'[6] In contrast, Kerr insisted that 'the whole aspect of the [dining] room ought to be that of masculine importance.'[7] It was in keeping with the nineteenth-century insistence on gender as a guiding principle in categorizations of human behaviour that even the rooms within a private home should take on a gender identity.[8] Up until the eighteenth century, dinner parties had been hosted by men for men. During the nineteenth century, the responsibility for hosting the dinner party came to shift from the host to the hostess, but there remained an underlying sense that cuisine was a masculine pleasure, and that dinner parties were occasions for male hosts to impress male guests.[9]

English dining-room furniture was, ideally, solid and serious, demonstrating stability and authority. Kerr argued: 'the style ... is always somewhat massive and simple ... on the principle, perhaps, of conformity with the substantial pretensions of both English character and English fare.'[10] Booth felt that the dining room was a less interesting room to furnish than the drawing room. According to Booth, the drawing room was the room in which luxury and taste were to be displayed, while the dining room 'should be suggestive of comfort and social convenience, for it is the apartment where the owner dispenses his hospitality.' He also advocated 'solid and substantial' furniture for the dining room.[11] *The Lady* published examples of dining-room furniture that avoided the frills associated with Victorian drawing rooms. Others used words such as 'grave, rich and stately' to describe what they felt should be the attributes of the dining room furniture.[12] Wheeler advocated dark woods for dining-room furniture, such as old oak and old Spanish mahogany.[13] He also discussed the general appearance of the dining-room, stating that the colours used should be stately and unobtrusive, and that if paintings were hung on the walls, 'the selection should be limited to a few pleasant, rich and cheerful designs.'[14] Apart from when a meal was actually being eaten, the chairs would be placed along the walls. Kerr felt that this gave the room a 'substantial and hospitable aspect.'[15] Robert Edis [*Decoration and Furniture of Town Houses*, 1881] illustrated a dining room that combined strong masculine furniture with some more feminine ornaments.   (... p 55)

While the masculine identity of the dining room was represented in the furniture, the female mark was placed on the table setting. There may have been several factors contributing to this. One was the shift, as we have seen, from male to female responsibility for hosting the dinner party. As it was the task of the mistress of the house to welcome her guests, there had to be some outward signs of the effort she had made to create a pleasant meal for them.[16] Advice writers generally agreed that there should be no appearance of strain or effort on the part of the hostess. It was also agreed that to have appeared to have had too much to do with the cooking of the food itself was improper – the duty of the mistress of the house was to order the meal and oversee its preparation, but the actual cooking had to be done, or at least appear to have been done, by servants.[17] Decorating the table, however, was a task that a woman could undertake with no risk to her reputation. In fact, it was generally advised that this was one of her principal duties, as servants would not have the aesthetic sense of the middle-class housemistress when it came to tasks such as selecting and arranging flowers. While furniture was expensive and therefore tended not to be changed very often, flowers were perishable, and it was possible to change the fashion in flowers with every new season.[18] Owing to the frequency of changes in fashion, advice about table decoration tended to appear in women's magazines more than in etiquette books.

Flowers and place settings were the principal elements of table decoration with which women were concerned. One author commented that: 'the best meal in the world is not appetising on a barren or soiled tablecloth.'[19] Mrs Loftie advised her readers to use restraint when setting the table. She warned against putting more glasses on the table than were likely to be needed: 'Many people, particularly old gentlemen, are fidgeted by finding five or six glasses at their elbow, all liable to be overturned or broken.'[20] She did, however, insist on the importance of finger glasses, for both aesthetic and practical purposes.[21] She also discussed the important question of what silverware was appropriate for use at respectable dinner parties, referring to this as the 'knife and fork question:' 'there is a serious question anxiously debated at many dinner parties as to the superiority of three prongs to four. The "three-prongians" hold their own against the "four-prongians," except in the matter of young peas.'[22] Choosing the right cutlery meant being aware of current debates, and also showed the extent to which a hostess cared about the ease of her guests. Just as the organization of house and furniture revealed the inner morality of household members, so the choice of cutlery and the arrangement of the table had moral as well as aesthetic implications.

The decoration of the table for a dinner party showed what the mistress was really made of.[23] Mrs Loftie pointed out the practical dimension of floral decorations: 'Flowers and fruits are at all times desirable on the table ... even to look at it is nice, and a bunch of sweet fresh flowers seems to give one appetite.'[24] An author in *La Salle à Manger* emphasized the more aesthetic principle, comparing a well-decorated table to a well-dressed woman: 'The arrangement of a table is like the toilette of a women, its success often rests on few things.'[25] As the capital of both cuisine and fashion, Paris saw itself as the arbiter of taste in floral decorations. Parisian women's magazines featured countless articles advising and educating readers on the subject, while the women of London were seemingly assumed to be able to decorate their tables without advice.   (... p 57)

Notes
1   In this issue, Penny Sparke, 'The "Ideal" and the "Real" Interior in Elsie de Wolfe's *The House in Good Taste* of 1913', *Journal of Design History*, vol 16 no 1, 2003, pp 63–76; and Emma Ferry, '"Decorators May be Compared to Doctors:" An Analysis of Rhoda and Agnes Garrett's *Suggestions for House Decoration in Painting, Woodwork and Furniture* (1876)', *Journal of Design History*, vol 16 no 1, 2003, pp 15–33; both look at specific cases of such publications.
2   See for example, Erika Rappaport, *Shopping for Pleasure: Women in the Making of London's West End*, Princeton University Press (Princeton NJ), 2000, and Lisa Tiersten, 'The Chic Interior and the Feminine Modern', Christopher Reed (ed), *Not at Home: The Suppression of Domesticity in Modern Art and Architecture*, Thames and Hudson (London), 1996.
3   Jonas Frykman and Orvar Löfgren, *Culture Builders: A Historical Anthropology of Middle-Class Life*, trans Alan Crozier, Rutgers University Press (New Brunswick), 1987, p 6.
4   Nancy Armstrong has argued that advice literature exposes ideology in its purest form. See Nancy Armstrong and Leonard Tennenhouse (eds), *The Ideology of Conduct: Essays in Literature and the History of Sexuality*, Methuen (New York), 1987.
5   See for example, *The Lady*, 19 September 1895.

6 Gervase Wheeler, *The Choice of a Dwelling: A Practical Handbook of Useful Information*, John Murray (London), 1872, p 221.

7 Robert Kerr, *The Englishman's House; or, How to Plan English Residences, From the Parsonage to the Palace*, John Murray (London), 1864, p 105.

8 While advice authors often conceived of the gendering of the house in terms of oppositions, the reality was far more complicated, with shifting boundaries and fluid meanings. For one thing, both men and women inhabited all the various rooms of the house, in spite of the assertions of various writers that some rooms were feminine and others masculine. For a second thing, in houses that were too small to have separate dining and sitting rooms, one room needed to reflect both masculine and feminine characteristics. The possibility of this made it clear exactly how blurred were the boundaries which separated masculine and feminine areas of the home. Finally, women were given the responsibility of furnishing the home, as an extension of their role of protectors of the domestic sphere. However, the furniture that they chose for the so-called masculine rooms of the house was intended to reflect the taste of their husbands.

9 In French advice literature and first-hand accounts there were frequent references to male-only dinner parties, but not to women-only ones. In contrast to this, English advice writers emphasized that lunch at home was a principally female meal. This is significant in that dinner was the highest-placed meal in the hierarchy of the meals of the day.

10 Kerr, *Englishman's House*, p 104.

11 Lorenzo Booth, *A Series of Original Designs for Decorative Furniture*, Houlston & Wright (London), 1864, pp 37–8.

12 Thomas Morris, *A House for the Suburbs, Socially and Architecturally Sketched*, London, Simpkin, Marshall, 1870, pp 161–2.

13 Wheeler, *Choice of a Dwelling*, p 217.

14 Wheeler, *Choice of a Dwelling*, pp 216–17.

15 Kerr, *Englishman's House*, p 105.

16 *Salle à Manger*, December 1890.

17 Isabella Beeton, *Beeton's Book of Household Management*, SO Beeton (London), 1861, p 12; Elphège Boursin, *Le Livre de la femme au XIXème siecle*, E Rome, 1865, pp 275–7. Bonnie Smith argues that the bourgeois women of the Nord, in France, never cooked the meals they served at dinner parties, but that while the cooking was done by servants, it was the hostesses' reputations which were affected by the food served; see Bonnie Smith, *Ladies of the Leisure Class: The Bourgeoises of Northern France in the Nineteenth Century*, Princeton University Press (Princeton), 1981, pp 66–7.

18 Furniture-purchasing patterns of the Parisian middle classes are discussed in Lisa Tiersten, *Marianne in the Market: Envisioning Consumer Society in Fin-de-siècle France*, University of California Press (Berkeley, Calif), 2001; and Leora Auslander, *Taste and Power: Furnishing Modern France*, University of California Press (Berkeley, Calif), 1996.

19 *The Lady*, 26 December 1895.

20 Mrs Loftie, *The Dining Room*, 'Art at Home Series (London), 1876, pp 102–3.

21 Loftie, *Dining Room*, pp 102–3.

22 Loftie, *Dining Room*, p 91.

23 Mme Louise D'Alq, *Le Maître et la Maîtresse de Maison*, 2nd edn Aux bureau du journal les modes de la saison, Paris, 1875, p 212; Pierre Boitard, *Guide manuel de la bonne companie*, Passard, 1851, p 277.

24 Loftie, *Dining Room*, p 34.

25 *La Salle à Manger*, March 1891.

Rachel Rich, 'Designing the Dinner Party: Advice on Dining and Décor in London and Paris, 1860–1914', *Journal of Design History*, vol 16 no 1, 2003, pp 49–61.

© 2003 The Design History Society. Reprinted by permission of the Design History Society. (Excerpts pp 50–7)

'Hi Honey, I'm Home'

Joyce Henri Robinson

psychological ● 1996

late 19th century decoration

Curator and art historian Joyce Henri Robinson discusses the affective power of interior decoration on the mind and soul of the late nineteenth-century dweller. Here the psychological space of the domestic interior is conditioned by the male, whose daily return from work requires a place of order and serenity. This excerpt discusses homely pastoral aesthetics as a means to calm the fatigued occupant in an environment that requires no intellectual effort. Included in this text's argument are images and writings on the decorative landscape that participate in creating a domestic pastoral oasis.

Advice books for the young mistress of the house written in the final decades of the nineteenth century encouraged her to create a psychologically and emotionally serene environment for her husband. Clearly, this kind of domestic advice participated in the ever-prevalent 'ideology of separate spheres' which identified the female's domain as the interior, while the male was inevitably associated with the exterior realm of the forum.[1] Reiterating this commonly-held belief in 1892, Jules Simon pronounced that while man was made 'to fight and work outside,' it was the woman's task 'to maintain order in the house and there organize happiness.'[2] Like Ruskin's 'angel of the house,' she provided a shelter from the mental headaches and tribulations of quotidian existence; and, thus, the foyer, the interior, was identified as an important site for male recuperation.[3]

Handbooks and popular articles on interior decoration also aided the housewife in her creation of a quiet and restful enclave within the urban jungle. Implicit in such writings was the belief that the decoration of the home fell within the purview of wifely activities and the related assumption that such domestic activity was undertaken primarily for the benefit of the male occupant of the home. Typical of this pervasive opinion regarding the nineteenth-century female's aesthetic mission is the argument preferred by Jacob von Falke in *Art in the House* (1879):

> ... the husband's occupations necessitate his absence from the house, and call him far away from it. During the day his mind is absorbed in many good and useful ways, in making and acquiring money for instance, and even after the hours of business have passed, they occupy his thoughts. When he returns home tired with work and in need

of recreation, he longs for quiet enjoyment, and takes pleasure in the home which his wife has made comfortable and attractive … She is the mistress of the house in which she rules, and which she orders like a queen. Should it not then be specially her business to add *beauty* to the *order* which she has created? [original emphasis][4]

It is clear from this and other writings on the decorative in the second half of the nineteenth century that order, beauty, and serenity were the pre-eminently desirable qualities in domestic decoration. While public decoration might be expected to challenge the mind and provoke thought, the decor of the home was intended to calm, rather than excite, the mind and nerves of the city dweller.

The *femme au foyer's* salubrious mission was often referenced in contemporary journals such as *Art et décoration* and *L'Art décoratif*, which featured any number of articles discussing the 'psychology of rooms'[5] and recommending appropriate colors and lines for the creation of a restful and welcoming interior, a wonderfully domestic variant on the modernist expressive self-sufficiency of pictorial elements. The desired goal, simply stated, was the creation of a pastoral realm for physical and mental reflection in which the decor contributed to, rather than detracted from, the refreshing of the weary brain-worker.

> The function of décor is not to arouse particular emotions, but to give the milieu a character in accord with the man who must live there, without compelling his thoughts to focus on the image of a concrete reality, without forcing them to be objective when the hour of subjective refuge awaits them.[6]

Not unexpectedly, this French author had the tired intellectual worker in mind when he advocated the creation of a decor that would not inspire analysis or force the weary brain to decipher its mysteries. Simply stated, the decor of the home should not encourage or inspire intellectual effort of any kind, since the fatigued businessman was forced to exhaust his mental energies on the diurnal routine of the forum. Concomitantly, paintings destined for the interior, it was believed, should not inspire mental headaches but participate in the restful ambiance of the domestic environment. Arts and Crafts architect M. H. Baillie Scott, an advocate of integrated and harmonious home design, ardently expressed this conviction in his *Houses and Gardens* (1906) in which he clearly privileged the place of the (weary) man of the house.

> If we imagine, for instance, the tired man of business returning to his suburban home in the evening, it can hardly be supposed that he will be prepared to make the special mental effort involved in an inspection of his pictures; but whatever decorative quality they express in conjunction with their surroundings will at once enfold him as in an atmosphere which soothes and charms like harmonious music.[7]

The ubiquity of this belief that interior decoration and paintings destined for the domestic interior should calm the fatigued viewer is further evinced in the writings of the quintessentially world-weary Vincent Van Gogh. Regarding his *Bedroom at Arles*, Van Gogh noted to Theo that color was to be 'suggestive here of *rest* or of sleep in general.' 'In a word,' he concluded, 'looking at the picture ought to rest the brain, or rather the imagination.'[8]

Another source for this homely pastoral aesthetic are critical writings from the 1890s on the decorative landscape, a modern genre of landscape whose intent, according to critics, was not to elevate or teach the spirit, but 'to make it serene again.'[9] This mission was made clear in critic Alphonse Germain's article of 1891, 'Le paysage décoratif,' in which he outlined the transformative power of the decorative landscape and identified the domestic interior as its intended site.[10]

> What better way to transform our depressing hovels into oases where the spirit can rest after the worries of mundane existence ... Oh, to forget the ugliness of the street when we stand before an idealized landscape ... [11]

The choice of 'oasis' to characterize the foyer is clearly purposeful and suggests a transformation of the domestic realm into a place of refuge, a pastoral shelter, as it were, via the idealized landscape. Germain, along with Raymond Bouyer, was the principal critic responsible for formulating the stylistic parameters of this new decorative genre which was envisioned as a kind of modern apparition of the heroic landscape minus the thought-provoking intrusion of didactic subject matter. The primary stipulation for the decorative landscape was that it contain the 'skilful lines of the Old Masters,' and both Germain and Bouyer recommended that young artists consult Poussin and Claude in their creation of a modern synthetic landscape. Such esteemed ancestry suggests the conservative nature of the decorative landscape as envisioned by Germain and reveals the true intention of his article, which was to ground the nascent decorative landscape tradition in the French past. For Germain, the decorative landscape as practiced by the young Nabis artists, whom he derogatorily labeled 'deformers,' was merely an ornamental distortion of the natural world.[12] The critic scoffed at the 'néo-traditionnisme' advocated by Maurice Denis, the most vocal proselytizer for the young followers of Gauguin, and excoriated the apologist's primitivizing, non-western definition of the 'decorative.' Galvanized by Denis's writings, which he believed had effectively co-opted the 'decorative' for the modernist agenda and corrupted the term by associating it with Japanese, Byzantine, and Egyptian art, Germain essentially reclaimed the decorative for the French race. Promulgating a far more parochial understanding of the decorative landscape than would Denis or fellow Symbolist critic Albert Aurier, both Germain and Bouyer ultimately defined the genre as the serenely expressive rearrangement of natural forms via the heroic landscape tradition of Poussin.

Germain believed that *the paysage décoratif* could serve as an integral component of a decorative schema within the domestic setting and was convinced of the *affective* power of interior decoration on the mind and soul of the dweller.

> In general, our contemporaries do not give the decoration of the home the importance it merits and are not sufficiently convinced of its influence on character. Lines and hues exert as considerable an influence as that of pure air, spectacles of nature and flowers … It is, therefore, necessary to surround oneself with harmonious and serene effects, luminous colors with nuances evoking feelings of happiness and calm, and ornament inspired by nature.[13]

This belief in the expressive autonomy of formal elements (here within the context of interior decoration) and in the power of line and color to influence 'character' derives from Charles Blanc's highly influential *Grammaire des arts du dessin* (1867) and from the more contemporary writings of Charles Henry. Germain's short-lived critical support of the Neo-Impressionists in the early 1890s had familiarized him with the psycho-physical system of Henry (which essentially codified and provided scientific verification for Blanc's traditional and vaguely defined ideas),[14] linking linear movement, the emotional value of color, and viewer physiological response. Ultimately, Germain believed that the soothing formal qualities and idyllic theme of the decorative landscape could appease and provide solace for the weary spirit; as such, its destination was the private interior where it participated in the creation of a domestic pastoral oasis.

Throughout the early years of the twentieth century, critics continued to praise the restorative power of the conservative decorative landscape, repeatedly linking the genre, as had Germain, with idyllic pastoral themes. Writing of the little-known painter Jean-Francis Auburtin in 1912, critic Louis Vauxcelles (best remembered for providing the 'Fauve' group with its moniker) identified the decorative pastoral landscape as an important means of placing 'a little calm joy and hellenic fantasy on the walls of homes.' This task was undertaken, not unexpectedly, 'to comfort the worried soul of men overtaxed by their miserably frenetic and brutal condition.'[15]

To accomplish this comforting mission, the decorative landscape had to be serene, rather than frenetic, and produce sensations of calm and well-being, not anxiety, if it were to succeed in creating a restful interior for the weary (male) viewer. According to conservative commentators, many decorative landscapes featured in late nineteenth-century interiors were not successful in achieving the requisite state of serenity. A cartoon bearing the caption 'Serpentine painting' from an 1894 issue of *Revue illustrée* underscores the popular perception of the goal of domestic decoration as restful and the failure of the tentacular forms of Art Nouveau interiors in this enterprise. In the cartoon we see the typical petit-bourgeois male who, on contemplating this 'decorative panel for a dining room,' has become incapacitated by the undulating movement of the female nudes, over-stimulated, as it were, by this vision of serpentine shrews.

According to historian Debora Silverman, there were artists and writers in *fin-de-siècle* France who created interiors that were deliberately designed to arouse the senses and activate 'nervous vibration.'[16] The most notorious example is, of course, Des Esseintes in Huysmans's *À Rebours*, who crafted his decor around images of Odilon Redon and Gustave Moreau in order to 'shake up his nervous system by means of erudite fancies, complicated nightmares, [and] suave and sinister visions.'[17] Silverman argues that though the interior did function as a therapeutic refuge from the metropolis throughout the closing years of the nineteenth century, the 'over-stimulated citizen ... transported with him the propensity for animating the interior.' 'No longer,' she concludes, 'could the interior be construed as a stable and static historical setting.'[18]

Silverman's analysis of the *fin-de-siècle* redefinition of interior decoration via the 'new psychology' of Charcot and Bernheim highlights, I believe, the effete (aristocratic) exception that proves the (bourgeois) rule. The 'peinture serpentine' cartoon encapsulates the pervasive bourgeois belief that the interior should provide a stable, calm environment, and humorously demonstrates the conservative reaction to the mentally exhausting *fin-de-siècle* interior. Similar attitudes are amply evident in the critical response to Siegfried Bing's model rooms in his *Maison de l'Art Nouveau*, which offered the French public a glimpse of the latest in home design in 1895. Featured in Bing's Paris gallery was a dining room designed by Henry Van de Velde that included decorative paintings by the Nabis artist Paul Ranson and dinnerware designed by Édouard Vuillard. In the Ranson panels the theme of young women working in the fields might certainly be construed as pastoral and, therefore, appropriate for an idyllic decorative landscape; however, the ornamental deformation and contorted meanderings of the trees and human figures (echoing the arabesques of Van de Velde's inlaid copper decoration) made them, it was suggested by more than one observer, inappropriate for the intended domestic setting. René Boylesve commented that in front of such an image he would barely be able to make it to the meat course before having to beat a hasty retreat from the table, while Camille Pissarro described the Ranson panels as 'odious.'[19] Perhaps most telling, however, was the response of *Le Figaro* critic Arsène Alexandre who, though he found Ranson's panels 'simple and skilled,' said of his visit to Bing's gallery: 'I left exhausted, sick, exasperated, my nerves on edge and my head full of dancing nightmares.'[20]   (... p 106)

Notes

1   For a discussion of the doctrine of the *femme au foyer* and the ideology of separate spheres in late nineteenth-century France, see James F McMillan, *Housewife or Harlot: The Place of Women in French Society, 1870–1940*, St Martin's Press (New York), 1981.

2   Jules Simon, *La Femme du Vingtième Siècle*, Calmann-Lévy (Paris), 1892, p 67.

3   In 'Of Queens' Gardens' (1865), Ruskin championed women as keepers of the home and hearth and praised their ability for 'ordering, arrangement and decision.' Consequently, the domestic interior

served as a protective place of refuge for the male dweller after 'his rough work in open world.' For Ruskin, the home's true function was to provide shelter and a 'place of Peace' amidst the chaos of modern life. See John Ruskin, 'Of Queens' Gardens', *Sesame and Lilies*, J Wiley and Sons (New York), 1887, pp 99–100.

4   Jacob von Falke, *Art in the House: Historical, Critical, and Aesthetical Studies on the Decoration and Furnishing of the Dwelling*, Prang and Company (Boston), 1879, pp 315–16.

5   Gustave Soulier, 'Une Installation de Château', *L'Art décoratif*, vol 4, May 1902, p 84.

6   O Gerdeil, 'L'Intérieur', *L'Art décoratif*, vol 3, June 1901, p 126.

7   MH Baillie Scott, *Houses and Gardens*, G Newnes (London), 1906, p 53.

8   Vincent Van Gogh to Theo Van Gogh, October 1888. Excerpted in translation in Herschel B Chipp, *Theories of Modern Art*, University of California Press, Berkeley, 1968, pp 40–1.

9   Alphonse Germain, *Le Sentiment de l'art et sa formation par l'étude des oeuvres*, Bloud and Cie (Paris), 1902, pp 145–6. This text is a reprint with some modifications of 'Pour le beau,' which appeared originally in *Essais d'art libre*, vol 3, February–March 1893, and was published in book form as *Pour le beau. Essai de kallistique*, E Girard (Paris), 1893.

10 For an extensive discussion of the critical formulation of the decorative landscape, see Joyce Henri Robinson, 'A "Nouvelle Arcadie:" Puvis de Chavannes and the Decorative Landscape in Fin-de-Siècle France', PhD dissertation, The University of Virginia, 1993. See also Roger Benjamin, 'The Decorative Landscape, Fauvism, and the Arabesque of Observation', *The Art Bulletin*, vol 75 no 2, June 1993, pp 295–316.

11 Alphonse Germain, 'Le paysage décoratif, *L'Ermitage*, vol 3, November 1891, p 645. 'Quel meilleur moyen de transformer nos cases maussades en oasis où puisse halter l'esprit retour des soucis vulgaires! ... Oh! oublier la laideur des rues devant le paysage idéalisé ...'

12 Alphonse Germain, 'Théorie des déformateurs: exposé et réfutation', *La Plume*, vol 3, September 1891, pp 289–90. On Germain's early career as a Symbolist critic, see Michael Marlais, *Conservative Echoes in Fin-de-Siècle Parisian Art Criticism*, University Park, Pennsylvania State University Press, 1992, pp 171–80.

13 Germain, *Le Sentiment de l'art*, pp 151–2.

14 Robert Herbert, *Neo-Impressionism*, Solomon R Guggenheim Foundation (New York), 1968, p 21.

15 Louis Vauxcelles, 'Francis Auburtin', *Art et décoration*, September 1912, p 78. For a discussion of Auburtin within the context of late nineteenth-century pastoral painting, see Joyce Henri Robinson, 'La représentation de l'Age d'or', Christian Briend *et al*, *Jean-Francis Auburtin, 1866–1930*, Délégation à l'Action Artistique de la Ville de Paris (Paris), 1990, pp 65–81.

16 Debora L Silverman, *Art Nouveau in Fin-de-Siècle France: Politics, Psychology, and Style*, University of California Press (Berkeley), 1989, p 77.

17 Joris-Karl Huysmans, *Against Nature*, trans Robert Baldick, Penguin Books (New York), 1959, p 63.

18 Silverman, *Art Nouveau in Fin-de-Siècle France*, p 79.

19 René Boylesve, 'Les Arts: Salon de l'Art Nouveau, Galerie Bing', *L'Ermitage*, 1896, p 116. Camille Pissarro, Letter to Lucien Pissaro, 27 December 1895, as quoted in Nancy J Troy, *Modernism and the Decorative Arts in France: Art Nouveau to Le Corbusier*, Yale University Press (New Haven and London), 1991, p 25.

20 Arsène Alexandre, 'L'Art nouveau', *Le Figaro*, 28 December 1895, 1, as quoted in translation in Silverman, *Art Nouveau in Fin-de-Siècle France*, p 278.

Joyce Henri Robinson, '"Hi Honey, I'm Home": Weary (Neurasthenic) Businessmen and the Formulation of a Serenely Modern Aesthetic', *Not At Home: The Suppression of Domesticity in Modern Art and Architecture*, ed and introduced by Christopher Reed, Thames and Hudson (London), 1996.

(Excerpt pp 102–6)

Curtain Wars[1]

Joel Sanders

In this text, architect and academic Joel Sanders exposes distinctions, antagonisms and historical factors that situate the interior design and architectural professions as oppositional practices. He highlights how social anxiety about gender and sexual identity, particularly cultural constructions of the heterosexual male architect and homosexual interior decorator, open space for a gendered discourse on interior design. Yet as gender roles become more flexible and modes of sexuality transcend the decorator/architect divide, Sanders suggests it is time for a new hybrid design vocabulary capable of merging the best of this divide within the domestic realm.

Curtains, that element of the domestic interior on which the hands of the decorator and of the architect come directly into contact, embody many of the tensions and prejudices that have divided interior designers and architects since the emergence of the professional decorator in the late nineteenth century.[2] Here the hard walls designed by the architect meet the soft fabric that is the decorator's trademark, in a juxtaposition that confirms the common perception that architects work conceptually, using durable materials to shape space, while decorators work intuitively, adorning rooms with ephemeral materials and movable objects. Window treatments underscore the divergent design approaches of architects and decorators. Architects typically repudiate curtains, believing that this element that modulates vision compromises the architect's conception, obscuring and softening the precise geometry of architectural forms.[3] Decorators, for their part, consider curtains essential; veiling sunlight and views, curtains make domestic privacy possible and offer relief from the austere spaces created by architects often obsessed with form at the expense of comfort. Ironically, the 'curtain wall,' the iconic modernist glass facade that has come to embody so many key values of modern architecture – logic, structural integrity, and stripped-down form – takes its name from the curtain, the signature element of the interior decorator. But are architecture and interior decoration really oppositional practices, or are they, as the term 'curtain wall' suggests, more interdependent than we think? Here I would like to argue that the supposed incompatibility between these two rival but nevertheless overlapping design practices evokes deeper cultural conflicts that are themselves bolstered and sustained by profound social anxieties about gender and sexuality.   (... p 14)

Curtain Wars implicate more than sex and gender; they also participate in the cultural construction of sexuality. Consider, for a moment, scenes from two Hollywood films, the 1949 adaptation of Ayn Rand's *The Fountainhead* and *Any Wednesday*, made in 1966. Both movies reinforce the image of the 'macho' male architect; simultaneously, they fine-tune a newer cultural cliché – the gay interior decorator.

In *The Fountainhead*, Howard Roark, as played by Gary Cooper, personifies the architect as the epitome of masculinity. In the climactic trial scene, Roark defends himself for dynamiting his own project rather than seeing it disfigured by collaborating designers; the concept of masculinity is at the heart of his self-defense. A real man, says Roark, refuses to compromise his integrity and independence; the architect must follow his own vision rather than capitulate to the client's whim. In the final moments of the movie, Roark's adoring wife is conveyed upward by a construction elevator to the top of the architect's latest project – a high-rise, of course – where he awaits her. Throughout the scene the camera's mobile eye is fixed worshipfully on Roark, who stands atop and indeed seems to surmount the skyscraper – an image that literally conflates the architect with manhood.

In *The Fountainhead*, professional identity is reinforced too by sartorial style. The clean hues of Howard Roark's dark suits, echoing the simple geometry of his buildings, indicate his heterosexual manliness. Similarly, in *Any Wednesday*, in a scene in which the male decorator consults with the newlywed played by Jane Fonda, the silk handkerchief that accessorizes the decorator's blazer betrays not only his design sensibility but also his sexual identity. And his flamboyant speech and gestures (which match the outrageous fees he freely admits to charging) call up the ubiquitous but suspect stereotype of the gay interior decorator.

If the history of the professional decorator has been neglected, the subject of homosexuality and interior decoration has been largely ignored.[4] Interestingly enough, two of the field's earliest and most influential members – Edith Wharton's collaborator Ogden Codman, Jr. and his notorious contemporary Elsie de Wolfe – were both homosexuals. A review of Codman's work in *Architectural Record* criticizes his interior designs for gaining 'variety at the expense of virility.'[5] While historians have described how decorating came to be considered a woman's pastime, they have yet to account for its emergence as a gay profession. One likely explanation is that interior design – like two allied design fields, fashion and theater – attracts a disproportionate number of gay men because gay men, already marginalized for their apparent femininity, are less reluctant to assume occupations that have traditionally been deemed feminine. But it is hardly coincidental that interior design, much like fashion and theater, is a discipline invested in the notion of self-fashioning through artifice. Borrowing the useful concept developed by feminist and queer theorists of sexual identity as 'performance,' I have argued elsewhere that architecture participates in the staging of individual identity.[6] According to this view, masculinity and femininity are constructed through the repetition of culturally prescribed norms, including gestures, mannerisms, and clothing. Daily life resembles theater, a stage where men and women learn to act culturally sanctioned roles. Extending this analogy, we can compare interiors to stage sets that, along with costumes and props, help actors create convincing portrayals. Because of their outsider status, many gay men, like women, are acutely aware of the performative nature of human subjectivity. Could it be that this awareness, which some consider a survival instinct, allows gay men to be unusually well represented in decorating, a craft in which applied surfaces – fabrics, wallpapers, paint colors – are manipulated in order to fashion personality?

The idea that interiors express human and in particular feminine identity is a message reiterated in periodicals like *House Beautiful* and *Metropolitan Home*. Like apparel, décor is said to disclose the secrets of selfhood. Perhaps the most exaggerated and paradoxical examples of this staple of design journalism are photo spreads showcasing celebrity homes. Inviting us to identify with the camera's voyeuristic eye, magazines like *Architectural Digest*, *Vanity Fair*, and *In Style* urge us to peek into the homes of stars like Madonna and Cher. Suspending disbelief, we delude ourselves momentarily into believing that these contrived and often outré environments reliably mirror the authentic selves of their occupants.

Patrons have long looked to designers to outfit both themselves and their homes to communicate self-image to the outside world; but the rich and famous are not the only ones savvy enough to understand the importance of a well-appointed home. Since the nineteenth century, publications aimed largely at middle-class women have instructed amateurs on how to fashion themselves and their domestic environments to reflect who they are or aspire to be. With the feminization of the bourgeois home comes a new conception of the domestic interior: a unique abode that mirrors the temperament of its (female) homemaker. Taste, once considered an expression of class and breeding but now freed from its aristocratic associations, thus becomes understood as an expression of personality. Following a literary model established by architectural theorists from Vitruvius to Marc Antoine Laugier, two early and influential decorating texts – Wharton's *The Decoration of Houses* and de Wolfe's *The House in Good Taste* – counsel readers that decorating, much like architectural design, is essentially a rational process, based not upon whim or whimsy but rather upon objective principles. But as the genre of the decorating book evolved during the twentieth century, a contrary tendency emerged, one that sought to distance interior design from architectural precedent. Two popular books written by designers known for working with celebrity clients – Dorothy Draper and Billy Baldwin – illustrate this trend by upholding womanly taste, not manly reason, as a prerequisite for practice. Both counsel women on how to express themselves through décor.[7]

One might expect that this subjective design approach would make interior designers unnecessary: consult your inner decorator rather than hire a professional. However, as Draper's and Baldwin's texts both demonstrate, decorators quickly learned to take advantage of this union of décor and 'womanly intuition,' employing professional empathy as a strategy to distinguish themselves from 'arrogant' male architects reputedly indifferent to client needs. Unlike stubborn architects who wilfully impose their own ideas and values on patrons, the ideal decorator is a facilitator. According to Baldwin, 'A decorator must first consider the kind of people for whom he works, how they lived, and their stated budget. Then, and only then, can he execute their wishes and requirements according to the best of his trained taste and experience.'[8] Capitalizing on a seemingly innate ability to forge close and familiar client relationships, some decorators even came to resemble psychics, mediums who enable housewives to channel their inner selves through their domestic furnishings.

True to the genre of decorating literature, both Draper and Baldwin gloss over a fundamental contradiction posed by their endorsement of the intuitive creator: the attempt to teach skills that ultimately cannot be taught. Moreover, although both authors claim to disavow the 'signature designer,' the books ultimately validate this figure. Peppered with personal anecdotes, both volumes double as publicity memoirs. Ignoring the incontrovertible fact that people hire decorators precisely because they believe that 'taste' can be purchased, Draper and Baldwin strive to convince the reader that hiring a famous designer will result in self-actualization.

Despite the sex of their authors, the subliminal portrait of the decorator painted in both these interior design books is of a female, thus playing into two of Western culture's long-standing associations with femininity: artifice, fabricated through the application of adornment, and subterfuge (while apparently submissive, women ultimately get their way by creating the illusion that others are in control). Not necessarily oppressive and limiting, these stereotypes have sometimes proved professionally beneficial. Under the right circumstances, the reputation of the cooperative and feminized decorator, when opposed to the figure of the domineering and unsympathetic architect, can pay off. ('I don't build for clients,' says Howard Roark, 'I get clients in order to build'). The gay male decorator's intimacy with his female patrons – coupled with his first-hand understanding of the crucial role interiors play in human self-fashioning – permits him to be trusted, to become, in a sense, 'just one of the girls.'

The popular perception of interior decorating as inherently feminine, conducted by either women or effeminate gay men not only accounts for the field's inferior status, it also effectively threatens the self-esteem of many architects. For some practitioners, the unstable borders separating architecture from interior design touch directly on the vulnerability that lies at the core of manhood. Whether seen from the vantage of psychoanalytic theory or cultural history, masculinity, while seemingly invincible, is fragile.[9] The biological penis can never live up to the mystique of the cultural phallus. Architects are inevitably asked to perform certain 'decorating' activities – like picking furniture and fabrics – that call into question their manliness. Already insecure about their attraction to tastes that society deems 'unmanly,' for some practitioners the architectural profession represents a strange sort of closet, a refuge that allows them (albeit with some discomfort) to engage in practices considered otherwise unacceptable for 'real' men. Still, many architects feel they must defend against the sneaking suspicion that inside every architect lurks a decorator. Ultimately, architects disavow interior design as a way of overcompensating for masculine vulnerability; they are compelled to draw emphatic limits between two professions whose contours inevitably overlap.

At this point in history, with interior design finally beginning to receive greater professional and cultural recognition, Curtain Wars underscore the low self-esteem in much of the architectural profession, exacerbating the male architect's doubts about his self-determination and empowerment. The cultural priority accorded to architecture over interior design was never all that secure. Despite the grand historical narratives promoted by art historians, architecture, although an ancient craft, is nevertheless a relatively new profession that has struggled for respect. To this day architects sometimes have to fight to overcome their image as aristocratic amateurs.[10] In the absence of public belief that architects provide indispensable skills, architecture is often viewed as an expendable luxury. Why hire an architect when many states allow clients to enlist professional engineers or contractors to do the job? Although they endure similarly lengthy training and demanding apprenticeships, architects typically command significantly lower fees than do other professionals such as doctors, lawyers, and yes, even interior designers. And while the public image of the architect is as a dashing and sometimes charismatic figure, rarely does this positive appeal translate into actual value in the marketplace.   (... p 19)

Notes

1   Many of the themes and issues explored here were raised in the 'Curtain Wars' conference that I organized at Parsons School of Design in 1996.
2   The term 'decorator', which originally designated an individual who practiced what we today call interior design, is now considered both obsolete and pejorative: it evokes the image of 'decoration', a culturally denigrated concept that I will call into question. In the same spirit in which the gay community has revived the once-reviled term 'queer', I will use the labels 'decorator' and 'interior designer' interchangeably, to both politicize and historicize the activity of 'decorating' domestic space.
3   Frank Lloyd Wright never used curtains and thought of them as 'unhygienic'. Charles Gwathmey is

quoted in the October 2001 *Architectural Digest*: 'Interior design "is a reductive process," he asserts. "Decorators think of coming in and adding to 'enrich', and I think of our work as the opposite. The interior does not want to be covered up; it does not want to be added to ... If I design a window wall, the details of that window wall – its materiality, its proportion, the fenestration, the way we control the light – are all integrated and thought about. The idea of coming in and saying, "Let's put a curtain over that!" Is totally antipathetical and totally contradictory"' (p 100).

4   One of the few authors to address the prominent role of gay and lesbian practitioners in interior design is Aaron Betsky, who takes up this topic in *Queer Space: Architecture and Same-Sex Desire*, William Morrow and Co (New York), 1997.

5   'Some Recent Works by Ogden Codman, Jr', *Architectural Record*, July 1905, p 51.

6   See Joel Sanders (ed), *Stud: Architectures of Masculinity*, Princeton Architectural Press (New York), 1986, pp 11–25.

7   Counseling female readers on how to express themselves through décor, Draper writes: 'Your home is the backdrop of your life, whether it is a palace or a one-room apartment. It should be honestly your own – an expression of your personality. So many people stick timidly to the often-uninspired conventional ideas or follow some expert's methods slavishly. Either way they are more or less living in someone else's house.' Dorothy Draper, *Decorating Is Fun! How to Be Your Own Decorator*, Doubleday, Doran, and Co (New York), 1941, p 4; Billy Baldwin, *Billy Baldwin Remembers*, Harcourt Brace Jovanovich (New York), 1974.

8   Baldwin, *Billy Baldwin Remembers*, p 73.

9   Although they offer different explanations, both cultural historians and psychoanalytical theorists argue that modern masculinity is in crisis. Historians attribute this to the aftermath of the Second World War that transformed traditional roles in both the workplace and the home. See Michael S Kimmel, 'Consuming Manhood: The Feminization of American Culture and the Recreation of the Male Body, 1832–1920', Lawrence Goldstein (ed), *The Male Body: Features, Destinies, Exposures*, University of Michigan Press (Ann Arbor), 1994. For a psychoanalytic reading of masculinity as masquerade, see Kaja Silverman, *Male Subjectivity at the Margins*, Routledge (New York), 1992. Several recent books explore the crisis of masculinity in terms of the depriving yet felt-to-be-necessary distance boys create from their mothers in order to feel like independent, 'manly' beings, a distance girls feel less need for (see, for instance, *The Reproduction of Mothering*, by Nancy Chodorow, *In a Time of Fallen Heros*, by William Betcher and William S Pollock, and *I Don't Want to Talk About It*, by Terrence Real).

10 The professional standing of the architect is a relatively recent invention. During the Middle Ages, architects belonged to guilds and were considered artisans. While the names of some master builders have been recorded for posterity, it was not until the Renaissance that the status of architects, along with that of artists, was elevated from anonymous craftsmen to individual creators. Even then, professional recognition did not come quickly. From the Renaissance through the mid-nineteenth century, architecture was still considered an 'art' largely practiced by amateurs like Thomas Jefferson, who personified the self-taught 'gentleman architect'. Not until the establishment of academies like the Beaux-Arts in Paris in the nineteenth century do architects define themselves as experts who learn not on the job but in school, a change in status that leads to the licensing of professional architects in the early twentieth century.

Joel Sanders, 'Curtain Wars: Architects, Decorators, and the Twentieth-Century Domestic Interior', *Harvard Design Magazine*, no 16, 2002, pp 14–20.
Reprinted by permission of Joel Sanders.
(Excerpts pp 14–19)

Productions of Incarceration: The Architecture of Daniel Paul Schreber

Felicity D Scott

psychological space 2002
early 20th century

Architectural historian Felicity Scott uses the space of the paranoiac Daniel Paul Schreber to test traditional notions of interiority and femininity. From her analysis, this particular interiority is no longer autonomous but is a depletion that is filled through participation in a larger system, such as the authority found in an asylum. Scott makes a link between Schreber's self-acquired knowledge of psychosexual and bodily development of the modern self with one of his own architectural projects, the placement of a cipher on the domestic facade of his own house. Focusing on the demarcation between a subject and its domestic surroundings, Scott's text unfolds a multitude of associations whereby language, ornament, habits and mental constructions figure as signifiers of interior moments and interior perceptions.

For the paranoiac, Freud explained, the 'external world' was in fact a projection, an unreal or hallucinatory outside such as the forest Schreber had viewed through his window in Leipzig. Nominated 'the holy forest,' this impossibly dense vegetation 'had not the slightest resemblance to the garden at the University Nerve Clinic.'[1] In fact, many of Schreber's hallucinations took place through the mediation of such architectural openings. A significant moment of his withdrawal from the 'actually existing world' took place when he looked upon his wife as a 'fleetingly improvised' person through a window in 'a room opposite' his own.[2] A peephole into an internal passage, moreover, produced for Schreber a disturbingly racially marked picture of 'yellow men' whom, he imagined, he needed to be 'prepared to fight.' While the presence of the 'yellow men' through the peephole was rejected as hallucinatory, in his dreams Schreber built a castle to protect himself against them: 'I traversed the earth from Lake Lagoda to Brazil and, together with an attendant, I built there in a castle-like building a wall in protection of God's realm against an advancing yellow tide: I related this to the peril of a syphilitic epidemic.'[3]

Articulating the mechanism of projection, Freud explained, 'An internal perception is suppressed, and, instead, its content, after undergoing a certain kind of distortion, enters consciousness in the form of an external perception.'[4] This projection of an internal perception had an important reconstructive role in which the paranoid rebuilt his subjective world: 'The paranoiac builds it again, not more splendid, it is true, but at least so that he can once more live in it.' Thus, Freud concludes, 'The delusional formation, which we take to be the pathological product, is in reality an attempt at recovery, a process of reconstruction.'[5]

This was not, however, the only lesson of paranoiac projection. Schreber's construction of the 'castle-like building' was not a projection from an organic interior but rather, as he had himself suggested, an anomic practice that registered the very depletion of that interiority. 'It was incorrect to say that the perception which was suppressed internally is projected outwards;' Freud noted, '*the truth is rather, as we now see, that what was abolished internally returns from without.*'[6] In Schreber's world we are not subjects with an autonomous interiority – indeed the sense of interiority has been lost, heightening the feeling of always already participating in a larger system. Nor, however, are we empty subjects gradually filled, since there remains an excess of desire beyond that system of representation, a voluptuousness experienced in opposition to ideological structures. In Lacan's translation of Freud: what is foreclosed in the symbolic returns in the real, registering the failure of a subject's inscription into a symbolic system.[7] 'Wherever sense ends,' writes Kittler, 'enjoyment begins: a pleasure in the margins that a discourse network of pure signifiers leaves to its victims.'[8]

While Schreber's 'private' space was always a public space, this did not mean that he retained no position of privacy. Schreber found a space of privacy, even of intimacy, in his own phantasmagoric religion and in his cross-dressing, practices which he assured the Saxon legal profession would remain covert if he were released.[9] Indeed he outlined his capacity for social propriety by arguing that these practices would not involve an improper squandering of money (private property) on trinkets and ribbons – in other words, that his ornament would not be a crime – and that the sanctity of the family's privacy would not be breached by the contents of his *Memoirs*. With some parody, it was precisely on the basis that he understood this socially condoned separation of the public from the private that Schreber framed his 'Grounds of Appeal.' He insisted that the law and juridical power should not have access to his body or to his privacy, but rather be limited to the mandate to assess his capacity for autonomous behaviour. Furthermore, the law should only have cause to engage a subject in terms of the conventional signifiers written into *its* code – such as disturbance of the peace or inability to manage finances. Schreber argued that hidden indiscretions could not be sufficient reason to incarcerate him against his will, despite his self-avowed insanity. It was on these grounds, along with his demonstration of a responsible attitude towards his domestic needs, that a judgment was passed in July 1902 to rescind his tutelage, enabling him to return to the 'outside world.' The 'feminine' space that Schreber constructed and occupied was in this sense deemed to be beyond the bounds of the law, or strictly speaking, obscene. What went on within this space was, as Schreber ironically invoked the law to insist, outside the limits of its authority. The feminine domain, understood by Schreber as that which was outside the system of symbolic authority, was thus a site of strategic avoidance of symbolic mandates.

At this point we can perhaps understand Schreber's architectural project, his own version of writing on the walls. Condensed in the image of the 'S' that was situated in the relief of the grillwork of his domestic facade, Schreber had perhaps figured his 'thou art that,' the 'cipher of mortal destiny' of Lacan's limit of analysis.[10] And the figure of the *cipher* entails a number of relevant operations which Schreber articulated, albeit elliptically: 1. a secret, or disguised, way of writing; 2. the arithmetic symbol 'o' denoting ... no amount but used to occupy a vacant place in decimal numeration; 3. the interlaced initial of a person or company, etc.: a monogram; 4. the continuous sounding of an organ-pipe caused by mechanical defect.

Perhaps rather the 'S' stands for Semite, symptom, syphilis, *Subjekt, Seele, Seelenmord, selig* ... [11] To the compulsive thinker the list is endless, and within the instability of meaning of Schreber's allegorical world the sign could in fact sustain this endlessly generated proliferation and substitution. However, while Schreber questioned the status of proper names, of nominations and their role in the construction of identity, it was their unfounded nature that facilitated his radical project. Unlike Muthesius's wish for an organic relation between a subject and their domestic surrounds, the ornamental 'S' was to be read as a constructed representation, a reflection or speculation on subjectivity itself placed over the unrepresentable intimacy of a subject's interior. Through ornamental signification Schreber parodied the system of language, using it as front for his erotic activities. Sensual pleasure at the expense of phallic signification had become phallic signification masking sensual pleasure. While the nomination *Senatspräsident* might not have been properly assimilated by Schreber, nor the family name assured, when connected to a domicile the inscribed 'S' – which names the house and its occupants – was a gesture pointing to the unfounded nature of such institutions, the pact sustaining social relations.[12]

In architecture, Judge Schreber had found a key to the inscription of institutional and symbolic authority, a representation, in stone, of social law. In his account, architecture, like the law and the institution of the family, was a prison house, the boundaries of which required reconstruction. Schreber researched possibilities of other modes of tenancy during his incarceration, finding a space of dwelling both in his feminization and, more literally, in his attempts to occupy the very space of the window opening in order to defend himself against the destruction of his reason. 'For some time I put my feet through the iron bars of the open window ... As long as I did this the rays could not reach my head ...'[13] Arendt argued that the law was originally identified with the 'boundary line' between the private interior and 'exterior appearance.' In ancient times, she explained, this 'was actually still a space, a kind of no man's land between the public and the private, sheltering and protecting both realms while, at the same time, separating them from each other.' The law of the *polis* retained traces of that 'original spatial significance.' 'Quite literally a wall' was required to constitute cities, and political communities.[14] It was the many possible articulations of that wall that Schreber foregrounded in his *Memoirs*.

Schreber provided, furthermore, a proto-theorization of the limits of the performative dimension of domestic architecture. Conceived as an iterative structure that operated through modes of inhabitation, architecture participated in setting the terms of the habitual daily occupation of environments. As such it inscribed a limited logic of habit on the body. Providing a frame for participation, architecture not only structured habituation, but embodied a means of transmission or communication as well, figuring a dialectical counterpart to Walter Benjamin's affirmative reading of the reception of architecture in a state of distraction.[15] Schreber's *Memoirs*, after all, were collected by Benjamin amongst books authored by the mentally ill.[16]

Yet even these effects did not fully circumscribe the terms of inhabitancy, since they acknowledged no place for intimacy. Prohibited by the law, desire had a way of returning to pervert that system of interdiction; indeed, according to Lacan, it was a dialectical counterpart produced by that prohibition. For Schreber, the body remained centrally a site of incorporation of the 'outside world,' but to this he added 'the cultivation of voluptuousness,' a more radical, even delirious engagement with desire. This provided an instability to the performative dimension, figuring a provisional agency, albeit within existing codes. While architecture prescribed fixing, it also provided the scene of a transgressive exit. In his articulation of a line of escape, Schreber might be understood as effecting a shift from an apparently dystopic lack of privacy and interiority to a redemptive anti-essentialist notion of the position of the subject within a broader social sphere. For as with the parodic fixing in stone of both his own body in the asylum's garden – described in the *Memoirs* as a fixing in which he became a 'marble guest' – and later the 'S' fixed to his domestic facade, Schreber's rejection of the organic conception of such relations allowed him to introduce the possibility of 'appearance' as well as that of reworking one's social self through external trappings and their potential duplicities. Schreber's transgressive occupations thus provide a form of critique in which depth, fixity, and enclosure are revealed as traces of an outdated epistemology.   (… p 66)

Notes
1   Daniel Paul Schreber, *Memoirs of My Nervous Illness*, trans Ida Macalpine and Richard A Hunter, Harvard University Press, Cambridge 1988, p 88; originally published 1955. Published in German as *Denkwürdigkeiten eines Nervenkranken nebst Nachträgen und einem Anhang über die Frage: 'Unter welchen Voraussetzungen darf eine für geisteskrank erachtete Person gegen ihren erklärten Willen in einer Heilanstalt festgehalten werden?'* Oswald Mutze, Leipzig 1903. Also included were 'Documents from the Court Proceedings placing me under tutelage', such as medical reports, Schreber's grounds of appeal, and the judgment of the Royal Superior County Court of Dresden of 14 July 1902 that rescinded his tutelage.

Chapter 3, which was to have contained matter pertaining to 'other members' of Schreber's family, was omitted, however, having been deemed 'unsuitable for publication',

2 Schreber, *Memoirs*, p 68.

3 Schreber, *Memoirs*, p 87.

4 Sigmund Freud, 'Psychoanalytic Notes on an Autobiographical Account of a Case of Paranoia (Dementia Paranoides)' [1911], James Strachey (ed), *The Case of Schreber, Papers on a Technique and Other Works*, The Hogarth Press and the Institute of Psychoanalysis (London), 1858, p 66.

5 Freud, 'Psychoanalytic Notes', p 70.

6 Freud, 'Psychoanalytic Notes', p 70.

7 Jacques Lacan, *The Psychoses* 1955–1956, Jacques-Alain Miller (ed), *The Seminar of Jacques Lacan*, trans Russell Grigg, WW Norton (New York), 1993, p 191.

8 Frederich A Kittler, *Discourse Networks 1800/1900*, trans Michael Metteer and Chris Cullens, Stanford University Press (Stanford, CA), 1990, p 303.

9 See Eric Santner, *My Own Private Germany: Daniel Paul Schreber's Secret History of Modernity*, Princeton University Press (Princeton, NJ), 1996, pp 80–3. Schreber's notion of privacy is, however, one that defers to the will to scientific knowledge. 'I can do no more than offer my person as object of scientific observation for the judgment of experts,' he explained. Schreber, *Memoirs*, p 251. Freud relied on this suggestion that the scientific gaze is divested of responsibility towards individual privacy to argue that his case study did not constitute a breach of privacy. He explained that Schreber 'urges upon Dr. Flechsig, however, the same considerations that I am now urging upon him himself. "I trust," he says "that even in the case of Geheimrat Prof. Dr. Flechsig any personal susceptibilities that he may feel will be outweighed by a scientific interest in the subject-matter of my memoirs."' Freud, 'Psychoanalytic notes', p 10.

10 Jacques Lacan, 'The Mirror Stage as Formative of the Function of the I as revealed in Psychoanalytic Experience' [1949], *Écrits: A Selection*, trans Alan Sheridan, WW Norton (New York), 1977, p 7: 'In the recourse of subject to subject which we preserve, psychoanalysis can accompany the patient to the ecstatic limit of the "Thou art that', wherein is revealed to him the *cipher* of his mortal destiny, but it is not in our mere power as practitioner to bring him to that point where the real journey begins.'

11 The German word *selig* translates as blessed, deceased, overjoyed; *Seele* as soul or mind. The other words we have encountered earlier in the text. On the relation of souls and bliss in Schreber's thinking see Lacan, *Écrits*, p 210.

12 In Walter Benjamin's reading of the law, it is precisely such a violence that fills the gap that represses the fact that something is missing. See Benjamin, 'Critique of Violence', Peter Demetz, (ed), *Reflections: Essays, Aphorisms, Autobiographical Writings*, trans Edmund Jephcott, Schocken (New York), 1986, pp 277–300.

13 Schreber, *Memoirs*, p 146.

14 Hannah Arendt, *The Human Condition*, University of Chicago Press (Chicago, Il), 1958, pp 63–4.

15 Walter Benjamin, 'The Work of Art in the Age of Mechanical Reproduction', [1936], trans. Harry Zohn, Hannah Arendt (ed), *Illuminations: Essays and Reflections*, Schocken Books (New York), 1968, pp 217–51.

16 This is noted in Samuel Weber's introduction to the 1988 edition of Schreber's *Memoirs*, p xiii.

Felicity D Scott, 'Productions of Incarceration: The Architecture of Daniel Paul Schreber', Bernie Miller and Melony Ward (eds), *Crime and Ornament: The Arts and Popular Culture in the Shadow of Adolf Loos*, YYZ Books (Toronto), 2002.
© Felicity D Scott. Reprinted by permission of YYZ Books of Canada.
(Excerpt pp 62–6)

Ornament and Order

Jacques Soulillou

philosophical • 2002
achronic decoration

Essayist and art theoretician Jacques Soulillou offers a philosophical reflection on the crisis of ornament and fear of excess, suggesting that ornament has an ordering function. To this extent he proposes that ornament is necessary for order's appearance but does not itself have an ordering function, whereas the decorative is that which escapes or opposes the ordering system, indicating loss of an order's authority. For architecture ornament also reveals sexual differentiation through the ground plan, a distinction made from left to right and from upper to lower that coincides with social and hierarchical divisions found in traditional societies. Central to Soulillou's thinking is the shift from ornament as visual elaboration to understanding it as a catalyst of cultural upheaval and perpetual reordering.

What is the purpose of ornament? Above all, it has an ordering function. Not in the sense of putting a room back in order, for that would assume that order exists before ornament. If ornament has an ordering function, it is in the sense of allowing the order to appear, as one says that something appears in the light.

Ornament is primary not in the naive chronological sense, but because it does not superimpose itself on a pre-existing order, as accident on essence in traditional metaphysics. It might rather be order that is viewed as accident in relation to ornament. Among ornament's salient properties is a tendency to assume a polymorphous appearance, without hierarchy, without order, insofar as everything is potential material for decorating – flowers, bone, rock, glass, metal, plastic, paper, etc. – and that these forms are infinite in number.

If order requires ornament in order to appear, this ally may just as well turn out to be its most dangerous enemy. For ornament is essentially chaos that threatens to subvert order if the latter does not pay attention. With respect to ornament, order will always have to be on guard, so to speak. For example, what first attracts one's attention when walking down a street, or visiting someone, is this chaos in which the ornament seems to contribute nothing to order, but rather to disorder. In other words, the order that appears through ornament is at once lit up and flooded from all sides by the ornament's powerful illumination, at the heart of which order looks like an island of precarious stability.

One of the formal means of preventing ornamental display from degenerating into chaos is by containing it in a more or less defined grid system (*grille ou maillage*). Without such a system, which we often notice implicitly in ornamental display – in particular on the superficies – the display would run off in all directions. In twentieth-century art, which has done much to eliminate all ornament, minimalism laid bare this formal substratum like no other movement before it. The absence (*le vide*) of the ornament is not nothing, it is the grid. However, when we reduce the ornament to its formal properties of symmetry and repetition, we have already surreptitiously introduced order into the ornament. To reveal itself, ornament has no need of symmetry and repetition, which form specific modalities of appearance, related to power in accordance with the double orientation of rationality and economy. Order, through the ornament, gives itself an air of symmetry and repetition. This signifies simply that it takes the path of least resistance, consistent with the objectives of power.

With the emergence of order in the ornament, it does not follow that the ornament has an ordering function in the obvious sense, as in the grid format of wallpaper or a carpet. The appearance can maintain its chaotic, disordered, anarchic character, even while forming a favourable context for the purposes of the ordering function. More than any other art form, fashion exemplifies this connection whereby the ordering function does not depend on the materials themselves, but in how they are used. The most common effect aimed at by this secondary ordering function could be characterized as distinction: the distinction of pure otherness as embodied by the famous photograph taken at the beginning of the twentieth century, showing a Melanesian man wearing a Kellogg's box by way of finery, or hierarchical distinction. So it is not by means of systematic presentation, in a grid for example, that the ordering function is realized, but rather through abundance, affectation, rarity. The convergence of the primary and secondary ordering functions, as can be observed in interior and exterior architecture, presupposes the constraint of an authority, primarily that of the sponsor.

The appearance of order in ornament is produced according to what I would call a ground plan (or original matrix), traversed by a double polarization: transversal in one respect, as in the male/female opposition, and vertical in another, as in the superior/inferior opposition. The latter may take on a sexual significance, but not necessarily. Expressed another way, sexuality and power are the forces which sustain the ground plan. Or, if one prefers: order initially appears through that feature of the ground plan where the sexual relation is intersected by the power relation. For if, in its horizontal axis, the ground plan refers to the inter-sexual differentiation of man/woman, the vertical axis is revealed by the intra-sexual dimension where the dominating male is opposed to the dominated male and, more generally, free man to the non-free.

In traditional societies ornament is revealed according to this plan: from left to right, without hierarchy, ornaments for men, ornaments for women; from upper to lower, with hierarchy, ornaments for the prince, the nobles, free men in general, and the slaves. Every anthropologist knows that, in this plan, order is anything but decorative. The decorative constitutes that which escapes the encoding that order practices on ornament, a kind of wild outgrowth that order seems unable to tame.

Thus Kant was justified in saying that a man abandoned on a desert island would not enjoy the pleasures of ornamentation. Why would he decorate a building or adorn himself, in a solipsistic situation where he is confronted with neither the inter-sexual differentiation, nor the intra-sexual differentiation of hierarchy? On the contrary, it is unlikely that this man (or this woman, but not both at once) could give himself unrestrainedly to any decorative pleasures. To ornament there must be two. Ornament is born under the gaze of another, as a flower blossoms under the light. It is the mark of socialization. This word 'mark' should be taken in the sense of something impressed (imprinted) on the flesh because, for epochs past, it is not the individual who appropriates the ornament but, on the contrary, the ornament that appropriates the individual with the purpose of assigning a place in a social or cosmic order. This explains why ornamentation has so often been inseparable from cruelty. One is reminded of what Nietzsche said about the creation of memory in *The Genealogy of Morals*. By means of a practice which is sometimes extremely cruel – of which our 'body piercing' is a distant ancestor, leaving ineradicable marks on the body – ornament has played a central role in the creation of memory. The performers of these 'ornamental' mutilations and deformations were able to find beauty in them. They were willing to be marked on their flesh by them, to ensure access to social individuation and desire (desire for the Other). This shows how the link between ornament and beauty, which seems self-evident, is intelligible only through the mediation of order. The ornament is beautiful, even as mutilation, if it registers one in an order with implicit or explicit laws. And this is equally true for the woman of ancient China whose feet have been bound, for the middle-class person who hangs a Warhol print in his living room, for the Western man of the seventeenth and eighteenth centuries wearing a wig, and for the Japanese noble staining his teeth black. Louis XIV, apparently, would never be seen without his wig, even at night. These are clear enough illustrations of the appropriation of the individual by the ornament.

However, for order to appear in the ornament, it is not enough that it monopolize it. It must literally produce it, and this production is not without a cost. Cosmetics are an economy of order, administering the ornamental costs to produce a symbolic yield. *Kosméô* in ancient Greek means 'I adorn,' 'I decorate,' and in doing so I produce order, I reproduce an order in initiating the appropriate expenses to honour a certain situation or figure. And all this happens at the same time: not just decorate, then order, or order then decorate, but *decorder* if I may so put it. This 'administration' has nothing to do with the economy of restraint in which the expense is incurred in function of an economic rationality, such as when an individual spends no more than he has. As an economy of order, cosmetics are a general economy in which the level of expense is set according to a symbolic rationality, in keeping with the status of the person.

'A high social circle,' says Norbert Elias in *La Société de Cour*, 'obliges a member to own a house and ensure it is beautiful. Although bourgeois morality sees this as nothing but waste ("If he's going to fall into debt, why doesn't he lower his standard of living?"), it is in reality an expression of the ethos of lords.'   (... p 90)

Order can never ultimately establish itself because ornament works to undermine it. The history of relations between order and ornament is one of permanent combat, of constant eruptions. Order is obliged to not only re-found but also to re-establish the rules of hierarchy, to proceed to exclusions, to affirm precedents.

This permanent re-founding of order, behind which loom the stakes of power, results in the double movement of election and exclusion; it aims, through ornament, to reaffirm certain divisions, certain hierarchies judged indispensable to its perpetuation.

In this respect, in the famous passage from Plato's *Gorgias*, where Socrates expounds his theory of flattery (*kolakeia*), we are not always aware that the four categories of sophistry and legislation, dress and gymnastics, rhetoric and justice, cooking and medicine, coincide with other oppositions that assume not only moral but social significance. When Socrates says that dress (*kommô* = to decorate, which we could compare with *kosméô*) is a pernicious substitute for gymnastics, he is simply contrasting the natural with the artificial, or perversion with integrity, illustrating an opposition that, from ancient society to the beginning of modern times, is of fundamental significance: the opposition between a free man (*eleùtheros*) and he who is not. When the sophist Antiphôn attacks Socrates in front of his students – all of them from a noble or wealthy milieu – he focuses on this fact: the philosopher does not have the dignified look of a free man; in summer and winter he wears the same coat and goes barefoot.

The character of he who is free cannot be dissociated in Greek language and thought from the exterior appearance and the ornamentation that goes with it. In Hegelian terms one might say that the appearance is the essence; there is no appearance which could conceal or contradict the essence. *Eleùtheros* means 'one who talks or acts like a free man,' 'one who is compatible with the station of a free man' and also, speaking of the exterior aspect of certain animals, 'of noble appearance.' In the West, an entire genealogy is expressed in this opposition between the free and the not-free in the visual field. To begin with, there is the basic opposition between the liberal arts and the mechanical arts, the development of which produces the opposition between the arts (sometimes called 'noble') and the applied arts, also called decorative. And when Kant says that art is that which is realized through freedom, this declaration – apparently exempt from all social considerations – carries in itself the age-old opposition between the free and the non-free.

Is the decorative unworthy of the free man? Does it reflect a servile origin or mentality? The problem is not so simple. In fact, if the opposition between the free and the non-free is a fundamental given of Western aesthetic judgement, the decorative will come to occupy the pole of both the free and the non-free. Thus in Kant the pure decorative gravitates toward the pole of the free inasmuch as beauty is not subject to the demands of a concept, as is the case, for example, with the beauty of a building. On the other hand, when Gleizes and Metzinger or Léger, and many others, posit the purpose of a work of decorative art as subject to a specific space, in contrast with a work of art whose purpose is free, the decorative is once again drawn to the pole of the not-free. The entire aesthetic of Ruskin or Wörringer is in the same way controlled by this opposition. For Ruskin, the ornaments produced by the artisans of the Middle Ages are beautiful because one can decipher in them the imprints of a free man. These imprints can no longer be discerned in the ornamental production of the ancient Greeks, Egyptians, or Romans – a production that, in its very perfection, betrays a servile origin. For Wörringer, abstract ornamentation, which can be traced back to a state of human evolution testifying to the submission of man before the forces of nature, is a clue to the enslavement of man, whereas the works of the ancient Greeks, through the realism of their representation of the human body, testify to the freedom and fulfilment of man. These constructions of Ruskin and Wörringer form veritable fantasies, raising fundamental questions which we can here only pose: Can one imagine the decorative outside the horizon which delineates the opposition of free and not-free? And this horizon itself, does it belong specifically to Western thought – an idea determined by metaphysics – or is it, on the contrary, an horizon encompassing all understanding of ornament?

Behind the opposition between free man and not-free stands another opposition, equally fundamental, between man and woman. It coincides with, without being fully reducible to, the opposition between the natural beauty provided by gymnastics (which was practised in the nude, needless to say), and the artificial beauty with all its accessories (*attirail* – which is one of the original meanings of the word 'ornament,' especially in Latin).

Book VIII of Quintilian's *Institutio Oratoria* thus established an opposition between strong and pure ornamentation, which is said to go well with the orator's discourse (and the orator is always a man ...), and that which is attached 'to the effeminate refinements' and 'the deceiving effects of make-up.' It renews, by displacing – and without entirely exhausting – the man-woman opposition. The feminine pole can in turn experience a new division opposing the 'woman without affectation' for whom 'simple beauty has no need to enhance itself with pearls, face powder, artificial whites and reds' (Cicero, *The Orator*

XXIII), to the 'woman with make-up' and all her accessories. And to conclude (if it is ever possible to conclude with this process of division), these oppositions of status (free man/not-free) and sex experience a new displacement caused by the territorial opposition noted in rhetoric between atticism (Western) and the orientalism characterized by ornamental abundance, excess of show – in short, bad taste.

Through this endless process of displacement one comes close to that which no longer resembles a logic of ornament – centred on the idea of order – but to what looks like a logic of the decorative, which would refer to the very spacing between these pairs of opposites incessantly dividing and displacing themselves. One could say that the logic of ornament, as the illuminated space at the heart of which order appears, serves to establish oppositions (man/woman, free/not-free, appropriate/inappropriate, etc.), whereas the logic of the decorative serves to displace and endlessly re-divide them, by intercalating additional terms.

These ancient debates are not foreign to the debate about modernity. Even the post-war polemic opposing Abstract Expressionism to what was called the School of Paris cannot be understood except in reference to this play of oppositions that we have just evoked: Abstract Expressionism proclaiming itself as the pole of virility in opposition to the decorative mannerism of the School of Paris, the new West in relation to a decadent, effeminate orientalism.

With the socio-economic changes experienced by Western societies since the end of the Middle Ages and Renaissance, the ground plan underwent ever greater distortions. Although the man-woman opposition did not experience fundamental changes (the sartorial image of nineteenth-century man seems, on the contrary, to go one better in the abandonment of showy ornamentation), the opposition between free man and not-free gradually lost its meaning. While the social hierarchies did not disappear, their borders no longer seemed so rigid, so insurmountable. With the decline of the aristocracy, their gradations seemed less pronounced. All this resulted in the fact that other strategies, related to other discourses, were forced into operation, since the old oppositions could no longer be relied upon.

Reason was one of the new tools to be promoted in this context. It was new not only with respect to order, but in the way it was used to justify the precedence of a certain type of ornamentation. For the first time the rationality of the ornament was asserted outside all consideration of 'class.' Thus it was no longer said that ornamentation admired by workers was in bad taste because it was of an inferior class, but because it was not 'rational.' While princes or aristocrats could declare ornaments beautiful and in keeping with order – because they were linked to their past – this strategy of re-founding proved impossible for the middle class to put into operation. Authority still faulted it for

319

founding an order which drew its legitimacy from the very status of that which it affirms through the ornament. As a result, there occurred a detour of rationality, which gradually emerged in Europe during the first half of the nineteenth century. It reached its apogee in the modernist architectural movement, with which one was to associate design. The rational re-founding of ornament aimed at preventing subversion of the new order, based on presuppositions outside the system itself, by summoning up a supra-rationale, historically legitimized as only an aristocracy could do it. The rationality of the ornament was to impose itself not only in coercive fashion, but on the basis of an authority whose principle lay within itself.

This is the *coup d'état* attempted by the reformers of the applied arts and the architects after them. For in effect, this movement, which took as its object the totality of the visible, first belonged to these 'minor' arts. But the *coup d'état* was doomed to failure, because what these upholders of the new pretended to forget was that no rationality could found ornament, which was anti-rational in its essence. On the other hand, despite its chaotic character, ornament could be exploited by rationality to establish its will to power.

Where, then, can the decorative be situated? Is it not simply another way of referring to ornament, or does it have its own specificity? Two things can be said in this regard. First, in conformity with the double movement of selection and exclusion that accompanies the continuous re-founding of order, the decorative is situated on the side of that which is an object of exclusion: dress and rhetoric in the *Gorgias* for example. From this perspective the decorative appears as the eternal double of ornament, which the latter agrees at regular intervals to denounce, to prevent it from threatening order.

We have seen that, in appearing in ornament, order produces oppositions: the man's body enhanced by gymnastics/the woman's body enhanced with accessories; the body of the prince or noble enhanced with the apparel appropriate to their station/the ordinary man's body adorned with simple apparel, etc. But these oppositions, which appear natural, are not self-evident; they require a continuous call to order. Their bare foundations demand a work of consolidation, insofar as the new oppositions appear to displace and weaken those in place. For example, we saw that we cannot simply oppose man and woman with respect to ornament, for there are women who are modest in their use of finery, just as there are men whose conduct is more typical of women, etc. And with a single blow, the whole structure seems extremely fragile. We are definitely in front of a facade, but it is full of cracks. It appears to be ordered, but there are outgrowths almost everywhere. Like a phantom, the decorative always walks in the tracks of ornament, which it doubles and ends up blurring. From which comes ornament's call to order: 'Down with the decorative!' In facilitating the appearance of order, ornament simultaneously betrays it, by failing to prevent the proliferation of the decorative along the very trails it had opened through these fundamental oppositions.

Historically, with respect to Europe, the need for a call to order was felt most urgently in the eighteenth and nineteenth centuries. The hierarchies, which appeared to guarantee the stability of the ground plan, were no longer tenable, and leaks began to appear almost everywhere, especially in the idea of propriety, which was gradually emptied of all meaning. The conditions were thus ripe for another logic to emerge, one which would no longer be a logic of the organization of the visible as in the case of ornament, but a logic which could be called spectral, doubling the first.

The spectral logic of the decorative emerges when the logic of the ordering function of the visible is no longer able to halt the re-dividing of the founding oppositions, endlessly displacing them. One of the classic calls to order that sanctions this displacement is the denouncement of the excessive use of ornament. Each time this denunciation appears in ancient or modern texts this call to order involves positions of power. The denunciation is paradoxical inasmuch as we know that, from the point of view of the general economy, the excess is a requisite condition for the logic of order to endure. It would be pointless for order to appear in the ornament if it had to deprive itself of the possibilities of excess, which is why the ornamental expense is exclusively thought of in terms of legitimate or illegitimate, in keeping with a certain status. Ruskin, Gombrich and many others, including Norbert Elias, have clearly shown that excess does not have any meaning – except perhaps a blasphemous one! – in the religious context, and that there were never enough ornaments, neither in quality nor quantity, to pay homage to the divinity (the original meaning of 'magnificent' does not refer to beauty, but to the largesse of the expense).

The idea of excess is a perfect indicator of this connection between the logic of ornament and the spectral logic of the decorative. From the viewpoint of the logic of ornament, the evaluation of excess only makes sense in relation to the general economy, according to which it acquires legitimacy, predicated on the worth of the consignee or the sponsor. In other words, nothing appears to be excessive. At the core of this logic, the denunciation of excess appears more or less directly from the call to order, that order rest on the hierarchies of legitimacy in the ornamental expense. The *Encyclopedia* of Diderot and D'Alembert is one of the last great Western texts to recall this – at the very moment it had run its course.

The second point is that from the moment the markers of the ground plan began to loosen, to unravel, the seemingly self-evident connection between ornament and order had to justify itself. Though presenting themselves as 'rational,' these justifications constantly betrayed the strategies of power which passed through them, forcing them to stigmatize as 'decorative' whatever got in the way of the creation of a new ornamental order. What strikes us when we examine the ornamental artifacts of the reformers of taste in the applied arts of the nineteenth century is that, although supported by rationality, they are no less weighted with ornament than those that they put on trial. These new strategies of the ordering function of ornament provide an insight into this paradox – the invisible character of the decorative, in the sense that I never verify visually the rationality of the reformer's discourse. I simply observe two different orders of ornament, one of which calls the other too decorative. This 'too decorative' does not refer to a set of visually verifiable signs, but to an internal organization of the discourse, consigning to the decorative whatever opposes it in its hegemonic strategy. The decorative is the invisible mark of the crisis of ornament, which results from the loss of authority of an order whose 'justice' does not depend on rationality to make its views prevail. Thus when rationality claims to dictate the rules of ornament and it turns out it lacks the means – the illusion that design still upholds, for those who believe that the armchair of Mies van der Rohe is more 'rational' than a *Bergère Louis XVI* – the Pandora's box of the decorative is opened.   (... p 99)

Jacques Soulillou, 'Ornament and Order', trans Mark Heffernan, Bernie Miller and Melony Ward (eds), *Crime and Ornament: The Arts and Popular Culture in the Shadow of Adolf Loos*, YYZ Books (Toronto), 2002.
© Jacques Soulillou. Reprinted by permission of YYZ Books of Canada.
(Excerpts pp 87–99)

'The Things Which Surround One'

Penny Sparke

Notions of taste and comfort are explored in this text by design historian Penny Sparke in light of Victorian attitudes towards females as housewives and agents of beauty. In this case, beauty is linked with nature through the application of naturalistic imagery and the importation of natural organic objects into the interior. While popular and consumer culture promoted furnishing the interior as a measure of good taste, Sparke points to criticism that condemns this commodious display of decadence and decoration as nothing more than frivolous and nostalgic. The breach between taste and design, particularly concerning matters of comfort, is investigated through discussions on furnishings, dress, the dining room and the parlour as a means of exposing the breadth and depth of the struggle for aesthetic dominance.

A house is a dead give-away.
Elsie De Wolfe[1]

> Taste is molded, to a very large extent, by the things which surround one, and the family taste is trained by the objects selected by the homemaker. There is, therefore, a distinct obligation in the home to set the highest standards of beauty ... Since art is involved in most of the objects which are seen and used every day, one of the great needs of the consumer is a knowledge of the principles which are fundamental to good taste.[2]

So wrote two American 'taste' advisers, Harriet and Vetta Goldstein, in 1932. Their words could have been published a century earlier as they applied equally to the mid-nineteenth-century housewife whose job it was to 'beautify' the home. A century earlier, however, the term 'taste' was more likely in advice books than the elaborated 'good taste.' Used alone the word 'taste' implied the presence of 'goodness' and 'beauty.' In the mid-nineteenth century a housewife either had, or didn't have taste, and her home either did or didn't manifest this. This monolithic notion of taste was rooted in an earlier historical period when only the elite had had the means to participate in the world of taste and fashion. With the democratisation of the capacity to consume goods with which to demonstrate social status – as opposed to being judged by the number of cows in one's possession – came the need on the part of the custodians of the dominant culture to create two categories of taste – good and bad – as a form of social and cultural distinction. It was a means of distinction which, by the end of the nineteenth century, was to have overtly gendered connotations.

Within the culture of mid-Victorian, middle-class domestic femininity, ideological values were made manifest in the physical reality of the home. To a significant extent it was the design of artefacts – their forms and appearances determined during their manufacture in the public sphere – which led to this link between the ideological and the material. Within the feminine culture of domesticity there were many connections between appearances and values which provided an insight into the way people led, or rather were expected to lead, their lives.

Taste was an active agent within the consumption and disposition of goods, and within the process of domestic display. Design can be seen as a passive respondent to its demands. Adopting this perspective permits a regendering of the conventional discussion about material culture in this period and a reassertion of the importance of the feminine sphere, marginalised by an emphasis upon 'design' at the expense of 'taste.' Inevitably, however, discussions about taste and design overlap each other. In mid-Victorian Britain and America, the goods which made up the material culture of domesticity – those objects with which the housewife chose to represent her ideal image of home – were mostly made and 'designed' outside the home. Once consumed by the housewife and brought inside they were arranged and integrated into an interior setting according to her aesthetic preferences. Thus, in this context, the term consumption encapsulated the whole process of selection and use, and the concept of taste necessarily complemented that of design. Nonetheless, an analysis of the aesthetic content of the goods and interiors of the mid-century, middle-class home suggests that taste was controlling design and not vice versa.

As we have seen, many middle-class family homes, both in Britain and the USA in this period, could be found in the new suburbs. One of the main appeals lay in the large gardens which came with such houses. James Luckcock, for instance, sought a 'small comfortable house, and a good sized garden.'[3] In America, suburbs constructed from the 1870s onwards included Shaker Hills outside Cleveland; Chestnut Hill outside Philadelphia; Ravenswood outside Chicago; and Queens outside Manhattan. Los Angeles also developed 60 new communities to accommodate the expansion of its population from 6,000 to 100,000 between 1870 and 1877. The main selling point, and undoubtedly a central appeal of the new suburban housing, was its links with nature. This was reflected in the materials and designs of the houses themselves: 'Picturesque site planning and natural building materials evoked a return to nature, to a lost innocence and an earlier stability.'[4] This was evoked in the use of 'rough limestone, wide clapboards, cedar shingles, green patina on slate tiles' in addition to colours which 'simulated the hues of nature.'[5] The recurring rhetoric surrounding suburbia stressed its role as a safe secure haven from the immorality and pressures of city existence and the stresses and strains of commercial life.

The same appeals generated the British rush to the suburbs begun a few decades earlier. London's population more than doubled between 1800 and 1840 and Henry Mayhew wrote in the *Mornington Chronicle* in 1850, that 'Since 1839 there have been 200 miles of new streets formed in London, no less than 6,405 new dwellings have been erected annually since that time.'[6] Unlike their American equivalents, most British suburbanites rented rather than owned their new houses. Writing rather disparagingly about the new London suburbs the architectural historian, John Gloag, explained that:

> North, south, east and west of London, mile after mile of streets were lined with these drab houses, each with cast-iron railings and front gates of identical pattern, bay windows and porches with fussy Gothic trimmings, and drain-pipes carrying water from gutters and bathrooms disfiguring the facade.[7]

Gloag's reactions were typical of a generation of historians and critics brought up on a diet of anti-Victorianism. Notwithstanding, his account is perceptive, highlighting as it did the central values which underpinned the construction of the Victorian suburban home – the emulation of the grander rural dwellings of the aristocracy – and the functionally and sexually-defined areas within them.

Above all, Gloag focused on the central concept of 'comfort' which lay at the very heart of the mid-Victorian home, both in Britain and the USA. The language of domestic comfort depended heavily upon its references to the natural world. Whereas the realm of technological progress which lay outside the sphere of the home was linked to the idea of culture, that of nature stood boldly in opposition to it, suggesting a lost innocence, a rural idyll which had to be retained if Victorian citizens were to maintain a balance between the spiritual and the material aspects of their lives. Ironically, this will to spirituality was expressed in the home in an overtly material manner through the consumption of goods and decorations which evoked nature in a variety of ways.

The furnishing and embellishments of the mid-Victorian home served to bring nature inside the domestic sphere. Potted plants and the addition of a conservatory filled with greenery achieved this literally, as did collections of flowers and small plants in bay windows. Many housewives also brought 'real' nature inside in the form of shells and other natural objects used as decorative items. In *The American Woman's Home*, Catherine Beecher and Harriet Beecher Stowe encouraged the use of natural objects in the forms of picture frames of pinecones, moss and seashells; hanging baskets for plants;

climbing ivy trained around the cornice; a large terranium furnished with ferns, shells, trailing arbutus, and partridge berries which offered a 'fragment of the green woods brought in and silently growing.'[8]

Gwendolyn Wright confirmed that such advice was heeded when she observed 'displays of shells, seeds, corals and other objects of natural history' in the American Victorian suburban home.[9] Aquaria filled with fish and a profusion of water plants were also a popular feature and they were frequently given the same kind of decorative treatment as an intricately carved piece of furniture, festooned with ornament inspired by natural forms and images. Stuffed animals also appeared in abundance from snakes encircling tree stumps to the more conventional hunting trophies.

John Gloag pinpointed a similar obsession with plants in and around the British house and quotes the advice literature of the time:

> 'whenever it is possible, climbing plants should be trained up the house and round the windows' said *The Young Ladies' Treasure Book*, adding that 'More than any invention of carving, friezes, stucco, paint, or outward adorning, does nature's greenery decorate the house.'[10]

Glass domes covering plants and other natural items were also a familiar sight.

> The domed glass case, under which ferns and other plants were used in conjunction with a small table supported by a pillar resting on claws or a solid base, was known as a Wardian case. It was a popular item in Victorian furnishing, introduced in the mid-nineteenth-century, and named after Nathaniel Bagshaw Ward who, in 1829, discovered accidentally the principle which led to this method of growing and transporting plants in glass cases.[11]

These inclusions of nature maintained the ideological imperatives of the Cult of Domesticity, suggesting a sense of continuity with the not too distant past. They also served as educational tools with which the housewife could introduce her children to the value system which underpinned their culture and they helped to create the image of domestic comfort which required familiar forms and soft, organically-derived decorative effects in the household.   (... p 36)

Notes
1   Elsie de Wolfe, quoted in J Banham, S Macdonald and J Porter, *Victorian Interior Design*, Cassell (London), 1991, p 12.
2   Harriet and Vetta Goldstein, *Art in Everyday Life*, Macmillan (New York), 1932, pp 2–5.
3   Leonore Davidoff and Catherine Hall, *Family Fortunes: Men and Women of the English Middle*

Class, 1780–1850, Routledge (London), 1987, p 17.

4 Gwendolyn Wright, *Building The Dream: A Social History of Housing in America*, Pantheon (New York), 1981, p 93.

5 Wright, *Building The Dream*, p 106.

6 Henry Mayhew quoted in Banham, Macdonald and Porter, *Victorian Interior Design*, p 10.

7 John Gloag, *Victorian Comfort: A Social History of Design From 1830–1900*, AC Black (London), 1961, p 27.

8 Quoted in SJ Bronner (ed), *Consuming Visions: Accumulation and Display of Goods in America 1880–1920*, WW Norton and Co (New York and London), 1989, p 161.

9 Wright, *Building The Dream*, p 107.

10 Gloag, *Victorian Comfort*, p 36.

11 Gloag, *Victorian Comfort*, p 35.

Penny Sparke, *As Long As It's Pink: the sexual politics of taste*, Pandora Press (London), 1995.

© Penny Sparke 1995. Reprinted by permission of Rivers Oram Press Limited.

(Excerpt pp 31–6)

Decorating Culture

Xiaobing Tang

social ● 1998
late 20th century decoration

This essay makes the connection between consumption and display as a sign of personal success rather than invidious distinction. Literature scholar Xiaobing Tang undertakes a close reading of He Dun's novella Didi nihao *(Hello, My Younger Brother) through Jean Baudrillard's 'system of objects,' the sign language of commodities. The text reiterates contemporary China's rapid absorption of the spectacle of desire, a cosmetic revolution in which external and ostentatious signs of modernity indicate consumptive mobilisation. Within this world, the transformed domicile is seen as an emergent form of interiority, which is connected to a new sense of private interior space and the mechanism of interiorisation.*

Toward the end of his much acclaimed novella 'Didi nihao' (Hello, My Younger Brother), He Dun, an energetic literary newcomer based in the provincial capital, Changsha, arranges for the hero of his story to enjoy a meaningful moment of peace and contentment.[1] Throughout the narrative, Deng Heping, his period-specific given name meaning 'peace,' is referred to as 'my younger brother' and is continuously cast in the awkward role of a rebellious and estranged family member. Disrespectful of his orthodox, revolutionary father and showing great ingenuity in capitalist entrepreneurship, Heping embodies a post-Cultural Revolution generation that, reaching its adulthood in the early 1980s, appears both familiar and yet ominously uncontainable in Chinese society in the 1990s. The novella begins in 1988, when Heping is twenty-six years old and definitely beyond his formative stages. In that year, because of a series of misdeeds, one of which is to impregnate his nineteen-year-old girlfriend, Heping finally manages to enrage 'my father' to such a degree that he is barred from visiting his parents' apartment for good. Incidentally, as the narrator coolly comments, 'my father,' at the same promising age of twenty-six, had also expelled his own land-owning father when he led a brigade of Communist guerrillas and ransacked his estate in 1948.

As the dense and fast-paced narrative winds to a sudden halt, we reach the wet December of 1992 and realize that 'my younger brother' has apparently 'made it.' In hurriedly following the protagonist around, we quickly get absorbed in, even fascinated by, his world of objects, desire, money, and action. The novella, together with He Dun's other narratives about contemporary Changsha, indeed offers a raw account of the widespread capitalist drive that has become a concrete passion for this generation of Chinese urban youth. Through all the rough and often sordid ups and downs in his fortunes and emotional life, Heping emerges as a self-made and self-confident hero, inspiring as much envy as admiration from the narrator, his ambivalent but ultimately sympathetic older brother. Even the young man's physique undergoes a significant metamorphosis in the process of assiduous self-fashioning. Gone are the two diseases, fistula and hyperthyroidism, that put him at a disadvantage when he was a constant annoyance to his parents and superiors. Radiating a robust glow, he now proudly rides an expensive Honda motorcycle and is preparing for a second marriage. The woman he loves and whom he will marry on New Year's Day of 1993 was the neglected but beautiful wife of Heping's one-time boss, a local Mafia leader who made his wealth through heroin trafficking and was eventually arrested and condemned. Since Dandan, a successful hairdresser, is now visibly pregnant, they need to get the wedding ceremony out of the way soon. Heping, however, is busier than ever, because he retails materials for building decoration, and 1992 happens to be a year when the entire nation, so chronicles the reserved narrator, is consumed by a craze in 'real estate, construction, gas and water-heater installation.'[2] To take full advantage of the new fad in home improvement, Heping has to leave his wife-to-be behind and shuttle nonstop, usually by truck, between Changsha and Guangzhou, scrambling for supplies that are now in great shortage. One afternoon, after another bumpy trip, he comes back exhausted, only to find his one-bedroom apartment totally transformed.

> Younger Brother languidly pushed open the door and was taken aback. The living room was completely redecorated. What used to be soft green walls were now covered with crimson red wallpaper with brick designs on it; overhead a soft red drop-ceiling of plywood was added. The original paneling of chestnut-colored plywood was now replaced with the same material in pink. 'She moved her Red Hair Salon here,' Younger Brother muttered to himself. The four walls of the bedroom, from bottom to top, were all covered with ash boards, and the floor was parqueted in a basket weave pattern. The furniture was now a luxuriant deluxe set, of a pleasant maroon color. The old white composite set was nowhere to be found. 'She knows how to spend money,' Younger Brother threw himself onto bed and marveled. 'But this is pretty comfy.'[3]

This newly decorated interior space that Heping enters comes as both a surprise and a reassurance. Everything he sees is new and unfamiliar, but together they win his recognition, almost instantaneously, and are accepted as his own possessions. He immediately claims this showroom as his home by throwing himself onto the comfortable bed. Although Dandan is not there to greet him, the meticulous design loudly bespeaks her presence. In fact, her absence conveniently allows him to take a close examination of their new home, of her anticipation for their future life together. Through her choice of objects, materials, and design, Dandan creates a private and concrete space that mirrors their private and concrete desires. It is also at this moment that Heping, the intrepid small-business owner, fully experiences, as if stepping outside himself, the seductive power of consumption and translates the home interior surrounding him into a sign of his social success. Hence his appreciative comment to Dandan when he wakes up hours later: 'This feels just like staying in a four-star hotel.'[4]

In fact, throughout the story, Heping is consistently studied as a conspicuous consumer, for whom consumption is more of a practiced ideology than a satisfaction of whimsical needs. He readily embraces what Jean Baudrillard describes as the 'system of objects' and, with great proficiency, commands the sign language of commodities.[5] He and his cohorts demonstrate an instinctive grasp of the status symbolism associated with brand names, foreign products, and luxury items. While the cigarettes he smokes continually evolve from domestic to American brands, his footwear also progresses from generic 'pointy and shiny black shoes' to 'Italian-made crocodile skin shoes,' which he is quick to put up on a table as means to convince his friends of his ambition. When the business of his Hongtai Decoration Materials store flourishes, bringing in a net profit of 700,000 Yuan (equivalent to U.S. $85,900), he rewards himself by upgrading his motorcycle from a Chinese-made Nanfang to a Royal Honda, and he makes a point of visiting all his friends and acquaintances on this handsome Honda equipped with twin tailpipes. Yet nothing gives him as deep and complete a gratification as the new domestic setting which he finds at home. For this is effectively the first time that, instead of demonstrating to others what he likes and can afford, he gets to view his own wealth and accomplishment splendidly displayed for his consumption alone. In a sense, he is now invited to read the sign of his own success rather than parade it around as an invidious distinction.

Deliberate display is what this particular scene of interior renovation brings to the foreground. It is also the intended effect of such detailed description. For both the character in the story and the related narrator, the pleasure derived from registering those ornamental details is irrepressible and functions as a driving force behind the narrative. An obsession with the ornament, of which Heping, owner of Hongtai Decoration Materials, is a professional promoter, penetrates the fictional world, both its form and content. Not only does the young hero of the story gradually learn how to distinguish himself through costly designer attire, but the narrator also continually relies on naming various objects and spelling out prices in order to make realistic his representation. Meticulous care is taken in the narrative to specify, yet often in an offhand fashion, whether a fountain pen is from America or a bicycle is just an ordinary domestic Phoenix. The reality effect of novelistic discourse now relies on recognizing the differentiating function that commodities are called upon to serve as everyday objects. All commodities, indeed, participate in an ingenious 'social discourse of objects' that contributes to what Baudrillard once described as a general 'mechanism of discrimination and prestige.'[6] According to the French sociologist, reflecting on the logic of rising consumerism in post-World War II Euro-America, there always exists a 'political economy of the sign' in which commodities or objects are consumed not so much for their utility or use value, as for their explicit sign value. Parallel to the signifying operation of all languages, the sign value of objects enforces a logic of differentiation and establishes, through display and conspicuous consumption, a distinctive hierarchy of taste, status, and identity.

> Signs, like commodities, are at once use value and exchange value. The social hierarchies, the invidious differences, the privileges of caste and culture which they support, are accounted as profit, as personal satisfaction, and lived as "need" (need of social value-generation to which corresponds the "utility" of differential signs and their "consumption").[7]

Human needs, further observes Baudrillard, are never a natural experience or objective perception, but they always have an ideological genesis from above and in the privileged. In fact, needs are necessarily constructed to provide the alibi or self-evident rationale for any given stage of 'consummative mobilization,' which proves to be a central legitimizing process of the late capitalist mode of production.[8]   (... p 535)

'Nineteen ninety-two was a year of decoration craze in the city of Changsha,' the narrator of 'Hello, My Younger Brother' describes with considerable ambivalence. 'Many shops were torn down beyond recognition, but overnight they would all be decorated absolutely anew. As if caught in a fierce competition, one store after another rushed to have itself remodeled. Some big department stores may just have had a face-lift in the first half of the year, but soon they would break everything into pieces and start all over.'[9] Such extensive and rapid restyling no doubt affects the appearance of and life in the city; it helps set off a new visual regime and sign system that directly contributes to the urban spectacle of desire. Tellingly enough, it is the shops and department stores that are most ready to undergo such cosmetic renovation, to present themselves as at the cutting edge of the latest fashion, and, ultimately, to package their commodities with an external, and ostentatious, sign of modernity. Heping's flourishing business, therefore, can be taken as an index to a culture that demonstrates a new sign-consciousness, one for which the production of difference through sign exchange becomes an instrumental operation. Sign exchange, suggests Baudrillard, is no less than the central logic of a consumer society's political economy.[10]

The enticing spectacle generated by a pervasive consummative mobilization turns out to be, not unlike the neon signs in a concentrated shopping district, an illusion of differentiation that colorfully decorates the stark reality of commodity exchange based on the principle of equivalence. The art of design and decoration, therefore, is the quintessential enterprise that at once advertises and disguises the truth of a consumer culture. It is mass production coupled with mass consumption, observes Penny Sparke in her history of design and culture in the twentieth century, that puts 'design in the centre of the picture as it is design that provides the variation that is so essential to modern society.'[11] With the alchemy of design, an industrial product is transformed into a deliberate object that signifies its invested difference and, consequently, systematic meaning. It is Bauhaus, the pioneer school of modern industrial design in the 1920s, that, in the words of Baudrillard again, 'institutes this universal semantization of the environment in which everything becomes the object of a calculus of function and of signification. Total functionality, total semiurgy.'[12] When it penetrates into the domestic interior and incorporates personal space into sign exchange, design encounters a situation where commodified difference is dramatized even further: The home interior has to signify a private domain as such, both to its occupant(s) and to a conceivable public. In comparison with the exterior decoration that makes over shop windows, buildings, or the city as a whole, interior design is compelled to address an individual rather than a projected crowd, to speak a more intimate *parole* with accented variations. It is only logical, then, to anticipate that interior design, as a business and generator of sign value, will cash in on personal preferences, encourage hobbies and idiosyncrasies, and profit from the notion of multiple identities. At the same time, interior design, by instilling a sign-consciousness in our most private and personal sphere, serves to acculturate us to the system of sign-objects – namely, to interiorize the political economy of the sign. At this point, the discourse of interiority gathers not only a legitimizing impetus from the market but also a concreteness that promises to atomize and undermine the metaphysical dimension of the interior. Instead of articulating a spiritual or psychic structure of depth, interiority may now describe a new frontier market for customized products of sorts.

This transmutation of a charged intellectual concept can be best examined in the widespread interest in interior design in contemporary China. Partly due to the new housing policy that requires residents to purchase their apartments from their respective work units, and partly due to the opening of the real estate market, urban Chinese now view their dwellings as their most significant investment. After more than a quarter of a century during which the idea of a private home was systematically erased and interior design was an alien concept, city dwellers now invest a great deal of money and time in decorating and remodeling what they can claim as their own living space. Privatization in this area necessarily gives rise to homeowner awareness different from an aesthetics of austerity bred by publicly subsidized, therefore standard and communal, housing projects.   (... p 542)

What complicates the situation greatly, however, is that He Dun's narratives refuse to stop at a triumphant moment where the hero may be seduced into believing that the world of his creation answers to his aspiration. A symbolic crumbling always follows. There is always a pause, a suspension of normal goings-on, or even absurd death, that puts in disarray all splendid displays of success, material as well as spiritual. Within his narratives of fast urban life, a specter of the unconsoled is created to haunt the city landscape. In the particular story that we have been examining, a traffic accident kills Dandan and the three-month-old fetus inside her. This occurs the day following Heping's coming home and, as is made clear in the narrative, before the night of passionate lovemaking that she promises him. The much-anticipated evening would have made the remodeled apartment really a part of his intimate being, an extension of his interior world. As it is now, the new home interior stands only as a reminder of the porcelain fragility of the world of objects; more ominously, the death of the unborn child hints at the impossibility for a potentially gratifying everyday life or relationship to reproduce itself. The symbolism of having Dandan thrown off Heping's powerful motorcycle and crushed to death is too strong to ignore. This scene of devastation reaffirms, in a cruel fashion, the need for an interior space to cushion the impact of the outside world. Until this instant Heping shows little concern with his world of fast and fragmented experience, and even less interest in the generally unanswerable questions of causality and meaning. In her gruesome death, Dandan is transformed, literally and figuratively, from an inspiring designer of home interior into the announcer of an injured form of interiority. The last sentence of the novella reverberates to the primal, haunting scream uttered by Dandan, and it is her voice that penetrates deep into He Dun's entire being: 'It was no longer a human cry, but the cracking sound of glass. For a long time, it hovered over the intersection, humming and parading like a phalanx of spotty-legged mosquitoes. One of those mosquitoes quickly took hold of my younger brother's ear, and fastened itself, like a thumb nail, onto his eardrum, permanently ...'[13]

The productive question to be asked about He Dun's fast-paced narratives, therefore, is not what alternative there is in an age of no interiority, but what function interiority, now recommended as spiritual resilience at a moment of worldly crisis or breakdown, is called upon to serve. It is by far much thornier to determine, for instance, whether or not those instances of putting one's faith and strength to the test actually interrogate the interiorization of consumer needs. Do the evocations of a transcendental longing at the end actually add to the legitimacy of massive consummative mobilization? Put differently, the question may have to be: What if interiority is served as an *alibi* in a culture that of necessity decorates and accessorizes everything for recognition? Or, conversely, does the injured form of interiority that Dandan articulates in her death reveal a fundamental structure of interiority – its success in failure? Of greater theoretical relevance could be a general question about the astonishing speed in which 'interiority,' as a central value and practice of Euro-American modernity, gets recycled and appropriated, for all intents and purposes, in contemporary Chinese culture. Is this a necessary process before the notion becomes once again exhausted and ripe for historical inquiry; what does the rapidity of

333

its transmutation entail insofar as a legitimating narrative of modern capitalist cultural logic is concerned? Does it suggest that ours is still part of the moment when interiority and its corollaries are conjured globally only to undermine their pertinence?   (... p 547)

Notes

 1 He Dun, 'Didi nihao' (Hello, My Younger Brother), *Shenghuo wuzui* (Life is not a crime), Huayi Chubanshe (Beijing), 1995.
 2 He Dun, 'Didi nihao', p 354.
 3 He Dun, 'Didi nihao', pp 355–6.
 4 He Dun, 'Didi nihao', p 356.
 5 Jean Baudrillard, *For a Critique of the Political Economy of the Sign*, trans Charles Levin, Telos Press (St Louis), 1981, p 29.
 6 Baudrillard, *Critique*, p 30.
 7 Baudrillard, *Critique*, p 125.
 8 Baudrillard, *Critique*, pp 130–42.
 9 He Dun, 'Didi nihao', p 354.
10 In 'The Ideological Genesis of Needs', Baudrillard (*Critique*, p 75) argues that 'consumption does not arise from an objective need of the consumer, a final intention of the subject towards the object; rather, there is social production, in a system of exchange, of a material of differences, a code of significations and invidious (*statuaire*) values. The functionality of goods and individual needs only follows on this, adjusting itself to, rationalizing, and in the same stroke repressing these fundamental structural mechanisms.' For a lucid discussion of Baudrillard's development of Marx's analysis of the capitalist mode of production, see Douglas Kellner, *Jean Baudrillard: From Marxism to Postmodernism and Beyond*, Stanford University Press (Stanford, CA), 1989, especially pp 19–25.
11 Penny Sparke, *An Introduction to Design and Culture in the Twentieth Century*, Allen and Unwin (London), 1986, p xxii.
12 Baudrillard, *Critique*, p 185.
13 He Dun, 'Didi nihao', p 360.

Xiaobing Tang, 'Decorating Culture: Notes on Interior Design, Interiority, and Interiorization', *Public Culture*, vol 10 no 3, 1998, pp 530–48.
© 1998 Duke University Press. All rights reserved. Reprinted by permission of Duke University Press.
(Excerpts pp 532–47)

In Praise of Shadows

Jun´ichirō Tanizaki

philosophical light 1977 achronic

Japanese novelist Jun´ichiro Tanizaki's book on shadows is as much a reminder of cultural differences toward space and light as it is specific to the subtle nuances within Japanese thought and practice of inhabiting in variations of darkness. Defending mystery and ambiguity as primary atmospheric conditions of interior space, Tanizaki speaks of rooms as having charm, repose, and ethereal glow brought upon delicate distinctions between material surfaces that glimmer, glint, lustre, gleam or shine through the application of gold, lacquerware, brocade and ivory. Instead of being bewildered by the lack of clarity or visibility, shadowed interiors provoke a sense of harmony based on faith in effect rather than truth in light.

In making for ourselves a place to live, we first spread a parasol to throw a shadow on the earth, and in the pale light of the shadow we put together a house. There are of course roofs on Western houses too, but they are less to keep off the sun than to keep off the wind and the dew; even from without it is apparent that they are built to create as few shadows as possible and to expose the interior to as much light as possible. If the roof of a Japanese house is a parasol, the roof of a Western house is no more than a cap, with as small a visor as possible so as to allow the sunlight to penetrate directly beneath the eaves. There are no doubt all sorts of reasons – climate, building materials – for the deep Japanese eaves. The fact that we did not use glass, concrete, and bricks, for instance, made a low roof necessary to keep off the driving wind and rain. A light room would no doubt have been more convenient for us, too, than a dark room. The quality that we call beauty, however, must always grow from the realities of life, and our ancestors, forced to live in dark rooms, presently came to discover beauty in shadows, ultimately to guide shadows towards beauty's ends.

And so it has come to be that the beauty of a Japanese room depends on a variation of shadows, heavy shadows against light shadows – it has nothing else. Westerners are amazed at the simplicity of Japanese rooms, perceiving in them no more than ashen walls bereft of ornament. Their reaction is understandable, but it betrays a failure to comprehend the mystery of shadows. Out beyond the sitting room, which the rays of the sun can at best but barely reach, we extend the eaves or build on a veranda, putting the sunlight at still greater a remove. The light from the garden steals in but dimly through paper-paneled doors, and it is precisely this indirect light that makes for us the charm of a room. We do our walls in neutral colors so that the sad, fragile, dying rays can sink into absolute repose. The storehouse, kitchen, hallways, and such may have a glossy finish, but the walls of the sitting room will almost always be of clay textured with fine sand. A luster here would destroy the soft fragile beauty of the feeble light. We delight in the mere sight of the delicate glow of fading rays clinging to the surface of a dusky wall, there to live out what little life remains to them. We never tire of the sight, for to us this pale glow and these dim shadows far surpass any ornament. And so, as we must if we are not to disturb the glow, we finish the walls with sand in a single neutral color. The hue may differ from room to room, but the degree of difference will be ever so slight; not so much a difference in color as in shade, a difference that will seem to exist only in the mood of the viewer. And from these delicate differences in the hue of the walls, the shadows in each room take on a tinge peculiarly their own.

Of course the Japanese room does have its picture alcove, and in it a hanging scroll and a flower arrangement. But the scroll and the flowers serve not as ornament but rather to give depth to the shadows. We value a scroll above all for the way it blends with the walls of the alcove, and thus we consider the mounting quite as important as the calligraphy or painting. Even the greatest masterpiece will lose its worth as a scroll if it fails to blend with the alcove, while a work of no particular distinction may blend beautifully with the room and set off to unexpected advantage both itself and its surroundings. Wherein lies the power of an otherwise ordinary work to produce such an effect? Most often the paper, the ink, the fabric of the mounting will possess a certain look of antiquity, and this look of antiquity will strike just the right balance with the darkness of the alcove and room.

We have all had the experience, on a visit to one of the great temples of Kyoto or Nara, of being shown a scroll, one of the temple's treasures, hanging in a large, deeply recessed alcove. So dark are these alcoves, even in bright daylight, that we can hardly discern the outlines of the work; all we can do is listen to the explanation of the guide, follow as best we can the all-but-invisible brush strokes, and tell ourselves how magnificent a painting it must be. Yet the combination of that blurred old painting and the dark alcove is one of absolute harmony. The lack of clarity, far from disturbing us, seems rather to suit the painting perfectly.

For the painting here is nothing more than another delicate surface upon which the faint, frail light can play; it performs precisely the same function as the sand-textured wall. This is why we attach such importance to age and patina. A new painting, even one done in ink monochrome or subtle pastels, can quite destroy the shadows of an alcove, unless it is selected with the greatest care.

A Japanese room might be likened to an inkwash painting, the paper-paneled shoji being the expanse where the ink is thinnest, and the alcove where it is darkest. Whenever I see the alcove of a tastefully built Japanese room, I marvel at our comprehension of the secrets of shadows, our sensitive use of shadow and light. For the beauty of the alcove is not the work of some clever device. An empty space is marked off with plain wood and plain walls, so that the light drawn into it forms dim shadows within emptiness. There is nothing more. And yet, when we gaze into the darkness that gathers behind the crossbeam, around the flower vase, beneath the shelves, though we know perfectly well it is mere shadow, we are overcome with the feeling that in this small corner of the atmosphere there reigns complete and utter silence; that here in the darkness immutable tranquillity holds sway. The 'mysterious Orient' of which Westerners speak probably refers to the uncanny silence of these dark places. And even we as children would feel an inexpressible chill as we peered into the depths of an alcove to which the sunlight had never penetrated. Where lies the key to this mystery? Ultimately it is the magic of shadows. Were the shadows to be banished from its corners, the alcove would in that instant revert to mere void.

This was the genius of our ancestors, that by cutting off the light from this empty space they imparted to the world of shadows that formed there a quality of mystery and depth superior to that of any wall painting or ornament. The technique seems simple, but was by no means so simply achieved. We can imagine with little difficulty what extraordinary pains were taken with each invisible detail – the placement of the window in the shelving recess, the depth of the crossbeam, the height of the threshold. But for me the most exquisite touch is the pale white glow of the shoji in the study bay; I need only pause before it and I forget the passage of time.

The study bay, as the name suggests, was originally a projecting window built to provide a place for reading. Over the years it came to be regarded as no more than a source of light for the alcove; but most often it serves not so much to illuminate the alcove as to soften the sidelong rays from without, to filter them through paper panels. There is a cold and desolate tinge to the light by the time it reaches these panels. The little sunlight from the garden that manages to make its way beneath the eaves and through the corridors has by then lost its power to illuminate, seems drained of the complexion of life. It can do no more than accentuate the whiteness of the paper. I sometimes linger before these panels and study the surface of the paper, bright, but giving no impression of brilliance.

In temple architecture the main room stands at a considerable distance from the garden; so dilute is the light there that no matter what the season, on fair days or cloudy, morning, midday, or evening, the pale, white glow scarcely varies. And the shadows at the interstices of the ribs seem strangely immobile, as if dust collected in the corners had become a part of the paper itself. I blink in uncertainty at this dreamlike luminescence, feeling as though some misty film were blunting my vision. The light from the pale white paper, powerless to dispel the heavy darkness of the alcove, is instead repelled by the darkness, creating a world of confusion where dark and light are indistinguishable. Have not you yourselves sensed a difference in the light that suffuses such a room, a rare tranquillity not found in ordinary light? Have you never felt a sort of fear in the face of the ageless, a fear that in that room you might lose all consciousness of the passage of time, that untold years might pass and upon emerging you should find you had grown old and gray?

And surely you have seen, in the darkness of the innermost rooms of these huge buildings, to which sunlight never penetrates, how the gold leaf of a sliding door or screen will pick up a distant glimmer from the garden, then suddenly send forth an ethereal glow, a faint golden light cast into the enveloping darkness, like the glow upon the horizon at sunset. In no other setting is gold quite so exquisitely beautiful. You walk past, turning to look again, and yet again; and as you move away the golden surface of the paper glows ever more deeply, changing not in a flash, but growing slowly, steadily brighter, like color rising in the face of a giant. Or again you may find that the gold dust of the background, which until that moment had only a dull, sleepy luster, will, as you move past, suddenly gleam forth as if it had burst into flame.

How, in such a dark place, gold draws so much light to itself is a mystery to me. But I see why in ancient times statues of the Buddha were gilt with gold and why gold leaf covered the walls of the homes of the nobility. Modern man, in his well-lit house, knows nothing of the beauty of gold; but those who lived in the dark houses of the past were not merely captivated by its beauty, they also knew its practical value; for gold, in these dim rooms, must have served the function of a reflector. Their use of gold leaf and gold dust was not mere extravagance. Its reflective properties were put to use as a source of illumination. Silver and other metals quickly lose their gloss, but gold retains its brilliance indefinitely to light the darkness of the room. This is why gold was held in such incredibly high esteem.

I have said that lacquerware decorated in gold was made to be seen in the dark; and for this same reason were the fabrics of the past so lavishly woven of threads of silver and gold. The priest's surplice of gold brocade is perhaps the best example. In most of our city temples, catering to the masses as they do, the main hall will be brightly lit, and these garments of gold will seem merely gaudy. No matter how venerable a man the priest may be, his robes will convey no sense of his dignity. But when you attend a service at an old temple, conducted after the ancient ritual, you see how perfectly the gold harmonizes with the wrinkled skin of the old priest and the flickering light of the altar lamps, and how much it contributes to the solemnity of the occasion. As with lacquerware, the bold patterns remain for the most part hidden in darkness; only occasionally does a bit of gold or silver gleam forth.   (... p 23)

Jun'ichirō Tanizaki, *In Praise of Shadows*, trans Thomas J Harper and Edward G Seidensticker, Leete's Island Books (Stony Creek, CT), 1977.
English translation © 1977 by Leete's Island Books, Inc. Reprinted by permission of Leete's Island Books, Inc.
(Excerpt pp 17–23)

Architecture and Interior: A Roam of One's Own

Mark Taylor

gender ● 2001

late 20th century space

This text operates in two significant ways towards expanding an understanding about the interior: first, it recalls Virginia Woolf's essay A Room of One's Own *and the important role it has played in inspiring women to claim space and authority over their own domain. Second, through the use of close and gentle observation, it positions intimate detail and temporality in the discourse of interior design as a creative act. Speaking directly to the question of interior design needing a room apart from architecture, Mark Taylor reflects upon the dualisms that might hamper interior design's liberation, naming it as a physical and psychological refuge – a space within and yet with physical atmosphere.*

'When you asked me to ... '[1]

write about architecture and the interior I wondered where does one turn? What construction of history and theory is invoked when undertaking such a task? What position is given architecture and the interior in such writing? Might it be interiors and what they are like; might it be architecture and interiors they create; might it be architecture and interiors they write; might it be written by the interiors encountered and the books read? I am reading Virginia Woolf's *A Room of One's Own* and I read 'Lies will flow from my lips, but there may perhaps be some truth mixed up with them; it is for you to seek out this truth and to decide whether any part of it is worth keeping. If not you will of course throw the whole of it into the wastepaper basket and forget all about it,'[2] a necessary condition for establishing a shift in thought and expression over that which is held as authoritative and immovable. Unexpected thoughts on the interior.

I turn back the page, a page in history, and read the deeply powerful and provocative opening line in which she remarks 'But you may say, we asked you to speak about women and fiction – what has this got to do with a room of one's own?'[3] Woolf's realisation is that writing by and for women can only be constructed when they write their own history outside patriarchy, epitomised by the need for independent means. Perhaps – and this is why I use her work – the same can be said of the interior. This line I read sitting in the 'architectural interior' of a Melbourne designer café, prompting the thought that perhaps the interior requires liberating from architecture and offered independent means: a room (*Raum*), or should I say a *roam* of its own.

Further, her writing and intellectual position upholds the notion of woman as something discovered rather than built. Perhaps by acknowledging the role of women in relation to the interior, we might parallel this argument; the interior is discovered not built. Perhaps the interior, if it is to be displaced from architecture, needs to be sought, not necessarily in re-reading canonical architectural texts from an interior perspective but in finding new modes of expression for the interior.

'So thinking, so speculating, I found my way back to my house by the ...'[4]

    sea where the wind lashed the windows and rattled the boarding. Across the desk lay scattered notes, two pens and a broken pencil, books piled high and a coffee cup from Paris – a single cup, perhaps a Benjaminian reminder of the occupant as failed collector, after all he asserts 'The interior was the place of refuge of Art. The collector was then true inhabitant of the interior.'[5] Does Benjamin, in suggesting that the interior is there to house our collections – our prehistoric markings on cave walls – see it as a conscious thing measuring one's knowledge and ability in relation to societies' values? Or does he confuse enclosure with interior?

'This melancholy lady, who loved wandering in the fields and thinking about unusual things ...'[6]

    a thousand pities. Thinking is never easy; not when laughed and sneered at, and forced to anger; not here in late October; when spring is coming and one wave intermingles with another as a thousand white-horses fringe the edge of the earth. I leave my room and make for the ocean hesitating momentarily to take from the shelf a *Thousand Plateaus*, Deleuze and Guattari's attempt to displace prevailing centrisms, unities and strata, and read how in *The Waves*, Woolf's 'Bernard' has an individuality designating a multiplicity: 'Bernard and the school of fish.'[7] Nothing seems static any more. Think. Think – that thinking involves 'a wrenching of concepts away from their usual configurations, outside the systems in which they have a home, and outside the structures of recognition that constrain thought to the already known.'[8] Could interior be thought of as haecceity – an element of existence on which individuality depends? Might the non-human architectural body need to be rethought away from oppositional dualisms such as structure/decoration, exterior/interior, masculine/feminine, etc., that continue an unhelpful homogenised binary position? For architecture (to have suggested that the inside is also the outside and the outside is also the inside) fares no better, since 'Bisexuality is no better concept than the separateness of the sexes.'[9] The architectural body. The body. The Deleuze and Guattari body is discussed not in terms of binary opposites but as a 'discontinuous, non-totalisable series of processes, organs, flows, energies, corporeal substances and incorporeal events, speeds and durations,' through 'the body without organs.'[10] In suggesting that a body is not defined by the form that determines it, one could say that room becomes interior in a molecular or atomic sense and that becoming-interior is ever-changing.

When later I survey this room in an evening light that hides things in shadows and catches others in lingering rays, it is day becoming night: and this room is my life's wealth, it is 'decorated' by numerous things self-gathered and inherited, both consciously and unconsciously, it is room becoming interior; after all with a room of one's own, one is free to do this. Are these really 'collections' or the emphasised traces that Benjamin asserts we leave behind in the interior along with everyday imprints on loose covers and protectors?[11] Or, as Woolf observes 'there are many rooms – many Bernards,' and that the room could determine our way of being, with different rooms reflecting different aspects of character, or character changes to suit the room.[12] The desk and reading, the room and anger, the door and coming and going, the threshold and pausing. Multiple narrations are now possible that subvert the form of the room (as internal) for the interior.

'Lamps were being lit and an indescribable change had come over ... '[13]
    the land as I draw the blinds and light the lamp, not of power or reason, nor the one 'in the spine [that] does not light on beef and prunes,'[14] but of the interior the vast inner land, the outback; the outcast.

With this in mind I opened Edith Wharton's *Decoration of Houses*, to find an advocation of classical regularity made through an appeal for a rationally determined relation between architecture and its parts. She reveals that the ordered plan removes unexpected encounters and expresses carefully controlled patterns of movement, forming a 'projection of the idealized self, a retreat, a series of protective enclosures.'[15] Planned in relation to social traditions her own house 'The Mount' constructs the interior in relation to patterns of movement, but which in turn can be read as 'patterns of stillness.'[16] And the interior is a result of decorating in relation to a controlled and ordered set of spatial constructs, that places social and societal encounters at the mercy of a greater force. But what of this argument that advocates decoration as adding to: yet is subservient to architecture; does it realise the dilemma faced by the interior; does it release the interior from the bounds of architecture? You see whereas Wharton depicts the plight of women from a woman's perspective no such position is afforded the interior which is still 'in a certain sense, "inside" architecture and its history.'[17]

Looking back I saw that Woolf's writing on the room is made in relation to the outside, the room is a refuge, a place of order, 'dry land,' whilst the outside is dark and watery, the site of psychological and physical chaos.[18] I pondered this, took my dry Parisian cup and made some dark watery coffee understanding as I did her reference to the 'deep waters of depression' and the 'dark places of psychology.'[19] The room as a metaphor for the mind is sometimes full and occupied, but what if it is locked or even empty, because for Woolf although empty rooms are rooms 'devoid of human beings,' they still endure. Could it be that the interior is constructed in relation to a physical and mental being; a place of reflection and withdrawal from the chaos of 'out there?' But what if 'out there' becomes ordered and controlled, as occurred with renaissance planning and the interior became re-described from the city, then there would be no withdrawing for they are spatially the same. Might the descent of Lily Bart, the heroine of Wharton's *The House of Mirth*, from a rigidly ordered plan to one of complete disorder culminating in her tenement room suicide, be evidence of the necessary beneficial correlation of order for the interior, in which dominance and continuity are maintained, or the inevitable ending for one that strives to subvert an order that is endemic in a patri-architectural society? Was her 'downward path … through a series of actual houses'[20] an inevitable descent? Is the nineteenth century practice of covering surfaces both a cry and an attempt to escape this imposed order that in certain circumstances leads to madness and suicide?

But then again this refuge, this fortress protecting from the confusion without, may also be 'a prison, constructed of conventions and illusions,'[21] that we return to with predictability. And what if that confusion and pointlessness is brought within the prison or place of confinement, generating madness as befell the heroine of *The Yellow Wallpaper*?[22] Might this be the same pointlessness of bringing the city within the home, and its haunting ability to control a situation in a curious undefined way? Might our sense of 'interiorness,' our interpretation of the interior depend on whether we, as inmates, are confined of our own accord, have encounters we initiate, and the manner in which we re-live memories and are moved by them?

'And I looked at the bookcase again. There were …'[23]

the classic architectural theorists, Vitruvius, Alberti, Laugier, Le-Duc, Le Corbusier and many others; great men who had experienced anger, sorrow, pain, suffering, joy, love, birth and death from both afar and within their rooms, within their memories. Could the same be said of these men? I pictured them in their chambers described by ornaments and decorations; the surfaces enriched with their traces; how they moved from room to room as their minds went from thought to thought; how they escaped inclement weather and drew chairs close to fires; how much time was spent within the buildings yet none thought to include a chapter, book or lamp on the interior. Did Alberti as he divided the whole into homogenous parts, through *partitio*, *area* and *proportio*, think ornament only in relation to physical form when he so beautifully suggests it 'has the character of something attached.'[24] The-wind-blows-the-curtain; the-door-creaked-as-it-opened? Did Alberti cleanse the room and re-surface it white in order to arrest and mask the fluidity of becoming-interior? Did the 'Abbe' use the frontispiece Muse to illuminate an architectural ambiguity between structure and decoration, in order to objectify and fix a fluid state?[25] Let us look closer at Laugier's 'influential' image that was used to 'point out' or 'point to' the ancients as the object of desire, in the process of which an opposed organism, a dominant history is fabricated[26] for the primitive hut, one in which structure and form is privileged over the decorative and ornamental. Would Laugier's sister have 'pointed to,' if she could have produced an equivalent work? Might she be tempted to see not objects and 'forms,' but relations of movement and rest, moments of walking, crying and singing that occur alongside things; becoming; a moment that sees room becoming-interior, as when Woolf cried 'The thin dog is running in the road, this dog is the road?'[27] Might the Muse be Laugier's sister, that would amuse. As Woolf realised, Shakespeare's sister could never be, so is the fate of Laugier's sister who would find her maternal space obliterated and her destiny sealed behind masculine modes of thought. This as Grosz observes, is the construction of an 'artificial' concept of architecture utilising a spatiality that reflects men's own representations.[28] Further, if one transposed her argument one could say that architecture in disavowing this maternal debt has left the interior in dereliction, homeless; it has touched itself from the outside (the city) in order to homogenise and recapture the sensation of the inside of a body; it has hollowed out its own 'interiors' and projected them outward and now requires interiors as supports for this hollowed space.

'Thus I concluded, shutting ... '[29]

Marc-Antoine Laugier's life and pushing away the rest. I mused how the ex-Jesuit priest's desire for order, simplicity and naturalness reflected a male-centred Spartan existence; one that accorded with a desire by theorists to bring the wild excesses of women, home and decoration under control. Perhaps the classic architectural theorists, still in the bookcase, could not write the interior because it lacks determination: like haecceities they are indeterminate. But I wonder is there – in this text – a nugget of pure truth to take away, shepherded from an avalanche of books. Or has it remained distracted, caught up in a web of its own making. I turned to Woolf again to see what light she cast in the text and found it near the window. That is, in another use of light. Used to differentiate between types of light, the window is protective and transparent revealing both the external light of nature and the controlled light of within, from which the sun's light is associated with truth while candles and lamps foster illusions and circumscribe our world.[30] This world-of-within I like. When we encounter this candle-lit world, one is struck by the manner in which the interior concerns 'capacities to affect,'[31] rather than it being defined or described by fixed moments or things such as geometry, order, artifacts and objects. But it becomes events, 'in assemblages that are inseparable from an hour, a season, an atmosphere, an air, a life.'[32]

Never again will Mrs Dalloway say of herself,
'I am this, I am that ... '.[33] (...p 21)

343

Notes

1 Virginia Woolf, *A Room of One's Own* [1929], M Barrett (ed), Penguin Books (London), 1993, p 3.
2 Woolf, *Room of One's Own*, p 4.
3 Woolf, *Room of One's Own*, p 3.
4 Woolf, *Room of One's Own*, p 3.
5 Walter Benjamin, *Charles Baudelaire: A Lyric Poet in the Era of High Capitalism*, trans Harry Zohn, NLB (London), 1973, p 168.
6 Woolf, *Room of One's Own*, p 55.
7 Gilles Deleuze and Felix Guattari, *A Thousand Plateaus, Capitalism and Schizophrenia*, trans B Massumi, University of Minnesota Press (Minneapolis), 1987, p 252.
8 Elizabeth Grosz, *Space, Time and Perversion*, Allen and Unwin Pty Ltd (St Leonards), 1995, p 129.
9 Deleuze and Guattari, *Thousand Plateaus*, p 276.
10 Elizabeth Grosz, *Volatile Bodies: Towards a Corporeal Feminism*, Allen and Unwin Pty Ltd (St Leonards), 1994, p 164.
11 Benjamin, *Charles Baudelaire*, p 169.
12 C Ruth Miller, *Virginia Woolf: The Frames of Art and Life*, St Martin's Press (New York), 1988, p 84.
13 Woolf, *Room of One's Own*, p 35.
14 Woolf, *Room of One's Own*, p 16.
15 Edith Wharton and Ogden Codman, *The Decoration of Houses*, Scribner's (New York), 1892, p 73.
16 Wharton and Codman, *Decoration of Houses*, p 74.
17 Grosz, *Space, Time and Perversion*, p 136.
18 Miller, *Virginia Woolf*, p 78.
19 Miller, *Virginia Woolf*, p 78.
20 Judith Fryer, *Felicitous Space: The Imaginative Structures of Edith Wharton and Willa Cather*, University of North Carolina Press (Chapel Hill), 1986, p 75.
21 Miller, *Virginia Woolf*, p 81.
22 Charlotte Perkins Gilman, *The Yellow Wallpaper* [1899], Virago, (London), 1981.
23 Woolf, *Room of One's Own*, p 78.
24 Leon Battista Alberti, *On the Art of Building in Ten Books*, trans Joseph Rykwert, Neil Leach and Robert Tavernor, MIT Press (Cambridge, Mass), 1988, p 156.
25 Marc-Antoine Laugier, *An Essay on Architecture* [1753], trans Wolfgang and Anni Herrmann, Hennessey and Ingalls (Los Angeles), 1977.
26 Deleuze and Guattari, *Thousand Plateaus*, p 276.
27 Deleuze and Guattari, *Thousand Plateaus*, p 263.
28 Grosz, *Space, Time and Perversion*, p 121.
29 Woolf, *Room of One's Own*, p 50.
30 Miller, *Virginia Woolf*, p 80.
31 Deleuze and Guattari, *Thousand Plateaus*, p 261.
32 Deleuze and Guattari, *Thousand Plateaus*, p 262.
33 Virginia Woolf, *Mrs Dalloway* [1925], Grafton Books (London), 1976, p 13.

Mark Taylor, 'Architecture and Interior: A Roam of One's Own', *IDEA*, vol 1 no 2, 2001, pp 14–22.
© Mark Taylor. Reprinted by permission of IDEA – Interior Design/Interior Architecture Educators Association.
(Excerpt pp 15–21)

Boredom and Bedroom: The Suppression of the Habitual

Georges Teyssot

psychological ● 1996

space

19th–20th century

Psychological disturbance, whether from disease, deprivation, or suppression of the comforting habitual and repetitive nature of everyday life, forms the subject of Georges Teyssot's essay. In this critical theorised historical account he discusses privateness and inwardness through painterly representation, in which the world outside the window is clearly distinct from the interior, the inner world of inner consciousness. Windows, mirrors and reflections acquire similar status when the mirroring of interior life, as an exaggeration of introspection, turns into boredom.

Happiness enjoys itself completely only if it doubles its own image in the mirror of reflection. Happiness wants to be both subject and object: the subject of its object and the object of its subject. There is no happiness if one is alone; happiness must be shared, it needs a public. If there is no one else, one needs a mirror to reflect the self. The nineteenth-century Danish philosopher Søren Kierkegaard, living in a small apartment, regarded the subject as the only truth and believed that reality consisted only of his thinking within his room. Anything that happened outside his window, any public representation, was merely an illusion – exactly contrary to what Hegel had been saying in Berlin. Kierkegaard was perhaps the first theorist of privateness, the first theorist of the inwardness that the German had defined under the word *Innerlichkeit*. This 'inwardness' is usually associated with the interiors of middle-class households, which, from a stylistic point of view, described the Biedermeier period between 1820 and 1850.

One might consider the watercolor *Drawing Room in Berlin*, circa 1820–1825, by Johann Erdmann Hummel, a contemporary of Caspar David Friedrich. During this period in Germany, a genre was developing within painting that represented the space between an interior and what is outside, seen through a window. Within this space is an 'inner world,' the world of the 'inner conscious.' Occurring in this inner world are both personal feeling and private thinking, moments traditionally identified by idealism as 'reflection.' Thus inner space becomes the space of reflection. In the seventeenth century, private space was often defined as the place of the relationship between an individual and God, the place of prayer. During the eighteenth and nineteenth centuries, this place was transformed into a space of intimacy. Intimate spaces, then, are those where the individual may have his own reflections and feelings. Were one homeless or without 'a room of one's own,' one could not belong to this world of reflection.

Hummel's painting makes a clear division between the interior and the world of things outside the window. The large room is like a box, on one side of which the viewer is situated. A mirror centered between the two windows reflects the closed door on the opposite wall, the wall where the observer, or the painter, should be. But the observer is absent. The viewer of the painting looks into a room that looks back at him through a mirror; but he does not appear. One might interpret this absence as an inclusion of the subject in the room. Because he is not represented within the room, it is as if the subject has become part of the room itself. One might also note the manifold reflections within the room: not only the reflection along the central axis, which emphasizes the general symmetry of its boxlike aspect, but also the reflections that occur among different mirrors. The windows, too, are reflected in the mirrors, by which an important transformation takes place. Both mirrors and windows, because they acquire the same luminosity and chromatic weight, become the same kind of object within this painterly representation. And, if the windows are mirrors, perhaps the exterior is a total illusion: there is no outside world. Here, the outside world is but a kind of representation. One exists only within this *Innerlichkeit*, this inwardness. It has been written that German interiors are ruled 'by the principle of mirroring and doubling.'[1]

Consciousness is recognizing one's image in the mirror; but at the same time, as the individual approaches the self reflected upon the glass, the mirror fogs with one's own breath. The self disappears; an attempt is made to wipe the mirror, yet one cannot help breathing. The image is blurred by a covering mist. This interior refers to happiness, to protection; but it contains as well the seeds of boredom. Perhaps because it protects too much, this mirrored interiority leads to a kind of excess of interior life, an exaggeration of introspection.

The refuge of the interior apparently offered an alternative to boredom, as Benjamin described in his notes on the arcades of Paris: 'Boredom is a warm gray cloth that is padded on its inside with the most glowing, colorful silk lining. Into this cloth we wrap ourselves when we dream. Then we are at home in the arabesques of its lining. But the sleeper looks gray and bored under it. And then, when he wakes up and wants to tell what he dreamt of, he communicates often only this boredom. For who would be able to turn inside-out in one motion the lining of time?'[2] Perhaps it is possible to turn inside-out this lining of time, which is not only the arabesque of the box, but also the design of the carpet, of the wall, and of the reflection between the mirrors and the windows. To understand this relationship between the subject and the mirror, one might examine Léon Spilliaert's washed pastel drawing *Self-Portrait at the Mirror* of 1908 or observe Max Klinger's etching *The Philosopher* of 1909, from the series *Of Death*, illustrating the tense relation among the notions of interior, reflection, and introspection. These images might, in turn, be associated with the mirror in which Igitur, a literary creation of Stéphane Mallarmé, sees himself. Here, in one of his most obscure and interesting texts, the poet describes a collapse among the past, the present, and the possibility of a future. At the moment of his suicide attempt, as Igitur sees himself in the mirror, past, present, and future merge to form the pure time of boredom, crystallizing only at the instant of death: 'The understood past of his race which weighs on him in the sensation of finiteness, the hour of the clock precipitating this ennui in heavy, smothering time, and his awaiting of the accomplishment of the future, form pure time, or ennui.' As he dies, Igitur searches for himself in vain in 'the mirror turned into boredom.'[3]

Two kinds of experience have been defined: First is that of the dandy or *flâneur*, the man who has time to waste. He strolls in the streets, stopping at anything that happens, any event, any accident. The city and the crowd are a huge spectacle for him. Second, on the other side, is that of the philosopher, best personified by Kierkegaard, or the man within the bourgeois *intérieur*. Theodor Adorno called Kierkegaard the *flâneur* who promenades in his room: 'the world only appears to him reflected by pure inwardness.'[4] For the philosopher, 'inwardness' and 'melancholy' are the constituents, 'the contours of "domesticity," which ... constitute[s] the arena of existence.' Adorno continues: 'He who looks into the window mirror, however, is a private person, solitary, inactive, and separated from the economic processes of production. The window mirror testifies to objectlessness – it casts into the apartment only the semblance of things – and isolated privacy. Mirror and mourning hence belong together.'[5] In Adorno's reading of Kierkegaard, one finds this remarkable connection between the mirror and the notion of boredom.   (... p 53)

Notes

1   Ulrike Brunotte, 'Innerwelten/Inner Worlds', *Daidalos*, 36, June 1990, speaks of 'Prinzip der Spiegelung und Verdoppelung'.
2   Walter Benjamin, *Das Passagen-Werk*, Rolf Tiedemann (ed), vol 5, bks 1 and 2, of the *Gesammelte Schriften*, Suhrkamp Verlag (Frankfurt am Main), 1982, bk 1, D2a, p 1.
3   Stéphane Mallarmé, 'Igitur ou la folie d'Elbehnon', *Oeuvres complètes*, Gallimard (Paris), 1985, p 440: 'Le passé compris de sa race qui pèse sur lui en la sensation de fini, l'heure de la pendule précipitant cet ennui en temps lourd, étouffant, et son attente de l'accomplissement du futur, forment du temps pur, ou de l'ennui;' English trans in Grange Woolley, *Stéphane Mallarmé, 1824–1898*, Madison (New Jersey), 1942, p 161.
4   Theodor W Adorno, *Kierkegaard: Construction of the Aesthetic* [1933], trans Robert Hullot-Kentor, University of Minnesota Press (Minneapolis), 1989, chap 2, 'Constitution of Inwardness', p 41.
5   Adorno, *Kierkegaard*, p 42, 'Spiegel und Trauer gehören darum zusammen'.

Georges Teyssot, 'Boredom and Bedroom: The Suppression of the Habitual', *Assemblage*, no 30, 1996, pp 44–61.
© 1996 by the Massachusetts Institute of Technology. Reprinted by permission of MIT Press Journals.
(Excerpt pp 50–3)

Visitors

Henry David Thoreau

Henry David Thoreau's interior is a small cabin made of scavenged building materials deliberately distanced from society and the luxuries of culture. While such a constructed space houses a place for introspection, deep self-reflection and interiority of the most profound sort, the single-room dwelling is seeped with influences and inferences to the complexity of social interaction necessary to confirm existence as well as the essential accoutrements to live. As a writer and poet in the first half of the nineteenth century, Thoreau articulates upon the purpose and meaning of chairs and how, as modest chattels, they signify the rules of exchange and engagement spatially and philosophically.

My furniture, part of which I made myself, and the rest cost me nothing of which I have not rendered an account, consisted of a bed, a table, a desk, three chairs, a looking-glass three inches in diameter, a pair of tongs and andirons, a kettle, a skillet, and a frying-pan, a dipper, a wash-bowl, two knives and forks, three plates, one cup, one spoon, a jug for oil, a jug for molasses, and a japanned lamp. None is so poor that he need sit on a pumpkin. That is shiftlessness. There is a plenty of such chairs as I like best in the village garrets to be had for taking them away. Furniture! Thank God, I can sit and I can stand without the aid of a furniture warehouse. What man but a philosopher would not be ashamed to see his furniture packed in a cart and going up country exposed to the light of heaven and the eyes of men, a beggarly account of empty boxes? That is Spaulding's furniture. I could never tell from inspecting such a load whether it belonged to a so-called rich man or a poor one; the owner always seemed poverty-stricken. Indeed, the more you have of such things the poorer you are. Each load looks as if it contained the contents of a dozen shanties; and if one shanty is poor, this is a dozen times as poor. Pray, for what do we *move* ever but to get rid of our furniture, our *exuviæ*; at last to go from this world to another newly furnished, and leave this to be burned? It is the same as if all these traps were buckled to a man's belt, and he could not move over the rough country where our lines are cast without dragging them – dragging his trap. He was a lucky fox that left his tail in the trap. The muskrat will gnaw his third leg off to be free. No wonder man has lost his elasticity. How often he is at a dead set! 'Sir, if I may be so bold, what do you mean by a dead set?' If you are a seer, whenever you meet a man you will see all that he owns, ay, and much that he pretends to disown, behind him, even to his kitchen furniture and all the trumpery which he saves and will not burn, and he will appear to be harnessed to it and making what headway he can. I think that the man is at a dead set who has got through a knot-hole or gateway where his sledge load of furniture cannot follow him. I cannot but feel compassion when I hear some trig, compact-looking man, seemingly free, all girded and ready, speak of his 'furniture,' as whether it is insured or not. 'But what shall I do with my furniture!' My gay butterfly is entangled in a spider's web then. Even those who seem for a long while not to have any, if you inquire more narrowly you will find have some stored in somebody's barn. I look upon England to-day as an old gentleman who is travelling with a great deal of baggage, trumpery which has accumulated from long housekeeping, which he has not the courage to burn; great trunk, little trunk, bandbox and bundle. Throw away the first three at least. It would surpass the powers of a well man now-a-days to take up his bed and walk, and I should certainly advise a sick one to lay down his bed and run. When I have met an immigrant tottering under a bundle which contained his all – looking like an enormous wen which had grown out of the nape of his neck – I have pitied him, not because that was his all, but because he had all *that* to carry. If I have got to drag my trap, I will take care that it be a light one and do not nip me in a vital part. But perchance it would be wisest never to put one's paw into it.

I would observe, by the way, that it costs me nothing for curtains, for I have no gazers to shut out but the sun and moon, and I am willing that they should look in. The moon will not sour milk nor taint meat of mine, nor will the sun injure any furniture or fade my carpet, and if he is sometimes too warm a friend, I find it still better economy to retreat behind some curtain which nature has provided, than to add a single item to the details of housekeeping. A lady once offered me a mat, but as I had no room to spare within the house, nor time to spare within or without to shake it, I declined it, preferring to wipe my feet on the sod before my door. It is best to avoid the beginnings of evil.   (… p 59)

I had three chairs in my house; one for solitude, two for friendship, three for society. When visitors came in larger and unexpected numbers there was but the third chair for them all, but they generally economised the room by standing up. It is surprising how many great men and women a small house will contain. I have had twenty-five or thirty souls, with their bodies, at once under my roof, and yet we often parted without being aware that we had come very near to one another. Many of our houses, both public and private, with their almost innumerable apartments, their huge halls and their cellars for the storage of wines and other munitions of peace, appear to me extravagantly large for their inhabitants. They are so vast and magnificent that the latter seem to be only vermin which infest them. I am surprised when the herald blows his summons before some Tremont, or Astor, or Middlesex House, to see come creeping out over the piazza for all inhabitants a ridiculous mouse, which soon again slinks into some hole in the pavement.

One inconvenience I sometimes experienced in so small a house, the difficulty of getting to a sufficient distance from my guest when we began to utter the big thoughts in big words. You want room for your thoughts to get into sailing trim, and run a course or two before they make their port. The bullet of your thought must have overcome its lateral and ricochet motion, and fallen into its last and steady course, before it reaches the ear of the hearer, else it may plough out again through the side of his head. Also, our sentences wanted room to unfold and form their columns in the interval. Individuals, like nations, must have suitable broad and natural boundaries, even a considerable neutral ground, between them. I have found it a singular luxury to talk across the pond to a companion on the opposite side. In my house we were so near that we could not begin to hear – we could not speak low enough to be heard, as when you throw two stones into calm water so near that they break each other's undulations. If we are merely loquacious and loud talkers, then we can afford to stand very near together, cheek-by-jowl, and feel each other's breath; but if we speak reservedly and thoughtfully, we want to be farther apart, that all animal heat and moisture may have a chance to evaporate. If we would enjoy the most intimate society with that in each of us which is without, or above, being spoken to, we must not only be silent, but commonly so far apart bodily that we cannot possibly hear each other's voice in any case. Referred to this standard, speech is for the convenience of those who are hard of hearing; but there are many fine things which we cannot say if we have to shout. As the conversation began to assume a loftier and grander tone, we gradually shoved our chairs farther apart till they touched the wall in opposite corners, and then commonly there was not room enough.   (... p 126)

Henry David Thoreau, *Walden, or Life in the Woods* [1854], Oxford University Press (London, New York and Toronto), 1906.
Reprinted by permission of Oxford University Press.
(Excerpts pp 57–9, 125–6)

The Chic Interior and the Feminine Modern

Lisa Tiersten

gender · 1996

late 19th century decoration

Historian Lisa Tiersten's feminist reading of late nineteenth-century Parisian life credits bourgeois women as the guardians of class and gender identity through their use of interior décor as a form of self-expression. Embracing the everyday as an aesthetic experience, such housewives were considered self-learned artists. Their skill at creating comfortable and intimate interiors previews the modernist's value of the creative individual, whereby body, self and interior are reflective and in harmony with one another.

The construction of the housewife-as-artist in the discourse on decorating may be characterized as an essentially modernist undertaking. In contrast to the traditional feminine role of refined appreciator of and midwife to the arts, the bourgeois woman of taste of the late nineteenth century was portrayed as a modern artist, herself a creator. In the modernist spirit, decorating was perceived as a form of self-expression, an exercise in the cultivation and expression of one's particular artistic individuality. Accordingly, the style and decor of a room were to aim toward the creation of an aesthetic harmony and unity out of disparate elements, rather than conformity to a set standard.

Although the Impressionist art of the 1870s was intended by its practitioners and seen by the bourgeois public to be deliberately anti-bourgeois, modernist aesthetics were gradually assimilated by bourgeois culture over the course of the next twenty years. The immense popularity of Impressionist art among the middle-class public of the 1890s, in contrast to Impressionism's negative reception by the same public twenty years earlier, is one index of the influence of modernism on bourgeois aesthetics; another is the adaptation of a modernist rhetoric of self-expression by the fashion magazines, home decorating manuals, and advertising of the late nineteenth century. By the turn of that century, the notion of an 'art of everyday life' was as much a guide to chic for an emergent middle-class elite as it was a slogan of the avant-garde.

Anticipating the way Art Deco clothing of the 1920s mimicked the Cubist geometric perspective, and the advertising of the 1930s adopted Surrealist iconography, decorative arts reformers and journalists of the ladies' press of the 1890s introduced modernist aesthetic values into home decorating by establishing parity between art and decor. The numerous decorating handbooks of the period disseminated the views of these writers among bourgeois housewives, expounding rules of design which echoed the tenets of modernism: self-expression, truth to materials, harmony of color, and the construction of an aesthetic unity. Decorative arts reformers such as Vachon taught women that 'a piece of furniture is just as valuable as a painting,' and that the decorator's tasks of juxtaposition and arrangement were as creative as any aspect of artistic production. They instructed bourgeois women to think of decorating as a form of painting and to compose a room as they would a canvas, paying scrupulous attention to the distribution of color and light, and the organization of lines and angles.[1]

A paradigm of modernism that was feminine and domestic was thus elaborated in these handbooks. This paradigm differed in important ways from canonical modernism, but was nonetheless fundamentally related to it, in ideological and, to a lesser extent, in stylistic terms. As ethos, to be modern was to be individual. As method, the feminine modern was based primarily on techniques of imitation, appropriation, and pastiche of a variety of historical and modern stylistic motifs; yet, even in its reliance on the past, it was oriented psychically and aesthetically toward the present and future. Bourgeois historicism may be seen as a response to a sense of aesthetic weightlessness; decor played the role not so much of creating a past or emulating the culture of the aristocracy, but rather of forging a particular bourgeois aesthetic out of disparate elements. The historicism of the *fin-de-siècle* bourgeois salon commodified the past: it invoked an attitude toward history not unlike that of the consumer toward the goods in a department store, and far removed from that of the spectator toward the objects in a museum.

Art historians have tended to overlook the evidence of the feminine modern, taking modernists too much at their word by conceiving of the clinical eye of the male *flâneur* as the heart of the modernist project. In fact, the perceived polarity between masculine high modernism and feminine decorative domestic culture concealed an underlying intimacy between the two aesthetics. Although there existed no direct female analogue to the male *flâneur*, modernism did engender the creation of a feminine point of view, one which was situated in the bourgeois interior rather than in the street. This aesthetic at first competed with the dominant male forms (a conflict manifest in the opposition between modernist painting and the decorative arts movement of the 1880s and 1890s), but by the time of the post-war Art Deco movement came to complement the modernist mainstream. Conversely, the Impressionists' belief in the sensory basis of aesthetics implied that women's supposedly sensate natures were intrinsically aesthetic and imbued the domestic ideals of comfort and intimacy with aesthetic purpose and meaning. For the decorating expert Emile Cardon, for example, the aesthetic knowledge required by the painter was the same as that required of the housewife-decorator; the only difference between the two was that women who attained this knowledge came to it by instinct, and not by a rational learning process: 'woman, no matter how incomplete her artistic education, has an innate feeling for artistic things, and the most fine and delicate taste; she lacks the science of art, but she guesses; she doesn't know, she feels.'[2] By emphasizing the decorative, defining creativity as reactive rather than active, and aestheticizing the everyday, modernism unintentionally mobilized what were regarded as elements of feminine subjectivity.

However, early modernists themselves ardently disavowed these 'feminine' elements. By maintaining a rigid distinction between high art and decorative art, between the male and female spheres of artistic practice, modernists sought to protect art from its appropriation by amateurs and – as in the case of many other male occupations – to professionalize in order to prevent the entry of women (among others) into the discipline. More importantly, the decorative art commentators and journalists who codified the feminine modern themselves drew on a number of fundamental high-modernist assumptions. Thus, even within the popular discourse of decorating, basic distinctions were implicitly preserved between the feminine modern and the high modern. Although they characterized the bourgeois woman as an artist, decorative arts reformers themselves ultimately permitted the male modernist to retain a virtual monopoly in the production of high art. Even though they celebrated the housewife, rather than the male professional, as the creator of the domestic interior, they relegated her to a lower sphere in the aesthetic hierarchy.

The confining of women to a lesser aesthetic role was accomplished in several ways. First, the power ceded women was more or less limited to the spheres of the home and of consumption. To that extent, decorative arts reformers and capitalists formed an unintended, and at times uneasy, alliance in mediating modernism to bourgeois women. Decorative arts reformers were concerned with the preservation of the crafts and with standards of decorative beauty in the age of mechanized production; capitalists wished to promote consumption by elevating it from a household routine into an artistic and personal ritual. In a sense, decorative arts reformers and journalists for the ladies' press inhabited a middle ground between the commercial marketplace and the world of high art: they accepted the machine age and the cultural power of the bourgeoisie – in short, modernity – and sought to create an aesthetic out of these building blocks. But as much as they sought to educate the housewife's aesthetic instinct toward this end, they clearly limited her purview to shopping for the home and arranging its objects.

Second, the subordination of the feminine modern was accomplished by positing a feminine intimacy with objects so great that the bourgeois woman herself became a part of the decor. The decorating guides conveyed two conflicting messages to women: that they were artists, yet that they were themselves objects of art. Decorating handbooks and magazine columns so emphasized the need for aesthetic harmony and unity between the woman and her home that the *body of* the bourgeois housewife became an integral part of the interior, a decorative object to be harmonized with the other objects of the home. 'Use your rugs and curtains to dress yourself,' suggested one journalist. Bourgeois wives were not to select the fabrics in vogue, but to pick those which best blended with their hair-color and skin tone; blondes were said to be best set off by rooms with accents of sea-green, sky-blue, or cherry-red, while brunettes were supposedly flattered by backgrounds of olive, gold, or deep blue. As the journalist Marcelle Tinayre put it, 'Our home ... is the extension ... of our personality. Our furniture, our bibelots, chosen by us, reveal our secret tastes, our ideas, our conceptions of happiness and beauty. When an unknown visitor awaits us alone in our salon, he first meets our objects, the witnesses and confidants of our lives.'[3]

Tinayre portrayed the bourgeois woman as a dedicated consumer who gathered objects for the purpose of her private delectation. Her remarks pointed toward a broader distinction drawn between masculine and feminine modes of display. Men were said to exhibit objects in both public and private venues for the spectatorial pleasure of others; women, by contrast, did not so much display objects as surround themselves with them. Men collected objects as evidence of their erudition and taste, or of their economic and social power, but these objects remained separate from the man himself. By contrast, the objects in a woman's home played a synecdochal rather than a symbolic role in relation to her identity; a room decorated by the bourgeois housewife was ultimately not so much her creation as an extension of her very being. In this intimate, organic relationship posited between woman and thing, women became the objects, more than the subjects, of modern art.

Finally, the domain of the feminine modern was limited to the extent that women were taught to express themselves artistically, but not that they were 'original,' in the way that male artists were said to be. As an eclectic style, the bourgeois decorative did in fact place new emphasis on the choice and, especially, the juxtaposition of objects, and exert new 'creative' demands on the housewife. However, despite the glorification of the chic woman's creativity, the concept of originality implicit in chic was considerably more limited than that of artistic modernism. In contrast to the supposed freedom of the modernist artist, the chic woman was confined to skilful variation within a more or less rigidly-defined code, her originality measured by her talent for the composition of already existing objects and styles. Henri de Noussane hinted broadly at the distinction between feminine decoration and masculine art-making:

> I don't ask you to *create* a style. Just arrange the furniture ... to your own taste, aided by your imagination ... You have old furniture, some imitations of ancient pieces,

some modern trinkets, a portrait by Largillière, a landscape by Corot: be inventive in the play of the rugs and wall-hangings, and in harmonizing the disparate elements to make an elegant unity. You will thus be able to add a personal note ... to this composite mélange.

According to the journalist Louise de Salles, the bourgeois woman knew 'how to be original within the limits of the permissible.'[4]

Despite the rhetoric of individuality used to figure the bourgeois woman, she was construed as a talented imitator as much as an inventor, an *objet d'art* as much as an artist. Although the fashion journalists, decorating experts, and advertisers of the late nineteenth century depicted decorating as a form of self-expression, they also drew upon broad cultural assumptions about femininity which were ultimately incompatible with their conception of art; while they ceded new aesthetic power to the bourgeoisie, they simultaneously undermined and restricted that power by reinscribing the feminine and decorative modern within the hierarchy elaborated by canonical modernism, promoting the aesthetic development of bourgeois women not only to help them become artists, but also to make them into good wives and smart shoppers. Like the modern artist, the chic woman's originality was said to lie in truth to a personal vision; her best means of realizing that vision, however, was to hone her skills as a consumer. For the modernist artist, on the other hand, the culture of domesticity expanded the purview of art, yielding the rich interior vision and decorative complexity of early twentieth-century painting.   (... p 32)

Notes

1   Marius Vachon, *La belle maison: Principes et lois de l'esthétique pour aménager, meubler, et orner sa demeure*, J Deprelle et M Camus (Lyon), 1925, pp 12–13. The book was based on a course he gave in 1913. See Adeline Daumard, 'Conditions de Logement', *Le Parisien chez lui au XIX siècle*, Archives Nationales (Paris), 1977, for confirmation that nineteenth-century French bourgeois families tended to move and to refurnish their homes several times in a lifetime.
2   Emile Cardon, *L'Art au foyer domestique*, Renouard (Paris), 1884, p 29.
3   Frisette, 'La femme chez elle', *Femina*, no 149, 1 April 1907, p 166; Louise de Salles, 'A propos de l'ameublement de style', *Paris-mode*, 20 January 1892, p 1; Marcelle Tinayre, 'L'Art de parer son foyer', *Femina*, no 221, 1 April 1910, p 189.
4   Henri de Noussane, *Le goût dans l'ameublement*, Firmin-Didot et Cie (Paris), 1896, p 19; Salles, 'A propos de la Parisienne', *Paris-mode*, 20 March 1892, p 1.

Lisa Tiersten, 'The Chic Interior and the Feminine Modern: Home Decorating as High Art in Turn-of-the-Century Paris', *Not At Home: The Suppression of Domesticity in Modern Art and Architecture*, ed and introduced by Christopher Reed, Thames and Hudson (London), 1996. © 1996 Lisa Tiersten. Reprinted by kind permission of Thames and Hudson Ltd, London.
(Excerpt pp 28–32)

Inside Fear: Secret Places and Hidden Spaces in Dwellings

Anne Troutman

psychological space

late 20th century

1997

In this semi-autobiographical account of childhood spaces, Anne Troutman suggests that dwelling holds an intimate, mirror-like relationship so that we dwell in the home and the home dwells in us. This Freudian connection, dividing and connecting inner and outer selves, gathers hidden spaces with visible house, and cloaks the visual with other senses such as fear, terror, fright and anxiety. Discussed this way the storyteller's relived world is contingent on conscious and unconscious associations that redefine the interior through psychological space.

I do not believe the house is a safe place. For me, it is a collision of dream, nightmare, and circumstance, a portrait of the inner life. The primal shelter is also the site of primal fears. Its interiors are a map of the conscious and unconscious, with conscious securities and insecurities visible in the main rooms, and unconscious ones lurking in smaller, peripheral spaces. There is danger in the house. Though I passionately wish for calm nourishing warmth and spaciousness, 'the promise of home,' I am irredeemably caught in the house Edgar Allan Poe built: the one in which someone has been buried behind the wall, alive.

In the middle of the middle of the middle of the night ... in the middle of the middle of the middle of the room ... in the middle of the middle of the middle of your mind ...

In the middle of the land rises the fortification; in the middle of the fortification, the town; in the middle of the town, the castle keep; within the keep, stone walls, the tower; within the tower, walls, attic, eaves; within the walls, stairs and chambers, passages, panels, cabinets, a locked cabinet; within the cabinet ... Within the fortress walls, we believe ourselves safe from whatever lies without, but what of what lies within those walls – what is within the locked cabinet?

Closets, hallways, stairways, doors and windows, attics, basements, eaves, and cabinets expand and contract with fear and desire. They are the night side of the house, in which the identity and security of domestic life is symbolically tested. Incorporated within the house, they form another realm where daily life is displaced, condensed, fragmented.

Disturbing dreams and repressed fears transform surface into cavity, large into minute, the miniature into the overwhelming. These curious places become the refuge of the half-realized. Wishes, dreams, fantasies, fears, desires are the inhabitants of the internal boundaries of our everyday environment: the place of the other, the imagined, the double, the dream.

To get in or out of the back bedroom we have to pass through the linen hall. Narrowed by cabinets that reached upwards along one side, it seems longer than its fourteen feet. The high ceiling disappears in gloom. Only one cabinet towards the end, reserved for linens, smells sweetly of lavender. The rest of the cabinets are filled with old things in boxes and various containers that smell of metal, wood, and oil. The hallway contains a small vertical shaft for an old dumbwaiter that has long since fallen into disuse. The empty shaft, dark and smelling of dust and rope, is the locus of lost things, never to be recovered. It is in these long dusky hallways and cabinets with box latches that my memories of the losses and loneliness of late childhood resonate.

A parallel world inhabits the borders of my waking life. This parallel world is one of refuge and passage, quiet places in which to nest and dream, dark places in which to hide or from which to flee. They are the spaces behind, between and through which I enter the larger 'rooms' of my daily life. They are spaces in which I am usually alone or on the way to somewhere else: the hall, the stairs, the closet, the attic. These spaces, internal to the house's structure yet external to its principal rooms, are the expanded boundaries of the house and my consciousness. They are condensed spaces, tight spaces, often storage spaces, repositories of the activities and memories just beyond and within the main episodes of my life. Without them, I am uncomfortably fastened to the present, limited to the surface.

In my brother's closet there is a small rounded door, no taller than a small child. It is hidden behind all the clothes that are hung on the rack in front of it. The door sticks slightly when pulled and opens into the dark recesses of the eaves where we have our club. We set up our table and benches (old boxes) and store the necessary things to the right, along the length of the eaves as they stretch toward and behind my parents' bedroom, from which there is another small door, like our own, but one that we never use.

As a child, I explore these hidden spaces in order to explore my fears. From within the safety of the house, I can venture to its edges, its perimeters, and, undetected, experiment with facing my fears of the dark, of the adults, of a large noisy world. In the eaves I escape, I huddle, I frighten myself, I cry and whisper and laugh and plot. In this hollow between the self I know and see and the one I do not know and cannot yet see, but sense,

I test my own limits and learn my own secrets. In these hollow walls dwells the unknown, the in-between, the impossible, the unseen. Exploring them, I am hero and master of the unknown; I stare fear in the face and survive.   (... p 147)

As a natural extension of the primal need for protection and nurture, the dwelling is also a defense against the primal fear of loss of protection. Occupying the territory between reality and illusion, the dwelling could be considered a creative 'space' that defends the individual against the anxiety of being alone.[1] My experience of dwelling in dreams and in reality both reflects and mitigates this anxiety. The house is a transitional space – a combination of inner and outer, open and closed, celestial and temporal. It has an 'illusory,' malleable, adaptive character that assimilates unexpressed and unacknowledged anxieties and feelings of loss.

I am inside a small old house. It is picturesque, the kind that you would find in an English countryside village – a comfortable slouch of thatch and wood and stucco. As I explore it, I realize that it is empty, abandoned, and feel the emptiness of the rooms as a cold pressure drawing me deeper inside. I flee out the door and stand on the threshold, my gaze fastened on the door, feeling in its solid dark thickness the shape of foreboding.

Long hallways, dark staircases, and chimney flues are sometimes also the stage of this primal anxiety. Freud distinguished anxiety from fear (*Furcht*). Anxiety is a reaction to a perception of danger; fear requires a definite object of which one is afraid. He defined anxiety as an adaptive function – essential in humans and animals to their survival – in response to the flooding of psychic apparati with stimuli. He considered birth the first experience of anxiety, later the absence of the mother, whose presence is essential to the gratification of instinctual demands.

I am climbing upward through an endless series of rooms. The rooms become smaller, tighter, darker until finally I am within a wall, climbing an old staircase. It twists and winds and sometimes levels off, but always become tighter and more uncomfortable, until I can barely fit my shoulders through the next opening. Disheartened and afraid, I rest on the landing.   (... p 151)

Sensuous detailing within the skin of a dwelling has always been an emblem of security in my life, making comprehensible even the grandest spaces to my senses. I think the security of detail stems from the period of early childhood, when the child, beginning to distinguish itself from 'mother,' relies on the acquisition of increased physical capacities to bring the external world into grasp and focus. Houses that I remember with texture and detail in their structure – window, floor, door, walls – feel safe to me; inhabited by smells, sounds, textures, and detail, they mitigate the anxiety of the outside world and hone my focus and insight, giving me a sense of comfort.

I am sitting on a horse-hair pillow covered in green velvet, inside the window. I can smell the dusty scent of the old velvet and feel the coolness of the small-paned leaded window on my cheek. I study the soft joints of the solder. We slept in an old bed that sank in the middle and whose headboard was filled with ancient National Geographics that we used to pore over after our parents said goodnight (oh spears and large dangling breasts!) There are two old pump organs in the room with foot pedals for air and hundreds of ivory knobs promising exotic sounds and combinations ... tympanum, flute, voice ... at the foot of the bed is an old tallboy; in the drawers are thousands of treasures: poker chips, golf tees, polished stones.

In counterpoint to the safety of detail and things experienced as near are the dream spaces of terror and fright that are claustrophobic: spaces diminishing abnormally or spiraling endlessly, creating a sense of distance and emptiness, endlessness, unreachableness – an unfriendly confusion of inside and outside.

The back bedroom is the only room in the apartment except the kitchen that is directly connected to the back stair and thus to the basement sixteen stories below. A large heavy metal door with two locks, a bolt, and a chain divides this dark room from the back hall. The wind whistles through the shaft, and we hear strange noises at all hours.

Like the storyteller's hypnotic suggestion to enter the space of his story at more and more intimate scales until the voice seems to come from within, we daily recreate within our dwellings the intimate internal landscape of our fantasies, the spaces of our primal needs and fears. Consciously and unconsciously, we assign meaning to every surface, every cavity, visible and invisible until certain types of spaces become associated with specific feelings and begin to form pockets or sites for the contents of our inner lives. From within these pockets we may occasionally glimpse our hopes and desires or sense our fears and anxieties.   (... p 156)

Note

1   'The capacity to create such an illusion [of transitional phenomena] defends the child against the anxiety of being alone, without the mother', Laurie Adams, *Art and Psychoanalysis*, Harper Collins (New York), 1993, p 178.

Anne Troutman, 'Inside Fear: Secret Places and Hidden Spaces in Dwellings', Nan Ellin (ed), *Architecture of Fear*, Princeton Architectural Press (New York), 1997.
© 1997 Nan Ellin. Reprinted by permission of Anne Troutman.
(Excerpts pp 143–56)

The Pleasure of Architecture

Bernard Tschumi

political ● 1977

late 20th century space

In this excerpt, architect and philosopher Bernard Tschumi champions pleasure through words such as decadence, eroticism, excess, sensual, geometry, bondage and voluptuous. This is undertaken with the knowledge that in modern architectural theory pleasure is considered decadent, even sacrilegious. Appealing to the subjective and the non-dialectic, he elucidates numerous fragments that constitute architecture's figural mask. And while Tschumi asserts that such pleasure is located within each of us as individuals and our desire to reconcile desire with reason, he positions it relative to architecture's ability to instigate social, cultural and political change.

In the following paragraphs, I will attempt to show that today the pleasure of architecture may lie both inside *and* outside such oppositions – both in the dialectic *and* the disintegration of the dialectic. However, this paradoxical nature of their theme is incompatible with the accepted and rational logic of classical arguments. 'Pleasure' obviously does not readily surrender to analysis, so there will be no theses, antitheses and syntheses here. The text is thus composed of fragments that only loosely relate to one another. These fragments – *geometry, mask, bondage, excess, eroticism* – are all to be seen not only in the reality of 'ideas' but also in the reality of the reader's spatial experience, a silent reality that cannot be put to paper. The illustrations are connected to the text in the same indirect way. They are extracted from a series entitled *Advertisements for Architecture*.

Fragment 1: A Double Pleasure (reminder)
The pleasure of space: This cannot be put in words, it is unspoken. Approximately: it is a form of experience – the 'presence of absence;' exhilarating differences between the plane and the cavern, between the street and your living room: symmetries and dissymmetries emphasising the spatial properties of my body: right and left, up and down. Taken to its extreme, the pleasure of space leans towards the poetics of the unconscious, to the edge of madness.

The pleasure of geometry and by extension, the pleasure of order – that is, the pleasure of concepts: Typical statements on architecture often read like the one in the first edition of the *Encyclopedia Britannica* of 1773: 'architecture, being governed by proportion, requires to be guided by rule and compass.' That is, architecture is a 'thing of the mind,' a geometrical rather than a pictorial or experiential art, so that the problem of architecture becomes a problem of ordinance. Doric or Corinthian order, axes or hierarchies, grids or regulating lines, types or models, walls or slabs, and, of course, the whole grammar and syntax of the architectural sign are all pretexts for sophisticated and pleasurable manipulation. Taken to its extreme, such manipulation leans towards a poetics of frozen signs, detached from reality, into a subtle and frozen pleasure of the mind.

Neither the pleasure of space nor the pleasure of geometry is (on its own) the pleasure of architecture.

Fragment 2: Gardens of Pleasure
In his *Observations sur l'Architecture*, published in the Hague in 1765, Laugier suggested a dramatic deconstruction of architecture and its conventions. He wrote: 'Whoever knows how to design a park well will have no difficulty in tracing the plan for the building of a city according to its given area and situation. There must be regularity and fantasy, relationships and oppositions, and casual, unexpected elements that vary the scene; great order in the details, confusion, uproar, and tumult in the whole.'

Laugier's celebrated comments, together with the dreams of Capability Brown, William Kent, Lequeu or Piranesi, were not merely a reaction to the Baroque period that preceded them. Rather, the deconstruction of architecture which they suggested was an early venture into the realm of pleasure, against the architectural order of time.

Take Stowe for example. William Kent's park displays a subtle dialectic between organised landscape and architectural elements: the Egyptian Pyramid, the Italian Belvedere, the Saxon Temple. But these 'ruins' are to be read less as elements of picturesque composition than as the dismantled elements of order. Yet, despite the apparent chaos, order is still present as a necessary counterpart to the sensuality of the winding streams. Without the signs of order, Kent's park would lose all reminders of 'reason.' Conversely, without the traces of sensuality – trees, hedges, valleys – only symbols would remain, in a silent and frozen fashion.

Gardens have had a strange fate. Their history has almost always anticipated the history of cities. The orchard grid of man's earliest agricultural achievements preceded the layout of the first military cities. The perspectives, diagonals and archetypal schemes of the Renaissance Gardens were applied to Squares, Colonnades and designs of Renaissance cities. Similarly, the romantic picturesque parks of English empiricism pre-empted the Crescents, Arcades and the rich urban design tradition of 19th century England.

Built exclusively for delight, gardens are like the earliest experiments in that part of architecture that is so difficult to express with words or drawings: pleasure and eroticism. Whether 'romantic' or 'classic,' gardens merge the sensual pleasure of space with the pleasure of reason, in a most *useless* manner.

Fragment 3: Pleasure and Necessity
'Uselessness' is reluctantly associated with architectural matters. Even at a time when pleasure found some theoretical backing (*delight* as well as 'commodity' and 'firmness'), utility always provided a practical justification. One example among many is Quatremère de Quincy's introduction to the entry on 'architecture' for the *Encyclopédie méthodique* published in Paris in 1778. There you will read that 'amongst all the arts, those children of *pleasure* and *necessity*, with which man has formed a partnership in order to help him bear the pains of life and transmit his memory to future generations, it can certainly not be denied that architecture holds a most outstanding place. Considering it only from the point of view *of utility*, architecture surpasses all the arts. It provides for the salubrity of cities, guards the health of men, protects their property, and works only for the safety, repose, and good order of civil life.'

If De Quincy's statement was consistent with the architectural ideology of his time, the social necessity of architecture has, two hundred years later, been reduced to dreams and nostalgic Utopia. The 'salubrity of cities' now obeys the logic of land economics, and the 'good order of civil life' is often the order of corporate markets. As a result, most architectural endeavours seem caught in a hopeless dilemma. If, on one hand, architects recognise the ideological and financial dependency of their work, they implicitly accept the constraints of society, renouncing any hope of an architecture autonomous of such constraints. If, on the other hand, they sanctuarise themselves in an 'art for art's sake,' their architecture is of course accused of elitism. This is an uncomfortable situation to be in. To simply remain silent implicitly signifies the prospect of the shameful suicide of architecture in the last quarter of the 20th century with a switch to the mere production of buildings and their processes.

Of course, architecture will save its peculiar nature, but only wherever it negates itself, wherever it negates or disrupts the form that a conservative society expects of it. For if architecture is useless, and radically so, this very uselessness will mean strength in any society where profit is prevalent. And, as there has lately been some reason to doubt the necessity of architecture, *then the necessity of architecture may well be its non-necessity*.

Rather than an obscure 'artistic supplement' or a cultural justification for financial manipulation, architecture recalls the 'fireworks' example. Fireworks produce a pleasure that cannot be sold or bought, that cannot be integrated in any production cycle.

Such totally gratuitous consumption of architecture is ironically *political* in that it disturbs established structures. It is also quite pleasurable.

Fragment 4: Metaphor of Order – Bondage

Unlike the 'necessity' of mere building, the 'non-necessity' of architecture is indissociable from architectural histories, theories and other precedents. These bonds enhance pleasure. Here is how: The most excessive passion is always methodical. In these moments of intense desire, organisation invades pleasure to such an extent that it is not always possible to distinguish the organising constraints from the erotic matter. For example, the Marquis de Sade's heroes enjoyed confining their victims in the strictest convents before mistreating them according to rules carefully laid down in a precise and obsessive logic.

Similarly, the game of architecture is an intricate play with rules that one may accept or reject. Indifferently called 'Système des Beaux-Arts' or Modern Movement precepts, this often undetected but pervasive network of binding laws entangles architectural design. These rules, like so many knots that cannot be untied, are generally a paralysing constraint. When manipulated, however, they have the erotic significance of bondage. To differentiate between rules or ropes is irrelevant here. What matters is that there is no simple bondage technique: the more numerous and sophisticated the restraints, the greater the pleasure.

Fragment 5: Rationality

In *Architecture and Utopia,* the historian Tafuri recalls how the rational excesses of Piranesi's prisons or his Campo Marzio took Laugier's theoretical proposals of 'order and tumult' to the extreme. The classical architectural vocabulary is Piranesi's self-chosen form of bondage. Treating these classical elements as fragmented and decaying symbols, Piranesi's architecture battled against itself – in that the obsessive rationality of building types was 'sadistically' carried to the extremes of irrationality.

Fragment 6: Eroticism

We have seen that the ambiguous pleasure of rationality and irrational dissolution recalled erotic concerns. A word of warning may be necessary at this stage. Eroticism is used here as a 'theoretical' concept having little in common with fetishistic formalism and other sexual analogies prompted by the sight of erect skyscrapers or curvaceous doorways. Rather, eroticism is a subtle matter. It does not mean simply the pleasure of the senses, nor should it be confused with sensuality. Sensuality is as different from eroticism as a simple spatial perception is different from architecture. *Eroticism is not the excess of pleasure, but the pleasure of excess.* This popular definition should make my point clear. Just as contentment of the senses does not constitute eroticism, so the sensual experience of space does not make architecture. On the contrary, 'the pleasure of excess' requires consciousness as well as voluptuousness. The pleasure of architecture simultaneously contains (and dissolves) both mental constructs and sensuality. Neither space nor concepts alone are erotic, but the junction between the two is.

The ultimate pleasure of architecture is that impossible moment when an architectural act, brought to excess, reveals both the traces of reason and the immediate experience of space.

Fragment 7: Metaphor of Seduction – the Mask

There is rarely pleasure without seduction, or seduction without illusion. Consider: sometimes you wish to seduce so you act in the most appropriate way in order to reach your ends. You wear a disguise. Conversely, you may wish to change roles and *be* seduced: you consent to someone else's disguise, you accept his or her assumed personality, for it gives you pleasure, even if you know that it dissimulates 'something else.'

Architecture is no different. It constantly plays the seducer. Its disguises are numerous: Facades, Arcades, Squares, even architectural concepts become the artifacts of seduction. Like masks, they place a veil between what is assumed to be 'reality' and its participants (you or I). So sometimes you desperately wish to read the reality behind the architectural mask. Soon, however, you realise that no single understanding is possible. Once you uncover that which lies behind the mask, it is only to discover another mask. The literal aspect of the disguise (the Facade, the Street) indicates other systems of knowledge, other ways to 'read' the city: formal masks hide socio-economic ones while literal masks hide metaphorical ones. Each system of knowledge obscures another. Masks hide other masks and each successive level of meaning confirms the impossibility of grasping reality.

Consciously aimed at seduction, masks are of course a category of reason. Yet they possess a double role: they simultaneously veil and unveil, simulate and dissimulate. Behind all the masks lie 'dark' and unconscious streams that cannot be dissociated from the pleasure of architecture. The mask may exalt appearances. Yet by its very presence, it says that, in the background, there is 'something else.'

Fragment 8: Excess

If masks belong to the universe of pleasure, pleasure itself is no simple masquerade. The danger of confusing the mask with the face is real enough never to grant asylum to all parodies and nostalgia. The need for order is no justification for imitating past orders. Architecture is interesting only when it masters the art of disturbing illusions, creating breaking points in a game that can start and stop at any time.

Certainly, the pleasure of architecture is granted when architecture fulfils one's spatial expectations as well as embodying architectural ideas, concepts or archetypes, with intelligence, invention, sophistication, irony. Yet, there is a special pleasure that results from conflicts: when the sensual pleasure of space conflicts with the pleasure of order. The recent widespread fascination for the history and the theory of architecture does not necessarily mean a return to blind obedience to past dogma. On the contrary, I would suggest that the ultimate pleasure of architecture lies in the most forbidden parts of the architectural act, where limits are perverted and prohibitions *transgressed*. (By limits and prohibitions I refer to the laws of nature, the scientific laws and the utilitarian ones, the economic laws and the political ones, the limits of reason and the ones of the senses, the social taboos and the sexual ones.) The starting point of architecture is the distortion the dislocation of the universe that surrounds the architect. Yet such a nihilistic stance is only apparently so: we are not dealing with destruction here, but with excess, differences and left overs. *Exceeding* functionalist dogmas, semiotic systems, historical precedents of formalised products of past social or economic constraints is not necessarily a matter of subversion, but a matter of preserving the 'erotic' capacity of architecture by disrupting the form that most conservative societies expect of it.

Fragment 9: Architecture of Pleasure
The architecture of pleasure lies where conceptual and spatial paradoxes merge in the middle of delight, where architectural language breaks into a thousand pieces, where the elements of architecture are dismantled and its rules transgressed. No metaphorical paradise here, but discomfort and unbalanced expectations. Such architecture questions academic (and popular) assumptions, disturbs acquired tastes and fond architectural memories. Typologies morphologies, spatial compressions, logical constructions, all dissolve. Inarticulated forms collide in a staged and necessary conflict: repetition, discontinuity, quotes, clichés and neologisms. Such architecture is perverse for its real significance is outside any utility or purpose and ultimately is not even necessarily aimed at giving pleasure.

The architecture of pleasure depends on a particular feat, which is to keep architecture obsessed with itself in such an ambiguous fashion that it never surrenders to good conscience or parody, debility or delirious neurosis.

Fragment 10: Desire/Fragments
There are numerous ways to equate architecture with language. Yet such equations often amount to a *reduction* and an *exclusion*. A reduction, insofar as these equations usually become distorted as soon as architecture tries to produce meaning (which meaning?, whose meaning?), and thus ends up reducing language to its mere combinatory logic. An exclusion, insofar as these equations generally omit some of the important findings made in Vienna at the beginning of the century, when language was first seen as a condition of the unconscious. Dreams were analysed as language as well as through language. Language was called 'the main street of the unconscious.' Generally speaking, it appeared

as a series of *fragments* (one may remember that the Freudian notion of fragments does not presuppose the breaking of an image, or of a totality, but the dialectical multiplicity of a process). So too, with architecture when equated with language. It can only be read as a series of fragments which make up an architectural reality.

Fragments of architecture (bits of walls, of room, of streets, of ideas) are all one actually sees. These fragments are like beginnings without ends. There is always a split between fragments which are real and fragments which are virtual between experience and concept, memory and fantasy. These splits have no existence other than being the passage from one fragment to another. They are relays rather than signs. They are traces. They are an in-between.

It is not the clash between these contradictory fragments that counts, but the movement between such fragments. This invisible movement between fragments is neither a part of language nor of structure.

('Language' or 'structure' are words specific to a mode of reading architecture which does not fully apply in the context of pleasure). This movement is nothing but a constant and mobile relationship inside language itself.

How such fragments are organised matters little: volume, height, surface, degree of enclosure or whatever. These fragments are like sentences between quotation marks. Yet they are not quotations. They simply melt into the work. (We are here at the opposite of the collage technique). They may be excerpts from different discourses but this only demonstrates that an architectural project is precisely where differences find an overall expression.

An old 50s film had a name for this movement between fragments. It was called 'desire.' Yes, *A Streetcar Named Desire* perfectly simulated the movement towards something constantly missing, towards absence. Each setting, each fragment was aimed at seduction, but always dissolved at the moment it was approached. Every time it was substituted by another fragment, 'Desire' was never seen. Yet it remained constant. The same goes for architecture.

In other words, architecture is not of interest because of its fragments and what they represent or do not represent. Nor does it consist in *exteriorising*, through whatever forms, the unconscious desires of society or its architects. Nor is it a mere representation of those desires through some fantastic architectural images. Rather it can only act as a recipient in which your desires, my desires can be reflected. Thus a piece of architecture is not 'architectural' because it seduces, or fulfils some utilitarian function, but because it sets in motion the operations of seduction and the unconscious.

A final word of warning. *Architecture* may very well activate such motions, but it is not a 'dream' (a stage where society's or the individual's unconscious desires can be fulfilled). It cannot satisfy your wildest fantasies, but it may *exceed* the limits set by them.   (… p 218)

Notes
For a detailed discussion of some of these fragments, please see:
Fragments 1 and 3: 'Questions of Space', *Studio International*, vol 9–10, 1975.
Fragment 2: 'The Garden of Don Juan', *L'Architecture d'Aujourd'hui*, vol 10–11, 1976.
Fragments 6 and 8: 'Architecture and Transgression', *Oppositions*, vol 2, 1977.

Bernard Tschumi, 'The Pleasure of Architecture,' *Architectural Design*, vol 3, 1977, pp 214–18.
(Excerpt pp 215–18)

Domestic Doyennes: Purveyors of Atmospheres Spoken and Visual

John C Turpin

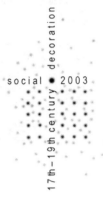

social ● 2003

17th–19th century decoration

The art of conversing and the art of living are, according to John Turpin, linked through the need for expression. The social challenge, the demand for mental acuity and the game-like aspects of conversation are explored in this text via a discussion of late nineteenth-century French salons and English drawing rooms. Turpin's historical examination of this interior environment points to the aural spatial affect of conversations that are driven and influenced by the presence and interaction of company in such interior settings. The tangible design of such spaces is revealed to be equally manufactured and contrived as the temporality of conversation that occurs within it.

Between conversation and civilization, the art of talking and the art of living, there has always been a vital link.
Peter Quennell[1]

If examined closely, Quennell's quote speaks of a phenomenon that is critical to human existence: the need for expression. Whether verbal or physical, humankind has continually devoted significant time and energy to the process of self-expression. Why? According to John Kasson, 'the protocols of conversation is one example of a ritual that establishes the structures by which individuals define one another and interact, defining social identities, social relationships, and an individual's perception of their social reality.'[2] Katherine Grier offers a similar view, but very clearly includes the significance of both etiquette and decoration which 'express the progress of civilization; both [are] ... a way of choosing language that reflects the presence of some cultural framework for organizing many kinds of human experiences.'[3] Both Kasson and Grier support Quennell's views by identifying how human expression, whether through direct human interaction (conversation) or the stage for its performance (decoration), are intimately tied to each other and the development of a culture.

Interestingly, correlations have been made between verbal communication and the notions of space. In his 1926 essay, *Talking*, John Priestly categorizes certain types of dialogue as 'atmosphere creating.'[4] He posits that various aspects of a verbal exchange help define an experience that in some ways creates an implied space. For example, the proximity of individuals during a conversation may evoke the feelings of an intimate space as the participants reveal information of a sensitive, personal nature. By choosing to confide in a specific individual, the speaker projects an aura of security onto the event. Priestly further relates the physical environment with the spoken word by stating, 'Such words as we use shall be but extra shutters and curtains and blazing coals and cushions.'[5] These allusions of a warm, comfortable interior environment are equated with the similar effects of an intimate verbal exchange.

Since Priestly's publication, little scholarship on the relationship between conversation and the environment has surfaced. This article will attempt to revive Priestly's discussions by asking a primary question: Is there a relationship between the ritual of conversation and the art of decoration? ...

In the first half of the seventeenth century, a new exclusive space developed for the nurturing of the elite culture. Originally referred to as an *alcove* or *ruelle*, today it is known as a *salon*. Here, conversation created its own social space with carefully marked boundaries as French women began redefining the criteria for inclusion and exclusion into the strata of the social elite. The vehicle for change would be the restructuring of etiquette.

The history of etiquette as a well-defined entity begins in Renaissance Italy with the development of a new literary genre, the courtesy book.[6] The Florentines regarded the art of civility as a branch of rhetorical theory. From these rather philosophical beginnings, etiquette eventually evolved into a political tool for social advancement and control in seventeenth-century France. Ambitious courtiers manipulated courtly politics during the reign of Louis XIV by exploiting increasing opportunities of the commercial classes. Through refinements in social conduct, courtiers meticulously refashioned their social selves.[7]

In 1630 Nicholas Faret altered the design of human relations by rejecting the military metaphors of the past.[8] Typical of male posturing in social events, French males demonstrated an impatient desire to engage in the rhetoric of combat. Acknowledging that the military was a classic gentleman's profession, Faret viewed military prowess only as an accomplishment for the model courtier. With the exclusion of a male-only topic such as the military, Faret facilitated the participation of women in a new definition of elite sociability. Due to their 'natural' taste, women soon became proprietors of good manners and civility. As a result, the best social education emanated from cultivated women, the gatekeepers of elite society.

For purposes of studying manner and wit, the women of highest rank began initiating carefully constructed meetings, where noble and scholar stood on equal ground. During such encounters, French women like Madame Geoffrin and Madame Lespinasse maintained high levels of control over carefully selected participants. In these situations, the women created atmospheres both spoken and visual to ensure a successful event. By the middle of the seventeenth century the salons began to separate themselves from the court society of the Louvre. One example is the infamous *Chambre Bleu* of Madame Rambouillet. She gave architectural proportions to this new concept of exclusivity. A description of the *Chambre Bleu*, the first known salon, follows:

> [The Marquis'] house featured numerous relatively small, well-proportioned rooms, instead of the great hall and central staircase. Passing through a series of ornately finished rooms, a visitor arrived at last in the famous chambre bleu, whose intimate proportions and daring use of color established an elegant and fresh tone. The chambre bleu had waist-high painted and gilded panels lining its walls, which were hung with patterned blue tapestries encrusted with gold and silver. Paintings and Venetian mirrors hung on the walls. The focus of the room was the blue, damask-hung bed in the second alcove where the Marquis de Rambouillet reclined.[9]

The physical design of the Hotel de Rambouillet with its architectural features facilitated movement between the rooms, creating a more unified interior space, with tall windows and doors offering the occupants enlarged exterior perspectives. Similarly, ideal conversation had to permit both a smooth pattern of movement between the participants and a broad view of the world outside.[10]

The art of conversation in the salon was unique in that nobles and scholars engaged on equal ground. Ideal conversation was possible only if all participants were confident of their equal standing within the group.[11] Domination, dispute, interruptions and inattentiveness were not permitted. An atmosphere of peace and tranquillity was far removed from the sometimes-hostile engagements between the gentlemen. The salon would be considered a failure and that particular *salonnière* would lose her most valued position if the environment was not perfect.[12]   (... p 44)

From the standpoint of the women, this new, distinct influence was significant in its retention of feminine qualities of tact, sympathy and mental alertness, as opposed to the masculine diversions of politics and letters. Without compromising the integrity of their gender, these women created a new position in society for themselves based on the ability to enhance human relations through controlled conversations.[13] Thus, French women clearly aided in defining the cultural standards of the seventeenth and eighteenth centuries through their skilful manipulation of the interior environment and the ritual of conversation.

Across the channel, nineteenth-century England set a completely different stage in which to socially interact. Both their interiors and manners were highly manufactured. The salon continued to slowly fuse itself with the culture of the English upper class, but without the emphasis on enlightened discussions occurring in France. With the increase in the wealth of the nation, the rise in the standard of living, and the growth of the middle classes, English ladies experienced a new way of living. However, the salon itself was not as popular as a room type. The drawing room was a more affordable choice. Here, participants focused on anomalous conversation with the sole intent of social and political advancement. The motivation for social events in Victorian England was far different than those in France. The relations between men and women delineated roles based on a patriarchal system. Compared to the more liberated French women, the English ladies were not permitted as much self-expression. For example, a wife was legally bound to uphold the husband's social status.[14] This was accomplished in two ways. The first was the presentation of the home. The second required the acquisition of new manners. Similar to the French madams, failure in crafting a successful public image meant ostracism, ridicule and exclusion from sources of power and wealth; in other words, a swift social and political death for the husband.

English gentlemen demonstrated their success in business by making enough money such that the wife no longer required additional income. As a result, women left the labor force. However, since a woman should not be idle, she spent a considerable amount of time on more 'appropriate' tasks, including the furnishing and maintaining of larger houses, social occasions and festivities. The profuse interior decor, with which the Victorian period is identified, was itself a product of all that female energy going into ornamenting the home.[15] Women flooded their drawing rooms with upholstered sofas with brightly embroidered cushions ornamented with beadwork, grand pianos, heavily layered windows, and elaborate chairs.

Due to the strong sense of guilt for such excessive expenditures, Victorian women justified the extreme opulence and extravagance by invoking the idea of social duty. Clearly, the women were experiencing conflict between social responsibilities and the religious teachings of the church. The women often applied self-imposed restrictions in order to soothe guilt. Ironically, such 'sins' were acceptable for women, but not for the men.[16] In English society the women clearly played a secondary role to their male counterparts. Even though they were given the responsibility of hosting events to maintain the couple's social status, society refused to allow them to stand alone. 'The great hostess must be a wife or nothing. No hostess counts without a host.'[17] However, it is the case that the English ladies, much like the French madams, were considered to be the gatekeepers of society. Again, etiquette bestowed the power.   (... p 46)

Unlike the enriching discussions of the French salons, the English drawing rooms were filled with pretentiousness and vacuity. The goal was neither to offend nor inform. By subduing intellectual growth, the social elite defined their status more or less by simply being in each other's presence. The aura of elitism found expression on elaborate stages where the significance of the actors' visual performance surpassed their verbal utterances. Staccato conversations permitted all present to participate in the creation of an atmosphere characterized by a 'false view of life.'[18]

Mentmore, the estate of Baron Meyer Amschel de Rothschild, manifests the extremity of elitism and arrogance in both its architecture and interiors. The disposition of spaces within the floor plan enhanced the primary function of Victorian social events, to be seen. Impressive foyers, such as the one at Mentmore, required guests to ascend to the Grand Hall, a pretentious metaphor communicating the superior status of the host and hostess. Upon reaching the level of the gala event, guests anxiously awaited their public announcement of arrival. After a momentary glance from other participants, the primary function of the guest had been accomplished. They were seen.

In opposition to the ascension of the guest, the Lady of the house often waited until her company had arrived so that they may witness her descent from the Grand Staircase axially aligned with the Grand Hall. The remainder of the rooms were arranged in a manner that permitted guests to mingle from room to room continuing their performance on the grandest of stages.

The interior of the Grand Hall is decorated with all the pretentiousness of most Victorian homes. Count D'Orsay's rules of conversation are supported by the stage set. For example, the avoidance of long stories in polite conversation prevents any one individual from being a point of focus. Conversation is to move freely and rather rapidly from one to another. In similar style, the Victorian interior is riddled with objects, each so spectacular in form and ornamentation that the eye of the guest is never permitted to rest. Unintentionally, the interior's demand for a roving eye may have lubricated the ritual of being seen as accidental glances imparted unintended meanings.   (... p 47)

America realized the absence of a native hereditary aristocracy prevented the infusion of etiquette into a society whose masses were mainly middle class. Yet, the need for direction was becoming increasingly important. Women quickly took charge of the issue and were viewed as the principal guardians of decorum in the middle and upper classes. By the turn of the twentieth century, basic etiquette regressed as the bustling American city interfered with ceremonious intercourse. An added obstruction was the exodus to the suburbs, which physically limited social interaction.[19] Prior to the appearance of the likes of Emily Post and Lillian Eichler, a new professional arose to fill the cultural void and embrace the need for etiquette.[20] Enter the interior decorator.   (... p 48)

372

Clearly fueled by her views of etiquette, Elsie de Wolfe expounds her rules regarding entertaining and decorating in her publication, *The House in Good Taste*. Within only a few pages, de Wolfe lays claim on both entertaining and decorating as female responsibilities. 'It is the personality of the mistress that the home expresses. Men are forever guests in our homes, no matter how much happiness they may find there.'[21] In the true spirit of the French madams and the Victorian ladies, Elsie de Wolfe would combine the ritual of entertaining and etiquette and the practice of interior decoration into a cohesive whole.

De Wolfe draws quite a few direct correlations between conversation and interior decorating and the manner in which they guide each other. In setting her own precedents, de Wolfe admits to being heavily impacted by the French culture. She refers to the Hotel Rambouillet and how it was 'devised for and consecrated to conversation, a new form of privilege.'[22] According to de Wolfe, while Americans use the terms 'drawing room' and 'salon' interchangeably, there is an appreciation for the term salon for its implication of brilliant conversation.[23]

De Wolfe utilizes the projects in her book as a means of disseminating the lessons of the salon. 'Your sense of the pleasure and meaning of human intercourse will be clear in your disposition of your best things, in your elimination of your worst ones.'[24] From the standpoint of decoration, the atmosphere should be warm and inviting by utilizing textures, materials, color, lighting, and seating arrangements. In her own home on 55th Street in New York City, de Wolfe describes a 'room made for conversation.' 'In this drawing room there is furniture of many woods, there are stuffs of many weaves, there are candles and chandeliers and reading-lamps, but there is *harmony of purpose* and therefore *harmony of effect*' [italics by author].[25] Her formula is further developed through the arrangement of numerous conversation centers, intimate in spirit, such that no one chair is isolated.   (... p 49)

Notes
1   Peter Quennell, *Affairs of the Mind: The Salon in Europe and America From the 18th to the 20th Century*, New Republic Books (Washington DC), 1980, p 9.
2   John F Kasson, *Rudeness and Civility: Manners in Nineteenth-Century Urban America*, Hill and Wang (New York), 1990, p 4.
3   Katherine Grier, *Culture and Comfort: Parlor Making and Middle-class Identity, 1850–1930*, Smithsonian Institution Press (Washington DC), 1988, p 1.
4   J Priestly, *Talking*, Jarrolds Publishers (London), 1926, p 10.
5   Priestly, *Talking*, p 14.
6   Quentin Skinner, *The Foundations of Modern Political Thought*, Cambridge University Press (Cambridge), 1978, p 14.
7   For further details see Jolanta Pekacz's *Conservative Tradition in Pre-Revolutionary France: Parisian Salon Women*, Peter Lang Publishers (New York), 1999.
8   Nicholas Faret, *L'Honnête homme ou l'art de plaire a la cour*, PUF (Paris), 1925.

9 Bonnie Anderson and Judith Zinsser, *A History of Their Own*, Oxford University Press (New York), 2000, pp 103–4.

10 Elizabeth Goldsmith, *Exclusive Conversations: The Art of Interaction in Seventeenth-Century France*, University of Pennsylvania Press (Philadelphia), 1988, pp 44–6.

11 Goldsmith, *Exclusive Conversations*, pp 44–6.

12 Pekacz, *Conservative Tradition*, p 125.

13 Helen Clergue, *The Salon: A Study of French Society and Personalities in the Eighteenth Century*, The Knickerbocker Press (New York), 1907, p 3.

14 Leonore Davidoff, *The Best Circles: Women and Society in Victorian England*, Rowman and Littlefield (Totowa, NJ), 1973, p 40.

15 See Anderson and Zinsser, *History of Their Own*, for a discussion on women's roles in England.

16 Davidoff, *Best Circles*, p 39.

17 Philip Guedalla, *Bonnet and Shawl: An Album*, Books for Libraries Press (New York), 1970, p 157.

18 Joan Wildeblood, *The Polite World: A Guide to English Manners and Deportment from the Thirteenth to the Nineteenth Century*, Oxford University Press (London), 1965, p 76.

19 Arthur M Schlesinger, *Learning How to Behave: A Historical Study of American Etiquette Books*, Macmillan Company (New York), 1946, pp 49–50.

20 In 1918, a prolific wave of publications on etiquette flooded the market. Between 1918 and 1945, over 140 books intended to educate the American public on what was considered to be socially acceptable behavior; the success of which Schlesinger (1946) attributes to the 'many earnest souls [searching] for a steadying hand in a period of bewildering flux in social conventions.' Within a 23 year period, Lillian Eichler's *Book of Etiquette* (1922) sold over a million copies; a far cry from the socially deemed queen of manners, Emily Post, whose publication, *Etiquette* (1923), reached over 65 million homes in roughly the same period of time. For the first time in American history, etiquette was disentangled from the religious-based ethics of the past and now accepted as a generalized pattern of behavior designed to lubricate social intercourse.

21 Elsie de Wolfe, *The House in Good Taste*, Atheneum (New York), 1913, p 5.

22 De Wolfe, *House in Good Taste*, p 11.

23 De Wolfe, *House in Good Taste*, pp 135–6.

24 De Wolfe, *House in Good Taste*, p 15.

25 De Wolfe, *House in Good Taste*, p 49.

John C Turpin, 'Domestic Doyennes: Purveyors of Atmospheres Spoken and Visual', *In.Form: The Journal of Architecture, Design, and Material Culture*, vol 3, 2003, pp 42–54.
Published by the Kruger Collection in conjunction with the Interior Design Program of the University of Nebraska.
© The University of Nebraska. Reprinted by permission of the publisher.
(Excerpts pp 42–9)

The Lair of the Bachelor

George Wagner

In conjunction with contemporary discourse on women, feminism and architecture, architectural academic George Wagner's essay addresses space through the sexed body as male heterosexual. Noting that space is gendered masculine or feminine, Wagner exposes the possibility of space also assuming specificity according to sexual orientation or body. Exploring the governance of fantasy in the function of interior architecture, this text discusses pornography in parallel with urban utopia ultimately to face conditions of gender within the city fabric. Seeing the bachelor as an anomaly in this equation, Wagner examines how gender and sexuality burden interiors as signs of the loss of male authority, and position the 'penthouse' as a resistant bastion of male liberation.

The image of the bachelor's life advanced by *Playboy* provided a private fantasy escape for the man whose home had been appropriated as the domain of wife and family and whose office was the site of a definitive reality – the wage. The ideal, imagined reader of *Playboy* magazine was a playboy, and the playboy acquired a fantasized mobility because he was a bachelor. A bachelor is a single man, but some delicacy has always been required in the discussion of why the bachelor is single. *Playboy* espoused the virtue of playing the field, but we know that in the shadows of the cocktail party, the speculation is that the bachelor is a loser, or even worse – he's a queer. And as a result, the decor of the bachelor must be carefully calibrated not to send off the wrong signals.

Emily Post, the president of the Emily Post Institute and celebrated author of *Etiquette: The Blue Book of Social Usage* included in her tract of 1948 The *Personality of a House: The Blue Book of Home Charm* a chapter titled 'A House – or a room – for a man' and presented quite directly the delicate question of the bachelor's house.
Ms. Post writes, 'That every normal man should be repelled by any suggestion of effeminacy is only natural. But even so, there is no reason why the house of a man living alone should be furnished like the display room of a cement company.'[1]

Ms. Post is quite clear about how easily the problem can be derived. Bachelors are single men. Queers are single men. Bachelors are queer. And so her presentation of the masculine house, and the others I will discuss, begins from a defensive position. It is focused around the preservation of the myth that masculinity is the bastion of the natural and the utilitarian. In fact, her reference to the masculine and the cement company is meant to align the masculine with the immediacies of labor and imply the feminine's affiliation with leisure, consumption, and contrivance.

In *The Decoration of Houses*, Edith Wharton and Ogden Codman described men's taste as simple and 'uncomplicated by the feminine tendency to want things because other people have them, rather than to have things because they are wanted.'[2]

For Wharton and Codman the den (as in lion, the king of the jungle) is a man's room: 'The den is freed from the superfluous, is likely to be the most comfortable room of the house; and the natural inference is that a room, in order to be comfortable, must be ugly.'[3]

These arguments are laden with clichéd ideas about masculinity: that masculinity is not a construction, but natural, that it constitutes some authentic dimension of human behavior and is free from the codes of artifice that characterize the rest of culture – of femininity, for instance, or the elaborate interstitial codes of homosexuality.

It was Oscar Wilde who said, 'To be natural is such a very difficult pose to keep up.'[4]

Back to *Playboy* and the defensive position around which the virtues of the bachelor were established: in September 1958, Philip Wylie published an article in *Playboy* titled 'The Womanization of America.' Mr. Wylie's point was to warn against what he called the encroaching 'taffeta tide' – the feminization of the suburban domestic realm. Mr. Wylie says,

> On some not very distant day I expect to see a farmer riding a pastel tractor and wearing a matching playsuit. And as he ploughs, I'll realize with horror it's not a contour job; he'll be fixing his fields so the crops will match an "overall design-feeling" incorporated in his home by the little woman ... The only inanimate object I can think offhand which still has masculine integrity is the freight car, and even some of these are being glamorized.

Obviously this caustic text displays both apprehension and paranoia, but it also quite clearly lays out many of the fears for which the domestic fantasies of *Playboy* are meant to compensate. The humiliation felt at the loss of masculine control is represented by the farmer, whose pantsuit might be color coordinated with his tractor. The freight car, which becomes a venerated icon, is not a space of occupation – except for the vagabond or drifter. Mr. Wylie laments the loss of the man's private domain in the spaces of the city:

The American male had lost his authority as symbolized by the places where he drank. Sawdust vanished and the stand-up bar was rare; the new saloons were like tea shoppes ... America's females pushed and heckled their way into every private male domain.

Wylie describes a spatial and architectural emasculation which occurs not only within the city but also in the home, and is manifest not through behavior or personal interaction, but through design. Men have become spatial expatriates:

Those domestic improvements which reduce labor – machines that do dishes, dispose of refuse, cook automatically, ventilate, heat, vacuum, clean, air condition, mow lawns, harrow gardens, preserve food and so on – were all of them, invented, perfected, manufactured and distributed by males.

The rest of home design fell into the hands of women and decorators who were women or, when not, usually males in form only – males emotionally so identified with the opposite sex they could rout reluctant husbands because their very travesty made men uncomfortable. Sundry special magazines took up the cause. They were identified by women and by women-identified males. These homemaking magazines brought forth a welter of counsel on how to convert normal residences into she-warrens.

Where once man had had a den, maybe a library, a cellar poolroom, his own dressing room, he now found himself in a split level pastel creation ... All he knew was that the beloved old place now looked like a candy box without even an attic for his skis, his humidor or hunting prints ... The American home, in short, is becoming a boudoir-kitchen-nursery, dreamed up by women, for women and as if males did not exist as males.[5]

If the home is the space of the woman, and if space is either masculine or feminine, what constitutes male space, and what role do women, or homosexuals, play in it?

In the fifties and sixties *Playboy* published a number of commissioned designs for apartments, houses, pads, and penthouses as a way of imagining sites for the *Playboy* lifestyle.[6] One of the most fascinating aspects of this discussion is how tacitly it is assumed that spaces and objects become charged with the conditions of social and economic gender roles, but also with specific ideas about sexuality as well. These spaces can be understood to constitute a strategy of recovery of the domestic realm by the heterosexual male.

By grounding the bachelor's fantasy away from the suburban family, the urban sites of *Playboy*'s apartments engage the dangerous pleasures of the city's shadows. The penthouse sits above but within the city – in it but not of it – and allows the bachelor a controlling gaze of the urban spectacle. The penthouse implicitly evokes the image of the city at night and its illicit pleasures. These apartments are the fantasy sites of seduction, with the bachelor the wily predator and the woman the prey. All of the apparatus that fill these spaces – the remote controls, the furniture, the bar – are essentially prosthetic devices that expand the effectiveness of the bachelor in his seduction, or, put another way, the predator in conquest of his prey.

Playboy's Penthouse Apartment was published in September and October of 1956. The article began,

> A man yearns for quarters of his own. More than a place to hang his hat, a man dreams of his own domain, a place that is exclusively his. Playboy has designed, planned and decorated, from the floor up, a penthouse apartment for the urban bachelor – a man who enjoys good living, a sophisticated connoisseur of the lively arts, of food and drink and congenial companions of both sexes. A man very much, perhaps, like you.[7]

The plan of the apartment is fairly simple. It is a penthouse located high in a building of unusual configuration. The plan is open, 'not divided into cell-like rooms, but into function areas well delineated for relaxation, dining, cooking, wooing and entertaining, all interacting and yet inviting individual as well as simultaneous use.'[8]

There are some things you have to know about the bachelor. He has a lot of friends whom he likes to invite over spontaneously. He has no family; the bachelor is fantasized as a free agent. His apartment is new and facilitates his behavior through a dependency on technology. It is a space of imagined liberation, in which technology serves as an extension of sexual desire.

> And speaking of entertainment, one of the hanging Knoll cabinets beneath the windows holds a built-in bar. This permits the canny bachelor to remain in the room while mixing a cool one for his intended quarry. No chance of missing the proper psychological moment – no chance of leaving her cozily curled up on the couch with her shoes off and returning to find her mind changed, purse in hand, and the young lady ready to go home, damn it. Here, conveniently at hand, too, is a self-timing rheostat which will gradually and subtly dim the lights to fit the mood – as opposed to the harsh click of a light switch that plunges all into sudden darkness and may send the fair game fleeing.[9]   (... p 201)

Notes

1   Emily Post, *The Personality of a House: The Blue Book of Home Charm*, Funk & Wagnalls (New York), 1948, p 410. See also 'The Masculine Graces', *Amy Vanderbilt's New Complete Book of Etiquette: The Guide to Gracious Living*, Doubleday & Co (Garden City, New York), 1952.

2   Edith Wharton and Ogden Codman, *The Decoration of Houses* [1897], WW Norton and Co (New York), 1978, p 17.

3   Wharton and Codman, *Decoration of Houses*, p 152.

4   Oscar Wilde, *An Ideal Husband*, as cited in Susan Sontag, 'Notes on Camp', *A Susan Sontag Reader*, Farrar Strauss (New York), 1982, p 110.

5   Philip Wylie, 'The Womanization of America', *Playboy*, September 1958, pp 51–2, 77–9.

6   Between 1956 and 1970, *Playboy* published five commissioned designs for the bachelor's quarters. These spreads featured complete texts describing the 'lifestyle' of the bachelor and also displayed contemporary furniture. Throughout the same period the magazine also published a larger number of houses and apartments, including Charles Moore's house in New Haven ('A Playboy Pad: New Haven Haven', *Playboy*, October 1969, pp 125–8, 186).

7   'Playboy's Penthouse Apartment', *Playboy*, September 1956, p 54.

8   'Playboy's Penthouse Apartment', *Playboy*, p 60.

9   'Playboy's Penthouse Apartment', *Playboy*, p 59.

George Wagner, 'The Lair of the Bachelor', Debra Coleman, Elizabeth Danze and Carol Henderson (eds), *Architecture and Feminism*, Princeton Architectural Press (New York), 1996.
© 1996 Debra L Coleman, Elizabeth Ann Danze and Carol Jane Henderson.
Reprinted by permission of Princeton Architectural Press.
(Excerpt pp 195–201)

Ultrasuede

George Wagner

political ● 2002

mid 20th century material

Architect and academic George Wagner writes on postwar North American design's fascination with material furnishings. Noting a tendency to unify body, textile and furniture with building via surface continuity, and therefore an elimination of eclectic clutter, Wagner traces the development of spatial design through the evolution of surface design via Gottfried Semper, Eliel Saarinen, Billy Baldwin, and Jeffrey Schnapp. This text demonstrates the way in which material invention and industrial production influence the theoretical notions at play in interiors as well as how they reflect values of innovation and convention in a material oriented culture.

The instrumental vision of the modernist architect seems to have panned easily from the piece of furniture to the design of the city, and to have done so by subjecting diverse scales to the binding operations of aesthetic unity. This unity came at the price of the autonomy of the individual design disciplines, which were silenced by the ambitions and economic imperatives of larger orchestrations. This paper reflects broadly on the subject of textiles, the body, furniture, and buildings in postwar North America. At a moment of material invention and spatial expansion, the dialectical possibilities of architecture's constituent elements were overwhelmed by a broad complicity. As a result, the enveloping continuity of the whole and its governing surfaces subsumed and refigured the parts. My speculations begin with a discussion of materials but ultimately grounds itself in the social culture of postwar North America, in the animated jostlings between rebellion and freedom, institutional deliberation and bodily improvisation.

In 1958, articulating motives for the design of his pedestal furniture, Eero Saarinen wrote:

I wanted to clear up the slum of legs.[1]

Pondering this remark forty-four years later, I find it notable that the space under the dining table would be described using the physical and social context of the decaying postwar American city. But after the war, social issues and the domestic realm were frequently viewed together, just as the resettlement of the U.S. in the form of rampant suburbanization was an attempt to increase the physical distance between the two.

Saarinen's slum – the discordant collection of table and chair legs – was to be erased and the domestic landscape renewed with the elegant white cast-aluminum bases of his pedestal furniture. In nine words, Saarinen pans from city to interior, describing the broad scope of engagement in his practice of architecture. The form of the city is invoked to criticize the formal disunity of the dining set.

At least as interesting as the analogies Saarinen was drawing, is that he was looking: at the space under a table surrounded by chairs. It's not hard to imagine him as a child, sitting on the floor, cross-legged under the table, taking in the squalor, or perhaps, as an adult, with greater detachment and a taciturn gaze, regarding the havoc from a comfortable chair across the room. But that space, between table top and floor, waist and foot, is a charged zone of ergonomic action in the human body, and that action is projected onto the inhabitation of buildings, where it must accommodate and support multiple body postures and their functional needs.

Historically the wainscot demarcated the space of the body in the room. But the wainscot was merely a veneer applied to the wall in a building composed of planar surfaces. In an architecture that engaged monolithic materials for the purpose of generating plastic space and form (as Saarinen's became), another, more radical and discontinuous method was necessary.

Some of Saarinen's most innovative buildings fused floor and program, furniture and field – inflecting the floor itself to model a dynamic landscape for the body. Banishing furniture and its clutter, Saarinen designed conversation pits, as at the Noyes House of Vassar College, carving seating from the depth of the floor. At a larger scale, the continuous and organically-modeled ground surface of the TWA terminal further reflects a conception of the floor as more than inert surface, but as a domain actively inflecting to the project's functional and aesthetic dimensions.

Eero Saarinen came by this concentration on floor and furniture honestly. His father Eliel had been the Michelangelo of carpet, allowing it to transgress its place on the floor and actively mediate between horizontal and vertical. At Hvittrask, the elder Saarinen fixed a traditionally-patterned carpet to the wall, which allowed it to fall over a bench and onto the floor, serving as backrest, seat and floor covering. This carpet was not used, as carpets had been historically, as a unit of measure that figured and defined the space of the room, but as a textile that engaged and defined a localized space of the body and the zones of its tactile encounter. The rugs marked the body's posture in the room as it mediated between three different spatial zones.

Eliel Saarinen's grafting of the carpet between wall and floor allows us to see some of the provocative issues of textiles and architecture after the war. Because he used the carpets with the sensibility of a collagist, they animated the room because he brought his own intentions to bear against the authority of an authentic artifact. The carpets he used were traditional and handcrafted, and the significance of their unconventional position was registered through the conventions of their form.

Made by hand, knotted carpets have been venerated as folk artifacts that conjure and reflect the body through their crafting, pattern, pile and position. Their individuality is sufficient to suggest the muted presence of a narrative of their creation. The patterns of these carpets are discrete and individual. They bind space and give it scale, even as they declare their own formal autonomy.

Gottfried Semper theorized textiles in general, and wickerwork and carpets in particular, as important material artifacts – or motives – through which we can comprehend the origins of architecture. Semper hoped that this journey back to an elemental understanding of building materials and logics of fabrication would foster the preservation of meaning and continuity in architectural design. His writing did not focus on the carpets' appearance or pattern, but on the incremental technique of their fabrication – the knot, and the role it played in scenarios describing the evolution of prehistoric building. His was a way of figuring architecture that fuses decoration, structural forces, spatial dimension and human presence. His theories polarized the material distinctions between frame and wall, mass and space, seen and unseen, and imagined architectural origins in the gentle craft of textiles.

> Hanging carpets remained the true wall, the visible boundaries of space. The often solid walls behind them were necessary for reasons that had nothing to do with the creation of space; they were needed for security, for supporting a load, for their permanence and so on ... Even where building solid walls became necessary, the latter were only the inner, invisible structure behind the true and legitimate representatives of the wall, the colorful woven textiles.[2]

In the most sophisticated version of this scenario, the building's perceived reality and essential spatial unit are defined by the carpet. Other realities are unseen and buried within, behind the textile surface, perhaps inside the wall. Conceiving the origins of architecture through textiles did not offer a holistic model for architectural theorization, but did offer one that was necessarily complex and discursive in the relation of the parts. While Semper's writing implied the perceptual immediacy of the spatial liner before the hidden facts of structure, in *The Principle of Cladding* (1898), Adolf Loos recognized the differences between the two as driving the architectural process.

> Carpets are warm and livable ... But you cannot build a house out of carpets. Both the carpet on the floor and the tapestry on the wall require a structural frame to hold them in the correct place. To invent this frame is the architect's second task.[3]

Loos' reading of Semper did not attempt to imbue an ethical relation between wall covering and building structure; it is not an argument for articulation, or an ethical orchestration of parts. He wanted to theorize the surface itself, the covering, which he called 'the oldest architectural detail.' For him, the detail is not a point of connection or inflection, but a continuous veneer more a mask than a joint.

The ultimate strategy for manipulating this surface and the space to which it gives life, is described by Loos:

> But the artist, the architect, first senses the effect that he intends to realize ... He senses the effect that he wishes to exert upon the spectator ... These effects are produced by both material and the form of the space.[4]

Loos offers a way of conceiving architecture unburdened from responsibilities of ethical expression, from the belief that the rhetorical articulation of the material facts of building somehow lie within the territory of honesty or truth. The celebrated corner of Schinkel's Altes Museum projects onto the surface a description of the building's internal parts and juxtaposes them against the figure of the monolithic whole. Loos suggests it is neither the responsibility nor the duty of the architect to bring to the surface the elements that reside privately within the deep space of architecture.

Schinkel's lucid reasoning and the clarity with which he hybridized building morphologies never impeded but only heightened his skills in scenography and creating effect. These were his other avocations. His tented room at Charlottenhof (1826–33) used stretched and hung fabric to devise a purely local space suspended from the architectural motives of the building that encased it. Its atmospheric reverie invokes a realm beyond the villa, to the suggestion of a Roman campaign tent. It is the isolated world of monolithic and indulgent decoration, unlike the analytic and historicizing theory of Semper.

The detached reveries of Schinkel's tent room suggest most clearly the role that textiles came to play in the second half of the twentieth century: producing a purely local reality in a space with a continuous surface, eminently spatial and inwardly focused – a space for mental reflection and bodily suspension. In the 1970s, *Vogue* published a number of tented rooms as part of its monthly review of glamorous domesticity. The rooms are like boudoirs, and celebrate the possibility of an enclosed, bodily suspension from time and place. The character of these rooms is nothing like the images or sensibilities circulating through popular culture, the high arts, or the other pages of *Vogue*. They present their occupants in isolation from the world.

The decorator Billy Baldwin produced comparably detached interiors for his clients in New York. The element of separation from the world was the very commodity these spaces offered. The means employed to produce these effects were always similar: the room's interior surface was treated as continuous, and fabric, mirror or canvas (when paintings were used) were applied. Baldwin described Diana Vreeland's salon as 'a garden in hell.'[5] The bathroom of Mrs. Harding Lawrence (the advertising executive Mary Wells) was a hall of mirrors that surrealistically captured the movement of the city in an intimate space. 'The only passers-by are birds, she bathes in full view of the elements; lying back in her tub, she can look up in the mirrored ceiling and watch reflections of barges on the river and the traffic roaring fourteen floors below.'[6]

The walls and ceiling of Baldwin's bedroom for Si Newhouse were covered in brown velvet, 'a cave.'[7] The floor was taupe wall-to-wall carpeting. Paintings by Morris Louis and Mark Rothko on adjacent walls spanned from floor to ceiling, so that the architectural space of the room was subsumed by the pictorial space of the pictures. A print by Barnett Newman hung beside the Louis. The interiority of the room's soft enclosure found its visual foil in the two color field paintings in which the depth was as hermetic as the paintings were introspective. Clement Greenberg called this depth 'color-space.'[8] Greenberg admired another aspect of the spatiality of color field painting, calling it 'openness.'

> Yet the ultimate effect sought is one of more than chromatic intensity; it is rather one of an almost literal openness that embraces and absorbs color in the act of being created by it. Openness, and not only in painting, is the quality that seems most to exhilarate the attuned eye of our time.[9]

From an architectural standpoint (and it seems clear that Greenberg hoped that the relevance of his term would extend beyond painting), this openness is abstract, referring as it does to mere paint on canvas. The paintings in question, a Newman or a Rothko, are legible as metaphors for space because of their relative blankness. And, while Greenberg wrote of chromatic intensity, the openness of color field painting is more a product of chromatic restraint than intensity. Openness and its spatial implications are derived more from the field than from the image, and more from monochromatic subtlety than from chromatic intensity.[10]

The openness that Greenberg found can realistically be described in terms of enclosure, interiority and delimitation. With even greater conviction, Barnett Newman described the perceived opening of his paintings in their projection of a two-dimensional spatiality. Newman saw inside his work a 'space-dome' and hoped that the viewer would 'feel the vertical domelike vaults encompass him to awaken an awareness of his being alive in the sensation of complete space.'[11] He described without irony the architectural space of the room that held his painting as both 'chaotic and empty.' The space-dome of his painting 'should make one feel ... full and alive in a spatial dome of 180 degrees going in all four directions. This is the only real sensation of space.'[12]

The content of paintings mattered to Barnett Newman. Most paintings, he said, are full of 'object-matter,' a term borrowed from Meyer Schapiro, which can be applied either to the narrative subject matter of realist painting or to the emergent forms of the abstract: it is clutter either way. What Newman wanted to avoid he called the anecdotal and the episodic. Both terms seem to imply the presence of the narrative, the verbal, and the temporal, it seems clear that the enemy for Newman was the presence within the work of a specificity that might inhibit the spatial expanse. 'Instead of working with the remnants of space, I work with the whole space.' Ultimately, Newman's insistence on the visual perception of this imagined space (and against talking), might offer 'its assertion of freedom, its denial of dogmatic principles, its repudiation of all dogmatic life.'[13]

But what is of interest is the impulse to read pictorial blankness as space, and the possibility that the motive to do so might have corollaries in other disciplines, as Greenberg suggested. Certainly the Newhouse bedroom, with its textile surfaces and large canvasses was an attempt to conflate the space of architecture and painting – and to do so through the treatment of the room's surface. It could be that this openness required of architects a recalibration of the relation between buildings and their furnishings, with the result that the space of the building absorbed the furniture and the accessories of daily life – just as the openness of color field painting soaked up color according to Greenberg.

This absorption of furniture into architecture initiated a new formal economy. While previously architecture and furniture had mirrored each other, each with its own discourse and format vocabulary, these new interiors erased furniture, and replaced it with an inflection between a reprogrammed architectural shell and its object – throbbing space. Paul Rudolph referred to this energy, identifying the presence of 'spatial velocity,' the visible and generative force 'escaping from the room.'[14]

The North Christian Community Church (1959–63) was designed by Eero Saarinen for the new postwar suburbs of Columbus, Indiana where his father had completed the First Christian Church in 1942. The interior of Eliel Saarinen's church is stark white, and lit by a large concealed window flanking the altar.

Eero Saarinen's church is a sort of space dome; caught between a molded floor and an inflected roof, two shells in tension, pulled away so that they never touch. Religious iconography has been minimized, reduced in scale and made discreet, no larger than a body. The space is full of little but light, dim and wavering, filtering down through a baffled oculus and washing up under the eaves across the soft, porous plaster. As little as a passing cloud can produce tremulous modulations. The ceiling reads like canvas that absorbs all the light and reflects all the color. The interior is monolithic, monochromatic and very subtle.   (… p 95)

Notes

1 Eero Saarinen, *Eero Saarinen On His Work*, Yale University Press (New Haven), 1968, p 66. 'The undercarriage of chairs and tables in a typical interior makes an ugly, confusing, unrestful world.'

2 Gottfried Semper, 'The Four Elements of Architecture', *The Four Elements of Architecture and Other Writings*, trans Harry Francis Mallgrave, Cambridge University Press (Cambridge), 1989, p 104. See also 'The Textile Art', pp 215–63.

3 Adolf Loos, 'The Principle of Cladding', in *Spoken into the Void*, MIT Press (Cambridge), 1982, p 66.

4 Loos, 'Principle of Cladding', p 66.

5 Billy Baldwin, *Billy Baldwin Remembers*, Harcourt Brace (New York), 1974, p 136.

6 Billy Baldwin, *Billy Baldwin Remembers*, p 225.

7 Billy Baldwin, *Billy Baldwin Decorates*, Chartwell Books (New York), 1972, p 200.

8 Clement Greenberg, 'After Abstract Expressionism', C Harrison and P Wood (eds), *Art in Theory 1900–1990*, Blackwell Press (Oxford), p 768.

9 Greenberg, 'After Abstract Expressionism', p 768.

10 Donald Judd wrote about this spatiality in his essay 'Specific Objects' of 1965: 'The main thing wrong with painting is that it is a rectangular plane placed flat against the wall. Almost all paintings are spatial in one way or another. Anything on a surface has space behind it. Two colors on the same surface almost always lie on different depths. As even color, especially in oil paint, covering all or much of a painting is almost always flat and infinitely spatial. The space is shallow in all of the work in which the rectangular plane is stressed. Rothko's space is shallow and the soft rectangles are parallel to the plane, but the space is almost traditionally illusionistic. In Reinhardt's painting, just back from the plane of the canvas, there is a flat plane and this seems in turn indefinitely deep. Pollock's paint is obviously on the canvas, and the space is mainly that made by any marks on the surface, so that it is not very descriptive and illusionist. Noland's concentric bands are not as specifically paint on surface as Pollock's paint, but the blanks flatten the literal space more. As flat and unillusionistic as Noland's paintings are, the bands do advance and recede. Even a single circle will warp the surface to it, will have a little space behind it.'

11 Barnett Newman, 'Interview with Dorothy Gees Seckler', *Art in Theory 1900–1990*, p 765.

12 Newman, 'Interview with Dorothy Gees Seckler', p 765.

13 Newman, 'Interview with Dorothy Gees Seckler', p 766.

14 Paul Rudolph, in lecture at Roger Williams College, 1984.

George Wagner, 'Ultrasuede', *Perspecta: The Yale Architecture Journal*, vol 33, 2002, pp 90–103.

(Excerpt pp 91–5)

The Historical Tradition

Edith Wharton and Ogden Codman, Jr

Writing at the turn of the century, novelist Edith Wharton and architect Ogden Codman are credited with producing one of the pivotal texts for interior designers. Their book equates architecture and decoration as professional activities, with the latter wrestled from the domain of upholsterers and considered as a harmonious addition to the architecture. Wharton and Codman also attend to issues of taste in the context of cultural specificity, social status and functional purpose. Considered advice literature, this text is a champion of modern thinking and design values which privilege simplicity, appropriate proportion and sensible utilisation of ornamental style to define a new version of harmony for interior architecture.

A building, for whatever purpose erected, must be built in strict accordance with the requirements of that purpose; in other words, it must have a reason for being as it is and must be as it is for that reason. Its decoration must harmonize with the structural limitations (which is by no means the same thing as saying that all decoration must be structural), and from this harmony of the general scheme of decoration with the building, and of the details of the decoration with each other, springs the rhythm that distinguishes architecture from mere construction. Thus all good architecture and good decoration (which, it must never be forgotten, *is only interior architecture*) must be based on rhythm and logic. A house, or room, must be planned as it is because it could not, in reason, be otherwise; must be decorated as it is because no other decoration would harmonize as well with the plan.

Many of the most popular features in modern house-planning and decoration will not be found to stand this double test. Often (as will be shown further on) they are merely survivals of earlier social conditions, and have been preserved in obedience to that instinct that makes people cling to so many customs the meaning of which is lost. In other cases they have been revived by the archaeologizing spirit which is so characteristic of the present time, and which so often leads its possessors to think that a thing must be beautiful because it is old and appropriate because it is beautiful.

But since the beauty of all such features depends on their appropriateness, they may in every case be replaced by a more suitable form of treatment without loss to the general effect of house or room. It is this which makes it important that each room (or, better still, all the rooms) in a house should receive the same style of decoration. To some people this may seem as meaningless a piece of archaism as the habit of using obsolete fragments of planning or decoration; but such is not the case. It must not be forgotten, in discussing the question of reproducing certain styles, that the essence of a style lies not in its use of ornament, but in its handling of proportion. Structure conditions ornament, not ornament structure. That is, a room with unsuitably proportioned openings, wall-spaces and cornice might receive a surface application of Louis XV or Louis XVI ornament and not represent either of those styles of decoration; whereas a room constructed according to the laws of proportion accepted in one or the other of those periods, in spite of a surface application of decorative detail widely different in character, – say Romanesque or Gothic, – would yet maintain its distinctive style, because the detail, in conforming with the laws of proportion governing the structure of the room, must necessarily conform with its style. In other words, decoration is always subservient to proportion; and a room, whatever its decoration may be, must represent the style to which its proportions belong. The less cannot include the greater. Unfortunately it is usually by ornamental details, rather than by proportion, that people distinguish one style from another. To many persons, garlands, bow-knots, quivers, and a great deal of gilding represent the Louis XVI style; if they object to these, they condemn the style. To an architect familiar with the subject the same style means something absolutely different. He knows that a Louis XVI room may exist without any of these or similar characteristics; and he often deprecates their use as representing the cheaper and more trivial effects of the period, and those that have most helped to vulgarize it. In fact, in nine cases out of ten his use of them is a concession to the client who, having asked for a Louis XVI room, would not know he had got it were these details left out.[1]

Another thing which has perhaps contributed to make people distrustful of 'styles' is the garbled form in which they are presented by some architects. After a period of eclecticism that has lasted long enough to make architects and decorators lose their traditional habits of design, there has arisen a sudden demand for 'style.' It necessarily follows that only the most competent are ready to respond to this unexpected summons. Much has to be relearned, still more to be unlearned. The essence of the great styles lay in proportion and the science of proportion is not to be acquired in a day. In fact, in such matters the cultivated layman, whether or not he has any special familiarity with the different schools of architecture, is often a better judge than the half-educated architect. It is no wonder that people of taste are disconcerted by the so-called 'colonial' houses where stair-rails are used as roof-balustrades and mantel-friezes as exterior entablatures, or by Louis XV rooms where the wavy movement which, in the best rococo, was always an ornamental incident and never broke up the main lines of the design, is suffered to run riot through the whole treatment of the walls, so that the bewildered eye seeks in vain for a straight line amid the whirl of incoherent curves.

To conform to a style, then, is to accept those rules of proportion which the artistic experience of centuries has established as the best, while within those limits allowing free scope to the individual requirements which must inevitably modify every house or room adapted to the use and convenience of its occupants.

There is one thing more to be said in defence of conformity to style; and, that is, the difficulty of getting rid of style. Strive as we may for originality, we are hampered at every turn by an artistic tradition of over two thousand years. Does any but the most inexperienced architect really think that he can ever rid himself of such an inheritance? He may mutilate or misapply the component parts of his design, but he cannot originate a whole new architectural alphabet. The chances are that he will not find it easy to invent one wholly new moulding.

The styles especially suited to modern life have already been roughly indicated as those prevailing in Italy since 1500, in France from the time of Louis XIV, and in England since the introduction of the Italian manner by Inigo Jones; and as the French and English styles are perhaps more familiar to the general reader, the examples given will usually be drawn from these. Supposing the argument in favor of these styles to have been accepted, at least as a working hypothesis, it must be explained why, in each room, the decoration and furniture should harmonize. Most people will admit the necessity of harmonizing the colors in a room, because a feeling for color is more general than a feeling for form; but in reality the latter is the more important in decoration, and it is the feeling for form, and not any archaeological affectation, which makes the best decorators insist upon the necessity of keeping to the same style of furniture and decoration. Thus the massive dimensions and heavy panelling of a seventeenth-century room would dwarf a set of eighteenth-century furniture; and the wavy, capricious movement of Louis XV decoration would make the austere yet delicate lines of Adam furniture look stiff and mean.

Many persons object not only to any attempt at uniformity of style, but to the use of any recognized style in the decoration of a room. They characterize it, according to their individual views, as 'servile,' 'formal,' or 'pretentious.'

It has already been suggested that to conform within rational limits to a given style is no more servile than to pay one's taxes or to write according to the rules of grammar. As to the accusations of formality and pretentiousness (which are more often made in America than elsewhere), they may probably be explained by the fact that most Americans necessarily form their idea of the great European styles from public buildings and palaces. Certainly, if an architect were to propose to his client to decorate a room in a moderate-sized house in the Louis XIV style, and if the client had formed his idea of that style from the state apartments in the palace at Versailles, he would be justified in rejecting the proposed treatment as absolutely unsuitable to modern private life; whereas the architect who had gone somewhat more deeply into the subject might have singled out the style as eminently suitable, having in mind one of the simple panelled rooms, with tall windows, a dignified fireplace, large tables and comfortable arm-chairs, which were to be found in the private houses of the same period. It is the old story of the two knights fighting about the color of the shield. Both architect and client would be right, but they would be looking at the different sides of the question. As a matter of fact, the bed-rooms, sitting-rooms, libraries and other private apartments in the smaller dwelling-houses built in Europe between 1650 and 1800 were far simpler, less pretentious and more practical in treatment than those in the average modern house.

It is therefore hoped that the antagonists of 'style,' when they are shown that to follow a certain style is not to sacrifice either convenience or imagination, but to give more latitude to both, will withdraw an opposition which seems to be based on a misapprehension of facts.   (... p 15)

Note

1   It must not be forgotten that the so-called 'styles' of Louis XIV, Louis XV and Louis XVI were, in fact, only the gradual development of one organic style, and hence differed only in the superficial use of ornament.

Edith Wharton and Ogden Codman, Jr, *The Decoration of Houses*, BT Batsford (London), 1898.
(Excerpt pp 10–15)

Home: Territory and Identity

J Macgregor Wise

philosophical 2000 21st century material

In this text, J Macgregor Wise asserts that home and identity are grounded in the location of one's body and self. The territories of such regions are discussed as milieus impacted by stable bodies and objects in our midst. The effect of these milieus organises the territory known and experienced as 'home', Our possessions signal identity but their presence in the context of history and memory constitute home as an articulation of effect. Unlike other essays which situate making house and home as a form of self-expression, Wise contends that home is established by the act of territorialisation, the accumulation of habitual acts that are shown to be permeable, changeable and socially reinforced.

Gilles Deleuze and Félix Guattari relate a story of a child in the dark. The child, 'gripped with fear, comforts himself by singing under his breath.'[1] The song is calming, a stability amidst the chaos, the beginning of order. The song marks a space, the repetition of the simple phrases structures that space and creates a milieu. The milieu is 'a block of space-time constituted by the periodic repetition of the component.'[2] The song begins a home, the establishment of a space of comfort. Home is not an originary place from which identity arises. It is not the place we 'come from;' it is a place we are. Home and territory: territory and identity. This essay is about home and identity, though home and identity are not the same. They are of course inextricably linked, and they are both the product of territorializing forces.

We begin with the tunes that we hum to accompany ourselves, to fill a void, to reassure ourselves. Doing so, we create a milieu. Whistle while you work; whenever I feel afraid I whistle a happy tune. Songbirds mark space, an area of influence, by sound. The bass-heavy rhythm pounding from a car driving by shapes the space of the street, changes the character of that space. Heads turn (toward, away), feelings (repulsion, identification, recognition) arise. The resonant space thus created is a milieu. Milieus cross, 'pass into one another; they are essentially communicating;'[3] rhythms blend and clash. The car and its occupants cross from one milieu to the next as they venture down the street; a figure on the sidewalk is enveloped in the bubble of sound, by the milieu, and is then released again as the car turns the corner down by the light. The street had its milieus before the car arrived (quiet suburban, congested downtown) which are altered by the arrival of the car and its rhythm, but reassert themselves after it leaves.

But space is marked, and shaped, in other ways as well. It is marked physically, with objects forming borders, walls and fences. Staking a claim, organizing, ordering. The marker (wall, road, line, border, post, sign) is static, dull, and cold. But when lived (encountered, manipulated, touched, voiced, glanced at, practised) it radiates a milieu, a field of force, a shape of space. Space is in continual motion, composed of vectors, speeds. It is 'the simultaneous co-existence of social interrelations at all geographical scales, from the intimacy of the house-hold to the wide space of transglobal connections.'[4]

Beyond the walls and streets of built place and the song of the milieu, we mark out places in many ways to establish places of comfort. A brief list of ways of marking: we may mark space more subtly by placing objects (a coat saves the seat), or by arranging our stuff (to make sure no one sits beside us on the bus or the bench) or even our bodies (posture opens and closes spaces; legs stretched out, newspaper up). Smoke from a cigarette marks space (different types of cigarettes, like clove, inflect the shape of the space, and then there are pipes, cigars, reefers) as do spices and scents. Symbols also mark space from clothing style (preppie, biker, grunge) to words on a t-shirt, but also graffiti, posters, and so on. The very words we use, the language we speak, the accent we speak it in, the ideas we expound on, have an effect on the space about us (attracts or repels others, drawing some together around the same theme, or tune). In and of themselves markers are traces of movement that has passed. 'To live means to leave traces,' as Benjamin once wrote.[5] And as Ivan Illich put it: 'all living is dwelling, the shape of a dwelling. To dwell means to live the traces that past living has left. The traces of dwellings survive, as do the bones of people.'[6]

As practised, our life-world is flooded by the variant radiance of the milieus. Each milieu opens up onto others; indeed, it is these connections with other milieus beyond the immediate place that give the markers their resonance – 'the identity of place is in part constructed out of positive interrelations with elsewhere.'[7] An encountered photograph glows with memories (though not necessarily nostalgia) of experience, of history, of family, friends. What creates that glow is the articulation of subject (homemaker) to object (home-marker), caught up in a mutual becoming-home. But that becoming opens up onto other milieus, other markers, other spaces (distant in space and/or time). One's apartment opens up onto a distant living room in a house far away, or onto a beach with those waves. But it not only articulates with a then (memory-space), but nows (that building has been pulled down, he's now living in Phoenix, she's in law school). The milieu opened up to is not just memory, not just the 'real,' but also imagined places (where one has never been, photographs of objects that never existed, at least *in that way*). And it is not just photographs that open up in this way,[8] but all markers. A small figurine – a Ganesha, the elephant-headed Hindu god – sits on the shelf above my desk. Its milieu-radiance comes from associated meanings (Ganesha helps one overcome obstacles, an empowering reminder while at work), a childhood in New Delhi, my father who purchased the idol, and so on. No space is enclosed, but is always multidimensional, resonant and open to other spaces.

What creates the *territory* is an accretion of milieu effects. Each milieu affects the space, bends it, inflects it, shapes it. Compound these effects, but then make these effects expressive rather than functional.[9] The resultant space is the *territory*. Territories are more bounded; milieu markers are arranged to close off the spaces (even while they themselves open up onto others), to inflect a more common character on that space. 'An open system integrates closure "as one of its local conditions" (closure enables, without preceding, "the outside"): and closure and openness are two phases in a single process.'[10] Territories are not milieus. 'A territory borrows from all the milieus; it bites into them, seizes them bodily (although it remains vulnerable to intrusions). It is built from aspects or portions of milieus.'[11] A territory is an *act*, territorialization, the expression of a territory. The car with its rhythm, discussed earlier, creates a territory when the space it moves through does not just react to it, but when the car and its music expresses something. Though some objects are unique in the resonance they provide (the only photograph of a great-grandparent, a cherished childhood toy), what is most important for the milieu is the effect of the object rather than the object itself, the effects on the space. In terms of territory, what is important is how the object expresses (e.g. a home). So one might rid oneself of all one's possessions each time one moves, but might recreate a similar space, a similar home, with a similar feel (a sense of light, of leisure, of tension) in the next place, drawing around oneself an expressive space from a variety of markers and milieus. One makes oneself at home (and, indeed, is often asked to do just that).

My office in early morning reflected sunlight: most wall-space is covered in over-laden bookshelves, what's free is papered with calendars and posters from old conferences. The surface of my desk is well-hidden under rather random-seeming stacks of papers. I settle into my chair and turn on the computer, log on to email – a link from this space to a broader world (often to spaces of colleagues in offices much like mine). The shelf above my desk is cluttered with photographs, two Hindu idols, a Darth Vader action figure (facing off against figures of Scully and Mulder), a Batman PEZ dispenser, a dried rose.

Home, likewise, is a collection of milieus, and as such is the organization of markers (objects) and the formation of space. But home, more than this, is a territory, an expression. Home can be a collection of objects, furniture, and so on that one carries with one from move to move. Home is the feeling that comes when the final objects are unpacked and arranged and the space seems complete (or even when one stares at unpacked boxes imagining). The markers of home, however, are not simply inanimate objects (a place with stuff), but the presence, habits, and effects of spouses, children, parents, and companions. One can be at home simply in the presence of a significant other. What makes home-territories different from other territories is on the one hand the living of the territory (a temporalization of the space), and on the other their connection with identity, or rather a process of identification, of articulation of affect. Homes, we feel, are ours:

> It was not the space itself, not the house, but the way of inhabiting it that made it a home ... [12]

The process of homemaking is a cultural one. The resonance of milieus and territories are cultural in that the specific expression of an object or space will be differentially inflected based on culture. Culture is meaning-making, and so the meaning effects of the aggregate of what I am calling one's markers (one's personal effects) reflect (though not reflect, rather inflect or create) cultures. Cultures are ways of territorializing, the ways one makes oneself at home. ('Culture is judged by its operations, not by the possession of products'[13]). Personal objects open up onto culture (and open up culturally), we draw on that culture when we mark space with that object (or idea or symbol). A business suit articulates one into a particular culture, a rock poster into another. Culture is the expression of an aggregate of texts, objects, words and ideas, their effects, meanings and uses. One culture differs from another by territorializing differently. Though cultures can share objects and ideas, they arrange and inflect these differently (e.g. different cultures may use the same ingredients, but produce much different food). However, cultures cannot be reduced to a symbolic, or meaning-specific, plane alone; cultures are expressions, they exist only in their expressions (and their repetition, which we will address below). A characteristic cultural space (the feel of a Russian apartment, a Greek Villa, a Korean temple, a stuffy academic office) may not have 'meaning' *per se*, but it is cultural and has the effect of shaping space and therefore the experience of that space. Culture is a complex aggregate of meanings, complexly articulated to an equally complex aggregate of texts (thought broadly), and both in turn complexly articulated to yet another complex aggregate of practices.[14] Though one's spaces are singular iterations of more broad cultural spaces (or modes), a culture only exists as a sum total of its iterations.

To label a space 'home' in and of itself territorializes that space depending on cultural and social norms (though never absolutely). For instance, to use the term 'home' as I have throughout may strike one as odd in the regions of the world that this essay is most likely to circulate, because of strong articulations of the term to gender, passivity, leisure (gendered, again), both household and sexual labour, and so on. Home, as I am using it, is the creation of a space of comfort (a never-ending process), often in opposition to those very forces (Deleuze and Guattari cite a housewife whistling while she labours at home; it is the whistling and comfort-effect that is home, not the house necessarily). Indeed, much in the same way as it is essential to differentiate between nation and state and not conflate the two, it is crucial that we separate the ideas of *home* and *the home*, home and house, home and *domus*. The latter terms in these pairs of contrasts are proper, normative, and may have little to do with comfort. Indeed, the home may be a space of violence and pain; home then becomes the process of coping, comforting, stabilizing oneself, in other words: resistance. But home can also mean a process of rationalization or submission, a break with the reality of the situation, self-delusion, or falling under the delusions of others. Home is not authentic or inauthentic, it does not exist a priori, naturally or inevitably. It is not individualistic. The relation between home and the home is always being negotiated, similar to what Foucault once called 'the little tactics of the habitat.'[15] It is crucial because only then can we begin to disarticulate the idea of home from ideas of stasis, nostalgia, privacy, and authenticity (which, as Doreen Massey has argued, are then coded as female), and present a more open and dynamic concept that does not tie identity to static place or reproduce gender inequality by articulating women to enclosed prison-homes while the men wander free, wistfully nostalgic for the gal they left behind.[16] This is not to argue that homes are not gendered, they are. As Ivan Illich has put it:

> Gender shapes bodies as they shape space and are in turn shaped by its arrangements. And the body in action, with its movements and rhythms, its gestures and cadences, shapes the home, the home as something more than a shelter, a tent, or a house.[17]

One cannot deny that the car-space and office-space described at the opening of this essay are gendered male; the important point is not to universalize that experience – I mean to do just the opposite, to ground it in the specificity of forces. This is why it is so important to differentiate between home as I have been describing it and the home or house; home is a becoming within an always already territorialized space (the home, the house, the domestic). Witold Rybczynski, for example, in his book *Home: A Short History of an Idea*, focuses much more on the changing nature of The Home (or at least, the Western European home) than on the territorializing process itself.[18] His chapter titles clearly set out the normative (and gendered) dimensions of the home: nostalgia, intimacy and privacy, domesticity, commodity and delight, ease, light and air, efficiency, style and substance, austerity, and comfort and wellbeing. Home can be a site of resistance, a leverage point against normative structurations of space, especially as the home becomes a domestic network terminal[19] and the idea of homework further expands beyond unpaid gendered labour and the extension of education after school hours. (... p 301)

Notes

1 Gilles Deleuze and Félix Guattari, *A Thousand Plateaus: Capitalism and Schizophrenia*, trans Brian Massumi, University of Minnesota Press (Minneapolis), 1987, p 311.

2 Deleuze and Guattari, *Thousand Plateaus*, p 313.

3 Deleuze and Guattari, *Thousand Plateaus*, p 313.

4 Doreen Massey, *Space, Place and Gender*, University of Minnesota Press (Minneapolis), 1994, p 168.

5 Quoted in Svetlana Boym, *Common Places: Mythologies of Everyday Life in Russia*, Harvard University Press (Cambridge, MA), 1994, p 150.

6 Ivan Illich, *Gender*, Pantheon (New York), 1982, pp 1, 19.

7 Massey, *Space, Place and Gender*, p 169.

8 See Roland Barthes, *Camera Lucida: Reflections on Photography*, trans Richard Howard, Hill and Wang (New York), 1981.

9 Deleuze and Guattari, *Thousand Plateaus*, p 315.

10 Meaghan Morris, 'Crazy Talk is Not Enough', *Environment and Planning D: Society and Space*, vol 14 no 4, 1996, p 393, following from Brian Massumi, 'Becoming Deleuzian', *Environment and Planning D: Society and Space*, vol 14 no 4, 1996, pp 395–406.

11 Deleuze and Guattari, *Thousand Plateaus*, p 314.

12 Boym, *Common Places*, p 166.

13 Michel De Certeau and Luce Giard, 'Envoi: A Practical Science of the Singular', M De Certeau, L Giard and P Mayol (ed.), *The Practice of Everyday Life: Volume 2: Living and Cooking*, University of Minnesota Press (Minneapolis), 1998, p 254.

14 This culture-assemblage is by way of Henri Lefebvre, *The Production of Space*, trans D Nicholson-Smith, Blackwell (Cambridge, MA), 1991, but see J Macgregor Wise, *Exploring Technology and Social Space*, Sage (Thousand Oaks, CA), 1997, p 79.

15 Quoted in Daphne Spain, *Gendered Spaces*, University of North Carolina Press (Chapel Hill), 1992, p 1.

16 Massey, *Space, Place and Gender*; Meaghan Morris, 'At Henry Parkes Motel', *Cultural Studies*, vol 2 no 1, 1988, pp 1–47.

17 Illich, *Gender*, pp 118–19.

18 Witold Rybczynski, *Home: A Short History of an Idea*, Viking (New York), 1986.

19 Stephen Graham and Simon Marvin, *Telecommunications and the City: Electronic Spaces, Urban Places*, Routledge (New York), 1996.

J Macgregor Wise, 'Home: Territory and Identity', *Cultural Studies*, vol 14 no 2, 2000, pp 295–310.

© 2000 Taylor and Francis Ltd. http://www.tandf.co.uk/journals

(Excerpt pp 297–301)

The Material Value of Color: The Estate Agent's Tale

DJB Young

As a profession, interior design is actively engaged with the speculative fit out of office space, residential apartments and commercial retail shops. Such design opportunities are inherently driven by fashion trends in a market economy. Within the context of short-term leases and the never-ending consumer demand for stylish environments, interior design plays a very prominent role in both, setting contemporary design character through experimental and novel design that stems from a popular culture image of what is 'urban', 'modern', 'new' or 'in'. Material culture scholar Diana Young examines these issues in the context of an estate agent's perceptions of preparing an interior space for sale. Citing prevailing use of white and neutral coloured surfaces, she notes a resulting lack of uniqueness or distinction between interior spaces and a general oppression of personification by people to interior space. With this observation in hand, a building's interior is subdued in the effort to make it appealing for market, reducing interior space to a simple commodity.

The world of colour is opposed to the world of value.[1]

> It is important that potential buyers can visualise themselves in your home – make sure that you keep the decoration clean and neutral and hide the family clutter.[2]

The UK is popularly characterized as a culture obsessed with home ownership and with the housing market. This article concerns London estate agents'[3] advice to their clients and the agent's experience of what sells quickly and what does not. Although location, both the area and more the intimate locale, are the main factors in the market value, the materiality of the building itself also has agency and this article sets out to explore the specific connections between materiality, value, and people.

Anyone perusing the selection of photographs on estate agents' websites or in their shop window, might be struck by the uniformity of interiors shown. Pale walls, the occasional yellow – but muted – and wooden floors are ubiquitous. This uniformity increases the more central the location and where there is a predominance of 'apartments.' It is not a phenomenon confined to the UK. 'Neutral décor' is a phrase that currently advertises property for sale and rent in Australia and the USA as well. I will return to the material effect, agency, and historical construction of neutrality later.   (... p 6)

The embedded discourses that separate people from things are implicit in agents' marketing approaches.[4] Estate agents mediate between buyers and sellers – as one agent succinctly put it, 'We deal with clients not properties.' The 'property,' as it is in agents' parlance, is the vehicle through which they earn their living either by selling it or by letting it, the latter usually for a third party – the landlord. The property is the material thing through which buyers and sellers relate in each other's absence and agents often discourage any direct relationship between the vendor and prospective purchasers.

Agents are not, by their own admission, necessarily either makers of style nor arbiters of taste but their job involves knowing how to market property. The faster the turnover of property the greater the profit for the agent since fees are usually charged only if the property sells, either as a percentage of the price fetched by the property or as a flat fee. The agent must maintain a steady flow of properties to earn a living. The location of the property, that is the area of London, is the major determining factor in the value. Within this are different types and sizes of property and then smaller gradations of value relating to the street, the 'features,' and condition of the actual building inside and out. The agent must be alert to and familiar with these variables in order to produce a valuation. For the vendor and the buyer the property is somewhere to dwell, and in the case of 'buy to let,' for tenants to inhabit, producing an income for the landlord and a fee for the managing agent.[5] For this reason the questions asked of agents in this research were about their advice to both vendors and to landlords. As property is less easy to sell in 2003 than during 2002 and 2001, agents consider the 'presentation' of the property as increasingly important in effecting a swift sale.

Asked about the principal selling points of a property in their area agents listed location and nearness to transport links, neutral decorations, 'the right price,' large kitchens, modern kitchens, wooden floors, good bathrooms. Very few mentioned emotional reactions to property, as a factor in buying: 'It's the "X factor" – people feel at home there.' Rather, for agents there are a series of material factors in the property and the problematic personalities involved. Agents dislike working for vendors who are greedy, wanting more than the market rate for their property either as a sale or a rental. Such clients are seen as a waste of resources and marketing since prices are not soaring month by month as they were in the recent past, fulfilling such ambition, and the property will fail to sell or attract tenants.

The two types of property most often categorized by the London agents interviewed are 'loft apartments,' either newly built or converted – often from commercial buildings – and the 'period house' which constitutes a large proportion of London housing stock. Built by speculators as London grew, the latter date predominantly from the nineteenth century and early twentieth or more rarely the eighteenth century. There is also some post-Second World War housing in the London suburbs. Apart from these, almost all earlier housing was built to a similar pattern with a room to the front and back of the plot and a window in each. A stair, hall, and passage runs to one side of the plan and from this the rooms are accessed. This pattern of plan recurs regardless of the number of stories or the social class for whom it was constructed, but the ceiling heights and the quality of the joinery were carefully indexical of this.[6] What agents term 'original features,' such as fireplaces, paneled doors, picture rails, and cornices are apparently desired by many buyers of period property. Conversely the wish by buyers to replace old sash windows with plastic ones was cited as a reason to drop the price offered in some less-central areas.

The 'loft apartment' is everything the period house is not, the antithesis of suburban domesticity. Developed as a type over the last twenty years in London, it ideally has none of the compartmentalized rooms but a large open reception area and kitchen combined and perhaps a split-level mezzanine area as a bedroom.[7] An apartment for rent needs one bathroom per bedroom and this is said by agents to accommodate groups of tenants desirous of each having their own bathroom. Loft apartments are increasingly marketed by area (as square feet) something rarely done for other types of property, as well as more conventionally by the number of bedrooms. In this respect and others they resemble the commercial property they once were, being in agents' accounts more knowingly 'presented' by their owners, synonymous with their being more intensely commodified.

There is a further category of property and that is 'ex-local authority,' and in London this is most often a flat. These are generally post-Second World War although there are also earlier mansion blocks of flats built by philanthropic organizations, which later became owned by local authorities. Since the Tory government of the 1980s when council tenants were given the 'right to buy' their home, these properties are now bought and sold like any other.[8] These are more variable in layout and proportionately cheaper per square foot. 'Ex-local' dwellings are still marketed as 'flats' whereas all other flats have become translated into 'apartments' after the loft apartment.

I have sketched the spatial and material aspects of the housing types available in some detail because ideally all seemingly need to conform to the same set of desires in order to sell. That is, spaciousness, cleanliness, and neutrality. This is what buyers and tenants want according to agents. Clearly spaciousness is easiest to evoke in large rooms, which is what the loft apartment should offer, whereas the average terraced period house usually needs some adaptation to achieve this illusion.

When asked what they meant by neutral, agents listed white-, beige-, and magnolia-painted walls and, if a loft apartment or a rental,[9] a wood floor.[10] For example:

> We advise against strong colours – too much of a personal statement – neutral décor (Partner of agents in Islington, North London).

> White walls, wood floors. Neutrality sells – plainness (Agent in west central London dealing with 25-40 age group of 'city types').

Neutrality is supposed to help achieve the aim of spaciousness. In many marketing photographs of reception rooms even the furniture is covered in white or neutral fabric camouflaged against the neutral wall in an effort to make it disappear and create the illusion of space.

> We tell them [the vendor] to make it look more spacey [sic], airy … maybe laminate flooring and mirrors, keep the curtains drawn [back]. It all helps to make it look more spacey (Sales negotiator talking about selling ex local authority flats inner East End).

> It [white] gives you a blank canvas [pause] – and most people like white anyway. My place is all painted white. Some people hire an interior designer and have pink ceilings and purple walls. You might move in and think, 'I want that wall red' but then you have to sell it to someone with the same colour taste as you (Sales negotiator East London/Docklands).

Personal taste in color is to be avoided and extreme examples were used to illustrate the point. An agent in west London related, 'Colour is very individual to a particular person. For example a few years ago I had a property where one of the bedrooms was painted black …' This client was advised to repaint before marketing. Some agents were sensitive about offending their potential vendor's taste: 'most people are quite proud of their own taste.' And in south-east London:

> We had this lower ground floor flat in Peckham, a basement really and it really didn't have much light and the gentlemen had painted it bright red, right. We had it on for about a month and everyone that walked in there just walked right out again. So then we said well maybe you could paint it and he was quite happy, you know, to do that and he painted it magnolia and it sold. It's all about presentation.

The other wall surface which was mentioned as 'appropriate' in apartments converted from old industrial buildings is exposed brick work. This is indexical of industry and signals the 'authenticity' of the loft.[11] For example: 'exposed timber beams and brickwork in this authentic riverside conversion.'

Evidently there is some widely understood social consensus about neutrality. It does not mean gray, which is the color that Western color science would term neutral. Here it constitutes lightness, a feeling of space and is impersonal, a 'blank canvas' in the recurring description agents give. For example an agent's promotion of an unfurnished flat to rent, '... an excellent opportunity for someone seeking a spacious and fresh environment in which to add their personal furnishings.' Anything that is not neutral, i.e. is colored, is by implication, a personal idiosyncrasy that other people cannot relate to. Nonetheless neutrality is culturally constructed and a 'fashion,' just like the terracotta reds that were mentioned by agents marketing period houses as being ubiquitous a decade ago in certain areas.

Cleanliness relates to both integrity of surface and to the absence of traces of other people's lives. 'To live is to leave traces' wrote Walter Benjamin[12] but this is precisely what prospective buyers and tenants do not want to see, signs of others' occupation. Agents cited examples; mastic round the bath that has turned black with mildew, scuff marks on the wall, the 'tired' decorations, as signs requiring obliteration. New properties obviate the need for these erasures and agents speak admiringly of the properties that are 'like show houses' in their presentation, that is, they are pristine, yet stylish – and sought after.

Unlike the Kula shell valuables of the Melanesian islands which increase in value as they are transformed from white to red by handling, or the patina on a piece of period furniture, surfaces in the contemporary home must be kept uninflected with a life lived.[13] Or rather this is how they should be presented for sale. The analogy of Melanesian shell exchange networks is perhaps a useful one here on two further counts illuminating contrasting notions of the relationship of persons and things. The shells, exchanged in the Massim of Papua New Guinea, personify and spread the fame of the man to whom they are linked so that persons and shells are not distinct. The reddening of the shells animates them, making them materially more like persons, not only as a symbolic referent – they resemble foetuses – but also, and anthropology seldom engages with this, because of their material redness.[14] Color is an animating presence in the world and potentially intrinsic to the fetish. Colors have different spatial qualities and red is attractive, moves forward towards the gaze. In the housing market this quality of red, for example, makes rooms appear smaller but also seems to attach the property too closely to the vendor.

Secondly, is the matter of flow, something which has been explored for the shell networks.[15] In one of the economic arguments concerning the housing market, we are told that in order to keep that market buoyant, first time buyers must be able to afford to enter the exchange network and keep it mobile. Without these buyers the chain will halt. Materiality though may also impede the flow or speed it up. Multiple patterned surfaces offer such an impediment. When highly patterned interiors come on to the market they considerably decrease the value of the property.   (... p 10)

Notes

1 Jean Baudrillard, *The System of Objects* [1968], trans James Benedict, Verso, (London and New York), 1996, p 31.

2 The National Association of Estate Agents.

3 Anyone can set themselves up as an estate agent but there are various regulatory bodies of which the largest is the National Association of Estate Agents. It is possible to buy and sell property privately without estate agents but this is still a minority of property transactions in the UK. For a US study of internet property sales see R Palm and M Daniels, 'The Internet and Home Purchase', *Tijdschrift voor economische en sociale geographie*, vol 93 no 5, 2002, pp 537–47.

4 Prospective buyers may of course have a very different view from the agent of what they are looking for in a dwelling, hinted at by an agent reporting that some buyers liked to talk to the vendor at length, 'you'd think they were buying the people' perhaps indicating a personification of the house.

5 The 'buy to let' phenomenon has been extensively discussed and publicized in the UK. The explanation given for its efflorescence is an economic one although doubtless other factors were and are at play. The low interest rates on mortgages and the month-by-month acceleration of housing prices combining to make property an attractive investment yielding better returns than the ailing stock market. By 2003 there was, according to the agents interviewed, an oversupply of rental accommodation in London and the price accelerations had ceased although interest rates remained low. Agents reported that many people who had bought one extra property – most usually a one or two bedroom flat – were now selling this, while 'professional' landlords were still 'looking to acquire.'

6 A grander variation is the 'double fronted' house where the plan is symmetrical about the hallway. See for example Helen C Long, *The Edwardian House*, Manchester University Press (Manchester and New York), 1993 on the Edwardian house and John Summerson, *Georgian London*, Penguin (Harmondsworth), 1978 on the Georgian; also Roy Porter, *London: A Social History*, Penguin (London), 2000 for a broader social history of the capital.

7 See S Zukin, *Loft Living: Culture and Capital in Urban Change*, Johns Hopkins University Press (Baltimore, MD), 1982 on the original SoHo lofts of Manhattan and Julie Podmore, '(Re)reading the "Loft Living" Habitus in Montréal's Inner City', *International Journal of Urban and Regional Research*, vol 22 no 2, 1998, pp 283–302 for a study of loft apartments in Montreal. The new-build London apartment now bears only nodding acquaintance with its original open plan, big space template, something agents volunteered in this research.

8 See assessments such as John A Dolan, 'I've Always Fancied Owning me Own Lion', Irene Cieraad (ed), *At Home: An Anthropology of Domestic Space*, Syracuse University Press (New York), 1999, p 70: Thatcher's "property owning democracy" ... emphasis(ed) ownership and nation rather than selling;' and Stuart Hall and Martin Jacques (eds), *New Times: The Changing Face of Politics in the*

1990s, Lawrence & Wishart in association with *Marxism Today* (London), 1989.

9 I.e. landlords required this as tenants demanded it.

10 Two agents marketing loft apartments in the central area, both describing their marketing as 'at the cutting edge,' reported that in their newest recently completed lofts, limestone or granite tiles were replacing wood. These materials are still 'neutral' in effect, albeit indexing expensive and distinctive neutrality.

11 Podmore, '(Re)reading', p 297.

12 Used as the opening in Beatriz Colomina, 'The Split Wall: Domestic Voyeurism', Beatriz Colomina (ed), *Sexuality and Space*, Princeton Architectural Press (Princeton, NJ), 1992.

13 S Campbell, 'Attaining Rank: A Classification of Shell Valuables', J Leach and E Leach (eds), *The Kula*, Cambridge University Press (Cambridge), 1983, pp 229–49.

14 M Strathern, *Property Substance and Effect: Anthropological Essays on Persons and Things*, Athlone Press (London and New Jersey), 1999.

15 M Strathern, 'Cutting the Network,' *Journal of the Royal Anthropological Institute*, vol 2 no 3, 1996, pp 517–35.

Article originally published as 'The Material Value of Color: The Estate Agent's Tale', DJB Young, *Home Cultures*, vol 1 no 1, March 2004, Berg Publishers (Oxford and New York). www.bergpublishers.com

Reprinted by permission of Berg Publishers.

(Excerpts pp 6–10)

INDEX